COLONIAL
SOUTH CAROLINA

TORY

ROBERT M. WEIR

COLONIAL
SOUTH CAROLINA

A HISTORY

UNIVERSITY OF SOUTH CAROLINA PRESS

© 1983, 1997 Robert M. Weir

First edition published 1983 by KTO Press, New York, New York.

First paperback edition published 1997.
Published in Columbia, South Carolina, by the
University of South Carolina Press.

Manufactured in the United States of America

02 01 00 99 98 97   6 5 4 3 2 1

Library of Congress Cataloging-in-Publication Data

Weir, Robert M.
    Colonial South Carolina : a history / Robert M. Weir—1st pbk.
ed.
        p.   cm.
    Originally published: Millwood, N.Y. : KTO Press, © 1983, in
series: A history of the American colonies.
    Includes bibliographical references (p.   ) and index.
    ISBN 1–57003–189–4
    1. South Carolina—History—Colonial period, ca. 1600–1775.
I. Title.
F272.W46   1997
975.7′02—dc21   97–1517

FOR ANNE

CONTENTS

ILLUSTRATIONS

PREFACE

Since the hardbound edition of this volume first appeared in 1983, the study of South Carolina's early history has become a growth industry. Literally hundreds of relevant works have appeared in little over a decade. Nearly everyone, I imagine, is pleased to find that others share an interest in what he or she believes is a significant subject, but authors greet subsequent publications in the same field with mixed emotions. Hell for a scholar, one of them accurately observed, is "truth discovered too late." Faced with that possibility, one has two urges. The first is to run out and get the new work to see if it adds something important; the other is to ignore the intruder entirely on the assumption that it couldn't possibly contribute anything. The first reaction is of course the more sensible, but neither response is entirely satisfactory. However, the republication of the present work prompted me to make a systematic survey of recent scholarship on colonial South Carolina, and I am happy to report that much of it is very good, that its findings are important, and that more warm winds than scorching blasts are blowing out of the fiery pit. *Colonial South Carolina* stands up better in the light of the new research than I perhaps had any right to expect. Matters of fact and interpretation remain largely intact.

I am therefore most pleased that the University of South Carolina Press is making the book widely available in paperback form. Although extensive revisions have not been possible, typographical errors and the like from the 1983 edition have been corrected. In addition, I have added a supplemental bibliography that includes popular as well as scholarly works and a few items for younger readers. The result, I hope, is a book for the twenty-first century. The subject remains enduringly relevant; the new scholarship answers many interesting questions; and this book has once again benefitted from the expertise of historians whose knowledge of South Carolina history is unparalleled. Allan Charles, Charles Lesser, Terry Lipscomb, George Rogers, Jr., and Allen Stokes have suggested bibliography and called attention to errors, while Sarah and Tom Terrill kindly vetted this preface. The book is better for their efforts, and I am grateful to all of them.

ROBERT M. WEIR

Columbia, South Carolina
October, 1996

COLONIAL
SOUTH CAROLINA

A HISTORY

1

PROLOGUE TO SETTLEMENT

By right of discovery, papal sanction, and a treaty with Portugal, Spain claimed almost all of the New World at the end of the fifteenth century. How much territory this involved was not even dimly known, but within a generation a relative handful of explorers and conquistadors fanned out from island bases in the Caribbean and planted the Spanish flag from Mexico to Peru. At one time, it seemed that nothing, in the words of one Englishman, would keep the Spanish from "flowinge over all the face of... America." Attempts to settle the area that would eventually become South Carolina proved to be among the least successful parts of this extraordinary process, and Spain eventually gave up the attempt. The Spanish crown, however, continued to regard its title to the North American continent as valid. Nevertheless, the comparative weakness of Spanish power in the area made it inviting to other European powers. During the sixteenth century South Carolina—which was then still generally regarded as part of Florida—thus became a zone of international conflict foreshadowing much of the colony's later history. Like giants wrestling with their fingertips, as someone once described the contestants in a similar struggle, Spain, France, England, and the native Americans were engaged in intermittent hostilities along the southeastern coast of North America for the better part of three centuries. Because the European contestants were usually overextended on this relatively remote frontier, the actions were rarely conclusive. The continual struggle, however, did much to shape both the history of the colony and the outlook of its inhabitants who frequently faced the possibility of violent death.

The first Spanish attempt to settle the area was in some ways a harbinger of things to come. In 1520–1521, a local official of Hispaniola, Lucas Vásquez de Ayllón, sponsored a slaving venture which eventually reached the Carolina coast, from which it returned with about seventy Indians. By this time laws against such practices were being enforced, so Ayllón disavowed his original intent and liberated the slaves. Among the captives was a young man whom the Spaniards renamed Francisco de Chicora. Encouraged by his tales of the land called Chicora, Ayllón sought royal approval for his venture and, after receiving it, in 1526 assembled an expedition of six ships and more than 500 men and women. Exactly where he attempted to make his settlement is still uncertain. It may have been on Winyaw Bay near modern Georgetown, or farther south, perhaps around the mouth of the Savannah River, or even possibly among the sea islands of Georgia. What is certain is that Ayllón's largest vessel with most of the supplies aboard ran aground and sank, while Francisco and the other Indians who were to serve as guides and interpreters disappeared into the woods. Within a few months Ayllón died of a fever, his men mutinied, and local Indians attacked. Before the ordeal was over for those who straggled back to Hispaniola, some 350 of their companions were dead. Clearly, there were logistical and other problems to overcome before a settlement would be a success.

Hernando de Soto was the next Spaniard to lead an expedition through South Carolina, and it too eventually came to grief. Having landed in Florida, de Soto apparently crossed the Savannah River near what is now Augusta in the spring of 1540. There (or perhaps near modern Camden, South Carolina) he encountered "the Lady of Cofitachequi" who ruled the local Indians. Finding neither silver nor gold but appropriating foodstuffs and some pearls, de Soto forced a woman whom he erroneously took to be the ruler to accompany him westward. During the subsequent crossing of the Blue Ridge Mountains, she escaped; de Soto continued on into present-day North Carolina, Tennessee, Alabama, and westward to a watery grave in the Mississippi River.

The next Spanish effort involving Carolina was perhaps more carefully planned but equally disastrous. By midcentury the treasure ships from the Spanish Main of Central and South America usually made a last call at Havana before the long Atlantic crossing. The first part of their route was through the Bahama Channel, a narrow passage along the eastern coast of Florida, less than forty miles wide in places, through which the Gulf Stream flowed northward at up to seventy miles a day. Riding that current, the freighters soon reached latitudes where they could catch prevailing westerly winds, but the price for this advantage was a voyage along a coast often buffeted by hurricanes and frequented by French and, later, English corsairs. After two large treasure fleets were wrecked in the channel in 1550 and 1553, Spanish authorities sought to establish a post that could serve as a haven from hostile craft and storms. Thinking naturally focused on Port Royal Sound, known to the Spaniards as Santa Elena, which provided a good harbor. In 1557 King Philip II therefore placed Florida under the jurisdiction of the viceroy of New Spain and directed that it be settled.

Plans called for an expedition to the northeastern Gulf Coast from which it would then proceed overland to Santa Elena. Ultimately, it was thought, a road could be laid out over this route along which farmers would settle and the whole area would become an agricultural hinterland supporting the port of Santa Elena. Tristán de Luna, who had commanded Coronado's main force in the southwest, led the group which sailed from Mexico in 1559. While they were still disembarking supplies at Pensacola, a hurricane destroyed most of the fleet. The expedition, however, continued but apparently never made it much beyond modern Alabama. Luna and others underestimated the distance to Santa Elena, and his men may have found the swamps of northern Florida to be an insurmountable barrier. Some two years later, Angel de Villafañe took Luna's place, bearing orders to transport most of the men to Santa Elena by sea. Although Villafañe doubted his chances of success, he did as ordered, entered a bay he believed to be at Santa Elena, and in 1561 took formal possession of the area for Spain. Unable to find a site that satisfied him, Villafañe continued to explore the coast before a hurricane sank two of his ships. The remainder of the force then sailed for Havana. At this point Philip II temporarily concluded that the price of settling Florida was too high.

French visits to the Carolina coast dated from 1524 when Giovanni da Verrazzano, a Florentine sailing for Francis I, explored the eastern coast of North America. Hopeful that the area might produce tropical products, relatively certain that it would provide bases for attacking Spanish vessels, and envisaging the possibility of using it as a refuge for Huguenots in the event that things went badly for them in France, the admiral of France, Gaspard de Coligny, commissioned Jean Ribault to plant a colony on the southern coast of North America. In 1562 Ribault entered the sound at Santa Elena, to which he gave the name it still bears, Port Royal. There he built a small fort, Charlesfort, and, leaving volunteers to man it, returned to France for supplies and reinforcements. Before he could accomplish his task, the men left behind mutinied, chose a new commander, and, building a makeshift vessel, sailed for home. Eventually some made it, but not before they had resorted to cannibalism.

Meanwhile, Ribault arrived in France and found it in the throes of a civil war which prevented him from obtaining supplies. Because England was assisting the French Huguenots in the war, he sought aid in London. Though he was promised it, the English became disenchanted with their allies and Ribault was briefly imprisoned. With the return of peace in France, however, Coligny sent another expedition to Florida under the command of René Goulaine de Laudonnière who had been with Ribault on the first voyage. The result was Fort Caroline, constructed on the St. Johns River in Florida. Again, hardship, misfortune, and dissension wracked the settlement. Only Ribault's arrival prevented abandonment of the colony. Having been released from prison and once again commissioned by Coligny, he had come to supersede Laudonnière and, he hoped, to forestall the Spanish, since Philip II had changed his mind about Florida. Philip's choice for the task of occupying the area was an able and energetic seaman, Pedro Menéndez de Avilés. Arriving on the coast of Florida, Menéndez established St. Augustine to serve as a base before attacking Ribault. The Frenchmen, however, escaped, regrouped, and prepared to counterattack, but a storm scattered the French ships. Meanwhile Menéndez marched under cover of the gale, surprised Fort Caroline, and killed most of its garrison. Later, finding Ribault and some of his sailors shipwrecked, Menéndez summarily executed them.

The Spanish garrisons which Menéndez soon established on the coasts of Florida and South Carolina, an English sea dog later observed, served "for no other purpose, than to keep all other nations from inhabiting any part" of the area. Basically that was correct. Menéndez, however, hoped that these lands not only would provide a staging area for further expansion but in their own right would also prove to be richer than

Mexico or Peru. As a first step, he occupied Santa Elena and erected a fort, San Felipe, on what is today known as Parris Island. From there he sent out Captain Juan Pardo to explore the interior, and Pardo in turn scattered small garrisons across the countryside. In its heyday the settlement at Santa Elena, which included a mission and a small farming community, was considerably larger than St. Augustine.

Nevertheless, the Spanish were never able to consolidate their position. Lacking precious metals or a large Indian population to provide a labor force and a lucrative cash crop, Santa Elena failed to develop as Menéndez had hoped. It therefore remained vulnerable, and Indian attacks forced its temporary evacuation in the mid-1570s. Although the Spanish returned and built a new fort, San Marcos, Englishmen finished what the Indians had begun when Sir Francis Drake sacked and burned St. Augustine after raiding Spanish strongholds in the Caribbean. Only the danger of navigating an unknown sound prevented him from repeating the performance at Santa Elena. Nevertheless, the destruction of St. Augustine forced Spanish authorities to abandon the post at Santa Elena. Thereafter the Carolina coast reverted to a sort of no man's land, claimed by Spain but visited by French corsairs and English privateers.

Englishmen had been rather slow to develop much interest in the area, though their claims dated back to 1497, when John Cabot, sailing for Henry VII, visited the New World. But it was not until the reign of Elizabeth I (1558–1603) that Englishmen really entered the race for territory, and then increasing hostility between England and Spain made colonization subordinate to strategic considerations. Consequently, the southern coast of North America appeared most attractive as a base from which to harass Spanish shipping, and for a time Queen Elizabeth apparently thought Ribault's activities might prove to be a way of gaining an English foothold in the area. Although these ideas never came to fruition, other schemes, such as Sir Walter Raleigh's settlement at Roanoke, did. Thereafter, the outbreak of full-scale war in 1587 diverted attention from the Carolina coast by making home waters the center of action. Furthermore, the accession of James I (1603) and peace with Spain in 1604 meant that Englishmen would first resume colonial activities farther north where the affront to Spain was less direct and where, it seemed, providence had reserved the land for English exploitation. Consequently, there was a hiatus of half a century before Englishmen showed much active interest in the area that would become South Carolina.

In the interim, English readers had access to accounts of the French ventures in particular. Ribault published *The Whole and True Discoverye of Terra Florida* in London in 1563. About twenty years later, Richard Hakluyt the younger included it in his *Divers Voyages Touching the Discoverie of America,* and in 1587 an English version of Laudonnière's narrative appeared. Those who read these early accounts, or the Spanish chronicles (many of which remained in manuscript), would have found a mixture of fact and fantasy. To some extent, fusion of the two was an indigenous product of the New World, since in many ways it was truly fabulous. The inhabitants also sometimes regaled gullible Europeans with fables of their own. The Indian Chicora told Ayllón that the land north of Florida had recently been populated by a race of men with tails for which they dug holes in the ground when they sat down. Chicora also claimed to know a tribe that stretched children so that their leaders grew to enormous size. All this and more, a Spanish chronicler observed, Ayllón believed as though he had been listening to the twelve apostles. Ayllón's credulity is understandable, for European knowledge of the New World developed in the context of much older lore. Going back to antiquity, there were tales of a paradise in the west, and more than one fountain of youth occurred in medieval legend. Juan Ponce de Léon was probably actually seeking the fountain of youth as well as Indian slaves when he discovered Florida, and even Ribault remarked that he had come to the land called Chicora where "aged men go without staves, and are able to do and ron [*sic*] like the youngest of them."

Accordingly, many of these early explorers resemble figures from a chivalric romance. In reality, Ribault does seem to have been a remarkable man. Even Menéndez paid tribute to him, "I think it a very great fortune" that he is dead; "for the King of France could accomplish more with him and fifty thousand ducats, than with other men and five hundred thousand ducats; and he could do more in one year, than another in ten." And when he could do no more, Ribault is supposed to have died like a legendary knight or a Renaissance gentleman, above the vagaries of fortune. When Menéndez asked if the Frenchmen were Protestant or Catholic, Ribault is believed to have answered, "Protestant." Quoting from the Book of Genesis, "From earth we come and unto earth must we return," he observed that another twenty years of life meant little. By the time Englishmen began settling Carolina in the mid-seventeenth century, such *virtus* was largely out; economics and real estate were in. Yet, in one of history's paradoxical convolutions, the descendants of these early Carolinians would centuries later again make the Renaissance ideal fashionable. In the meantime, the native Americans may have understood Ribault and his kind somewhat better than their immediate successors.

2

THE INDIANS

From the very beginning, Europeans encountered native Americans, and their early narratives provide much information about the culture of the Indians in the sixteenth and seventeenth centuries. Unfortunately, these accounts also include much misinformation, for Europeans not only often misunderstood what they saw but their very presence soon changed it as contact between Indians and whites quickly modified both cultures. Thus, the testimony of Europeans must be handled with care. Even the term "Indian" is a misnomer resulting from Columbus's belief that he had reached the Orient; worse, such a generic term conceals the variety among Indian cultures.

The size of the aboriginal population also suffers from the miscalculations of the earliest chroniclers. Older estimates placed it at perhaps no more than 11,000 or 12,000 in the seventeenth and eighteenth centuries, a figure that is little more than an educated guess. More recent investigations of the Indian populations in other areas of the New World suggest that these figures are much too low. White men made the original counts, and they were not impartial enumerators, in part because one of the most common justifications for taking Indian lands was the doctrine of effective use. The smaller the Indian population, the greater the claim which Europeans could assert to the land. There is also considerable evidence that Indians suffered a catastrophic death rate from diseases introduced by Europeans. For example, scholars now believe there were as many as 8,000,000 Indians on the island of Hispaniola in 1492. In 1570 there were 125. That the aboriginal population of South Carolina declined as precipitously during the first hundred years of contact is almost inconceivable, but there can be no doubt that Indians were being decimated by disease as early as 1540 when Spaniards first cut through the central portion of the present state. Multiplying older figures by ten or even twenty as has been done in other areas, therefore, appears to be not unreasonable, though the most recent statistics for the southeastern United States are less than double the older figures. The present estimates ranging upward from about 20,000, are also plausible, though obviously very tentative. We know, on the one hand, that at least some Indians in this area lived in large towns of perhaps as many as 500 houses but that, on the other hand, there were large uninhabited areas between villages. It is probable that the region as a whole was sparsely populated, with clusters of relatively dense population.

The Indian settlements were linguistically diverse. Nearly fifty tribes representing four major language groups resided in the area. Using only some of the historically most important tribes as examples, one finds that the "Savanoes" who lived along the Savannah River may have been Shawnees, most of whom were located in Ohio and Kentucky. If so, they spoke an Algonkian language related to those in New England. The language of the Yamasees, who somewhat later also lived along the Savannah River, is now extinct, but it may have belonged to the Muskogean family, which also included the Creeks of Georgia and Alabama. Some scholars believe that the Catawba Indians of central South Carolina used a language most closely related to the Siouan tongues of the Plains Indians. The Cherokees of the southern Appalachian Mountains spoke three distinct dialects, all of which belonged to the Iroquois family. Some Indians appear to have been multilingual, and many may have understood one or more trade jargons.

For the sake of convenience, geographic locations have been attributed to the tribes mentioned above, and, speaking generally, the associations are accurate. But it is worth noting that questions of residence are as thorny as the matter of language. By the fifteenth century the Indians of the southeastern United States had long since ceased to be nomadic, and most lived in permanent towns. Nevertheless, there continued to be considerable geographic mobility. Some of it, as in the case of a few coastal tribes who traveled inland during the winter, amounted to seasonal migrations over relatively short distances. Other movement represented the peregrinations of splinter groups from larger tribes. Occasionally, an entire tribe moved. For example, the Westos, who probably appeared on the Savannah River shortly before 1670, may have come from Virginia. In 1704 most of the Apalachees who survived a raid by Carolinians left northwestern Florida for South Carolina, and a little over a decade later the Yamasees moved south to Florida. In short, even in cases where documentation is sound (which are relatively rare), it is frequently difficult to say where a particular group of Indians was located without being precise about dates. But that such movement existed has at least two important implications. One, to emerge throughout the ensuing discussion, arises because much of this movement was associated with white intrusion; the other stems from the surprising ease with which the remnants of one tribe joined others.

Such ease of fusion suggests that the tribes in question were culturally related, and other evidence confirms the inference. Archaeologists and anthropologists now recognize that, despite their linguistic variation, Indians of the southeast shared a common culture. Accordingly, though almost nothing is known about some of the smaller coastal tribes of South Carolina, like the Abbapoola, their social organization and cosmology were probably similar to that of the Creeks and Cherokees, and much has been learned about these larger groups. Moreover, the Carolina Indian trade involved not only the Creeks and the Cherokees but also, at one time or another, most of the major tribes in the huge area from the southern Appalachian Mountains to the lower Mississippi Valley. Contact between South Carolinians and the Indians to the northeast was less frequent (except during the Tuscarora War), and there seems to have been a rather sharp cultural discontinuity between tribes in the vicinity of modern Georgetown and those further north around the Cape Fear River. Less pronounced regional differences occurred elsewhere on the coast and in the mountains, but the relative homogeneity of Indian cultures southwest of Cape Fear, as well as the wide-ranging Carolina trade, make it possible to generalize about the Indians who affected the development of the colony by drawing evidence from tribes who lived well beyond the present boundaries of the state.

The most striking feature of the Indian culture in this area was its relatively high degree of sophistication. Indeed, the southeastern Indians were the most culturally advanced of any in the present United States, partly because of a long period of development. Humans crossed a land bridge from Asia to North America during the Ice Ages perhaps as long as 50,000 years ago; by 9000 B.C. they were definitely here. By at least 2000 B.C. they were making pottery, tempered or strengthened with vegetable fibers, and some of the oldest ware of this kind found in the United States has been discovered at a site on Stallings Island in the Savannah River near Augusta, Georgia. By 1000 B.C. Indians had begun to cultivate the soil and build burial mounds. Between 700 and 900 A.D., a sophisticated civilization developed in the region around the confluence of the Missouri and Mississippi rivers, from which it spread southward and eastward. Characterized by relatively intensive cultivation of crops which had originated in the tropics, the construction of flat-topped pyramids, and symbolic motifs which included the plumed serpent, this culture or "Mississippian tradition," as it is now termed, exhibited many Meso-American affinities. The precise source of the latter is unclear. Perhaps some traits were indigenous; the migration of peoples and diffusion of characteristics among adjacent populations could have accounted for others. Some characteristics may even have been spread by Aztec traders. Whatever the source, the height of the Mississippian tradition at approximately 1200 A.D. produced large and impressive civilizations based on agriculture, supplemented by hunting and gathering.

Corn, beans of various kinds, and squash were the main crops; and interestingly enough, these plants complemented each other in a number of ways. Beans and corn are both sources of protein, but the former supplies an amino acid, lysine, which the latter lacks. Thus together they provide a reasonably complete diet of vegetable protein. (Incidentally, the Indians treated the corn with lye made from wood ashes to make hominy in a process which also increased the amount of both lysine and niacin.) Being a legume, beans also replaced nitrogen in the soil which corn depleted. This semi-symbiotic relationship helps to account for the Indians' ability to cultivate the same fields over long periods of time without the use of fertilizer. (Contrary to current mythology, Indians in this area did not place a fish in each hill.) They did, however, plant the corn and beans in hills, and the vines entwined themselves around the cornstalks, which made picking easier. Piling additional soil on top of the hill as the plants grew also helped to support the corn, which has shallow roots, conserved moisture, and decreased erosion. It also reduced the amount of labor involved in

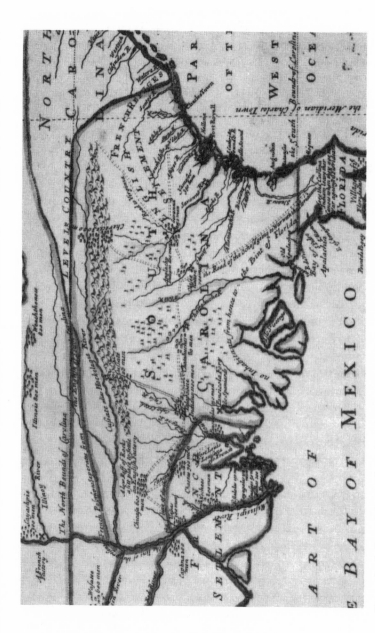

From the influential map by Edward Crisp entitled "A Compleat Description of the Province of Carolina in 3 Parts" (London, 1711). A detail of part two, "A Map of South Carolina *Shewing the* Settlements of the English, French, & Indian Nations *from* Charles Town *to the* River Mississippi *by Capt.* Tho. Nairn." *Courtesy of the Henry E. Huntington Library and Art Gallery.*

cultivation, which was done with sticks and hoes. Although clay soils would have been difficult to work with this technology, it was well adapted to the loose and alluvial soils of the river bottoms near which the Indian villages were located. Precisely how much of their diet came from these fields is difficult to say, and the amount obviously varied from year to year. Usually, however, the proportion was substantial, and it made the Indians vulnerable to attacks by whites who devastated their fields. The Cherokees, for example, suffered great hardships after the Carolinians destroyed their crops in 1760, 1761, and 1776.

Under such conditions gathering wild plants became essential, but normally it played only a supplementary role. Berries and fruits like the persimmon provided a doubtless welcome change and, unlike almost all other foods which were usually boiled, broiled, or barbecued, these were often eaten raw. After whites introduced peaches, figs, and watermelons, the Indians quickly adopted them. Nuts of many kinds, including especially chestnuts, were a source of oil. "Hickory milk," made by boiling hickory nuts and skimming off the oil which floated to the top, had an unusually delicate flavor. Acorns were normally bitter, but some Indians may have learned to neutralize the acid content with lye. They certainly knew much about the pharmacological if not chemical properties of other plants. Among the Creeks and perhaps other Indians, willow bark provided one of their most common remedies. It contains salicin, the active ingredient synthesized in our most commonly used medicine, aspirin. "Black drink," a tea made from a species of holly, was a potent source of caffeine; taken in large enough quantities, it became an emetic. In one form or another, its use was a constant accompaniment at council meetings and ceremonial occasions.

The latter, which, as we shall see, were a central feature of Indian life, derived from earlier hunting cultures, and hunting itself continued to be an important activity. Before the advent of the whites it was done with a bow and arrow, though some Indians such as the Cherokees also used a blowgun for birds and small game. Estimates of the effectiveness of bows and arrows differ, but Spaniards reported after one engagement that they found arrows which had penetrated oak saplings two inches in diameter. Nevertheless, the Indians quickly came to prefer guns. The main game animal, which probably accounted for well over 50 percent of the animal protein in the diet, was the white-tailed deer, and there is evidence to indicate that the Indians artificially increased its numbers by firing the woods. Such burning keeps down the underbrush and promotes the growth of grass. Hence, as Europeans noted, forests frequently had the appearance of parks, and as late as the Revolution, they were often open enough for the operation of horsemen. As a result, deer sometimes ranged in herds of up to 200 head, much larger than are now seen. Before white contact Indians hunted in groups, sometimes driving deer, sometimes decoying them by disguising themselves under deerskins to which the head and antlers remained attached. The hunting season ran from late fall to early spring; and the kill was proportional to the need for meat and clothing. But the deerskin trade which developed through Charles Town tapped an apparently insatiable English demand for buckskin breeches, and the resulting slaughter of deer boggles the mind. In 1748, Indians, hunting alone, using guns, and leaving the carcasses to rot, supplied approximately 160,000 skins for export from Charles Town, and by the end of the colonial period the cumulative total was probably several million. To be sure, that figure subsumes the better part of a century and a hinterland which often reached to the Gulf Coast and the Mississippi River, but the numbers involved suggest what would happen to the buffalo in the nineteenth century. Bison, incidentally, once occurred infrequently in South Carolina but were rare by the time Europeans arrived. Fish and small game — including turkeys, passenger pigeons, waterfowl, raccoons, and opossums — made up most of the rest of the Indians' diet. Bears furnished oil for cooking and cosmetic purposes.

Apparently alone among the game animals, bears could be killed with impunity; all others required an apology and a show of respect, lest their spirits inflict harm upon the hunter. Rheumatism, for example, was considered to be the deer's disease. Precisely why bears bore the brunt of this invidious distinction is not entirely clear. A Cherokee myth suggests that in a council of the animals they once revealed themselves to be too spineless to retaliate against man's insults and injuries. But the existence of such a myth raises more questions than it answers. Perhaps the bear's anomalous appearance and behavior were the source of its unenviable distinction. Though a four-footed animal, the bones of the paw resemble the bones of a human hand; a bear sometimes walks on its hind legs like a human and is also omnivorous. In short, bears appeared to stand at the borderline between the categories "human" and "animal." To an Indian, that made them objects of special concern and interest.

Like many preliterate societies elsewhere, the southeastern Indians subscribed to a system of beliefs in which all things material and spiritual were neatly categorized. According to the Cherokees, the world, which was flat and suspended by four cords, hung from a stone vault that lifted daily to permit passage of the heavenly bodies. Above the vault was an Upper World of purity, order, and stability inhabited by god-like beings, of which the sun and moon were the most important. Beneath this world was the Lower World of uncertainty and chaos inhabited by monsters, of which the Uktena was the most terrible. Possessing the wings of a bird, the body of a serpent, and the antlers of a deer, it combined normally separate categories of animals and thereby epitomized the awful consequences of confounding that which should be kept separate. Being balanced between opposing forces, this world and those that dwelled therein fared well when the balance was maintained. When the equilibrium was upset, evil and misfortune ensued. Thus, fire, which represented the sun from the Upper World, should never be extinguished with water, especially spring water which issued from the underworld. To mix categories was to create pollution.

Indian rituals and ceremonies were accordingly designed to maintain or restore purity. Whole villages bathed every morning; mothers sprinkled newborn infants or plunged them in creeks before permitting them to nurse; council members used the black drink before deliberating, and men fasted before joining war parties. Purity appears to have been the object in each case. Perhaps its importance can be seen most clearly in the "busk" or Green Corn Ceremony performed by virtually all of the southeastern Indians. A festival of fasting and feasting to celebrate the ripening of the corn crop, it was an occasion for wiping the slate clean and beginning anew. Thus the Chickasaws extinguished all fires, and a priest clad in white buckskin kindled a new one, which was then used to relight the fires of each household. Spouses could dissolve the tie that bound them, and offenders who had committed most types of crime received pardons.

The exception was a killer who remained liable for the death he had caused, even if it had been accidental. Unlike English criminal law, which was chiefly concerned with guilt, Indian legal systems were interested in questions of liability or responsibility for injuries inflicted.

The underlying principle was that of retaliation, "an eye for an eye or a tooth for a tooth." Although compensation of other kinds was accepted, at times, the usual sequence involved a life for a life. The life forfeited need not necessarily be that of the guilty party; it could be that of a kinsman. Both the responsibility for the initial wrong and for avenging it were collective; they belonged to the clans of which the individuals involved were members. Thus a Chickasaw once offered to die in place of his nephew who had killed a white man. Although the governor of South Carolina continued to demand the guilty party, the uncle's act was no mere gesture. His death would have satisfied the requirements of Indian law, which was designed to keep the peace. A life for a life evened the score, restored the balance and, at least theoretically, ended further retaliation. Colonists had some trouble getting this straight, perhaps because they frequently failed to understand the clan system.

The basic unit of Indian society was the clan, a kinship group which commonly traced the relationship of its members along matrilineal lines. An individual belonged to, for example, the deer clan because his mother belonged to the deer clan, and he was considered to be related to all other members of the clan. He could therefore expect special hospitality from kinsmen in other towns whom he might never have seen, and he was obligated to avenge their deaths. His father's clan was another matter. Most of its members were not considered to be his relations, and he might marry one of them whom we would consider to be closely related; nor was he obligated to retaliate for injuries done to them. Perhaps the most striking illustration of the close ties between the clan and legal systems arises out of the death of a child. For a father to kill his child was murder because they belonged to different clans, and he thus had committed a wrong which cried out for vengeance. However, if the mother killed her child, she did not commit infanticide because they were of the same clan and no one bore the responsibility for avenging the death. By the same principle, it would seem that members of the same clan might slay each other as adults without fear of retaliation. Actually, however, the moral sanctions against such behavior appear to have been strong enough to make it virtually unthinkable, and Indian societies apparently failed to develop institutionalized methods for dealing with these unusual occurrences.

At the same time, war—which was essentially an extension of the clan system of retaliatory justice—was common. Rarely, except perhaps at the peak of the Mississippian tradition, was it fought for territorial expansion or other economic gain; rather, its purposes were generally revenge or prestige. It was the way in which men acquired war names and other honors; one suspects that they regarded it as their essential function. Like hunting (which was also a man's business), war was seasonal. Men hunted game in winter and scalps in summer. Under most circumstances, annihilating the enemy would have been no more rational than annihilating the deer. War parties were therefore usually small-scale affairs, from two or three men up to perhaps twenty. Surprise was essential and, if discovered, such a party might turn around without engaging the enemy. One or two deaths on either side frequently ended a skirmish. If a party surprised and killed everyone in a small group of the enemy, it would leave some token—usually a war club—to reveal who had been responsible, lest the contest be without meaning. War waged by such rules ended without formal treaties, and peace was more a temporary respite than an extended condition.

Here again, Europeans had difficulty understanding Indian behavior. In particular, the rituals and ceremonies connected with war puzzled and frustrated them. For example, while forming a war party the Cherokees placed a sacred quartz crystal on a red pole and the warriors filed by. If one of them failed to see a flash of light, he dropped out of the undertaking. Similarly, a war party which encountered an unfavorable omen might turn around and go home. If Englishmen considered such behavior cowardly, they admired the Indians' prowess and courage in other contexts. As one Carolinian scornfully remarked in the late eighteenth century, local society had not progressed beyond the adolescent state in which men most respected physical accomplishments. Accordingly, whites marveled at the stature of Indian men, many of whom at 5 ft. 8 in. to 6 ft. were taller than most Europeans of this time. In addition, Indians were frequently in superb physical condition. According to one story, a trader, having wronged an Indian, escaped on horseback. Fifteen miles away, the Indian, who was on foot, overtook and killed him. No wonder that a British officer, seeking to describe the arduousness of a campaign in the mountains of western Carolina, summed everything up by noting, "Even our Indians were

Knocked up," or exhausted. Moreover, few whites would deny that when the end was inevitable Indians knew how to die.

In a sense, they had had lessons in dying from captives. To be a prisoner of the Indians was not to be in an enviable position. At one extreme, such persons, especially women or children, might be adopted and treated as full members of the tribe. Alternatively, they might be enslaved. Thereafter, they were walking scalps and lived precariously. Most men, however, were tortured and killed. The exact procedure varied from tribe to tribe, but a male captive was often tied to a frame or pole, his scalp taken or protected with clay, and he was then burned, sometimes by being impaled with resinous pine splinters which were lighted. Such burning may have been related to practices introduced by de Soto and other Europeans, but the taking of scalps seems to have been an indigenous custom. So, too, was the death song, which the captive was expected to sing while being tortured. Boasting of his exploits and showing contempt for his captors earned the dying man respect but seldom a reprieve. Betraying fear brought laughter and derision.

That women participated in torturing prisoners may seem surprising in view of the fact that war was predominately a male activity, and in many respects the sexes not only had very distinct roles but also remained apart much of the time. Yet these roles occasionally blurred, and Nancy Ward, who earned the title "War Woman," accompanied Cherokee warriors into battle during the 1750s and, after the Revolution, participated in peace talks. Actually the latter was not so unusual. Finding no women among white negotiators in Charles Town twenty years earlier, her uncle had inquired if whites were not also born of women. As his remark implied, Cherokee women, like those in most other southeastern tribes, enjoyed considerable influence if not power. A woman ruled Cofitachequi, the chiefdom in the interior of South Carolina visited by de Soto in 1540. And though they were probably more persuasive behind the scenes, women could speak in council meetings throughout the seventeenth and eighteenth centuries. To the extent that these tribes recognized private property (which did not include the communally worked fields), women—or the immediate lineage traced through women—also owned individual houses, and a new husband might move in with his wife. Like a man, a woman had virtually complete sexual freedom before marriage; thereafter—except among the Cherokees who continued to give her sexual privileges equal to those of her husband—something of a double standard applied, and she might have her ears cut off with a dull knife for adultery. Normally, women tended the fields and garden plot and did the gathering of vegetable foods; men supplied the meat. The latter skinned the animals; women processed the hides and made clothes. The rearing of girls was also the responsibility of women. Young men, however, came under the tutelage of their mother's brother or the senior male among her immediate relations. Although the pattern seems to have been somewhat modified by white influence, the father usually had only a minimal role in disciplining his sons. In fact, contemporary whites would probably not have used the term discipline to describe the restraints imposed upon boys who were reared in what appeared to be an extremely permissive environment. White observers undoubtedly underrated the power of ridicule and shame to shape behavior, but they were correct in believing that punishment seldom involved physical coercion.

Indeed, at least by the seventeenth century, coercion of anyone was very rare. At the height of the Mississippian tradition on the eve of European contact, there appeared to have been chiefdoms in which rulers exercised great discretionary, even arbitrary, power. Although the Natchez "Suns" continued to wield extraordinary authority, most chiefs—of which there were usually many in a tribe—were influential men who could persuade but not command. Each man and woman was a separate entity. Protected by their clans, they could not be compelled to act against their will. Perhaps nothing reveals the strength of this individualism more clearly than the siege of Fort Loudoun. In 1760, after surrounding the Carolina fort in what is now eastern Tennessee, Cherokee warriors settled down in uncharacteristic fashion to starve the garrison out. But Cherokee women who had husbands and lovers among the soldiers continued to supply them with food. Short of killing these women, there was no way to compel them to desist, and to kill them was to invite retaliation from their kinsmen. Indian decisions were arrived at by consensus, and treaties with whites, to be binding, required virtually unanimous approval.

Colonists sometimes called this anarchy but the goal was harmony, and Indians appear to have been generally quite successful in attaining it, not only in a social sense but in other ways as well. In particular, their beliefs formed a coherent whole in which almost everything was related to everything else. Furthermore, these belief systems, like many modern faiths and ideologies, involved abstract categories and tenets not easily susceptible to proof or disproof. Accordingly, the Indian way of life exhibited a toughness and resiliency in the face of white pressure that has been frequently overlooked.

Although whites often misunderstood the causes of what they believed to be the Indians' stubborn refusal to become "civilized," most colonial South Carolinians soon learned not to underrate it. The Spanish had rather mixed success in Christianizing Indians with their mission system and the English did considerably worse. The first Anglican missionary, who came to South Carolina in 1702, ostensibly to convert the Yamasee Indians, gave up without ever going beyond the white settlements near Charles Town. Few of his successors did much better, though the Society for the Propagation of the Gospel brought a young Yamasee "prince" to London some years later. He was among the first of several Indians who visited England under different auspices during the colonial period. Most notably, seven returned to London with Sir Alexander Cuming, a Scottish baronet who visited the Cherokees in 1730. A generation later, following the Cherokee War, several chiefs again went to London for a short stay. Frequently lionized and given royal audiences, such Indian visitors were exotics on the London scene and were usually being exploited for diplomatic or private purposes.

Something else seems to have been going on in the case of a German, Christian Priber, who lived among the Cherokees from 1736 to 1743. Priber was a fascinating and enigmatic figure who sought to erect a "kingdom of paradise" in the southern Appalachians. Unlike those utopian schemes which start from scratch, his seems to have involved a desire to preserve the best features of Indian society and some understanding of what they were. Among other things, he sought to educate the Cherokees about the white traders' techniques. Not surprisingly, the latter professed to believe that he was a Jesuit agent of the French crown. Seized by British traders and Creek auxiliaries, Priber died imprisoned in Georgia. James Adair was neither so colorful nor so eccentric, but he was an unusual trader, for he observed Indian life closely and sympathetically. Perhaps it is significant that he was unable to obtain enough subscribers in Charles Town to publish his *History of the American Indians*. Printed in London in 1775, it remains one of the basic sources for understanding native Carolinians.

Priber and Adair are notable because their attitudes towards Indians were exceptional. Daniel Hammerer deserves mention because his underwent a typical transformation. Another German, he concocted a scheme in the 1760s to civilize the Indians, for which he received support from the British ministry. Though skeptical, the lieutenant governor of South Carolina, William Bull, promised to aid; sometime later he reported that Hammerer had given up the task and turned instead to "trafficking" with the settlers of the backcountry. The whole episode epitomizes the English experience with the Indians. By the time Carolina was founded in 1670, Englishmen had the benefit of much prior contact with Indians elsewhere, but they were still not sure who the native Americans were and how they might behave. Some students of the matter suspected that they were descendants of the lost tribes of Israel, and as late as the early eighteenth century ministers in South Carolina frequently exhibited an otherwise puzzling interest in whether Indians were circumcised.

In general, however, most Englishmen appear at first to have believed that natives were merely human beings like themselves in what might now be called an earlier stage of social evolution. "Enlightened" Englishmen of the seventeenth and eighteenth centuries had descended from the "rude" Anglo-Saxons of the Dark Ages; so too, they thought, Indians would shortly become civilized. Such assumptions may have been partly responsible for the Carolina proprietors' liberal policy toward them, including the truly remarkable provision in the Fundamental Constitutions granting Indians complete religious toleration provided they acknowledge the existence of a God. Few did, in the Christian sense, and for entirely unrelated reasons the Fundamental Constitutions never became the law of the land. That provision and the assumptions undergirding it marked the road not taken. For conflict with the Indians soon convinced most South Carolinians that the likes of Hammerer were on a wild goose chase, and Bull represented the majority of those who came to believe that the Indians were locked in "savagism," destined not to evolve but to be brushed aside or crushed by the wheel of progress. He was therefore puzzled but not especially saddened by their fate. Concluding a report in 1770, he observed, "I cannot quit the Indians without mentioning an observation that has often raised my wonder. That in this province, settled in 1670...then swarming with tribes of Indians, there remain now, except the few

The Cherokee Indians who visited London in 1730 under the auspices of Sir Alexander Cuming. According to the original caption, they were (left to right) O Onaconoa, K Skalilosken Ketagustah, K Kollannah, Ok Oukah Ulah, T Tathtowe, C Clogoittah, and U Ukwaneequa. Engraving by Isaac Basire, London, 1730. *Courtesy of the South Caroliniana Library.*

Catawbas, nothing of them but their names, within three hundred miles of our sea coast;. . . nor [is there] any accounting for their extinction by war or pestilence equal to the effect." Expecting the same thing, whatever it was, to befall the Catawbas, he soon tried to make arrangements for his nephew to acquire their lands.

Few men in the seventeenth and eighteenth centuries were as humane as Bull; and many, not content merely to take advantage of the inevitable, were quite willing to assist in hastening it. Some of the Carolina traders were especially ruthless. One, irritated for some reason with an Indian woman, "caused" her, in the words of a contemporary observer, "to be scalloped." She lived for "two or three days in that miserable condition." Nevertheless, such random and gratuitous acts of violence, though perhaps more frequent than one would like to believe, could not have been common enough to have played a major role in reducing the Indian population. Bull, however, almost certainly underestimated the effects of disease. The long cold trek from Asia during the Ice Ages acted as a microbial filter, and by the time whites arrived in the New World, Indians had very little immunity to smallpox, whooping cough, measles, influenza, and other European diseases, let alone malaria and yellow fever which came from Africa. As we have seen, they died by the millions. During Bull's own lifetime, more than half the Cherokees succumbed to smallpox. Moreover, he probably overlooked the full impact of wars, which not only swiftly displaced or nearly annihilated whole tribes such as the Westos but also gradually eroded others. Whites had little or nothing to do with some of the attrition, but in other cases they instigated it for purposes of their own. Sometimes these were associated with the imperial ambitions of European powers; occasionally they involved the assumption that if Indians were not killing each other they would be killing whites; and more often than not, in the early days, they concerned the slave trade.

South Carolinians were *the* Indian slave traders of the North American continent. In fact, so many Indian slaves were exported from the colony that in 1715 Connecticut and some of the other New England colonies specifically barred their importation from Carolina. Historians have therefore frequently assumed that most captured Indians were sent to the Caribbean and elsewhere. Undoubtedly many were, but substantial numbers also remained in the province. In 1708, for example, the total slave population was approximately 4,300; 1,400, or about one-third, were Indians. Among the Indians were 300 children, 600 women, and 500 men. There are several ways of explaining these figures. Indian women were accustomed to agricultural labor, while their husbands were not. Whites therefore considered the Indian men lazy. Moreover, men were less tractable and more apt to run away or rebel. Many of those captured were accordingly sent to other markets or, usually it seems, killed. Certainly that is the implication of John Barnwell's statement following an attack on the Tuscarora Indians in 1712, to the effect that "while we were putting the men to the sword our Indians got all the slaves and plunder, only one girl we got." Similarly, at about the same time, an Anglican missionary condemned the Indian traders for instigating wars to produce slaves which could then be used to pay for goods. "And what slaves!" he continued. They were only "poor women and children; for the men taken prisoners were burnt most barbarously." Thus the 500 men on the tax list in 1708, or the 308 Indians presumably exported in 1716, are poor measures of the carnage wrought by the Indian slave trade. There is no way to estimate the number of warriors who died to produce these figures, but it must have been many times greater.

If Bull neglected the slave trade as a factor in the disappearance of the Indian, he may also have overlooked a few Indians who remained right at his own doorstep. Much has been written in the past about the breakdown of Indian cultures, the concomitant rise of alcoholism, and the growth of a degraded Indian population, eking out an existence in the interstices of white society. Although scholars are now more aware of the extent to which native Americans were able to retain tribal cultural integrity and tribal identities, the older view rested on considerable evidence. Like other diseases, alcoholism struck Indians especially hard. Why is not yet entirely clear. What is certain, though, is that some Indians continued to live among white settlements in South Carolina. Traces of them appeared in the record, especially in the seventeenth century, when they commonly served as hunters who, it was said, would keep a planter's table supplied with game for a mere trifle. By the 1740s, however, some ministers were reporting that there were few if any Indians left in their parishes. Yet as late as 1761 the governor observed that "there are among our Settlements several small

Tribes . . . , consisting only of some few Families each." Who they were and how they survived are questions which require further investigation.

How Indians perceived their eroding position also requires further study; their actions reveal patterns of both accommodation and resistance. The Catawbas, for example, kept their footing by becoming clients of the authorities in Charles Town. And unlike most of the southern Indians, they backed the winning side in the Revolution. Thus, despite some compromises—e.g., their "King" became a "general" during the Revolution—they were able to maintain much of their tribal culture and part of their lands. Today, still living in South Carolina, they are making attempts to obtain compensation for some of the rest. Indians also resented wrongs and retaliated in kind when they could. Thus many conflicts with whites were essentially traditional Indian wars in which the balance sheet of retribution might involve very precise calculations. At other times, as when Indians acted as auxiliaries with French or British armies, their own purposes were overshadowed and obscured.

The Yamasee War of 1715, however, appears to have been different and perhaps unique in character. Some contemporary South Carolinians blamed Spanish authorities for instigating the conflict; and Spaniards in Florida certainly provided a refuge for the Yamasees after the uprising failed, though modern scholarship tends to minimize the role of Europeans and attribute greater responsibility to the Creeks. Some historians have implied that the term "Yamasee War" is something of a misnomer that should signify no more than that the Yamasees, who were located near settlements in the southern part of South Carolina, attacked first. The most significant point, these scholars sensibly suggest, is not who started the war but the fact that before it was over about fifteen tribes were leagued against the whites. Yet an effort of such magnitude raises important questions about the Indians' intentions and ability to mount it, which are inseparable from the question of origin. One historian, Leitch Wright, has recently suggested that the Indian attacks were the dying gasps of Cofitachequi. Metaphorically speaking, he is of course correct, and vestiges of the organization of an earlier chiefdom, if they did persist, might well have facilitated a coordinated attack. Furthermore, if, as some scholars believe, the Yamasee language was widely understood among other tribes, it may have played an important part in the planning of hostilities. Thus it is perhaps significant that some knowledgeable Carolinians attributed the primary responsibility to the "Huspah King" of the Yamasees. In addition, the nature of the attacks suggest that for perhaps the only time in the colonial period, Indians in South Carolina both believed that they could wipe out the white settlements and attempted to act on that belief. If that supposition is correct, the war is probably appropriately named; for the Yamasee had reason to be especially confident of their own prowess and contemptuous of the whites'. In short, their grievances, which included intrusions on their lands as well as abuse and exploitation by avaricious traders, though serious, were common to other tribes, but their perspective on their problems and potential solutions may have been somewhat different.

Approximately three years before going to war with the colonists, a large number of Yamasee warriors had accompanied an expedition from South Carolina under John Barnwell, sent to assist the North Carolinians against the Tuscarora Indians. There the Yamasees could have made a number of relevant observations. First, the Tuscaroras nearly obliterated some of the settlements in North Carolina. They were also strong enough to force Barnwell to accept a negotiated peace. And finally, the Yamasees themselves may have been the best fighting men on the field; they certainly were the best in Barnwell's force, which eventually included quite a few white North Carolinians. In one engagement, the latter needlessly broke and ran, for which, Barnwell observed, several were "deservedly shot . . . in their arses." On the other hand, he was sure that his "brave Yamassees" would "live and die" with him. Nor was his confidence misplaced. "When all others left me in my greatest extremity," he later reported, they remained steadfast. In short, the Yamasees not only had reason to feel that subsequent mistreatment of them was a poor reward for their services, but they also had solid evidence to suggest that the Indians were capable of doing something about their plight. Significantly, a letter addressed to the governor of South Carolina was found on one of their dead after an early battle. It warned him to leave the province because the Indians intended to retake their country and they had, or soon would have, all the Indians on the continent with them. Such all-out efforts are frequently associated with more general attempts to revitalize threatened cultures. To what extent that was the case at this time is a question which also deserves more investigation.

The Yamasee War was the Indians' supreme effort at resistance in South Carolina and, in the end, it obviously failed. Leaving behind Pocotaligo and their other towns, the survivors withdrew to Florida, from which for many years they continued to harass the southern frontiers of their old homeland. Despite his oversights, Lieutenant Governor Bull was essentially correct. Like so many other Indians, the Yamasee were gone by his day, and Pocotaligo lives on today as a little hamlet, not far from Interstate 95 in Beaufort County. Musical names are a part of the local Indian legacy, but only a minor part. Textbooks in American history mention more important contributions to the colonial way of life—crops like corn and squash; techniques such as hilling for cultivating them, and ways of cooking them like cornbread and succotash. The list obviously could be extended to much greater length, but even this abbreviated version suggests both the limited nature and the character of much of this cultural transfer; it consisted of foods. Why the colonists were interested in Indian foodstuffs is perhaps obvious; precisely how they learned about them is not. One has to wonder if many South Carolinians visited Indian villages where they could have seen corn being grown and cooked. Whites in general could have picked up techniques from contemporaries who had been to Indian towns or from predecessors who were learning about such matters in Massachusetts and Virginia a half century or more before South Carolina was founded. The slave quarters were, however, a more direct route to the kitchen. Indeed, there is a chain of circumstantial evidence to indicate that this was in fact the chief channel of transmission. Indian women were in charge of growing and processing food in their own societies; Indian slavery was common in South Carolina; most Indian slaves were women; and planters usually permitted slaves to maintain their own garden plots. These gardens, one accordingly suspects, had a good deal more influence than the more elaborate experimental plantings made at the direction of the proprietors during the early years of the colony. Indian hominy lives on as grits, and soul food in general owes much to Indian cooking.

The relationship between Indians and blacks is difficult to categorize.

Throughout the colonial period whites tried hard to maintain separation and foster antipathy between free Indians and slaves. Blacks were forbidden to trade in the Indian towns, while Indians were encouraged to pursue runaway slaves. To judge from their own comments on the matter, white South Carolinians appear to have believed that their policy was successful. Indians, they claimed, hated blacks and blacks feared Indians. Perhaps so, but scattered evidence also indicates the contrary. A runaway black helped the Tuscarora Indians construct the fort which gave Barnwell such a hard time; runaway blacks and Indians inhabited Fort Mosé outside of St. Augustine, and both were among the ancestors of the Seminole Indians. If relations between Indians and blacks were this close outside of slavery, there is every reason to think that they were at least equally close within its confines, where many of the Indians were women while most of the blacks were men. Perhaps the complementary sex ratio helps to account for the natural increase among slaves, which probably began in South Carolina at a relatively early date. One can speculate even further about the effects of intermingling Indian and black slaves. Most African tribal societies were patrilineal, but black families exhibited many matrilineal features under slavery. Much of the change was undoubtedly due to the willingness of masters to disrupt the bond between father and son more often than that between mother and daughter. But for black South Carolinians the transition from one familial pattern to another may have been facilitated by the presence of Indian women. One also wonders about the role of "uncles." In the case of "Uncle Tom" and "Uncle Remus" the avuncular image is a neutered one. But Uncle Tom's forebears may have included an Indian warrior, for he was usually the one in charge of his sister's sons; and Uncle Remus certainly had Indian antecedents, for the trickster rabbit and the Tar Baby were characters in Indian myths. There is even another more remote but intriguing possibility. Shortly before the Civil War in Prince William's Parish, at least one slave foreman or driver was a woman. Such a thing was almost unheard of by this date, and it was probably rare at any time. Yet once again it is worth noting in their own societies Indian women exercised considerable authority and influence; they were familiar with agricultural techniques, and Indian slavery in South Carolina antedated the largest importations of blacks. Thus Indian women may well have been in a position to introduce newly arrived Africans to the routines of the plantation. Under these circumstances, it would not be surprising to find that some of them acted as drivers.

Certainly there can be no doubt that Indian slaves, especially women, were crucial vectors of the Indian cultural influence. This does not mean, however, that there were not other routes. White and Indian males met perhaps most memorably on the battlefield and in the council chamber. Indian men were at home in both. And, like Thomas Jefferson, white South Carolinians were frequently impressed by their eloquence. Thus, a few historians have attributed some characteristic features of Southern oratory to Indian influences. Nor does it seem unreasonable to suggest that Indians may have taught South Carolinians something else. At least William Gilmore Simms, the most prominent man of letters in the state during the antebellum period, carried admiration for their bravery far enough to express a fleeting regret that whites and Indians had not intermarried, for together they might have produced "the very noblest specimens of humanity... that the world has ever witnessed." To be sure, that statement was made after the Indians were no longer a real threat. But for more than a hundred years their presence had contributed very materially to a pervasive sense of insecurity which did much to shape the ethos of white South Carolinians. Insecure or not, however, Carolinians could not resist the lure of the land.

3

THE LAND

No doubt the Indians could have taught—and did teach—the settlers
much about the environment of the New World, but except for the
garden plot, the process of transmission is often obscure. What is
clearer is that Europeans learned and mislearned from each other.
Ribault, who observed that he had entered the River Jordan, "wherof
so muche hathe byn spoken," was obviously familiar with Spanish
efforts. Englishmen, too, knew about them, and in fact the record of
Spanish frustration and failure on the southern coast of North America
may have temporarily diminished their interest in the area. But Ribault's *The Whole and True Discoverye of Terra Florida* was intended to
stimulate, not discourage, English efforts. Thus he emphasized the
opportunities for Christianizing the natives, finding precious metals,
establishing naval bases, and settling the land.

By chance, however, Ribault landed in the part of Carolina where
the climate is the most semi-tropical. Having sailed into Port Royal
Sound, which he described as "one of the greatest and fayrest havens
of the world...where without danger all the shippes in the worlde
myght be harbored," he found "one of the goodlyest, best and frutfullest
culteres that ever was sene, and where nothing lacketh." There were
pepper trees and "the best watter of the worlde, and so many sortes of
fishes that ye maye take them withowt nett or angle, as many as you
will; also guinea foule and innumerable wildfoule." Laudonnière added
that some of the deer were so large and beautiful that Ribault ordered
his men not to shoot them. The place, Laudonnière continued, was so
pleasant that it was beyond comparison. "It was completely covered

with numerous tall oaks and cedars" and turkeys flew through the forest. Animals common to Europe abounded, and the whole "was a beautiful thing to see." Among them everywhere "were palm trees and many other kinds of trees, and flowers and fruit with rare shapes and attractive perfumes," and the air was laden with their scent. Readers no doubt recalled that the legendary air of Paradise was often perfumed; certainly, some twenty years later, Sir Walter Raleigh noted that palm trees were native to it, "for whereinsoever the Earth, Nature, and the Sun can most vaunt that they have excelled, yet shall the Palme-tree be the greatest wonder of all their workes: This tree alone giveth unto man whatsoever his life beggeth at Nature's hand." And palm trees grew in Carolina! Accordingly, he concluded that the Garden of Eden had been located in the same latitude. Thus, legend, chance, experience, and promotionalism came together, and for a moment at least it appeared that Carolina resembled our earthly birthplace.

But reality soon intruded. Indeed, men spent most of the seventeenth and eighteenth centuries coming to terms with the local environment. By the end of the eighteenth century, the boundaries of the state were approximately what they are today, and a reasonably accurate understanding of climate and topography prevailed. Not everyone who wrote about them was an equally keen and accurate observer. Promotional pamphlets, of which many were published in the late seventeenth century, were the equivalent of modern sales brochures. They accordingly provide a good index to the writers' assumptions about the values and aspirations of prospective settlers but not necessarily much accurate information about the environment. As one frequently reprinted work first published in 1682 described the colony, South Carolina was "a pleasant and fertile Country, abounding in health and pleasure, and with all things necessary for the sustenance of mankind." Tempered chiefly, if at all, by the need to maintain credibility as more was learned about the area, these pamphlets attempted to perpetuate the image of a land of milk and honey. Travelers' accounts were frequently not much more reliable, for, as a Virginian observed early in the eighteenth century, "there are no books (the Legends of Saints always excepted,) so stuff'd with Poetical-Stories, as Voyages; and the more distant the Countries lie, which they pretend to describe, the greater License those priviledg'd Authors take, in imposing upon the World." Settlers, on the other hand, though perhaps generally more truthful, seldom described their environment systematically and in detail. As might be expected, official and scientific reports were usually the most complete and accurate, and fortunately for the historian, a number of naturalists, including Mark Catesby and William Bartram, came through South Carolina in the eighteenth century.

What strikes the modern reader most forcibly about these early writings is their attention to details which only a few individuals would now notice, such as the direction of the prevailing winds, the height of the tides, and the consistency of the soil. These observations suggest something which should be obvious but is frequently overlooked in a period of technological and scientific hubris. During the seventeenth and eighteenth centuries, everyone, even the most wealthy and sophisticated, lived relatively close to nature. To say this is not to exhume long dead and properly interred notions of geographic determinism. Few now doubt that what man chooses to do with a given environment is usually more important than the environment itself in shaping his social institutions; but it is easy for an age which has sent men to the moon and returned them safely to forget how narrow the range of options often was for earlier generations. Physical geography made a difference in colonial South Carolina, indeed perhaps more of a difference there than in some of the other colonies where it impinged on the inhabitants more uniformly and perhaps less forcefully.

For a relatively small colony, South Carolina possessed an unusually varied climate and topography. On a map it now looks roughly like a triangular kite or shield tilted so that its coastal base runs northeastwardly from the mouth of the Savannah River while its apex points northwestwardly at the Appalachian Mountains. Charleston is at approximately the midpoint of the base; from it to the westernmost point is about 235 miles; the coastline stretches for approximately 190 miles. Thus, South Carolina contains slightly over 31,000 square miles or almost 20 million acres, which makes it somewhat smaller than Maine or Indiana. The elevation ranges from sea level to more than 3,500 feet; average annual rainfall varies from about forty-one inches in the driest central portions to as much as seventy inches in the wettest areas of the mountains, while the temperature may fluctuate from below zero to about 100°F. Portions of the state exhibit occasional seismic activity. An earthquake struck Charles Town at the end of the seventeenth century, apparently without inflicting great damage (unlike the one of 1886). Tornadoes and waterspouts, such as the one that capsized and dismasted ships in the Ashley River at Charles Town in 1764, were relatively infrequent and, in a sparsely populated colony, usually not very destructive.

Hurricanes, which occurred periodically and affected much wider areas, were a more serious matter. Following the storm of 1686, "the whole Country" seemed to one observer "to bee one entire map of Devastation," and two perhaps equally destructive hurricanes struck Charles Town in 1752. The possibility of such occurrences was therefore something which always had to be considered in coastal areas between June and October. For instance, American and French forces cut short their attempt to capture Savannah from the British in 1779 because the French naval commander was reluctant to remain on a hurricane-prone coast during the height of the storm season. In the nineteenth century planters began constructing brick towers (like windmill towers without the machinery) as hurricane shelters for slaves in the rice planting district around Georgetown. Before then, however, the loss of life in low-lying areas must have been substantial during storms.

The nature of the coast itself and the resulting pattern of settlement provided some protection, however, at least in the southern part of the colony. From Winyaw Bay northward, there are few if any barrier islands; from the bay southward, they dominate the coastline. The tidal creeks and estuaries separating them are frequently surprisingly large and deep. In part, it was the size of these estuaries and the apparent ease of access which they provided into the interior that made the area around Port Royal especially attractive to the early explorers. The Broad River there was big enough for a vessel sailing up it to disappear over the horizon, and the anchorage, as Ribault had noted, was large enough to hold all the navies of the world, including the British navy in the eighteenth century—a fact which was not lost on local boosters who repeatedly tried without success to convince the admiralty to establish a naval station there. But the very features that attracted mariners tended to repel settlers, for the tides in this area rose and fell, on an average, more than seven feet, and the resulting tidal currents were faster than small boats propelled only by paddles or oars could negotiate easily. As a result, everyday transportation was difficult. Conversely, the large plantation craft designed to carry heavy produce to market had trouble maneuvering in confined waters; they were decked to cope with rough water and went far enough out to sea to avoid shoals, something that British authorities had trouble comprehending when they tried to tighten maritime regulations on the eve of the Revolution. Thus the islands along the southern coast remained isolated and sparsely populated until late in the colonial period. Shifting slightly as beaches eroded and built up again over the years, they acted as buffers for the mainland, protecting it against storms.

Behind these islands and on the mainland are a number of distinctive features of the coastal plain. In the long run, perhaps the most important of these are the extensive salt water marshes (South Carolina now contains 25 percent of the salt marshes on the eastern coast of the United States), for such wetlands represent a rich and varied ecological system supporting a wide variety of aquatic life. During the colonial period, livestock sometimes grazed on them. Savannahs—treeless grasslands in otherwise forested areas*—provided better pasture, and local names, such as "Horse Savannah," often reflected their use. Their origin is still somewhat puzzling, but most experts now believe that the Indians' practice of burning the woods was a factor. The prevalence of savannahs, as well as the salt marshes which provided a year-round fodder, helped to make the southern coastal plain the center of the early cattle industry, from which it spread inland to the tributaries of the Edisto River. In fact, livestock were so fond of the cane which grew along these rivers that overgrazing almost wiped out the canebrakes.

Except for the Savannah, most of the true rivers in the southern part of the province, like the Edisto, are relatively short and slow moving, while those north of Charleston originate in the piedmont of North Carolina and carry a larger volume of water. Thus before the Santee was diverted into the Cooper River in the 1940s, the stream flow was sufficient to restrict salt water to the first two miles of river at high tide. In contrast, some of the southern rivers might be brackish thirty-five miles from their mouths under comparable conditions. The Ashley and Cooper rivers at Charles Town were both relatively short, but there was sufficient fresh water in their upper reaches to provide protection for ships which came up the rivers to escape the marine

---

*The term "savannah" was also sometimes used to denote fresh water marshland without trees.

organisms that attacked the bottoms of wooden ships in salt water. Neither of these two rivers nor the short streams in the southern part of the colony were subject to the severe flooding characteristic of the Santee system. "Freshes," as they were known, were, however, a seasonal occurrence almost everywhere. (Some erosion seems to have been almost constant in the watersheds, for navigational aids often mentioned that the sea was muddy several miles offshore.) There are indications, however, that both the severity of flooding and the loss of topsoil increased as more of the interior uplands came under cultivation. Much of the topsoil lost from areas upriver was deposited along the lower reaches, and this process contributed to the fertility of the fresh water swamps which were found to be the best for growing rice. Large cypress trees and dark brown loam were thought to signify prime rice land. Later, as planters learned to use the rise and fall of the tide to flood and drain fresh water from the fields, rice production came to be concentrated in a narrow band along the lower reaches of the rivers in the vicinity of Georgetown where conditions were ideal.

Inland, the character of the land changed. High ground in and around the swamps was usually covered with pine trees, and these became increasingly common as one went west. Quite early men began to develop the notion that the west was best, that perhaps the soil was better or that it was healthier there. To what extent this feeling foreshadowed the pull of the trans-Appalachian west is perhaps worthy of consideration elsewhere, but there was certainly a limit to the west's attractiveness to the earliest settlers in South Carolina. Approximately eighty miles inland, running parallel to the coast, were the sandhills, which supported thin stands of pine and scrub oak separated by areas of bare soil. The High Hills of Santee which rose abruptly to a height of about 200 feet above the surrounding countryside were the most notable features in this area. Located on the Wateree, not the Santee River, they were thought to be a healthy place, and their name may have arisen from the French word for health. The rest of the sandhill country received less favorable comment. In fact, Washington, who traveled through it from Columbia to Camden in 1791, termed it the "most miserable pine barren" he had ever seen. Being inhospitable, the area remained relatively uninhabited long after the regions on both sides contained substantial populations.

The sandhills therefore marked a more "real" line of separation than the imaginary "fall line." The latter term, though frequently used to refer to a line drawn on a map which would connect the first rapids in the several rivers, is misleading. No abrupt break marks the landscape and even the location of the rapids shifts with the season and the water level. But the sandhills do mark a geological zone running roughly parallel to the present coastline. On the eastern side, the land is flat or gently rolling; on the western it rises more steeply and becomes more broken. For the next 100 miles or so travelers going west would be among pines and an increasing number of hardwoods, including oak and hickory. By the time they reached the mountains, these hardwoods would predominate. The mountains themselves, though not especially high as mountains go, were fairly rugged. And though they did not act as a population dam holding settlements on the eastern side until sufficient pressure built up to flow over the crests (it never did in South Carolina), these mountains did help to protect the Cherokee Indians longer than most of the tribes in the southeast.

The climate varied as much as the landscape. Pleasantly cool in summer, the mountains could be miserably cold in winter. A traveler who penetrated deep into them in the 1760s reported that "the potts [were] ready to freeze on a slow fire: I must own," he continued, "I was never more sensible of the cold, even in Novascotia." Conversely, in summer the lowcountry was almost unbearable for those not accustomed to it. "We have been as if we were baked in an Oven," one woman wrote in 1711, and a half century later even Eliza Lucas Pinckney admitted that "4 months in the year is extreamly disagreeable, excessive hott." She could equally well have referred to the rain in February. A newly arrived official, who eventually became fond of South Carolina, concluded during his first winter in Charles Town that "this country is certainly the pisspot of the world." Little did he know that periodic droughts struck even some of the areas of highest rainfall. In short, despite its location on the 35th parallel, the climate was not Mediterranean. Rather, it varied from nearly subtropical on the southern coast, where the Gulf Stream comes close to shore, to Alpine in the mountains, and the seasonal range was considerably greater. For several years in the eighteenth century, it appeared that oranges might be grown successfully along the coast, and leases sometimes required tenants to plant a given number of trees per year. Most plantings died in the hard winter of 1748, though a few individuals continued to experiment with them.

Colonists could deal with the extremes of temperature, but disease proved to be an especially intractable problem. The earliest settlers believed that they had come to a healthy country, perhaps because they contrasted it to the West Indies, but within a decade South Carolina had begun to develop a reputation as a "charnel house." By the eighteenth century there was a German aphorism to the effect that those who wished to die quickly went to South Carolina. Contemporaries also nicknamed the characteristic sallow, sickly complexion of those who survived, the "Carolina Phiz" or physiognomy. Such morbid jocularity was founded on fact. During the eighteenth century over a third of the Anglican missionaries coming to the colony died or resigned because of illness within the first five years; more than 50 percent were either dead or seriously ill during the first decade after their arrival. One who stuck to his post was so weak and shaken with chills that he "was forced to write with both hands"; another reported that he had "not...one day or one Night's Ease or rest these four Months past, ... [and] now it affects me to such a degree that no less than fifteen times a night I am oblig'd to get up; & that accompanied by the Most excruciating pains in my Bowels, my back, my Loins."

He had one of the more common complaints known as the "bloody flux"; the man who could not hold the pen suffered from fever and "ague." In all probability these terms referred to dysentery and malaria, the two diseases—along with yellow fever—which were primarily responsible for the poor reputation of the colony. Immigrants and infants appear to have been most susceptible to dysentery, and, although it seldom killed adults outright, it debilitated them, making them vulnerable to other diseases. Much the same could be said about malaria, though the severity of its attacks varied widely. A relatively mild form of the disease was present in England before the settlement of South Carolina, but more virulent varieties, which apparently came to South Carolina from Africa by way of the West Indies, soon appeared. Almost certainly, yellow fever followed the same route, first appearing in Charles Town in 1699. Thereafter periodic outbreaks occurred throughout the eighteenth century. Unlike the other two diseases, yellow fever either killed those who contracted it or rendered them at least partially immune to future attacks. Blacks, having come from regions where yellow fever and malaria were common, possessed considerable natural immunity; whites did not. (Susceptibility to lung and respiratory diseases seems to have been reversed.)

Except for developing such natural immunities over time, there was little that contemporaries could do to cope very effectively with these diseases. Until the late nineteenth century no one knew that mosquitoes were the carriers of both yellow fever and malaria, though few doubted that these insects were "very Troublesome." Thus many who could afford it slept under mosquito nettings or "Pavillions Made of Catgut Gause," as one woman described them, and by the early nineteenth century ladies sometimes wore gauze pantaloons to cover their legs. Perhaps these measures helped some. Quite early, settlers also began associating disease with stagnant water and "the miasmas" of the swamps. Initially, Charles Town itself appeared to be more unhealthy than the surrounding countryside, and crowded conditions always made it the center of epidemics. It soon became apparent, however, that the farther one went from the swamps during the sickly season, the better off one was. Accordingly, the wealthy began going to Charles Town; later destinations also included the beaches, northern resorts such as Newport, Rhode Island, and in the era of the Revolution, the upcountry of South Carolina itself. In the eighteenth century, planters also began to associate pine trees (which require relatively dry land) with healthy locations. Consequently, they not only moved their houses farther away from the swamps but also at the end of the century established a number of little towns like Pinopolis on higher locations in the lowcountry. When all else failed, they took Peruvian or cinchona bark for the ague. Containing quinine, it was a reasonably effective remedy. But that at midcentury forty-five was still considered to be the average lifespan speaks volumes about the debilitating effects of disease throughout the colonial period.

If, as the popular saying went, South Carolina was "a hospital" in the fall, it was also "a paradise" in the spring, though many of the domestic flowers and shrubs now associated with it, such as the gardenia and the poinsettia (both of which were named for South Carolinians), as well as some azaleas, were introduced in the eighteenth and nineteenth centuries. Other varieties of azaleas, the flowering magnolia, the palmetto, and yellow jessamine, among other plants, were native.

So too were Spanish moss, live oaks, and the bald cypress tree. The former, which grows on trees near the coast, is an airplant once used by settlers for stuffing mattresses and pillows as well as feeding livestock. To Englishmen, live oaks and cypress were anomalous, for the latter sheds its needles while the former retains its leaves during the winter. Moreover, the cypress, which grows in water, is surrounded by protrusions from its roots known as "knees" whose purpose is not yet completely understood. Both trees were extremely useful to the colonists. Live oaks not only provided shade for man and beast over lowcountry roads—something so essential that trees along the right of way were protected by law—but also furnished a hard and durable wood, especially good for ship timbers. Cypress, on the other hand, was soft and somewhat oily. Easily worked and highly resistant to insects and rot, it was used for shingles, posts, and other building construction materials.

Most native animal life played a less essential role for the colonists, but some of it seemed to be fully as unusual as the plants. Deer and turkey (of which there might be fifty in a flock) provided the chief game for whites as well as Indians. Blacks, who were generally not supposed to possess firearms, relied more on small game such as ricefield rats, opossums, and raccoons—which, incidentally, some English visitors appear to have mistaken for foxes. Perhaps they looked more carefully if not closely at the alligators and snakes, both of which were continuing sources of fascination. The former, though a danger to some livestock, only rarely attacked humans. The latter, however, were a cause for some concern. Writing in 1725, a woman shopkeeper noted that in the vicinity of Charles Town there was something "called a Rattle Snake, so Named from Rattles in its Tail which you may hear at a very Considerable Distance, and a Large sort of Black Water Snake [the water moccasin], the Bite of both which are Mortal." Rattlesnakes in particular were sufficiently common and dangerous enough for the legislature to offer rewards for the discovery of cures for their bite, which more than one black collected. On the grounds that the reptile seemed to be immune to its own poison, a broth made from the rattlesnake itself was sometimes believed to be an antidote. Many individuals also considered the meat, which was said to taste like veal, to be quite good. Green and loggerhead turtles were also delicacies, and they were often sent as presents to friends and acquaintances in

"The Parrot of Carolina" sitting on a cypress bough, as depicted in Mark Catesby, *The Natural History of Carolina, Florida, and the Bahama Islands*, 2 vols. (London, 1731–1747). The Carolina parakeet is now believed to be extinct.

A rattlesnake, probably of the canebrake variety native to the Carolina low-country, as depicted in Mark Catesby, *The Natural History of Carolina, Florida, and the Bahama Islands*, 2 vols. (London, 1731–1747).

England. Then common enough to appear in the diet of indentured servants with sufficient frequency to raise complaints, these turtles are now endangered.

In the seventeenth and eighteenth centuries there was little indication any species would be in trouble, and most early South Carolinians were definitely not conservationists. For that very reason, however, even small indications of an increasing awareness that natural resources were not inexhaustible are especially noteworthy. Some of these indications are, to be sure, a bit misleading. Laws against night hunting or jacklighting deer probably had more to do with the protection of livestock—which roamed loose in the woods—and with control of a wandering population of hunters than with the preservation of deer. Yet by the mid-eighteenth century the *South Carolina Gazette* repeatedly condemned the "ill-judged" practice of seasonally burning the woods, not only because of smoke, which sometimes contributed to smog thick enough to prevent ships from entering port, but also because of the apparent damage to young timber and topsoil. Perhaps the printer had recently bought firewood and was therefore sensitive to such matters. Hauled in from a distance, fuel was becoming increasingly expensive in Charles Town by the end of the colonial period. Some residents therefore burned imported coal, and many complained about the price of wood. The British, who occupied the city during the Revolution, even cut down the protected trees lining nearby roads. Clearly, by this time, few individuals could have been oblivious to depletion of some natural resources. Fewer still, however, would have been willing to agree with Johann Martin Bolzius, a German minister who spent the middle third of the eighteenth century in South Carolina and Georgia. Lamenting the over-grazing of the canebrakes and the indiscriminate slaughter of deer, he exclaimed, "Oh, how good it would be for the present and future world if the abuse of freedom in this land would be limited a little."

John Drayton, who was governor of the state during the last decade of the eighteenth century, was not ready to go that far (though he was much disgusted with the common practice of cutting down chestnut trees to harvest the nuts), but he was clearly a pioneer in another sense. Reflecting on possible ties between the physical characteristics, the social configuration, and the history of his state, he may have been the first American to hit upon the basic concept of regional geography.

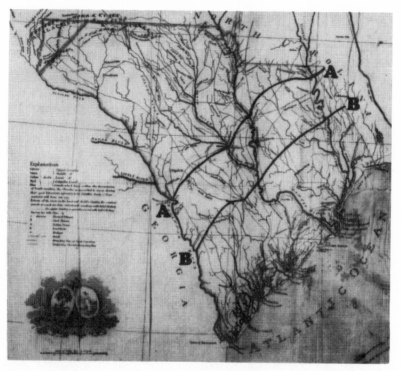

The pathbreaking map of South Carolina drawn to accompany John Drayton's *A View of South-Carolina as Respects her Natural and Civil Concerns* (Charleston, 1802). On the original hand-colored map, the area to the west of the curved line labeled here A-A was outlined in green to designate the "Upper Country." The region between A-A and B-B was left white to denote the "Middle Country," while the area southeast of B-B had a yellow border indicating that it represented the "Lower Country." The irregular diamond along the boundary of North Carolina, which designated the land set aside for the Catawba Indians, was outlined in red. *Map courtesy of the South Caroliniana Library.*

His *View of South Carolina* (1802) went beyond Jefferson's *Notes on the State of Virginia* by containing a map depicting the "low," "middle," and "upper" country. That map, geographers have noted, was "the first one authored by an American on which regions are given definite and logical expression." That a South Carolinian should be perhaps the first to think in such terms says much about the power of the environment in shaping the history of the state.

For most of the colonial period, however, South Carolina consisted almost exclusively of only one of Drayton's regions, the lowcountry. Despite its hardships and the dangers of disease, settlers came. Some died quickly and a few fled, but many persisted, learned, and prevailed. Part of the lure was of course the ownership of land, any land, and what it could produce. Yet, for those who came and stayed, the attractions soon went deeper, and though they are difficult to put into words, two contemporary vignettes provide illustrations. One is from a planter's daybook kept early in the nineteenth century; the other from the letters of a loyalist written shortly after the Revolution. Walking through his fields one day, the planter watched as lightning hit a live oak tree and its Spanish moss dropped in a shower of fire. Sitting in far off London, the loyalist remembered the natural glories of Carolina, including the "innumerable hosts of fireflies," its thunder and lightning, and "fine peaches." The Kennedy peach, he recalled, exceeded "in richness and flavour any other fruit or what ever fancy can suggest—a taste the cold clime of Albion with all her art can never emulate." Homesick as he was, Alexander Garden—and perhaps most South Carolinians—would nevertheless have been quick to realize that peaches were not a native plant but a domesticated fruit introduced by Europeans.

4

THE SEVENTEENTH CENTURY

During the seventeenth century Englishmen succeeded where the French and Spanish failed, and by the end of the period South Carolina was a well-established, if not exactly flourishing, colony. At first, however, the result of English efforts was scarcely more encouraging than that of their predecessors. Not a great deal is known about these early seventeenth century ventures, which often seem to have involved much negotiation and many legal complications but few settlers. Nevertheless, their story is instructive because it suggests by contrast some of the conditions that contributed to later success.

The first prominent Englishman to become involved with the area that would later become South Carolina was the attorney general in the 1620s, Sir Robert Heath. More willing to challenge Spanish power in the New World than James I had been, Charles I in 1629 granted Heath an immense tract named "Carolana" (for Charles himself) which stretched southward from Virginia to Spanish Florida and westward to the Pacific Ocean. Precisely what connection Heath had at this time with a number of Huguenot refugees who had fled France after the Protestants' defeat in a civil war is unclear: perhaps he planned to settle his colony with them; perhaps, however, they were his competitors for a grant. Whatever their initial relationship, these Huguenots—like Ribault before them and others of the same persuasion after them— saw the possibility of establishing a religious refuge in Carolina, and they were soon cooperating with Heath. Extended negotiations occupied much of 1630, during which the Huguenots helped to formulate plans for establishing salt works in the colony. These schemes proved to be unrealistic, and matters dragged on. In 1632, however, the group dispatched a vessel to explore the Carolina coast, and the following year some forty prospective settlers, who intended to stop in Virginia enroute, set sail aboard the *Mayflower* (not the Pilgrims' vessel). They seem never to have progressed farther than Virginia. By this time Heath appears to have lost faith in the Huguenots, and an agreement with the crown that all settlers would be Anglicans may have been his way of disencumbering himself of the Frenchmen. Not long thereafter, Heath assigned his title to Carolina to a young nobleman, Henry, Lord Maltravers, whose attempts to settle the area in the late 1630s also failed. In each case, it seems, the project foundered on lack of funds, poor management, and bad timing, for this was a period in which the competition for settlers from Massachusetts, Virginia, and Maryland helped to undermine the Carolina project. A generation later, other colonies, which were by then overcrowded, would supply settlers, while new proprietors would provide better planning and more initial support.

In the interim, civil war in England diverted attention away from the southeastern coast of North America. The victorious Puritans nevertheless exhibited considerable interest in the empire. Under the Commonwealth, naval forces seized Jamaica from the Spanish, made war upon Dutch trade, and passed the first navigation act restricting colonial trade to English vessels. After the restoration of the monarchy in 1660, this trend continued. More navigation acts and more wars with the Dutch followed; the Duke of York, who would later become James II, captured and renamed New Amsterdam, while he—like many of his associates—invested in the colonial slave and fur trades. More important, in the next two decades men close to the crown founded four new proprietary colonies.

One of them was to become South Carolina; two of its eight proprietors were also the proprietors of New Jersey, and nearly everyone in the Carolina group was involved in one way or another in other colonial ventures or their governance. None of its members, however, was primarily a colonial entrepreneur; rather, all were politicians and men of affairs who sought to make money on the side from landed estates in the New World. One of the least influential politically but perhaps one of the more important for the subsequent history of South Carolina was Sir John Colleton. He had fought for Charles I, lost, and fled to Barbados where he became a planter. Barbados during this period was in the throes of rapid change. The great bonanza which accompanied the transformation from tobacco to sugar had come and not quite gone, but the acquisition of wealth for even the ruthless and lucky few was not as easy as it had once been. For the elite, increasing difficulty in obtaining land, greater commercial restrictions, and less political autonomy were the problems. For other men, pushed aside by the consolidation of the sugar estates, the island was clearly too crowded, and after 1650 more than 10,000 persons left. These developments, Colleton and others believed, created opportunities as well as problems.

In London to claim his reward for faithful service, Colleton enlisted the help of John and William Berkeley. William, who was also in the city on a mission of his own, was governor of Virginia, and for some time now Virginians had been drifting southward into the area around Albemarle Sound which was to become the nucleus of North Carolina. Most historians have therefore assumed that William Berkeley, like Colleton, was one of the prime movers of the Caroline proprietorship. Recently, however, a leading authority on the southern colonies in the seventeenth century, Wesley Frank Craven, has suggested otherwise, pointing out that Berkeley objected to the infringement of Virginia's claims inherent in Heath's charter and that he made no financial contribution to the Carolina project. Nevertheless he was the brother of Lord John, Baron Berkeley of Stratton, who was close to the Duke of York, who was, in turn, close to Sir George Carteret. (The duke would soon give New Jersey to these two.) In addition, Colleton was related to the Duke of Albemarle, who had helped to engineer Charles II's return to his father's throne. Eventually, the group included William Lord Craven, another loyal and powerful royalist, Lord Clarendon, the king's first minister, and Anthony Ashley Cooper, who would soon become Lord Shaftesbury. Without doubt, the skillfully assembled combination had political influence. Thus although Charles II would probably have preferred not to make the grant, the eight proprietors received Carolina in 1663.

Two years later, after the claims of Heath's successors had been disposed of, Charles issued another charter extending the boundaries of the colony to include the existing settlement at Albemarle on the north and St. Augustine on the south. Such an extravagant grant, which gave the Carolina proprietors a title to the upper Gulf Coast, was apparently designed to put pressure on Spain. If so, the scheme worked, for Spanish negotiators soon agreed to the Treaty of Madrid which recognized that England was in effective occupation of large portions of the North American coast southward as far as the site of modern Charleston. Precisely how effective the occupation of the southernmost point was might be a question open to debate, and, despite the treaty, Spaniards in Florida attempted to make the most of the doubt for many years to come. In other essentials, the two charters were similar. Like that given Lord Baltimore a generation earlier, the Carolina charters conferred upon the proprietors the land and all "Rights, Jurisdictions, Privileges, Prerogatives, Royalties, Liberties, Immunities, and Franchises of what kind soever within the Country, ... TO HAVE, use, exercise, and enjoy, and in as ample manner as any Bishop of Durham, in our Kingdom of England, ever heretofore have" exercised. The bishops of Durham had been the feudal overlords of a frontier county in which as late as the fifteenth century the administration of justice and government derived only indirectly from the crown. Thus the "true Lords and Proprietors" of Carolina were empowered to govern the province; to make laws—with the "advice, assent, and approbation of the Freemen"; to enforce the laws—"YEA, if it shall be needful . . . by taking away member and life . . ."; to maintain military forces, "to make War and pursue the Enemies . . . , as well by Sea as by land"; and, among other things, to grant such religious toleration as they, "their heirs or Assigns, shall, in their discretions, think fit and reasonable."

Given these sweeping powers, which also included the right to create a nobility (provided its titles were not the same as those used in England), what is perhaps most significant is the liberality with which the proprietors eventually acted. Perhaps they learned from early disappointments. Their hope, of course, was to attract as many settlers as possible, not necessarily from England—for it was then thought emigration might weaken the nation—but from the older colonies. In particular, New England as well as Barbados might be a source of experienced colonists, and the Puritans' success in establishing towns especially impressed the proprietors. Accordingly, they were pleased when a group from Massachusetts established a settlement on the Cape Fear River early in 1663. For reasons not entirely clear, it lasted only a few months before the settlers abruptly decamped, leaving behind a sign execrating Carolina. The desire to minimize the potentially adverse effects of this episode may help to explain the extraordinarily generous provisions of the Concessions and Agreements issued in 1665. This document, which was also used virtually without change by Berkeley and Carteret in New Jersey, promised all settlers almost complete self-government through an elected assembly having the sole right to tax inhabitants, freedom of conscience in matters of religion, and nearly free land under a headright system giving the first arrivals up to 150 acres for themselves and each dependent. In return for all of this, the proprietors retained the right to veto legislation and to collect a quitrent of a halfpenny per acre per year.

Meanwhile, a number of Barbadians were making their own plans for settling the area. The first group, known as the "Barbadian Adventurers," included Peter Colleton, the oldest son of the proprietor. Failure to come to a meeting of the minds with the proprietors over the arrangements for local government checked their efforts. However, another group, led by John Vassall, established another settlement at Cape Fear before coming to a final agreement with the proprietors. In the meantime, negotiations with still another group of Barbadians under Sir John Yeamans bore fruit in a formal agreement and his appointment as governor. Intending to plant settlements at both Cape Fear and Port Royal, Yeamans and his contingent at the end of 1665 joined men already at Cape Fear, superseding Vassall. The area proved to be more than a match for the Barbadians as well as the New Englanders. The largest vessel bearing most of the provisions ran aground and another dispatched for supplies encountered such adverse winds that its captain broke under the strain and leapt overboard. "A child," according to contemporary reports, brought the vessel safely into port, but even such apparently providential care failed to save the colony. By 1667 both the settlement at Cape Fear and the plans for another at Port Royal had been abandoned. Bad luck and trouble with the local Indians contributed to the failure, but friction between the two groups of settlers and poor leadership also played a part. Yeamans, for example, stayed only a few weeks before returning to Barbados.

Nevertheless, these unsuccessful efforts by the Barbadians had some lasting effects. The first group hired William Hilton (for whom Hilton Head Island is named) to explore the coast of Carolina; and the Yeamans-Vassall group sent Robert Sandford south from Cape Fear on a similar mission. Both men published glowing accounts of their voyages lauding in particular the area around Port Royal. Sandford also ceremoniously took possession of all the land in the name of the king and to seal the "bargain" left behind with the Indians an intrepid volunteer, Dr. Henry Woodward. Woodward was soon captured by the Spanish, taken to St. Augustine, rescued by an English pirate, shipwrecked, and eventually joined the expedition which founded the first permanent settlement in 1670.

Up to this time, the proprietors themselves had not been very active in attempting to exploit their holdings. No doubt they had not originally envisaged the need for personal efforts, but as others tried and failed they may have changed their minds. Events at home, however, would probably have precluded action, for in 1665 the Great Plague killed thousands, and in 1666 the Great Fire swept London, destroying more than 13,000 houses. Meanwhile war with the Dutch and French dragged on until 1667. That the proprietors did not do more is therefore not really surprising. The question is why Anthony Ashley Cooper was the one who suddenly galvanized them into action in 1669. He was not the palatine or head of the group (though the palatine did assign his powers to him after Cooper had organized the expedition). Cooper, who became Lord Shaftesbury in 1672, was something of an enigma to his contemporaries and remains one to this day. An extraordinarily able—if rather slippery—politician, he served both Cromwell and Charles II. Under the latter he was appointed lord chancellor before losing favor by attempting to exclude Charles's Catholic brother James from the succession to the throne. When legal methods failed, Shaftesbury helped to organize an abortive rebellion, for which he almost lost his life and did spend his last days in exile. Given the record, John Dryden's poetic description does not seem unduly unfair:

> For close designs and crooked counsels fit.
> Sagacious, bold, and turbulent of wit,
> Restless, unfixed in principles and place,
> In power unpleased, impatient of disgrace;
> "Absalom and Achitophel," lines 152–155

While his star was ascending, Shaftesbury certainly seemed at home in court. Fond of pomp and ceremony, he approached the throne one day in the full regalia of lord chancellor; the king, who wished to deflate him a bit, turned to some of his minions and in a stage whisper said, "Here comes the greatest whoremaster in England." Shaftesbury's quick reply was, "Of a subject, Sire." Except that he was obviously a man of nimble mind and great energy, Cooper scarcely seems the kind of person who would spend much time on a peripheral investment shared with seven others. Certainly, he had other things to do, and most contemporaries doubtless considered them to be far more important.

Yet Cooper was interested in colonial affairs. Not only had he once owned a Barbadian plantation but he had also invested in the slave trade. Moreover, he served on the Council for Foreign Plantations, an advisory body on colonial policy. Perhaps equally important, recent experiences may have caused him to put Carolina rather high on his list of priorities. In 1669 he was forty-eight years old and in the prime of his life. But the Great Plague and Fire probably gave him pause, and in 1668 an abscess of the liver almost killed him. Only major surgery supervised by John Locke saved him, and thereafter Cooper walked around with a permanent drain in his abdomen reminding him of his mortality. Locke remained a member of Shaftesbury's household where, more friend than servant, he acted as secretary for the proprietors as well as for Lord Ashley himself. Accordingly, the blueprint for colonial development embodied in the famous Fundamental Constitutions appears to have been a collaborative effort by the two men, with some contributions from other proprietors. Shaftesbury bore the primary responsibility; he was the one who came to call the Carolina project "my Darling," and the one who, after his fall, thought (futilely) of going into exile there. It therefore seems reasonable to believe not only that he was the author of some of the more utopian features of the Fundamental Constitutions but also that for a time at least he saw Carolina as his ticket to immortality. Although it did not happen quite as he planned, he was not far wrong. The Ashley and the Cooper rivers bear his names, and both Shaftesbury himself and the Fundamental Constitutions were more influential in the continuing history of South Carolina than is often realized. Sir Thomas More might dream of his *Utopia;* James Harrington might write about *Oceana;* but Shaftesbury could try to make Carolina a reality.

The Fundamental Constitutions of 1669 have been frequently described and frequently misunderstood. At one time it was fashionable for historians to trundle them out as exhibit A in the cabinet of anachronistic European curiosities which men were once foolish enough to try to impose on the New World. "Visionary, crude, incomplete, and impracticable" were the adjectives frequently employed. More recently, however, scholars have tended to look at them more sympathetically. Actually, at least one early student in the course of tracing the influence of James Harrington and his seminal work *Oceana* (published in 1656), read the Constitutions with considerable care and concluded that they were heavily indebted to Harrington's ideas. Other scholars have been less certain, arguing that many of the concepts that appear to be borrowed from Harrington were common at the time and easily could have had other origins. More important, these students imply, was the incorporation of several shrewd promotional devices. Religious toleration, coupled with state support for the Anglican Church, was a way to appeal to both dissenters and Anglicans. A clear statement to the effect that masters possessed absolute control over their slaves dispelled any doubts which might have arisen on that score. And what better way, one might also ask, was there to appeal to a substantial Barbadian planter like Sir John Yeamans—unless it was to offer him another title and the lands that went with it.

So much is clear, but historians have generally been puzzled over the proprietors' belief that some men would voluntarily bind themselves and their descendants to the soil as "leetmen" or serfs in return for ten acres of land to be leased to them upon marriage. Yet even this apparently strange assumption was reasonable in the light of the proprietors' experience with Barbados where they had encountered men without homes or hope. As Sir John Colleton had observed, such individuals were "of noe interest or reputation, of little innate Courage, being poor men that are just permitted to live, ... derided by the Negroes, and branded with the Epithet of white slaves." In a world in which it was believed necessary to stipulate, even in the harsh codes governing indentured servitude, that no master was to turn a servant out for illness, trading the shadow of freedom for the security of semi-bondage might not always have seemed to be such a bad bargain. Even the most appparently outlandish provisions of the Fundamental Constitutions sometimes owed as much to knowledge as to ignorance of the colonial situation.

All of this, however, though true enough, misses the essence of the document which is a pervasive attempt to balance the elements believed necessary to provide the orderly basis for a good society. If the proprietors wished to avoid "erecting a numerous Democracy," they had no more desire to establish an aristocracy in which the powerful few might exploit a politically impotent people. As Shaftesbury later noted, the Constitutions were designed so that "noe bodys power[,] noe not of any of the Proprietors themselves . . . is soe great as to be able to hurt the meanest man in the Country." This was to be achieved by giving each man a share in the political process sufficient to protect himself. Common sense—if not the commonplaces of contemporary political thought—suggested that no government in which the distribution of political power ignored underlying social realities could long endure. It is therefore not necessary to attribute the proprietors' attempt to match the possession of power and property to the influence of Harrington, though he may have been partly responsible for it.

Whatever the precise sources of the stipulations governing the distribution of land under the Fundamental Constitutions, these provisions were designed to provide the foundation for the entire social and political edifice. "Each Province" was to be divided into six counties of 480,000 acres; in turn, each county was to be subdivided into eight seigniories, eight baronies, and twenty-four colonies, each of 12,000 acres. Each proprietor was to receive one seigniory in every county. In addition, there was to be a nobility composed of landgraves and caciques. (The first was a German title; the second derived from a Spanish word for Indian chief which the English mispronounced "cassock.") To every county there was to be one landgrave, who would receive four baronies, and two caciques, each of whom was to have two baronies. The remaining land was reserved for the people at large.

Political power and legal authority followed ownership of land. Eight administrative courts or councils, each headed by one of the proprietors, were to supervise government business. At the top was the palatine court composed of the proprietors themselves and named for their senior member. The proprietors and the other members of the subordinate courts were to constitute the Grand Council. Probably modeled in part on the English Privy Council, it was to function both as a court of appeals and a collective executive. Parliament—like the Irish parliament which after 1494 could not consider legislation without the prior approval of the Privy Council—could only debate matters that the Grand Council had previously approved. Composed of the proprietors (or their deputies), the nobility, and elected representatives of the freeholders, parliament was unicameral. Votes in it and (explicitly by later revisions of the Fundamental Constitutions) elections to it were to be by secret ballot. Elected members needed 500 acres to qualify for a seat; voters, merely fifty to exercise the franchise. Laws were to be enforced by an elaborate legal system which included manorial courts. To prevent packing, juries (according to another revision of the document) were to be composed of individuals meeting requisite property qualifications whose names had been placed in a box and drawn by a child under the age of ten. It being "a base and vile thing to Plead for money," the Constitution forbade fees for such legal services. Similarly, no one was to write commentaries on the laws, which were themselves to terminate automatically every sixty years.

This last provision, which is misleading at first sight, requires further discussion. Superficially, it resembles Jefferson's later suggestion that constitutions should terminate every two decades. However, Jefferson's dictum derived from his belief that "the earth belongs to the living" who should be free from the tyranny of the past; the Carolina proprietors had something very different in mind. The trouble with laws which failed to expire, they believed, was that they proliferated over time and so "by degrees always change the Right foundations of the Original Government." Legal commentaries, which also tended to "obscure and perplex," had the same pernicious effect. Intending to start aright at the beginning, the proprietors wanted their constitution to be permanent, and they accordingly incorporated numerous impediments to change. If a measure being debated in parliament appeared to a proprietor to affect the Constitutions, he might so define it. In that event, not a simple majority but a majority of each order (proprietors, nobility, and commoners) composing the house was necessary to approve the bill. And even then the palatine court retained the right to veto it. Finally, by making everyone who received a grant of land or became a member of the assembly swear to uphold the Fundamental Constitutions, the proprietors sought to erect yet another safeguard.

Under a constitution which included some of the most advanced political thinking of the age, change was supposed to be almost impossible. If that now seems surprising, it may be because the modern world is no longer Machiavellian, except perhaps in a superficial sense. Machiavelli, it is worth recalling, was fundamentally concerned with the problem of mutability in the polity; Harrington, perhaps more than any other man, infused Machiavelli's ideas into the English political tradition; and Harrington's own *Oceana* described the constitution of what was supposed to be an "immortal commonwealth." According to the classical political theory upon which Machiavelli and Harrington both drew, only a balanced constitution, composed of monarchic, aristocratic, and democratic elements might escape the inevitable cycle of excess, degeneration, and decline which awaited any of its constituent parts in pure form. The balance in a mixed government was, of course, also subject to disturbances which, in Machiavellian thought, could be rectified only by a return to "first principles"—that is, the reestablishment of the original balance. Such a return to first principles might occur in a number of ways, including revolution (in the root sense of the term). The impediments to change embodied in the Fundamental Constitutions were therefore designed to prevent degeneration and obviate the need for renovation. In short, the proprietors sought to insure the stability of Carolina by anchoring the political system in the possession of land, balancing the distribution of power accordingly, and then making the superstructure as rigid as possible.

Equally noteworthy are the clauses governing religious toleration. "Since the Natives of that place, who will be concerned in our Plantations, are utterly Strangers to Christianity, whose Idolatry, Ignorance, or mistake gives us no right to expel or use them ill," and because settlers will be "of different opinions concerning matters of Religion, the liberty whereof they will expect to have allowed them," any seven individuals "agreeing in any Religion shall constitute a church or profession." Thereafter, provided they believed in a God and practiced public worship, members of such churches were guaranteed civil rights and freedom from molestation.

As an attempt to create a good society out of recalcitrant human materials, the Fundamental Constitutions stand with William Penn's liberal Frame of Government as an effort worthy of attention and respect. Carolinians, however, proved to be perhaps a bit more recalcitrant than the Quakers of Pennsylvania. As the proprietors were well aware, the Constitutions were also too elaborate for immediate application. In 1669 the document could only be a "Grand Model" toward which to work, "the compasse [we] are to steere by." While devising the compass, Cooper was also making headway on more mundane matters. In April of 1669 he convinced the other proprietors to pool £500 sterling apiece to finance an expedition and during the summer proceeded to organize it. By August, three ships and more than 100 colonists were ready to sail under the temporary command of Captain Joseph West. Going by way of Kinsale, Ireland, where they expected to pick up additional settlers but actually lost by desertions, the fleet arrived at Barbados apparently without further difficulty. From there on, however, the settlers ran into trouble. In November while at Barbados, one vessel, the *Albemarle,* sank in a late season storm. Yeamans, who superseded West as commander of the expedition, leased another. En route to South Carolina, a second storm struck, blowing the new vessel all the way to Virginia and wrecking one of the original ships, the *Port Royal,* in the Bahamas. (Not long thereafter, the proprietors applied for and received a grant for those islands.) Thereupon Yeamans suddenly decided that his presence was required in Barbados, so he named William Sayle, an experienced colonial administrator from Bermuda, to take his place as governor. Sayle was nearly eighty years old. But on March 15, 1670, all of them—including Sayle—aboard one of the original three vessels, auspiciously named the *Carolina,* anchored slightly north of modern Charleston in what is now Bull's Bay. They then worked southward to Port Royal, where, thanks to the reports of Hilton and Sandford, the proprietors had decided to locate the settlement. More than two months later, the vessel that had gone to Virginia arrived after having overshot Port Royal and losing several of those aboard who were captured by Spaniards on the coast of modern Georgia.

Obviously Port Royal was perilously close to the Spanish. That consideration, the low-lying ground, and the urging of an Indian, who had joined the settlers at Bull's Bay, induced them to move northward from Port Royal to his area along the Ashley River. Apparently, the cacique of Kiawah was seeking protection from the Westo Indians who had recently raided northward from their home on the Savannah River; the record is more ambiguous as to whether and when he began to wish for protection from the English. For the settlers themselves—who included about nineteen women—security was clearly the prime requisite. Thus their first permanent settlement, which came to be known as "Old Town," was located on relatively high land on the western side of the Ashley River several miles from the mouth. Keeping closely together at first, the new arrivals surrounded their huts and cabins with a palisade, confined themselves to ten-acre plots of land, and delayed taking up the larger grants to which they were entitled until an increase in numbers made it somewhat safer to disperse. Their precautions were justified, for in August three Spanish frigates, plus Indian auxiliaries, moved to attack the little town. After a preliminary skirmish, heavy weather forced the frigates to withdraw.

It was just as well that survival did not depend entirely on the Carolinians' own unity, for there were political divisions from the very beginning. Holding the Fundamental Constitutions in abeyance until the colony became more populated, the proprietors directed that a council composed of their deputies, five men elected by the freemen, and the governor act as a collective executive and judicial body. Elections for the five freemen were held at Port Royal. Thereafter, the council—which was frequently termed the "Grand Council," though it was not the Grand Council outlined in the Fundamental Constitutions—acted as the most important governing body, issuing ordinances and trying offenders. Organizing a parliament presented a problem. According to the proprietors' instructions, twenty members were to be elected, but when it came time to make their choice, there were not twenty freemen available. Thus the first parliament did not meet until July 1671. By then various individuals had already challenged not only the legality of the elections to the council but also the procedures for granting land. Although the challenges failed, they were productive of many "broils and heats" under the governorship of Sayle and his successor Joseph West. Sayle's age exacerbated the problems. "Being a person verie anchant or aged and verie feble," as one observer reported, "what small reason he had is almost taken from him. . . . He is one of the onfittest men in the world for . . . being Governor."

Before dying in March 1671, Sayle nominated West as his successor, but the new governor, who was both younger and abler, soon had to contend with the presence of Yeamans, who, as a landgrave and deputy of the palatine, was theoretically the senior man. Elected speaker of the first assembly, Yeamans mounted several flanking attacks on West before explicitly claiming the governorship on the basis of his rank. Although the council refused to accept his argument, his commission from the proprietors soon arrived, and Yeamans became governor. West certainly knew with whom he was dealing, and, according to him, so did "the people" who had begun "to murmur" at Yeamans's activities, "saying Sir John intended to make this a Cape Fear settlement," which bickering had helped to destroy. Even Shaftesbury soon lost whatever illusions he may have had about Yeamans. "If to convert all things to his private profitt be the marke of able parts," Shaftesbury observed, "Sir John is without a doubt a very judicious man." In the spring of 1674 the proprietors dropped Yeamans and replaced him with West who served for the next eight years.

Though not a very appealing individual, Sir John was an important figure in the early history of South Carolina, not only because he played a prominent role in the efforts which eventually produced a permanent settlement but also because he was in many ways the archetype of the aggressive Barbadians who made up a substantial proportion of the early immigrants. For about a third of those who arrived during the first decade, the place of origin is known, and about half of these came from Barbados. Moreover, many of the Barbadians—like Yeamans— were relatively wealthy, as well as aggressive. Thus they exercised a disproportionate influence in the government, and, like Yeamans, they often pursued self-interest most assiduously. He, for example, sold his own produce in Barbados while Carolinians were still short of food. The possibility of doing that is part of what attracted the Barbadians to Carolina in the first place, but Sir John was rushing things. That South Carolinians never had a real starving time, despite some temporary scarcity, was due fully as much to the support of the proprietors as it was to the likes of Yeamans, though the Barbadians' previous experience with the environment of the New World proved useful in establishing the colony. These men were, however, a major source of disappointment and frustration for the proprietors. What they had hoped to get for a ruling group in South Carolina is revealed in the oath prescribed for members of the council, which required them to swear to "doe equall right to the rich and to the Poore"; and not to "give, or be of Councill for favor or affection, in any difference or quarrell depending before" them, "but in all things" to "demeane and behave" themselves "as to equity and justice appertaines." What they largely got can be seen in Yeamans, who resembled a pirate ashore.

Not everyone in South Carolina during the early years was a scoundrel, though some individuals suspected that was the case. Alexander Hewatt, one of the earliest local historians, looked back from the eighteenth century and observed that South Carolina was populated by "bold adventurers, who improved every hour for advancing their interest, and could bear no restraints which had the least tendency to defeat their favourite views and designs." Men who were a generation closer to these early buccaneers were often less charitable. One governor who got along with them better than most observed that the largely Barbadian Anglicans were generally "ill-livers," and one of their own ministers was even more jaundiced in his assessment: "The people here generally speaking are the vilest race of men upon the earth. They have neither honor, nor honesty, nor religion enough to entitle them to any tolerable character." They are, he concluded, "a perfect medley or hotch-potch, made up of bankrupt pirates, decayed libertines, sectaries and enthusiasts of all sorts who have transported themselves hither . . . and are the most factious and seditious people in the whole world." These comments should not be taken entirely at face value. Some of the minister's harshest words were directed at the dissenters merely because they were dissenters. Others, including the proprietors, thought more highly of them.

During the 1670s the proprietors became increasingly disenchanted with the way things were going in Carolina. Not only had they contributed funds for the initial expedition, but in 1674 most of them agreed to invest an additional £100 per year in developing the colony. Moreover, they had agreed to forego all quitrents for the first twenty years. In return they expected but did not receive cooperation from the settlers. Arrangements to repay some of these cash advances fell through; the scheme for a systematic survey of lands failed completely because of the irregular coastline and many inland waterways; and after the very early days the settlers refused to establish themselves in compact townships, but spread out in isolated plantations along the rivers. Only the city of Charles Town itself, to which the settlers moved in 1680, met some of the proprietors' expectations. Laid out on the neck of land between the Ashley and Cooper rivers with streets intersecting at right angles according to their instructions, it was one of the first planned cities in North America. Contemporaries were convinced that these arrangements would enable them to "avoid the undecent and incommodious irregularities which other Inglish Collonies are fallen into for want of ane early care in laying out the Townes."

From the proprietors' point of view, however, other matters were not nearly so regular. By treating the Indians well they hoped to maintain peace; yet in less than a year the settlers were at war with some of the tribes in their immediate vicinity. Perhaps worse yet, despite explicit directions not to enslave the Indians "upon any occasion or pretence whatsoever," that was precisely what some Carolinians were doing. As a result, in 1677 the proprietors tried to head off further trouble and recover some of their financial losses by giving themselves a monopoly of the trade with the more distant Indians, especially the Westos. The Carolina traders broke that monopoly by precipitating a war which nearly exterminated the tribe. Exhibiting an equal disregard of law and the proprietors' wishes in other areas, many government officials winked at the presence of pirates who put into the port of Charles Town and brought coin.

These and other problems prompted the proprietors to seek remedies. As early as 1675, Shaftesbury envisaged a new settlement on the Edisto River to be called Locke Island. Although he sent an agent over to make preparations, the project never materialized, probably because of his increasingly heavy involvement in the labyrinthian byways of English politics. But in the early 1680s, while he was trying to find a way to prevent the Duke of York from becoming James II, Shaftesbury negotiated with a number of Scottish dissenters. Ostensibly, the purpose was to establish another separate settlement in South Carolina, but these plans may have been partly a cover for plots against the Stuart crown. Either way, the plans miscarried. Shaftesbury was forced to flee England, and the settlement at Stuart Town on Port Royal Sound was short-lived. Led by Lord Cardross, about 150 Scots landed at Charles Town in 1684. By the time Spaniards wiped out the settlement two years later, no more than twenty-five men were alive and well enough to bear arms, and Cardross himself had already returned to Scotland. Although the authorities at Charles Town made military preparations to avenge the destruction of Stuart Town as well as Spanish depredations nearer Charles Town, they shed few tears over the former. Cardross's settlement had been independent of their au-

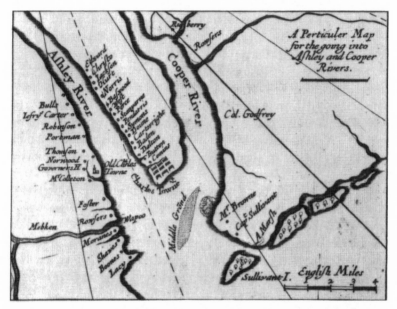

The area around Charles Town as depicted on "A New Map of Carolina" by John Thornton, Robert Morden, and Philip Lea (London, ca. 1685). *Courtesy of the Henry E. Huntington Library and Art Gallery.*

thority and there had been considerable friction between the two jurisdictions, especially over the Indian trade. But neither were the
Carolinians very pleased with the sequel of the drama, for the proprietors forbade retaliation against the Spanish with whom England was
then supposedly at peace.

Meanwhile, the proprietors had also been making vigorous attempts
to reform the settlement at Charles Town. Beginning about 1680 they
launched a recruiting drive aimed especially at Huguenots and English
dissenters, and their efforts met with considerable success. Augmented
by refugees who left France after 1685, when Louis XIV revoked the
protection hitherto afforded by the Edict of Nantes, the influx of
Huguenots brought nearly 500 individuals to South Carolina by the
end of the century. And before the pressure on dissenters in England
relaxed during the latter half of the decade, perhaps an equal number
of English Presbyterians and Baptists arrived, led by members of several
prominent families. Indeed, the proprietors seem to have tried to
capitalize on this last phenomenon by making an influential dissenter—
Joseph Morton—governor in the belief that he could attract more
men of his own persuasion. Accompanying revisions in the Fundamental Constitutions were also largely designed to appeal to dissenters.
Other steps gave the newcomers political power. Dissenters replaced
incumbents in several subordinate offices as well as the governorship,
and changes were made in the procedure for electing members of the
assembly. Three counties were to be established and serve as election
districts. Berkeley and Craven would jointly elect ten members of the
assembly; and Colleton was to have the same number. Because the
northernmost of the three, Craven County, was still largely wilderness,
the inequity was not precisely what it appeared to be. Rather, the
reason for the arrangement and a cause of the resulting friction lay in
the fact that Berkeley alone, which was composed of Charles Town
and the surrounding area, was considerably more populous than Colleton, which was the area being settled south of the Stono River. As
the proprietors envisaged it, Colleton County would be inhabited by
the dissenters, and the arrangement would give them disproportionate
voting strength in the assembly. Finally, in an attempt to insure their
own financial returns from the colony, the proprietors changed the
method of granting land. In the future, all grants were to contain a
reentry clause, which would give them a convenient legal device for

recovering their property in the event that quitrents were not paid promptly. Although none had yet become payable, the proprietors also announced that, when due, the rents would be receivable in coin.

These changes alarmed the hitherto dominant local politicians, many of whom were known as the "Goose Creek men" because of their residence in Berkeley County along a tributary of the Cooper River. Composed by and large of Barbadian Anglicans, this faction was led by Maurice Mathews, who had no trouble recognizing a challenge when he saw one. Accordingly, the attempt to use dissenters to build a proprietary party produced nearly three decades of fierce but unstable factionalism. Men sometimes changed sides as circumstances dictated, while a few Anglicans habitually supported the proprietors and some dissenters opposed them. Among the latter in particular were the Huguenots who, contrary to what one might expect, tended to align themselves politically with the Barbadians. Propinquity may be one explanation, since Craven and Berkeley counties were next to each other and their respective French and English residents shared representatives in the assembly. Huguenots have also assimilated well in widely dif-ferent societies, and in this case they may have perceived the local power structure as being Anglican. Certainly many of them later joined the Anglican Church (as did many English dissenters). The Huguenots' behavior suggests, and other evidence tends to confirm, that despite the tendency of factional alignments to coincide with religious divi-sions, the issues basically concerned power. Being newcomers, the dissenters wanted a share of it; by giving it to them, the proprietors sought to break the power of their (largely) Anglican opponents, and the latter, who sought to retain their power, defended the status quo. Thus the Anglicans presented themselves as champions of the liberties guaranteed by the charter in opposition to proprietary "innovations." To the dissenters, however, Mathews and his Goose Creek cohorts were beyond the pale. In the words of one of his enemies, their leader was "Metchivell Hobs and Lucifer in a Huge lump of Viperish mortality [with] a soull [as] big as a musketo."

Tenacious and resourceful—not to say cunning—the Goose Creek men and their successors ultimately broke the power of the proprietors, but the process took a while. That there were seven different admin-istrations during the decade of the '80s and five more during the first five years of the '90s suggests that the proprietors were initially as persistent as they were frustrated. Early in the '80s, they posed the crucial question when they asked Governor Morton, "Are you to govern the people, or the people you?" The implicit answer was clear enough, for he virtually capitulated to local leaders and permitted trade with pirates and exploitation of the Indians to continue. In 1686 the proprietors therefore dispatched James Colleton, a brother of one of the proprietors and a Barbadian, to cope with his own kind. He tried but failed after a combination of circumstances and deception on the part of his opponents started him off on the wrong foot. Countermanding the preparations to attack St. Augustine following the destruction of Stuart Town because royal authorities then wished to avoid antagonizing Spain, he quite properly opened negotiations with Spanish authorities in Florida and soon came to a limited agreement. Although it produced compensation for some captured slaves and could therefore be said to have had beneficial effects, the negotiations made Colleton look bad. For the sake of some "filthy lucre," his opponents charged, he had pusillanimously failed to avenge an insult and had come to terms with the traditional enemy. A little trickery by the Goose Creek men made him appear to be even more grasping. Assuring Colleton that they would support the measure, they suggested that he ask for an excise tax to augment his salary; but when he took the bait, they double-crossed him by joining the opposition.

With his local support thus weakened, Colleton was in a poor position to deal with one of the most important issues of his administration, the Fundamental Constitutions. The Goose Creek men refused to accept a revised new draft. That they had never approved the original version and that it was therefore never the law of the land did not seem to trouble them. In qualifying for earlier assemblies they had sworn, they said, to uphold the Constitutions of 1669 and they could not possibly swear to the version of 1682. Accordingly, under Colleton's predecessor more than half the members of the house refused to take their seats rather than qualify under the new document. The proprietors on the other hand maintained that there was nothing sacred about the 1669 version, which was but a copy "of an imperfect original"; the Goose Creek men replied, in effect, that something so mutable could not be a constitution. They preferred to rely on the royal charter. Trying to compromise, Colleton permitted a committee made up of members of both the assembly and council to examine the Fundamental

Constitutions in the hope of finding areas of mutual agreement. Soon the "worke grew voluminous" as well as acrimonious and that scuttled the effort. Colleton then managed to get along without calling the assembly for nearly two years. Late in 1688, however, the Glorious Revolution in England placed William and Mary on the throne, and William brought England into the continental alliance against Louis XIV. In the Caribbean, French forces seized an English island; and on the mainland, South Carolinians were soon convinced that they would be the next target of a French attack. Although the southern frontier was relatively calm during King William's War (which lasted until 1697) because England and Spain remained allies, Carolinians had no way of foretelling these events and were understandably concerned about the situation. Thus some local politicians, chiefly dissenters, urged Colleton to put the colony in a posture of readiness by declaring martial law rather than calling the assembly, and he complied. However, this action, as a contemporary observed, failed "to put a Lock on . . . Tongues," and the opposition party contended that it smacked of tyranny.

At this point, apparently by chance, Seth Sothell arrived in Charles Town. Having purchased Clarendon's interest, Sothell was a proprietor and had just served as governor in North Carolina (from which the local assembly had ousted him for malfeasance). Forgetting their opposition to the Fundamental Constitutions, the Goose Creek men invoked their provisions to argue that Sothell should assume the governship on the grounds that as a proprietor he outranked Colleton. Sothell proved to be amenable to such reasoning; Colleton was harder to convince and sought to protect his position by calling out the militia. Numbers proved to be a more effective argument than strained logic, and Colleton decided to listen to reason when it became apparent that he lacked the force to do otherwise. Thus Sothell peacefully assumed the governorship. Although Colleton's opponents may have taken heart from the contemporary developments in England which culminated in the overthrow of James II, events in South Carolina seem to have involved little more than a local factional turnover.

Despite Sothell's earlier record, his performance in South Carolina turned out to be mixed. Largely because most, if not all, of the laws had expired during the period in which Colleton had called no assemblies, the field was wide open for constructive legislation, and because of his cozy relationship with the Goose Creek men, Sothell was able to get much of it. A spate of acts dealing with everything from roads to the regulation of slaves issued from the assembly. It even passed the first act to regulate the Indian trade. There is some evidence, however, to indicate that Sothell intended the restrictions on local traders to be a step toward giving himself a monopoly of the trade. And, as his administration continued, he appeared to become increasingly rapacious. He also joined with the members of his assembly in passing punitive legislation against their opponents, who were barred from holding political office and, in the case of Colleton, exiled from the colony.

Until news of the latter arrived in London, the other proprietors appear to have been willing to go along with these unauthorized political changes because Sothell was a proprietor. The vindictiveness of Colleton's banishment as well as some of Sothell's other measures changed their minds. The proprietors accordingly disallowed all acts passed under his administration and in 1691 replaced him with the same man who had previously followed him in North Carolina, Philip Ludwell.* In addition, they changed the composition of the council by enlarging its appointed membership and excluding the elected representatives of the people. They also acknowledged the right of the lower house of the assembly to sit separately and, shortly thereafter, to initiate legislation. Perhaps these changes were designed to make the structure of the local government more like that of the royal colonies and thus more acceptable to imperial authorities. The proprietors, it seems, were also making a genuine effort to placate their local opposition. Responding to the repeated contention that attempting to rule by the Fundamental Constitutions was "unconstitutional" because the document had never been approved by the people of South Carolina, the proprietors agreed that "the Government of the said Province is to be

---

*Because Ludwell was given power to appoint a deputy for North Carolina, separation of North and South Carolina is often considered to date from 1691. The proprietors, however, still hoped that the Carolinas would eventually be governed by a single parliament meeting at Charles Town. But the trip proved unfeasible for North Carolina representatives, who continued to meet in their own house. Partly because deputy governors lacked the status to deal effectively with the legislature, beginning in 1712 the proprietors themselves commissioned governors for North Carolina, thereby giving official sanction to the separation of the two colonies.

for the future as it shall be directed by the Majority of Us the sd. Lords Proprietors... pursuant to the powers granted to us by our sd. Charter." The note of both exasperation and irony in their statement is clear, for the Fundamental Constitutions were intended to provide more protection for the people than the charter. If the latter did not see it that way, however, the proprietors were prepared to go along. This does not mean that they had entirely abandoned the Constitutions; as late as 1705 they were still futilely urging their adoption. But their immediate purpose, as they informed one of their agents, was "to Imbrace an Amicable Composition of matters." With the help of increasing prosperity at this time, they seemed to be succeeding for a while. Yet, as their new governor observed, the task really required a governor who was a proprietor with extraordinary powers.

The proprietors agreed and attempted to convince Shaftesbury's grandson to take the position. After he declined, they turned to John Archdale who had purchased one of the proprietary shares for his son. Archdale was a Quaker who had had experience in both Maine and North Carolina, and he retained enough interest in the colonies to induce him to go. No doubt recalling his fellow proprietors' warning to his predecessor, "beware the Goose Creek men," he arrived in Charles Town in 1695 equipped with broad powers to deal with the current issues. The first problem was political. Seeking to build as wide a base of support as possible, he would have preferred to work with the Huguenots who had been sitting in the assembly—thanks to instructions to the governor in 1691, which gave Craven County separate representation. However, the war with France augmented hostility to all Frenchmen—which was already high enough among local dissenters—and Archdale found that to get cooperation from the assembly he would have to go along with a demand for the exclusion of Huguenots. He therefore dissolved the first house and called for elections of twenty representatives from Berkeley County and ten from Colleton. Although successful in eliminating Frenchmen from the assembly, the maneuver established a dangerous precedent, for local dissenters of English extraction would soon find that similar games could also be played at their expense.

Nevertheless, Archdale got a cooperative house, which immediately tackled the increasingly thorny issue of land titles and quitrents. The latter had been due since 1690 and, though the proprietors had reluctantly agreed to accept them in commodities appropriate for the English market as well as in coin, South Carolinians had not been paying. Archdale and the assembly worked out a compromise. Speaking for the proprietors, he refused to give up the reentry clause previously incorporated into recent land grants but agreed to make no similar changes in the future without giving prior notice; he arranged for the outright sale of lands by the proprietors at a price considerably lower than what they had hitherto asked; he approved the payment of quit-rents in purely local commodities, and he remitted part of the currently overdue rents. In return, he asked that the assembly make provision to repay the funds advanced by the proprietors over the last twenty-five years, to enforce the payment of quitrents, and to build a fort at Charles Town. The assembly agreed to the last and, in lieu of the first, arranged to pay the back salary of several proprietary governors. More important, the house also passed a strict law designed to ensure the payment of quitrents (though some individuals still managed to evade them). Finally, because this reasonably comprehensive settlement was supposed to be perpetual, Archdale permitted the assembly to stipulate that these laws could not be changed without its consent. This was more than the other proprietors could bring themselves explicitly to approve, and they never formally ratified these acts. But their failure to exercise a veto permitted the laws to remain in force for more than twenty years, during which the assembly came to regard them as establishing its right to enact legislation with which the proprietors could not subsequently tamper. Later in the decade, the house also demanded the right to repeal acts which the proprietors had approved.

By not agreeing to this request, the proprietors could scarcely have fooled themselves or anyone else: there had been a wondrous change over the last thirty years. The center of political gravity had clearly shifted from their own meetings in London to the local legislature in Charles Town, where the Commons House had acquired the right not only to sit as a separate body and initiate legislation but also to control its own membership and elect its own speaker. Equally important, it was rapidly increasing its authority at the expense of the proprietors. The assemblymen were not engaged in a conspiracy to enlarge their own powers, but all of them were aware of the English House of Commons's struggle with the Stuart kings, and most politically con-scious South Carolinians understood the importance of a precedent. In most cases the local legislature enlarged its powers by an essentially ad hoc process in which local leaders resisted the exercise of the proprietors' authority because they wished to do something—such as trade with pirates—which the proprietors wished to prevent. The increasing local autonomy was largely a by-product of specific and sometimes rather sordid quarrels and to a great extent the same was true of resistance to the Fundamental Constitutions. But precisely because the latter was supposed to be *the* fundamental constitution it became a source of continuing contention with larger significance. Had the document gone into effect, it would have permanently relegated most local leaders to a subordinate and relatively passive role in the polity. Perhaps equally important, being the proprietors' prescription, the Fundamental Constitutions epitomized the unilateral imposition of outside authority on the people of South Carolina. This was precisely what local leaders wished to avoid and what the royal charter seemed to protect them against, for as Carolinians read it, the proprietors could frame constitutional arrangements and legislate only with the consent of the people. The Fundamental Constitutions, as Clarence Ver Steeg has perceptively noted, "had been and remained a symbol: the imposition of a government by the proprietors without consultation or agreement with the colonists." Invoking the charter, South Carolinians therefore became amateur constitutional lawyers. Whether they thereby established a tradition may be an open question; but they certainly created an impasse. Contests of this kind, in which the tangible and intangible stakes are very high, tend to take on a life of their own and spill over into other areas. Thus one reason that South Carolinians never developed much local government at the county level may be that the Fundamental Constitutions called for it, and local politicians threw the baby out with the bathwater. Entail, too, may also have been discarded in similar fashion. Certainly, when in 1712 the legislature adopted more than 100 English statutes, it not only failed to incorporate, but deliberately rejected, the concept of entail; this action was probably related to the provision in the Fundamental Constitutions stipulating that seigniories and baronies were to be entailed after 1700. If so, however, the step was more than a mere emotional reaction against the Constitutions, for it clarified the legal status of the large tracts granted by the proprietors.

If only in a negative sense, then, the Fundamental Constitutions had important effects on the subsequent history of South Carolina; at least equally important, however, was a positive legacy. The land system continued to operate under the headright arrangement outlined in the Constitutions, and for most of the colonial period possession of a single headright remained sufficient to qualify one for the franchise. Thanks in part to the Fundamental Constitutions, Carolinians enjoyed something very close to free, white manhood suffrage. Relatively few other colonies outside of New England used the secret ballot, and only South Carolina legally mandated its use. None, except Rhode Island, granted settlers more religious freedom than the South Carolinians had during the early days, and the dissenters who immigrated because of it continued to be an important part of the population. Juries continued to be impartially selected by the distinctive—not to say quaint—method spelled out by the proprietors. For most of the first thirty years, the legislature operated at least in a formal sense, as outlined in the document, with the council proposing legislation and a single house "parliament" accepting or rejecting it. In all probability, the fact that the legislature was known as the parliament helped to prompt the lower house, which called itself the Commons, to emulate its English counterpart. And finally, a responsible gentry did eventually develop, and its power was largely based on wealth in land. After the Revolution, representation in the legislature even came to be based on property as well as population. More intriguing yet, the notion of the concurrent majority advocated by John C. Calhoun during the nineteenth century resembles the procedure prescribed in the Fundamental Constitutions for dealing with constitutional questions.

This is not to imply that Calhoun was necessarily any more indebted to Shaftesbury and Locke than they, in turn, were to Harrington. Nevertheless, history is full of coincidences, and if some of these features and provisions did not exist, Carolinians would have had to invent them or something very like them. In fact, the appearance of apparent innovations in revisions of the document suggests that in some cases the proprietors may have been responding to practices already introduced by the colonists themselves. Separating influence from prescience is therefore virtually impossible. Perhaps the safest thing is to regard the Fundamental Constitutions primarily as a symbol, as much futuristic as feudal, emblematic of a striking propensity of South Carolinians throughout much of their history to combine widely divergent elements of the old and new. The ways in which they acquired both were not always what they appeared to be; for ironically much of the political culture that would ultimately help to transform the Carolina buccaneers of the early days into the responsible gentry of the eighteenth century could be found embedded in the Fundamental Constitutions. Harrington and such "neo-Harringtons" as Shaftesbury were among its most important progenitors. Yet South Carolinians apparently assimilated this political culture largely indirectly, not from Shaftesbury and the Fundamental Constitutions but from other figures in the first half of the eighteenth century. Perhaps it was just as well. If the Carolinians had seen it in the Fundamental Constitutions, they might have rejected it. Or at least in the 1690s the proprietors would undoubtedly have been sure of this, for there is evidence to suggest that they were about ready to give up on their colony.

5

TWILIGHT OF PROPRIETARY GOVERNMENT, 1700–1719

The years from the end of the seventeenth century until the revolution against the proprietors in 1719 constitute an eventful and complex period in the history of South Carolina. Stripped of subordinate themes and sometimes admittedly important but peripheral issues, the crucial political question of the seventeenth century came down to who was going to have the predominant voice in running the colony, the proprietors or the colonists. By the end of the seventeenth century, it was increasingly obvious that the answer was the colonists. One would therefore logically expect that the next controversy would be over who among the colonists would control local policy, and that certainly became one of the major issues of this period. The proprietors, however, did not entirely surrender the field, and for a number of reasons the crown took an increasing interest in South Carolina. Accordingly, it is almost impossible to disentangle and discuss the relationship among various developments without simplifying the complexities of the whole. But to make the account as coherent as possible this chapter deals first with events in the colony, then London, and finally returns to South Carolina to show how trends in both places culminated in the overthrow of the proprietary government.

Although both Governor John Archdale and his successor were dissenters, Anglicans benefited politically from their administrations. Under Archdale, the legislature disenfranchised Frenchmen and gerrymandered election districts so that the Anglicans of Charles Town and its surroundings had, to all intents and purposes, twice as many representatives as the dissenters from Colleton County. Later concessions to the French—which in 1704 gave them the vote though not the right to sit in Commons—earned their gratitude and enabled the Anglicans who dominated the assembly to perpetuate the advantage gained in the gerrymander. Moreover, the election in Charles Town was manipulatable. During the 1680s, it was said, some Indian traders boasted that they could control matters "with a bole of punch." By the first few years of the eighteenth century—if the dissenters' charges can be believed—the Anglicans further refined election techniques by recruiting unqualified voters and intimidating opponents. Although such methods were not foolproof, the Anglicans were in a strong position in the house by the opening of the eighteenth century. They also did well on the executive side. For several reasons, including the expansion of the economy and pressure from the crown, the proprietors appointed a number of additional officials about this time, and some of them proved to be strong figures as well as militant Anglicans. Furthermore, James Moore, who was elected governor by the council upon the death of his predecessor in 1700, was an Anglican.

Although that fact alarmed the dissenters, Moore seems to have been less interested in religious matters than in providing for a large family. This concern, dissenters claimed, was not entirely unrelated to lust for Spanish plunder and that, in turn, they believed, had something to do with his premature zeal to attack St. Augustine. (He was making preparations even before the outbreak of Queen Anne's War; the dissenters who lived on the exposed southern frontier were, for the most part, more pacific.) When the costs of Moore's expedition turned out to be higher than expected, the dissenters from Colleton County became, from the Anglican point of view, quite obstructionist about paying for it. Two dissolutions of the house and two turbulent elections weakened the dissenters' position, but not sufficiently to satisfy Moore's successor, Sir Nathaniel Johnson, who took office in 1702.

He undertook to solve "the problem" of the dissenters by excluding them entirely from the Commons. Normally, it took several days to assemble a quorum at the beginning of a session. Johnson apparently quietly notified his supporters and then called a special meeting of the legislature. The Anglicans promptly appeared in force and, before the dissenters could rally, passed an act requiring that to qualify for his seat each member of the Commons had to swear that he conformed to the Church of England. Shortly thereafter, the legislature enacted another bill establishing the Anglican Church as the official state-supported church of the colony. Designating seven parishes, the act presaged the use of public funds to construct Anglican churches and pay their ministers, who were given the exclusive right to perform legally recognized marriages.

There are basically two ways of interpreting these acts. One is to view them in the context of local politics. As might be expected, this is primarily what the dissenters did. The exclusion act was naturally grist for their mill: "Although nothing is more contrary to... the doctrine of the Church of England, than persecutions for conscience only," its preface stated, "nevertheless whereas it hath been found by experience that the admitting of persons of different persuasions and interest in matters of religion to sitt and vote in the Commons House of Assembly, hath often caused great contentions and animosities in this Province... Be it, therefore enacted...." Daniel Defoe, the great English writer and publicist who composed pamphlets for the Carolina dissenters, paraphrased this as follows: "Whereas the Laws of God, the Laws of Nature and Reason, the Christian Religion, the Doctrine of the Church of England, and the Constitution of this Country, are directly against, and do clearly condemn the Law now making," he wrote, and then continued, "yet in Defiance to them all, in order to carry on our own private Resolutions, for the Enriching [of] ourselves, and the Destruction of this Colony, we have resolved to enact...." Though perhaps a bit harsh in his assessment, Defoe was correct in perceiving that the exclusion bill could be understood at least partly in the context of the ongoing factional contest. From this perspective, the exclusion bill was the victors' penultimate step; the ultimate would be to eliminate the opposition. In a sense that is partly what the Anglicans both attempted and achieved by the act to establish the Church; for it created a lay commission with disciplinary authority over the clergy. That the commission soon sought to use its powers against the rector of St. Philip's, who had been one of the most vociferous critics of these high-handed measures, seems scarcely to have been a coincidence. Furthermore, as the Anglicans undoubtedly hoped would be the case, many dissenters gradually gravitated toward the seat of power and became members of the Church of England (and of South Carolina). To attribute either their actions, or those of the Anglicans who established the Church, exclusively to political motives would be mistaken. (Defoe had the excuse of partisanship.) The point here is merely that, in a political sense, the two acts were complementary.

The other major approach to understanding these developments is perhaps a bit less critical. According to several historians (and some contemporaries), the major impetus for the establishment of the Church came from London, and excluding dissenters from the assembly was not an end in itself but a preliminary step. There is also considerable evidence to support this point of view. Unusually active during the first decade of the eighteenth century, the Anglican Church bestirred itself in the missionary field by founding the Society for the Propagation of the Gospel (more commonly known as the SPG) which soon supplied ministers for many of the colonies, including South Carolina. Church-related issues also figured prominently in the politics of Queen Anne's reign when, beginning in 1703, the High Tories repeatedly attempted to bar dissenters from public office by enacting a bill against "occasional conformity" (the practice of taking communion in the Anglican Church periodically merely for purposes of the qualifying oath). Significantly, the preamble of the exclusion act passed by the South Carolina assembly was almost identical to that of the first bill against occasional conformity. That the colonial act was modeled on the English bill does not of course prove that it was instigated in London, but there are other reasons for believing that this was the case. One of the new Tory peers created at the beginning of Queen Anne's reign was Lord Granville, who was not only a proponent of the bill against occasional conformity, but also at this time the proprietary palatine. Circumstantial evidence suggests that he worked to have the Church established in both Carolinas. In 1701 the North Carolina assembly passed the first vestry act, a step that alarmed dissenters in South Carolina but failed to remain in force. Thus when a South Carolinian, Robert Daniel, became governor of North Carolina in 1704 he was instructed to pass another establishment act. It is also noteworthy that the proprietors selected Johnson and not someone else as governor of South Carolina at this juncture. Although he had lived in the colony for several years in comparative obscurity, he was not an obscure figure; rather, he had been a member of parliament and governor of the Leeward Islands. After the Glorious Revolution, however, he had refused to take the oaths of allegiance to William and Mary and instead emigrated to South Carolina. That Granville offered him the post or that he agreed to take it without an understanding about the Church seems highly unlikely. In short, there were two centers of authority involved, and developments in both London and Charles Town contributed to the establishment of the Anglican Church in South Carolina.

To be more precise, there were really three centers of authority involved, and a failure to be adequately mindful of that fact soon created difficulties for the proprietors and the Anglican faction. Outvoted and outmaneuvered at the local level, the dissenters sought protection from these measures by sending agents to England. One died before he could do much; the second received a cool reception from Granville, who was supposed to have said, "Sir, you are of one opinion, I am of another, and our lives may not be long enough to end the controversy. I am for the bill, and this is the party I will hear and countenance." The story may be apocryphal, but it suggests prevailing attitudes on both sides of the controversy. After the proprietors approved the act, Joseph Boone, the dissenters' agent, enlisted the aid of Defoe and other pamphleteers and took his case to the public, to the Anglican hierarchy, and to both houses of Parliament. Having rejected the English bill against occasional conformity, the House of Lords was an especially appropriate forum. In addition, because the Bishop of London was nominally in charge of the colonial clergy, the Anglican hierarchy would view the lay commission as an infringement upon his authority. Lest anyone fail to make the appropriate connections, the title of one of Defoe's two pamphlets on the subject was *Party-Tyranny, or An Occasional Bill in Miniature; as Now Practiced in Carolina,* and the dissenters worked hard to demonstrate, as another contemporary observed, that the creation of the lay commission revealed the "furious faction" to be "no friends to the Church of England." They were successful, and the House of Lords addressed the crown, asking it "to deliver the said Province from the arbitrary Oppressions under which it now lies"; the crown referred the matter to the Board of Trade and its legal advisors, who reported that the acts were improper. Whereupon the Privy Council directed the proprietors to disallow the legislation and instructed the attorney general to look into ways of vacating the proprietors' charter. Following notice of disallowance, the assembly in Charles Town repealed both acts, and then repassed the establishment act—minus the lay commission. Although the dissenters continued to protest it until about 1712, their efforts were less vigorous and less effective. The act of 1706, with some refinements added two years later, remained the law of the land throughout the rest of the colonial period.

One reason that the dissenters gave up relatively easily the second time around was that other issues were becoming more important. Defense and related matters in particular became increasingly central concerns (not that South Carolinians had ever felt very secure). But Spain in the late seventeenth and early eighteenth centuries was comparatively weak; France under Louis XIV was the foremost power of continental Europe. Having discovered and explored the Mississippi River in the 1680s, Frenchmen quickly established Biloxi (1699), Mobile (1702), and New Orleans (1718). Pushing north from the Gulf Coast, the French in 1717 also constructed Fort Toulouse at the forks of the Alabama River (near modern Montgomery). Meanwhile, a dizzying game of diplomatic musical chairs found the French and the Spanish at war during the 1690s, allied during the war of the Spanish Succession—known in the colonies as Queen Anne's War (1702–1713)—and once again at war from 1718 to 1720. During the first two contests, England and France fought each other, while during the last they were allied. In all probability, the intricacies of dynastic politics meant little to South Carolinians. What was clear to them was that the French presence to the southwest presented a major threat, both economically and militarily. This was the heyday of the deerskin trade, during which Carolina traders were pushing westward as far as the Mississippi River and beyond, even to modern Arkansas. Significantly enough, a governor who was himself deeply involved in the Indian trade told Spanish emissaries that Carolinians would soon occupy Pensacola. It turned out that he was wrong; the French did it temporarily in 1720—which was scarcely an improvement for South Carolinians.

Obviously, there were plenty of aggressive men on all sides, including James Moore. As we have seen, he was eager to attack St. Augustine, and after the assembly had received official notification of hostilities, it supported his attempt. Unfortunately for the governor, who led it himself, the expedition turned out to be a fiasco. Confronted by a force of about 800 Indians and whites, the Spanish, who had only about 400 soldiers, prepared the Castillo de San Marcos for siege and withdrew within it. Converted to stone in the 1670s and 1680s because of the threat posed by Englishmen in the Carolinas, the fort easily withstood the ensuing bombardment. Ordinary shot, as a contemporary later observed, penetrated the soft limestone like "a knife into a cheese," scattering few fragments and doing little damage. Moore therefore sent to Jamaica for large mortars and explosive shells. Meanwhile, the Spaniards summoned aid from Havana; the Spanish reinforcements arrived first. Judging it safer to withdraw overland, Moore burned his own ships as well as the town of St. Augustine and retreated. The shipowners were understandably distressed, and the assembly, instead of promptly paying for the expedition, launched an investigation into its failure. Angry recriminations, dissolution of the house, and a disputed election followed. Perhaps the most succinct and telling assessment of the whole expedition was made by a Yamasee Indian chief who observed that had he been in command he would not have treated his men so, and "though your Governour leaves you, I will not stir till I have seen all my men before me."

One year later, Moore sought to redeem himself by an attack on the Spanish settlements in northwestern Florida, then known as Apalache. Although he had the blessings of the new governor (Johnson, who was an old soldier), the assembly was less supportive. Moore financed the expedition himself. Undoubtedly, he expected his pamphet, *An Account of What the Army Did under the Command of Col. Moore, in his Expedition Against the Spaniards and the Spanish Indians,* published in 1704, to restore his military reputation. Among contemporaries and some later historians, it appears to have been effective; to others, however, he succeeded chiefly in indicting himself. Slaughtering and torturing both Indians and whites, Moore and his men plundered church silver and other objects of value as they laid waste the extensive mission system of the area. When they withdrew, they took with them about 1,000 Indians. Some of these became slaves; the others settled along the lower reaches of the Savannah River below modern Augusta. Moore reported that Apalache was "now reduced to so feeble and low a condition, that it can neither support St. Augustine with provisions, nor . . . frighten us." The Spanish seem to have agreed, for on one of their maps someone noted over the area, "wholly laid waste being destroyed by the Carolinians."

The blow to the Spanish in Florida was staggering, and a little over two years later they sought to redress the balance with French aid. Late in August the force sailed from St. Augustine; en route the vessel carrying the commander of the land forces and some 200 of his troops fell astern while engaging a Dutch warship. The rest of the fleet proceeded to Charles Town where the fortifications were incomplete. (The major work on James Island promised Archdale by the assembly would bear Governor Johnson's name, but it was not in use until 1709.) Johnson and the militia were prepared, however. Summoned to surrender within the hour, he is supposed to have replied that it would not take him a minute to refuse. Despite the absence of their commander and the men with him, most of the invaders landed and immediately met defeat. No sooner had the remainder withdrawn and weighed anchor for St. Augustine, than the delayed vessel put into a bay north of Charles Town and disembarked its troops. Unaware of what had happened to the others, these men advanced toward the city. Again, the Carolinians were victorious, not only defeating this detachment but also boarding and capturing the French vessel. All in all, the victory was an impressive one. At the cost of one man, according to some reports, the South Carolinians had killed about thirty and captured several hundred of the enemy.

The South Carolinians had given a good account of themselves, and they emerged from the encounter in high martial spirits. The French, the Commons House officially resolved the next year, should be ousted from Mobile. Pending something more ambitious, Carolinians provided a leaven of white troops among largely Indian forces which twice unsuccessfully attacked Pensacola in 1707. Meanwhile, Thomas Nairne, one of the most visionary among the Indian-trader politicians of Carolina, developed a plan for taking over the Gulf Coast as far west as the Mississippi River. For the next few years, intrigue was rife among the southern Indians as the French and Spanish as well as the Carolinians sought to marshal forces. But nothing conclusive came of all these efforts, perhaps in part because Nairne himself ran into trouble with Governor Johnson.

The issue was regulation of the Indian trade in which abuses had long been notorious. By the end of the 1690s, such unrestrained exploitation of the Indians was, as the Commons House observed, a threat to the safety of the colony. Yet no permanent arrangement for regulating the trade was adopted until nearly a decade later, apparently because most of the governors preferred a public monopoly while the Commons wanted a supervisory commission under its own direction. In 1707 the Commons had its way, and Nairne became the new commission's first agent. He was a good choice—perhaps, it turned out, too good since he soon prosecuted one of the leading traders. Unfortunately, the trader was also Governor Johnson's son-in-law, and Johnson retaliated by charging Nairne with treason. Although Nairne was eventually exonerated, the imbroglio crippled regulation of the trade at a crucial time.

In the interim, the Yamasee Indians in particular became increasingly unhappy. In the 1680s, when raids on Spanish territory by Indians instigated and backed by Carolinians had induced Spanish authorities to evacuate threatened tribes southward, the Yamasees refused to go and moved into South Carolina near Port Royal. In 1707 the legislature set aside the mainland between the Combahee and the Savannah rivers for their perpetual occupation. Four years later, however, the town of Beaufort was established on Port Royal Sound, and in 1712 the surrounding parish was organized. Although technically not encroachments on their area, the Yamasees were understandably concerned about these developments. Moreover, squatters and cattle did intrude on their land and the latter became fair game for the Indians. Thus trouble was soon brewing in the area.

If Moore's expedition to St. Augustine did little more than produce scorn for the white man's military prowess among the Yamasees, the Tuscarora War soon provided an object lesson in possible ways of remedying their grievances. Like the Yamasees, the Tuscaroras of North Carolina had been victimized by Indian traders; like the Yamasees, the Tuscaroras also had trouble with white settlement on their lands. Alarmed by the establishment of New Bern in 1710, the Tuscaroras and four other tribes in the area attempted to remove the settlers the following year. Attacks on other settlements followed, and more than 100 whites died. Officials sought help without much success from Virginia; they then turned to South Carolina. Scarcely in a position to ignore a request for aid from the proprietors' other colony, South Carolinians responded generously by appropriating £4,000 to finance an expedition led by Colonel John Barnwell. Accompanied by thirty-odd whites and several hundred Yamasee Indians, he arrived at the Neuse River near New Bern in January 1712. For the next four months he waged war with considerable success. Nevertheless, the treaty signed with the Indians in April was a negotiated peace. Barnwell thought his job was done; North Carolinians seem to have been less certain. On the march home, Barnwell was wounded, apparently by one of his own men, and other Carolinians violated the agreement with the Tuscarora Indians by seizing several as slaves. Renewed fighting soon broke out. Once again, North Carolinians asked for aid, and the South Carolina assembly dispatched a force commanded, this time, by James Moore, Jr. (a son of the former governor) and accompanied not by Yamasees but Cherokee, Creek, and Catawba auxiliaries. Moore, his men, and some North Carolinians decisively defeated the Tuscaroras, but peace did not really return until early in 1715.

By this time rumors of an imminent attack on South Carolina had begun to circulate. On Good Friday, April 15, at the Yamasee town of Pocotaligo, where Nairne and others had gone to negotiate in the hope of averting hostilities, the war began. Seizing the white men, some Indians tortured and killed them, while others attacked the settlements around Beaufort. Soon hostile Indians seemed to be everywhere, as one contemporary reported, "killing all they meet[,] destroying and laying wast the Plantations where they came plundering and then burning the Houses[,] Lying Sculking in the Bushes and Swamps...," so that "we know not where to find them nor could follow them if we did so that we may as well goe to War with the Wolfs and Bears." The governor at this time was Charles Craven, and leading the militia himself, he pushed the Yamasees back across the Savannah, but then Catawbas and other Indians north and west of Charles Town attacked from that direction. Craven and the militia pursued, and the Indians in the south returned, raiding plantations almost as far north as the Ashley River. For a time the defensive perimeter around Charles Town was scarcely more than thirty miles in diameter. Authorities drafted part of the militia for continuous service, armed some slaves, and sought aid from other colonies. Massachusetts provided arms and Virginia supplied a few troops—at exorbitant rates, South Carolinians believed. Worse yet, they also charged, guns from

Virginia appeared in the hands of the enemy. (Rivalry for control of the southern Indian trade long complicated relations between Virginia and South Carolina.) What eventually saved the day was diplomacy and assistance from the Cherokees. Traditional enemies of the Creeks and fairly secure in their relatively remote mountains, the Cherokee Indians at first elected to remain neutral. By autumn, however, they agreed to aid the Carolinians. When they failed to show up, Maurice Moore (a brother of James, Jr.) led a force of about 300 Carolinians into the Cherokee country. The maneuver, which was designed to impress the Indians, worked. The Cherokees murdered envoys sent by the Creeks and went to war with them, thereby taking much of the pressure off South Carolina. By the spring of 1716 the real crisis was over, but a "sculking warr" and sporadic raiding by both sides continued along the southern border for over a decade.

In the end, the South Carolinians won, but despite their technological superiority the issue was in real doubt for a considerable time. Not unreasonable estimates place the number of whites in the militia able to bear arms at not much over 1,200; the Indians may have had about seven times that number. As a result, the Yamasee War stands with King Philip's War as one of the bloodiest and most costly of the colonial Indian wars. In proportion to the size of the populations involved, the loss of 400 whites in South Carolina represented a casualty rate almost twice that of Massachusetts in the earlier war. The parishes south of Charles Town were devastated; and, it was estimated, approximately half of the cultivated land in the province was temporarily abandoned. Indeed, it was not until the 1730s that many men showed much interest in reclaiming abandoned plantations in the southeastern part of the colony. By 1717 the cost of defense alone amounted to £116,000 sterling, and the indirect costs of the war, in the form of damages, lost production, and increased prices for foodstuffs and commodities in short supply were undoubtedly many times higher. Contemporaries estimated that the conflict reduced the tax base by £236,587 sterling. The colony had suffered a blow that South Carolinians would long remember; and years later, long after the Indian danger was safely past, William Gilmore Simms, perhaps the best of the antebellum southern novelists, would give fictional treatment to the struggle in *The Yemassee*.

No sooner had South Carolina begun to recover from the war than another threat arose, one that was also later to be the subject of fiction but no less real at the time. This was piracy. During the seventeenth century when the colony was poor, pirates tended to be more welcomed for their trade than shunned for their plundering. As South Carolina became more prosperous, attitudes changed. The hanging of seven culprits in 1700 provides a symbolic turning point, but it failed to stamp out piracy. At the end of Queen Anne's War, seamen who had found adventure and profit in wartime activities were sometimes lured or forced into piracy. British authorities responded with a vigorous campaign against them, and by 1715 the royal navy had chased most of the pirates out of the Caribbean. Many of them took refuge on the coast of North Carolina from which, it was said, nearly 1,500 were soon operating. Among them were at least two who became legendary—Edward Teach (or Thatch), known as Blackbeard, and Stede Bonnet. A sailor from Bristol, Teach was basically a thug; Bonnet had been a major in the British army and thereafter a planter in Barbados. In June 1718 Blackbeard appeared off Charles Town with four vessels, carrying about forty guns, and proceeded to stop ships at leisure. Taking hostages, he went so far as to send word to the governor that, unless he received needed medical supplies, he would kill the hostages and, according to some reports, destroy the town. The medicines were sent. Bonnet and other pirate captains were only slightly less audacious. But by August the authorities were prepared to act. William Rhett led an expedition which caught Bonnet in the Cape Fear River. After a six-hour battle, Rhett supposedly promised to intercede for mercy, and Bonnet surrendered.

The sequel is a bit puzzling. While being held for trial, Bonnet escaped but was recaptured, convicted, and executed. Apparently some South Carolinians believed that he had been unfairly treated; an attempt was made to free him, and disorders ensued. Precisely who was involved and exactly why is not clear. Perhaps Bonnet was able to pay for assistance, or perhaps the sensational nature of his case elicited interest and sympathy. Possibly, however, he was perceived as a kind of Robin Hood. In remote rural areas, historians have recently noted, one sometimes encounters a kind of banditry in which outlaws express popular frustrations and are in turn supported by the people. To what extent pirates filled this role is an open question, but it is at least worth noting that, contrary to what one might expect, pirate commanders frequently seem to have been among the least authoritarian of ship-masters. Because they lacked legitimate sources of authority, they had to rule by force or consensus, and the latter often proved to be more effective. Not being a seaman, Bonnet initially encountered difficulty in controlling his crews. Whether this caused him to abandon the authoritarian style of his military background and how much the pop-ulace knew of his shipboard regimen are unclear. Rhett, however, apparently quarreled with the governor over the question of mercy, among other things. So when four ships, mounting seventy guns but disguised as merchantmen, put to sea in November, not Rhett but the governor himself, Robert Johnson, commanded. Again, the quest was successful and, after a running battle, Johnson captured another pirate vessel and "rescued" a shipload of convicts—including about thirty-five women—who before being taken by the pirates had been bound to the Chesapeake as indentured servants. The convicts were sold in Charles Town; forty-nine pirates were hanged. Meanwhile, forces from Virginia took Blackbeard. Thus by the end of 1718 Carolinians were relatively safe from pirates.

Although the local campaign against the pirates was dramatic and commendable, the efforts of the royal navy in the Caribbean largely provided the conditions for its success. These naval activities reflected a growing official interest in the colonies which would play an in-creasing role in the history of South Carolina. Not that royal authorities had ever entirely neglected the area. Following the treaty of Madrid with Spain in 1670, they were especially anxious to promote the slave trade with the Spanish empire. Accordingly, they sought to curb pirates whose activities worked at cross purposes with this policy, and they were particularly annoyed with the governor of the Bahamas who, in the late 1680s, commissioned known pirates as privateers to attack the Spanish while the two nations were at peace. To all intents and pur-poses, the proprietors of the Bahamas were by this time also the pro-prietors of the Carolinas; they appointed the governor; and though he had acted on his own initiative, the charter of the Bahamas, like that of the Carolinas, gave him authority to make war—but, crown officials noted, not on nations with which England was then in amity. Clearly such activities could jeopardize the proprietors' charters. Quickly mov-ing to arrest the governor in question, the proprietors repeatedly instructed their agents in South Carolina to curb the trade with pirates. Indeed, they seemed to have "pirates on the brain." However, their concern was justified, and, given the wider context, their otherwise puzzling remark, that if the Carolinians' countermanded attack on St. Augustine had been made in 1687, those who authorized it might have been hung, becomes understandable.

Illegal trade of all kinds was an increasingly sore point with royal officials. More with the intent of regulating trade by manipulating economic incentives than raising revenue, Parliament in 1673 imposed duties on the exportation of certain commodities from the colonies. As several customs officers in the Carolinas discovered, collecting these duties and enforcing the acts of trade were not easy tasks. In 1687 the local collector, George Muschamp, reported, for example, that local courts would not convict for illegal trade even when the evidence of guilt was clear. The charter, Carolinians claimed, exempted them from the provisions of the first navigation act because it had been issued after passage of the law. Under the circumstances, Muschamp noted, it was "difficult to maintaine the Acts of Navigation in due force here." Not long thereafter, he requested a transfer to Maryland. Needless to say, the crown's legal officers disagreed with the local interpretation of the law, and the proprietors recognized that the situation threatened their possession of the charter. Claims to such exemptions, they hastily noted, "must be the discourse of ignorant and loose people only and not of any concerned in the government." Their ability to curb such practices was distinctly limited, however, and though the Carolinas were notorious for irregularities during this period, imperial officials had reason to be concerned about most of the proprietary and corporate colonies.

In the 1690s the crown took measures to tighten up the system. Thereafter, proprietary governors required crown approval before being appointed, and their instructions stipulated that they enforce the acts of trade. Vice-admiralty courts (which operated without a jury) were also established in each of the colonies to deal with the problem of obtaining convictions. Many crown officials continued to believe that further steps were necessary. One of them, Edward Randolph, was the surveyor general of the customs service in North America, which meant that he was a roving investigator. In 1698 he arrived in South Carolina, and what he saw impressed him in several ways. There was, he believed, entirely too much illegal trade; proximity to the Spanish and the French on the southern frontier made South Carolina strategically important; and its increasing prosperity rendered it a valuable colony. More specifically, it appeared to be ideally suited for producing naval stores, which were crucial to English maritime activities. If the crown would take over the colony, Randolph observed, the king would be "the richest prince in Europe."

Although the hyperbole may have been new, the idea of assuming control over the proprietary colonies was not. Hoping to consolidate the colonies and centralize their control, royal officials sought to vacate independent charters during the 1680s. Had the distractions of English politics and the Glorious Revolution not intervened, there is good reason to believe that South Carolina would have become administratively part of the royal colony of Virginia. But, as the proprietors were well aware, their luck might not last, since imperial bureaucrats remained hostile to the notion of "independent" colonies. Thus Randolph's comments fell on fertile ground, and during the first decade of the eighteenth century Parliament considered two bills which would have vacated the Carolina charter (along with those of other proprietary colonies). Parliament, however, was reluctant to augment the power of the crown and leery of tampering with property rights, and the bills failed to pass. Theoretically, the courts could also have been used to invalidate the charter, and serious consideration was given to this approach, not only in the 1680s but also in 1705–1706 when the exclusion and establishment acts attracted the attention of the crown. But several of the proprietors were peers, and, as such, they enjoyed some immunity from legal actions. The crown's desire to royalize South Carolina was therefore not synonymous with achieving it. Nevertheless, after 1706 imperial officials were clearly committed to the idea, and bringing it about seemed to be chiefly a matter of time. Purchase of the proprietors' rights appeared to be the most promising approach, but that would require their consent and, most probably, sums not readily available during Queen Anne's War.

Yet straws in the wind clearly showed its direction, and there were able individuals among the proprietors who were quite capable of reading the signs. In 1702 imperial officials convinced the proprietors of New Jersey (with whom the Carolina proprietors were no longer connected) to give up their governmental rights without compensation.

The next year William Penn informed the crown that he was also willing to surrender Pennsylvania for a price. Negotiations ensued, and in 1714 he received the first installment of the agreed-upon payment. Then declining health and his death intervened, and Pennsylvania remained in the hands of his heirs. How close the Carolina proprietors were to similar negotiations is difficult to say, but they were obviously losing interest in their governmental rights as early as the 1690s. Ashley's grandson did not want the governorship, and Archdale, who was willing to take it, came, saw, conciliated—and left as quickly as possible. There was good reason for the proprietors' indifference. Carolina was the first Earl of Shaftesbury's pet project, but he and his colleagues were long since dead, and in most cases their successors were investors rather than descendants. As such, they had little reason to regard South Carolina any differently than they viewed the Bahamas—that is, as a profit-and-loss account.

A brief look at the proprietors' relationship with their other colony in this period casts light on their behavior toward Carolina. A haven for pirates and a hotbed of illegal trade almost from the beginning, the Bahama Islands had given the proprietors a headache for years. In 1702, believing that they had irretrievably lost control of the colony, they virtually abandoned it. Exposed to French and Spanish depredations during Queen Anne's War, the islands were repeatedly devastated; and thereafter, like floating derelicts in a shipping channel, they remained a hazard because of their strategic location. Angry imperial officials therefore put pressure on the proprietors who in 1717 decided to do something about the situation. Leasing the soil to a private individual for twenty-one years, they voluntarily surrendered their governmental rights to the crown. The islands, it was obvious, had become more trouble than they were worth.

From the proprietors' point of view, the same could almost be said about Carolina, where the crucial problem was defense. Being private individuals with relatively limited resources, they were in no position to contribute very much toward it, yet the struggle with France increasingly made protection of their colony a matter of national concern. Accordingly, the proprietors made some appropriate gestures—as when Archdale asked the assembly to build the fort at Charles Town—and they sent a few supplies, but as they and everyone else undoubtedly knew, South Carolinians would have to rely mainly on themselves and the crown for whatever protection they were going to have. Thus when the Carolinians petitioned the proprietors for aid, the latter referred the requests to the crown. Taking advantage of the situation, imperial officials noted that "if the Queen was at the Expence of protecting and relieving the Province, the Government thereof should be in the Crown." This, a contemporary observed, "first contracted in the Inhabitants in general, an opinion of their being very unhappy in living under a Government that could not protect them" and whose existence appeared to prevent the others from doing it.

Actually, some of the proprietors may have agreed with the crown. As early as 1701 when the first bill to royalize the proprietary colonies was being considered, Randolph believed that at least some of the Carolina proprietors were "indifferent" to the outcome and that others hoped to profit from it. Carteret, who was one of the most important of the proprietors, also told royal officials that, speaking for himself, he would prefer to give up the government of Carolina rather than deprive the colony of the crown's aid. Although both North and South Carolina came through Queen Anne's War relatively unscathed, the Tuscarora and Yamasee wars may well have convinced most of the proprietors that these colonies were nearly as great liabilities as the Bahamas. By 1717—the same year that they leased those islands— the proprietors were ready to try a somewhat similar arrangement on the mainland. Under it, the unsettled southern portion of South Carolina (which eventually would constitute much of Georgia) was to be converted into a separate colony known as the "Margravate of Azilia." As one could infer from the name, which was evocative of European border marches, the new settlement was to be a defensive buffer for South Carolina. How enviable that role might be was certainly open to question, and the proprietors were quite willing to have a Scotsman, Sir Robert Montgomery, receive all the glory if he would bear all the burdens. As margrave, he would be governor for life. Already having more proprietors and quasi-proprietors than they wanted, imperial officials vacillated and finally vetoed that particular plan on the grounds that the proprietors could not legally alienate their governmental rights to anyone except the crown. Thus the proprietors had reason to fear that they might be stuck with the problem of South Carolina and its defense.

It is tempting to conclude that at about this point the proprietors decided that the crown could protect their property more effectively than they could and that they should figure out a way of unloading their more onerous responsibilities on the king. One can therefore speculate that at least some of the proprietors may have deliberately sought to provoke the revolt which eventually occurred in South Carolina. But conspiracy theories, though sometimes accurate, are usually among the most implausible of historical interpretations; and in this case, though some of the proprietors may have believed that their chance for compensation was greater if they did not voluntarily tender their rights, there was no inherent reason why they could not have just turned over the government of South Carolina to the crown. Moreover, their subsequent bitterness toward the last governor who had lost control of the colony, as well as their futile attempts to regain it, suggest that if there was a covert scheme afoot not all of the proprietors were involved in it. The most probable explanation of their behavior toward South Carolina is that they were fed up with its problems and no longer committed to governing it. Though generally neglectful of colonial affairs (their secretaries handled most of the day-to-day business), they occasionally indulged in spasms of activity that now appear to have been foolhardy. That they did not realize they were taking high risks is almost inconceivable; that they were willing to run them is quite probable. Long believed by historians to have been "incompetent and helpless," the later Carolina proprietors were, in all probability, also calculating.

Which of these adjectives should characterize the behavior of the proprietary governors toward royal officials is a difficult question. Whatever the answer, there was always a good deal of jurisdictional rivalry and friction in the relationship, especially over the rights to vice-admiralty jurisdiction. In 1700, after the council had elected another one of its members as an interim governor, Moore managed to convince his colleagues to reverse their decision and choose him by pointing out that his rival had been disloyal to the proprietors in accepting a concurrent appointment as judge in the royal vice-admiralty court. The defeated candidate believed—apparently with some justification—that he was discarded because the council was convinced he would be more vigorous in enforcing the acts of trade. Under Moore the assembly passed, and he approved, a bill ostensibly "reforming" but in reality crippling the vice-admiralty court. Under pressure from the Board of Trade, the proprietors then backpedalled by removing Moore and directing his successor to obtain repeal of the offending act.

The friction between the customs officials and Governor Craven is more puzzling. Charles Craven, who served during the Yamasee War, is generally conceded to have been one of the most able of the proprietary governors; he was also a brother of a proprietor. His attitude toward the customs officials is therefore especially significant. If the latter's complaints in 1715 are to be believed, he deliberately attempted to impede them in the performance of their duties. If they seized a vessel for illegal trade, he would commandeer it on the grounds that it was required for public service and send it out of the colony. If they confiscated goods, he claimed them as his own. He also ordered shipmasters not to allow customs officials to board their vessels, and he actually had the fort fire on both the customs yacht and a royal naval vessel, apparently on the grounds that customs officials lacked the right to detain incoming vessels. In one case involving smuggling, he not only testified in behalf of the defendant but also supposedly whiled away the hours in court by making jokes about the acts of trade. Even if one accepts these charges at less than face value, they had enough substance to require some explanation. Perhaps, as the customs officials claimed, Craven was himself engaged in illegal trade, though that does not appear very probable. Perhaps he was courting the merchants, or maybe he was merely contemptuous of the local customs officials.

Jurisdictional rivalry alone could in fact help to explain Craven's rather strange appointment of Robert Daniel as his successor. An arbitrary and hot-tempered old soldier, Daniel took no guff from anyone, including customs officials, and the most notable event of his administration turned out to be a memorable confrontation with them. Having seized a vessel for an alleged violation of the acts of trade, the local surveyor general of the customs, William Rhett, came aboard to claim the crown's share of the cargo. Daniel ordered him to leave the ship until proceedings in the vice-admiralty court had been completed. Rhett refused; Daniel called out the militia and commanded them if necessary to fire on Rhett and his party—which included a detachment of sailors from the royal navy. Gunfire was avoided when Rhett left the ship screaming, "I will kill the old Rogue...God damn me I will kill the Dogg." That Craven and Daniel intended to goad authorities in London into action is of course very doubtful; but had that been their goal, it is difficult to see how they could have chosen a much better way.

Meanwhile, the proprietors' own activities combined with circumstances beyond their control to alienate many of their erstwhile supporters in South Carolina. Proprietary attitudes and behavior during the local exclusion crisis convinced many of the dissenters—who at one time had composed the most loyal faction—that the crown was a more reliable source of protection against arbitrary rule. Conversely, the proprietors' more recent alliance with the Anglicans was somewhat shaky for a number of reasons. In the first place, some of the Anglicans were the heirs and successors of the old Goose Creek men who had a long tradition of opposing the proprietors; and there is evidence to indicate that the movement to overthrow proprietary government may have originated among the planters of Goose Creek. Some of the aggressive Indian traders were also Anglicans, but anyone who had visions of tapping the deerskin trade of the Gulf Coast could scarcely fail to realize the advantages which might accrue from royal assistance in repelling French and Spanish competitors. Finally, officeholders, most of whom were Anglicans by this time, and merchants of all persuasions, who initially welcomed the proprietors' stance on economic issues, would seem to have been their natural allies. But even many of them became disenchanted in time. To understand why, the issue of paper money must be examined.

Between 1702 and 1718, military expeditions, Indian wars, and the campaign against the pirates had been extraordinarily expensive. How to pay for them therefore became an acute and divisive question. During the 1690s, Massachusetts had financed military measures by emitting the first colonial paper currency; following Moore's expedition against St. Augustine, the South Carolina assembly adopted the same expedient by issuing paper bills bearing interest at 12 percent. Theoretically, these were to be redeemed by tax revenues within the next two years. However, continuing expenditures for defense made it impossible to retire the issue as planned; instead, the legislature emitted more bills of credit, dropped the interest payments, and declared paper money to be legal tender. Although seven such issues were soon circulating, depreciation was not excessive until 1712 when the assembly tried something new—the first public land bank in the colonies. Printing more paper currency, the legislature established a fund for

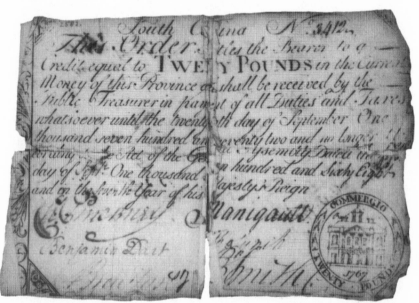

An example of paper currency. These twenty-pound notes were authorized by the legislature in 1767 and 1768 to finance construction of the Exchange, a building for the town watch, and a new poorhouse in Charles Town. Although the structure depicted has sometimes been thought to be the colonial State House, circumstantial evidence suggests that it is the Exchange. *Courtesy of the South Caroliniana Library.*

interest-bearing loans to be made on the security of landed property. Almost immediately, both the new and old issues of paper money began to depreciate and within the next four years declined in value by about 50 percent. What triggered the rapid fall is not entirely clear; but the magnitude of the last emission and the fact that it was designed to be a permanent currency rather than a temporary substitute may well have been primarily responsible. Further emissions to pay for the Yamasee War then led to even more rapid depreciation and by the end of 1717, £4 in paper money was worth only £1 sterling. Nevertheless, being legal tender, the local paper remained the nominal equivalent of sterling. The rapid depreciation had disparate effects in different areas. Where prices were free to move, a two-tier system developed in which the price in currency was adjusted to compensate for its depreciation, while the price in sterling remained relatively stable. But in areas where the nominal price counted—as in contracts, instruments of debt, and other legal documents—someone took a beating and someone made a killing.

Thus the impact of depreciation was substantially different on different economic interests, and individuals reacted accordingly. In general, men who had borrowed money and planters, whose commodities appeared to appreciate in value, benefited. Creditors and officials, whose salaries and fees were fixed by law, suffered. Merchants are more difficult to categorize because they frequently had multiple economic interests. Beginning in the 1690s the increasing volume of valuable exports (in the form of deerskins, rice, and naval stores) attracted the attention of British merchants who became heavily involved with the colony for the first time. Merchants in England naturally tended to take a dim view of a depreciated paper currency; their agents and local merchants who regarded themselves as primarily purchasers of local produce and providers of credit appear to have been almost equally hostile to the local currency. But others who had deep roots in the local economy and perhaps themselves owned plantations could often see the utility of some paper money. Although adequate for present purposes, these categories are too schematic to be a completely accurate reflection of reality—many men, for example, were both creditors and debtors. Perhaps only the proprietors can be safely placed in a pigeonhole (and even that is rather doubtful). They reacted like men who were not only trying to sell land at a fixed price but who were also exposed to the direct and indirect pressure of British merchants, and they opposed the local paper money. In this, as in so many other instances, they were not very effectual. As a result, it appears that they fell between two stools: their opposition alienated those who supported the emission of some paper currency, and their ineffectiveness eventually alienated those who opposed all paper money.

Nor were the proprietors much more successful in retaining the loyalty of their own officials. As early as 1712 one of their favorites, Rhett, whom they had just commissioned as receiver general of the quitrents, observed, "this is but a Lords proprietors Government and I wou'd wipe my Arse with the Commission." Such a remark by such an individual suggests that the remaining days of proprietary government were already numbered. It is therefore especially ironic that his employers' favoritism toward Rhett and his brother-in-law, Nicholas Trott, helped to shorten those days even further. Rhett, in addition to his post as receiver of the quitrents, was at various times—and sometimes simultaneously—naval officer (that is, keeper of the port records) and surveyor general of the customs. From 1711 to 1715 he was also speaker of the Commons House. Trott, a lawyer who was reputed to be the most learned man in South Carolina, was also, successively or simultaneously, naval officer, attorney general, judge of the vice-admiralty court, and chief justice. In addition, he was the moving spirit behind an attempt made by the assembly in 1712 to codify the English law in force in the colony, which apparently impressed the proprietors. The two brothers-in-law were reputed to hold "great Sway" with the voters of Charles Town, and they obviously had influence with the proprietors. In fact, the latter went so far in 1714 as to give Trott the authority to block all legislation of which he did not approve. This, and the fact that Rhett continued to remain in their good graces despite his derogatory remarks about them, suggest that the proprietors' understanding of the situation in Carolina was less than complete. The man who handled—and probably culled—their correspondence with local officials was their secretary, Richard Shelton, who also had a close working relationship with Trott and his brother-in-law.

Although Trott in particular was undoubtedly an able man, neither he nor Rhett was a complete asset to the proprietors. Both exploited their offices for personal gain, and the excessive concentration of power in their hands prompted resentment and opposition. The Commons requested that Trott's extraordinary powers be revoked and, somewhat later, that he be removed from at least some of his offices. Although the proprietors did rescind his special authority, Trott retained his posts; Rhett did not fare so well. Perhaps partly because of the voters' reaction to his brother-in-law's bloated powers, Rhett was not elected to the house in 1716. In his absence the Commons passed a bill barring from membership anyone who held income-producing offices. In addition, the house, modeling the act on Barbadian practice, changed the basis of representation from the counties to the parishes, stipulating that the elections were to be held at the parish churches. (Hitherto, despite the proprietors' earlier attempts to decentralize them, they had continued to be held in Charles Town.) The voters of Charles Town thereby lost control of sixteen of the twenty representatives previously elected by Berkeley County, and the two brothers-in-law lost much of their influence over the election process. Still, as one contemporary later remarked, they continued to have "too much Interest" with the proprietors "either for their Lordships or the Peoples Good." The extent to which these two men were responsible for the proprietors' reckless behavior during the last three years of the proprietary period will perhaps never be known. Contemporaries certainly blamed them, but the proprietors had other sources of information, and if Trott and Rhett misled them, it was because they chose to heed them rather than others. Perhaps the crux of the matter was that both sides emerged from the Yamasee War more alarmed than chastened, resolved that, one way or another, things in Carolina were going to be put on a more satisfactory footing.

Their agendas were naturally different. Local leaders began by tackling several problems. Abuses in the Indian trade had helped to cause the war; accordingly, the legislature forbade private trading and established a public monopoly. The lack of white manpower and the presence of black slaves made the colony especially vulnerable; the assembly therefore imposed a prohibitory duty on the further importation of Africans, confiscated the Yamasees' lands and used them to establish a homestead system under which new immigrants could acquire small tracts at no cost in return for settling on the exposed southern frontier. Expenditures for defense had created a large public debt, which had spawned paper money, which had in turn depreciated. The legislature consolidated the debt in a new issue of paper currency, enacted new taxes to retire it, and sought additional revenue by imposing a duty on imported goods.

The proprietors, on the other hand, were particularly concerned about the fate of their lands and not enthusiastic about measures taken by the Commons. They wanted a stricter law to insure collection of quitrents and somewhat smaller tracts under the homestead system. In addition, to compensate for the depreciation of the currency, they raised the price of their land. A bit later, the proprietors disallowed most of the legislation recently passed by the assembly. Although it came as a surprise, this action was not quite as arbitrary as it appeared. The crown, ever solicitous of British mercantile interests, directed them to repeal the import duties on British manufactured goods and slaves; complaints from local merchants—backed by Rhett—had given the proprietors a hostile view of the public monopoly of the Indian trade and the new fiscal policy, which seemed to them to be designed to soak the merchants and spare the planters; and the election law of 1716 (which they also disallowed) not only undermined the influence of their favorite duo but also dealt with an area which they considered to be within their purview. Convinced that the assembly was being extraordinarily recalcitrant, the proprietors ordered that it be dissolved and new elections held under the old system. Other instructions to the governor directed him to seek prompt retirement of existing paper currency and to permit no further emissions. Placing an embargo on further grants or sales of land, the proprietors ordered the surveyor general to lay out fifteen baronies for themselves in the area taken from the Yamasees. In addition, they restructured the council. Dropping the notion that councilors were their deputies, which had hitherto been the case, in order to undercut the Commons' contention that the principals could not repeal acts to which their surrogates had assented, the proprietors increased the membership to twelve, ousted most of their opponents and, in an attempt to woo local merchants, appointed a number of them.

By this time their governor was Robert Johnson, the son of Sir

Nathaniel. Though a popular and able man, he could not get out of the bind in which his employers had placed him. Nevertheless, he tried to mediate. Disobeying his orders, he neglected to dissolve the assembly and approved a bill reenacting the duties on imports. In return, the assembly passed a new quitrent law and opened the Indian trade to limited private involvement. The proprietors were not to be mollified. Learning that the same assembly was still in session, they vetoed its quitrent law, repeated their disallowance of the election act so that there could be no mistake about it, and once again ordered the house dissolved. This time, Johnson dared not disobey. Fully aware, however, of what the proprietors' heavy hand was apt to lead to, "he resolv'd for the future," as a contemporary observed, to rely on the advice of Trott and the (new) council members so that "they might be answerable for any ill Effects their future Councils and Transactions might produce." Johnson dissolved the assembly and called for new elections, to be held in Charles Town.

Given the cumulative effects of the proprietors' recent actions, the results of these elections were almost a foregone conclusion. Although the assembly had repeatedly requested that the crown add the province to those under its "happy protection"—and nearly 600 individuals, or about half the free white men in the province, had signed the most recent petition in 1717—the wording remained sufficiently ambiguous to indicate that many persons still had ambivalent feelings about the situation. (Protection, after all, could mean exactly that, despite the fact that some local leaders clearly intended it to mean royalization.) But so many apparently arbitrary acts coming so quickly angered many, and some of the councilors who had been removed from their posts were especially disturbed. Furthermore, reorganization of the council raised a serious constitutional issue; for if the proprietors could unilaterally change the composition of the upper house of the legislature, what about the lower? Given the proprietors' wholesale attack on the Commons's recent enactments, the implicit answer was not very reassuring. In addition, the proprietors' unwillingness, or inability, to accept import duties while they were equally opposed to paper currency presaged steeply higher taxes since this combination left no other way to cover past and current expenses. And public levies had already doubled in recent years. By the time the elections were held in November 1719, "the whole People in general" were, according to one observer, "prejudic'd against the *Lords Proprietors* to such a degree, that it was grown almost dangerous to say any thing in their Favour." As a result, holding the elections in Charles Town failed to help the dwindling proprietary faction which, it was reported, "could not get so much as a Man chose" to the Commons House. A revolt was clearly in the offing.

What finally triggered the revolution against the proprietors was another threat to the security of the colony. War had broken out between England and Spain, and a rumor reached Charles Town in 1719 that the Spanish were readying a fleet to attack the city. The report was accurate, but the expedition was diverted to another target. Local leaders could not know that, and they decided to waste no time. An association pledging signers to "support whatsoever should be done by their Representatives . . . in disengaging the Country from the Yoke and Burthen they labour'd under from the *Proprietors*" circulated widely and, according to a later report, "almost every body in the whole Province" signed it. In December, when the Commons met, it refused to recognize the authority of the new councilors, announced that it was "a Convention, delegated by the People, to prevent the utter Ruin of this Government, if not the Loss of the Province, until His Majesty's Pleasure be known," and asked Johnson "to take the Government upon him in the King's Name, and to Continue the Administration thereof until His Majesty's Pleasure be known." Johnson refused on the grounds that he could not betray his employers. The convention then chose the one-time ranking officer of the militia, James Moore, Jr., to be provisional governor and sent an agent to England with a petition requesting that South Carolina be made a royal colony.

Johnson made several fairly vigorous attempts to regain control, even to the extent of trying to use some naval forces in the harbor to cow his opposition into submission. The local leaders had cannon, however, as well as nearly 500 men from the militia under arms, and it was Johnson, not they, who backed down. Shortly thereafter the crown took advantage of the revolt to appoint a provisional governor (just as it had in the Bahamas under somewhat similar circumstances). For the next ten years the legal status of the colony remained in a kind of limbo during which the proprietors tried to sell their interests, and, at one time, sought to appoint a governor. In 1729, however, the crown bought out seven of the eight proprietary shares. Carteret, who refused to sell, eventually received title to an area in North Carolina known as the Granville Tract. So, for £17,500 sterling, plus a sum to cover arrears in quitrents, ended the remnants of Shaftesbury's faded dream: a utopian society flourishing under the benign auspices of the proprietors.

Obviously it did not work out quite the way he had planned. But if South Carolina had not become utopia, it was becoming distinctly more English. To imply, as many historians have done, that the revolution was not much of a revolution is correct, but to say no more is to overlook much of its significance. To be sure, it was not very violent and almost no blood was shed. (Only Rhett was wounded, and he was not sufficiently hurt to prevent him from later straddling the political fence.) Constitutional issues played only a minor role, and tyranny was not the focal point of the dispute; rather it was the failure of proprietary government to do what governments were supposed to do—that is, provide protection. In an age of increasingly modern warfare, proprietary rule was an anomaly. Had white South Carolinians been sufficiently numerous to feel capable of defending themselves, or had the colony been located in a relatively secure region, Carolinians would probably have been less restive under the proprietors, and they in turn might well have been more committed to the colony.

What is perhaps most important, however, is that to contemporaries, at least, from beginning to end this was a very English revolution. The election act, which the proprietors vetoed, had been passed, as one Carolinian remarked, because "it came nearer the Methods used in *England*"; in 1689, a convention parliament had offered the crown to William and Mary because, it declared, James II, having endeavored "to subvert and extirpate the Protestant Religion, and the Laws and Liberties of this Kingdom" and having withdrawn himself from England, "abdicated the Government." Thirty years later, the Commons House, calling itself a convention, asked the crown to assume direct control of South Carolina because the proprietors had by "their Proceedings, unhing'd the Frame of government, and forfeited their Right to the same." Looking back on the revolution from the mid-eighteenth century, a local historian observed that "British subjects in general abhor oppression, even from a supreme, and it could scarcely be expected they would tamely submit to it, from a subordinate jurisdiction." How many Englishmen were ruled, in the eighteenth century, by *"Lords Proprietors?"* Believing that they were acting like Englishmen, South Carolinians became, from their own perspective as well as ours, less provincial and more English in being able to say, not us.

6

THE TRANSFORMATION OF POLITICS, 1720–1748

The revolt against the proprietors was in part an expression of the Carolinians' desire to make themselves as much like Englishmen as possible, and royal government was obviously a step in that direction. So, too, was the ensuing ministerial policy of "salutary neglect." Despite sometimes heroic efforts, the proprietors had been largely unable to impose their vision of what a colony should be. Given a remarkable degree of autonomy while Sir Robert Walpole headed the ministry between 1721 and 1742, South Carolinians pursued their own vision. The result is replete with contradictions: under the proprietors, constitutions designed to produce harmony and prevent revolution contributed to endemic factionalism and ultimately revolt; under the crown, voluntary pursuit of the British constitutional model contributed to the decline of factionalism and, ultimately, the development of a political system in some ways more British than British authorities were willing to accept, though not quite as English as South Carolinians believed it to be.

That, however, was in the future. In the early 1720s imperial officials believed, as the secretary of the Privy Council observed, that "in the Plantations...Government should be as Easy and mild as possible." Thus for reasons of policy, as well as the press of other business, authorities did not look too critically at the actions of the insurrectionary government and permitted most of its work to stand. Not that there was a great deal, for the revolutionary regime largely confined itself to resisting attempts by Johnson and, later, William Rhett to restore proprietary authority, while it maintained order awaiting a royal governor. Nevertheless, during the interim, the legislature took steps to regulate the courts. Because this legislation—if the acts of an extralegal assembly can be termed such—foreshadows the way in which British precedents would fuse with local conditions to produce an increasingly unique combination in South Carolina, it is unusually interesting.

As has been seen, the concentration of power in Nicholas Trott's hands caused problems, especially since he had been both the chief justice (and the only judge in the common law courts) and a member of the council (and thus a key figure in the court of chancery as well). The rebels therefore stipulated not only that henceforth the chief justice was to have assistants but also that the council would no longer act as the court of chancery. In addition, apparently in part modeling its actions on the Act of Settlement (1701), which provided that English judges would hold office during good behavior, the assembly denied the governor power to remove judges. Although another act passed the following year restored the council's chancery jurisdiction—after the crown had removed Trott from all of his positions—the restrictions on the governors' power stood for nearly thirty years. Then an assistant judge invoked them to protect himself, and the crown's legal officers noted that, having been passed by an unauthorized regime, the act was null and void.

The cooperative, not to say permissive, attitude of imperial officials and the joy of most South Carolinians at the prospect of being rid of the proprietors combined to make Francis Nicholson's governorship a productive one. Appointed provisional governor by the crown in 1720, he arrived in Charles Town in May of the next year as perhaps the most experienced colonial official ever to serve in South Carolina. Then in his sixties, he had been governor of New York, Virginia (on two separate occasions), Maryland, and Nova Scotia. He was also a military man, an ardent Anglican, and an irascible character who distrusted dissenters. They were, he believed, imbued with "Common Wealth Principles" which made them hostile to the monarchy; and they in turn reciprocated his distrust. The Anglican clergy, on the other hand, considered him to be among the best of governors, for he spent his own as well as public money building churches and promoting education. Nevertheless, at least one Anglican failed to share their warm feelings. He was William Rhett, who was still surveyor of the customs. Within six months, Nicholson was convinced that Rhett was a "haughty, proud, insolent fellow and a cheating scoundrel" who, despite his office, engaged in illegal trade. Not to be outdone, Rhett charged that the governor himself was a smuggler and let it be known that he—Rhett— was to be appointed to the post. Rhett's death "of apoplexy" (according to Nicholson) soon disposed of the claim, but the charge—of which Nicholson was apparently innocent—eventually proved to be something of an albatross around the governor's neck.

In the meantime, Nicholson got along with the assembly considerably better than with Rhett. Consultation and cooperation among agents of the convention assembly, the Board of Trade, and Nicholson himself had led to the appointment of a council which, though composed primarily of men who had opposed the proprietors, included some of their supporters. The attempt to placate all factions paid off; irreconcilables like Rhett were in a distinct minority, and Nicholson's cultivation of both houses tended to make the majority even more cooperative. As a result, the legislature quickly passed two acts which drew on the governor's experience elsewhere and which, had they lasted, might accordingly have made later developments in South Carolina less idiosyncratic. The more ephemeral was the incorporation of Charles Town. Under legislation enacted in 1722, a corporation of nineteen men who would choose their own successors was given the right to govern Charles Town, henceforth to be known as Charles City and Port. This arrangement, which was similar to those prevailing in New York and Philadelphia, went into effect immediately, and William Gibbon became mayor. But complaints from a number of inhabitants, including some prominent merchants who had been excluded from the ruling body, prompted the crown to disallow the act on the grounds that it established the "Compleatest Oligarchy" ever seen.

An act to establish local courts was in force somewhat longer. In this case Virginia provided the model, and the act of 1721 established five county or precinct courts outside of Charles Town. Staffed by local justices of the peace, these courts were to handle minor criminal offenses as well as civil cases involving small sums. The courts functioned for a while but apparently—despite an attempt to strengthen them in 1727—never very effectively. Most of the difficulty appears to have arisen from relatively unskilled magistrates, a sparse population, and the unwillingness of urban merchants and lawyers to leave Charles Town. The latter's reluctance to become involved with the local courts was not merely a matter of convenience. Debtors, who were often small farmers, preferred trial before a jury of their neighbors; creditors, who were frequently Charles Town merchants, naturally preferred a jury of *their* peers. And thus the attempt to establish local courts got caught up in the controversy over the currency.

The debate over paper money did not end with proprietary rule. In fact, for a number of reasons it intensified during the 1720s. In 1723 floods destroyed about a third of the rice crop; five years later, a drought during the growing season combined with a hurricane just before harvest to do even more damage. Yet, in general, rice growers—or at least the larger ones—appear to have done relatively well during the decade. Prices remained good, exports increased rapidly, and planters bought slaves in large numbers. Those who produced naval stores primarily were, however, in increasing trouble. Many of them appear to have been relatively small operators without much capital, and the Yamasee War disrupted activities in the southern part of the province where Beaufort had been established to export their products. When the center of activities shifted to the more protected northeastern area, producers had to transship bulky products through the facilities and customs house at Charles Town. Production suffered from the weather and, worse yet, in 1724 Parliament dropped the bounty previously given on Carolina naval stores.* As a result, paper money became the most disruptive issue of the decade and perhaps of the entire colonial period. During 1720 and 1721 the legislature twice authorized the emission of so-called "rice-bills" or bills of credit which were to be redeemed by a tax in kind on rice. The combination of the short crop and the second emission produced considerable depreciation. Thus when the house considered a bill to print more money the following year, twenty-eight merchants (who constituted almost the entire merchant community in Charles Town) petitioned against the measure. Unfortunately, they made the mistake of charging that the house had committed a breach of faith in considering the bill, and the Commons responded by imprisoning them all for contempt until each had apol-

---

*For the rise and fall of this subsidy, see chapter 7.

ogized. The bill passed, despite some opposition in the council, and Nicholson, who understood the need for some additional paper money, signed it. The exchange rate between currency and sterling then fell to seven to one.

Merchants on both sides of the Atlantic protested to British authorities, and the Privy Council disallowed not only the last act but also the one before it. The acts had already gone into effect, so instructions were issued to Nicholson directing him to retire these issues as quickly as possible. That tipped the scales too far in the other direction. Even most of the local merchants were opposed to such a drastic reduction in the currency supply and petitioned British authorities accordingly. The act of 1724 was therefore a compromise measure having wide support. Instead of immediate retirement of the most recent issues, it provided for their gradual withdrawal. Meanwhile, the approximately £120,000 in circulation would be legal tender for limited purposes. At this point, complaints from British merchants to the effect that Nicholson was not only soft on paper money but also excessively hard on their legitimate trading activities combined with Rhett's old charges to prompt imperial authorities to suggest that he return home in order to justify his actions.

Nicholson's acting successor was Arthur Middleton, who had been one of the leaders of the revolt against the proprietors and subsequently president of the council. Unfortunately, his position was a bit anomalous. Although the governor's instructions stipulated that the eldest councilor be president, Nicholson had permitted an election. Middleton had been chosen, and the eldest, Landgrave Thomas Smith, by-passed. Middleton was therefore vulnerable, and he immediately made himself more so by selling minor offices, to which the Commons took exception.

Paper money was a more important issue. By 1727 farmers and naval stores producers were beginning to feel the full impact of the lapse of the bounty, and many of them were in serious financial trouble. Demanding that the legislature provide relief, inhabitants of the northern parishes banded together, refused to pay taxes, and forcibly prevented writs from being served on debtors. A remonstrance, addressed to Middleton, called for more paper money, the temporary suspension of taxes, trial by local courts, and the establishment of a port of entry north of Charles Town. When Middleton tried to avoid receiving the remonstrance, a mob forced him to change his mind; but he still failed to take action, apparently in part because he considered his role to be primarily that of a mere caretaker and partly because he himself opposed more paper money. Mass meetings followed, and Thomas Smith, who began to argue that his seniority entitled him to the governorship, emerged as a leader of the discontented. Middleton had Smith arrested for treason, and several hundred of the latter's followers marched on Charles Town. Middleton called out the militia and "found by experience," as he later observed, "that to employ the people to reduce themselves" was "a vain attempt"; the militia joined the mob. Middleton was therefore forced to agree to its demand that he call the legislature to consider current problems. When the Commons met, however, it turned its attention to the chief justice who had refused to release Smith in response to a writ of habeas corpus. To protect the judge, Middleton then prorogued the assembly. By the time it met again, Smith was out on bond, and continued raiding by the Yamasee Indians had become sufficiently threatening to prompt fears of another all-out Indian war. The legislature therefore authorized a small expedition against the Indian villages outside of St. Augustine and emitted some paper currency to pay for it.

Demands for more money continued, and the Commons and the council were soon deadlocked over the issue. Responsive to popular demands, the former wanted to enlarge the currency; the latter, though not entirely opposed to the idea, put various impediments in the way. Moreover, Smith's case was still unresolved, and the Commons tried to compel the chief justice to explain why. Whereupon, Middleton dissolved the house. Subsequent elections produced a new house but no change in its policies, and the impasse continued. Enough members then boycotted the Commons so that it could not make a quorum, and to all intents and purposes the legislature failed to meet between mid-1728 and 1731. In the meantime, taxes remained uncollected and the judicial system operated only intermittently. Yellow fever swept Charles Town in 1728, and so many died and "so quick was the putrefaction, so offensive and infectious were the corpses," that even relatives were reluctant to bury them, and planters refused to send food to town for fear of contagion. Accordingly, in one of its last meetings, the Commons appointed a committee to report on the state of the province which found what everyone knew: the colony was "in a very distressed and calamitous condition occasioned by the great losses which the Inhabitants in general have sustained by the late dreadful hurricane and storms, by the great mortality among them and their slaves, by the large and growing Debts of the Province, the scarcity of money, and the decay of public credit," all of which, "unless timely prevented by the care of the Legislature must produce fatal consequences to the Province." The legislature seemed unable to act, and about all a number of private individuals could do was to establish a small bank which lent out its own currency—bearing a picture of a drowning man.

One authority has accurately termed the end of the 1720s as the most "serious political crisis" in the history of the colony up to that time. However, a "new era," as one of the earliest local historians observed, was about to commence "in the annals of that country, which may be called the era of its freedom, security, and happiness." Activities and decisions in London laid much of the groundwork. Purchase of the proprietors' rights by the crown in 1729 removed a source of uncertainty and instability; successful lobbying by Samuel Wragg, a London merchant who acted as an agent for Carolina, and others induced Parliament to remove some of the restrictions on rice and to restore part of the bounty on naval stores. Further, designating Georgetown a port of entry about 1731 provided a convenient shipping point north of Charles Town. Perhaps most important, the crown also appointed Robert Johnson as the new royal governor. Not only was he a popular and able man but, having been the last of the proprietary governors, he was also well acquainted with the situation in South Carolina. In London since 1724 trying to secure the appointment, he was able to assist in drafting his own instructions, which also drew on the ideas of John Barnwell and other Carolinians who were especially concerned about military security. A group of twenty-one British merchants— most of whom owned land in South Carolina—also contributed. Agreeing with Johnson's contention that to lessen the amount of paper money in circulation and thereby increase its value "would ruin at least 19/ 20 of the Inhabitants," these merchants helped to convince imperial authorities to take a moderate position on paper currency.

Thus Johnson arrived in Charles Town in December 1730, having been directed to carry out what came to be known as "Johnson's township scheme." A carefully thought-out plan for solving several problems simultaneously, it called for the establishment of a number of frontier townships to be settled by white immigrants who would strengthen the militia, provide defense for the frontiers, and act as a counterweight to the increasing number of slaves. To induce them to immigrate— and at the same time alleviate the shortage of currency—monies set aside by the sinking act of 1724 for retiring bills of credit would be temporarily diverted to subsidize the newcomers. The legislature quickly enacted the essentials but decided to use about two-thirds of the diverted funds to amortize the public debt, which had recently become more burdensome because the treasurer had mixed public with private funds before going bankrupt. Johnson, interpreting his instructions broadly, approved the act; and in general it worked well, though his successor used revenue earmarked for the immigrants to pay provincial officials.* The reward for creditors was an act permitting them to choose the court in which they wished to enforce payment, and that option effectively killed the local courts.

Meanwhile, other developments helped to reduce the importance of paper money as a political issue. No doubt the most important was more widely distributed prosperity, but a relatively minor change in the way the legislature did business also contributed. After 1732 the government operated largely on credit—that is, it arranged to buy goods and services, audited the resulting accounts, incorporated them in the tax bill and, then, when it passed, issued certificates validating the amounts due. Although the "money" to cover these certificates was not collected until the following year, they could themselves be used to pay taxes and therefore in the meantime circulated as currency. Furthermore, in 1741 the courts held that debts due British merchants could be adjusted to compensate for depreciation in the local currency, thus removing most of their objections to it. Accordingly, despite a brief and relatively minor flare-up in the 1730s, paper money ceased to be a seriously divisive issue.

For several reasons land became the chief source of contention in the early 1730s. In the first place, more than a decade had passed since the proprietors closed the land office, and though they had made some grants and sales in England during the interval, they did not do the same in the colony. Secondly, the relatively good market for rice in the 1720s, combined with the removal of some restrictions on its export and the new bounty on naval stores, made men more interested in

---

*For the effects of these townships on the population, see chapter 9.

acquiring acreage, especially rice lands. Finally, the township scheme, the anticipated influx of new settlers, and plans for the establishment of Georgia promised better security on the southern frontier. All of this added up to an extraordinary demand for land in the 1730s. But before making new grants Johnson was directed to settle the matter of quitrents on current holdings. There was no difficulty in working out the basic terms of a new quitrent act with the legislature: in return for remission of arrears in payment, all who held land from the proprietors would be required to register it with the appropriate officials and receive new grants. Thus the crown would presumably have an accurate roll of all lands on which it would be collecting quitrents.

However, Johnson and the Commons (and, eventually, the council) disagreed over the question of how to deal with claims that had not yet been staked out. Many of these were so-called "baronial patents"— that is, rights to large tracts of land granted to landgraves, caciques, and others—which had then subsequently been sold in whole or in part. Further complications arose because good rice lands were limited, and some of the larger planters were relying on purchases of these rights to secure claims to part of the dwindling supply. The Commons therefore wanted to validate these titles, but the crown, seeking to encourage immigration, frowned upon the engrossment of large tracts for speculative purposes. Its legal officers argued that, not having been exercised before the crown acquired title to all unclaimed land, the rights had expired. The Commons insisted on validating these titles in the quitrent act, and Johnson signed it. Nevertheless, he continued to regard such titles as void; curiously, he also "misconstrued" his instructions so that men who had already been granted land under the proprietors' headright system apparently received additional land from the royal government for the same headrights. If this was not an implicit trade off, appearances are deceiving. Certainly, one way or another, some prominent men continued to hold land which they had originally claimed through purchase of baronial rights. As an early historian who was in a position to know observed, "each planter, eager in the pursuit of large possessions of land, which were formerly neglected, because of little value, strenuously vied with his neighbour for a superiority of fortune, and seemed impatient of every restraint that hindered or cramped him in his favourite pursuit." The rush continued under Johnson's successor, Thomas Broughton, when "many of the leading men of the colony scrupled not to practise impositions, and being eagerly bent on engrossing lands, the lieutenant-governor freely granted them warrants; the planters, provided they acquired large possessions, were not very scrupulous about the legality of the way and manner in which they were obtained."

Among those whose activities fit that description was the surveyor general himself, James St. John, who, apparently for purposes of his own, assumed a cloak of righteousness. Normally he would have been responsible for surveying the new townships, but he demanded excessive fees and lost the job. That put him at odds with Governor Johnson and both houses of the legislature. He, in turn, accused Johnson and others of attempting to engross land within the boundaries of the townships, which were supposed to be reserved for immigrants. In addition, St. John tried to convince imperial authorities to disallow the quitrent law on several grounds, including the fact that its validation of baronial patents dispossessed a number of men who had settled on what seemed to be vacant land near Beaufort. For a time it appeared that his argument would prevail. Yet his position was not entirely disinterested. A group of speculators operating under the name of Cooper, Rothmahler, and Company—with which St. John cooperated and in which his chief deputy was a silent partner—began surveying the lands in question and selling them to local squatters. A number of landholders in the area then protested the "illegal" surveys, and the Commons House responded by ordering the arrest of St. John and one of his confederates. A lawyer who attempted to have them released under a writ of habeas corpus joined them in jail; each of the prisoners had to make a formal apology to the house before being released. The chief justice who tried to support them did not get off quite so easily; the Commons withheld his salary during the remainder of his term. To quiet him and others like him who doubted the power of the Commons to imprison for contempt, the legislature passed a law denying the right of habeas corpus to anyone arrested by either house. Imperial authorities disallowed the law and paid the chief justice's successors out of the quitrent funds. However, in response to Johnson's pleas and intense lobbying by agents in London, the crown permitted the quitrent law to stand.

Evaluating all of this is not easy, and historians have been almost as divided as contemporaries over the controversy, but the most recent tendency has been to take a more favorable view of Johnson and the legislature. The quitrent act of 1731 seems to have been a conscientious attempt to deal with current realities, and in general it worked reasonably well—despite two loopholes. Nothing required that lands acquired by private conveyances be registered, and nothing covered future royal grants. Early in the 1740s, a special commissioner of the quitrents, Henry McCulloh, rather officiously tried to remedy these defects, but the legislature, which was unhappy with him, refused to cooperate until after his departure. Then it quickly passed the quitrent act of 1744, which dealt with these matters. McCulloh, however, objected to it because it permitted men to surrender surplus lands to the crown, and royal authorities failed to approve the act. All of this is not to suggest that South Carolinians were anxious to pay quitrents— individually, many of them were rather slack about it and, by the eve of the Revolution, perhaps less than 20 percent of the total due was actually being collected by royal authorities. But despite McCulloh's complaints, there is little indication that the legislature attempted to sabotage their collection.

About who got what in the great land boom of the 1730s, there is more uncertainty, and the question will not be entirely resolved until someone makes a definitive study of individual holdings. If the situation in the area which would shortly become the southernmost parish was typical, the evidence seems to point in two different—but not necessarily contradictory—directions. St. John was probably substantially correct in maintaining that all land fronting on freshwater within a hundred miles of Charles Town was taken up by the early 1730s, and not primarily by small farmers. On the other hand, Johnson obviously tried to curb speculation, and he probably did as well as could be expected under the circumstances. Certainly the majority of grants made during the period were for small to moderate-sized tracts (less than 2,000 acres), and the average grant on a typical day in the mid-1730s was 500 acres.

Interest in the southern region of the province on the part of both small and large planters was related to the prospect of improved military security. Partly in response to the lobbying efforts of colonial agents like Barnwell, imperial authorities dispatched an independent company of regular soldiers to the colony in 1721. Working under Barnwell's direction, this company built a wooden blockhouse, Fort King George, near the mouth of the Altamaha River, just northwest of St. Simon's Island. However, garrison duty at the remote and malarial outpost was anything but popular. Thus when part of the fort caught fire in 1725 the investigation was not merely a formality. The investigators found evidence not of arson but of inactivity; apparently the soldiers sat on their hands while the fort burned. At any rate, it was rebuilt and briefly reoccupied before the soldiers were withdrawn to Beaufort, where they provided some protection for the southern frontier, though the raid on the Yamasee village near St. Augustine in 1728 seems to have been more effective. Better yet was the founding of Georgia in 1733. South Carolinians therefore did much to assist the settlement at Savannah. An able member of the council, William Bull, Sr., accompanied James Oglethorpe and his settlers on the last leg of their journey from Charles Town southward, and Bull spent much of the next year in Savannah helping to organize the militia, survey the town, and conduct Indian diplomacy. Other Carolinians gave or lent supplies and manpower, and good relations between the two colonies prevailed as long as Johnson remained governor of South Carolina.

After Johnson's death in 1735, rivalry for the Indian trade caused trouble. The lieutenant governor who acted as Johnson's successor was Thomas Broughton, and he had been a trader himself. Consequently he was sympathetic to his old colleagues, who apparently wanted to drive the Georgians out of the business. The Indian trade, however, was as central to the safety and economy of the nascent colony as it had been to South Carolina a generation earlier. Modeling their regulations on the Carolina law, officials in Georgia therefore sought to curb abuses—and perhaps the Carolina competition—by requiring traders operating in the southern territory to obtain local licenses, even though they might already be licensed by South Carolina. Matters came to a head when authorities in Georgia seized the goods of some Carolinians for violating these rules. Broughton assumed a belligerent stance and then, perhaps deliberately, blocked attempts at compromise. Eventually, both sides agreed to refer the dispute to imperial authorities, who in turn sent it back, directing local authorities to work out the problem and suggesting that perhaps one license was sufficient for a trader. By this time, Oglethorpe, who had been in England during much of the dispute, had returned to Georgia, and William Bull had become the acting governor of South Carolina after Broughton's death in 1737. Not only were the two men good friends but Oglethorpe was also partly responsible for Bull's appointment as lieutenant governor. As a result, the controversy abated, even while Indian affairs continued to vex both colonies. Another conflict between England and Spain was in the offing, and the Cherokee in particular were restive. Smallpox caught from traders swept the tribe in 1738, or about the same time that Christian Priber sought to establish his projected Kingdom of Paradise among the Indians. As discussed earlier, he puzzled many South Carolinians, but few doubted that his presence was a threat. Oglethorpe dealt with the smallpox epidemic by sending food to the Indians and with Priber by eventually arresting him. Meanwhile Bull concentrated on improving local defenses.

In 1739 the War of Jenkins' Ear broke out between England and Spain, largely over questions of trade, and it in turn soon merged with a general European war involving the succession to the Austrian throne. Lasting until 1748, King George's War, as it was known in America, had a profound effect on South Carolina, both militarily and economically. During the late summer of 1739, Oglethorpe, who was commander-in-chief of all military forces on the southern frontier, met with Creek Indian chiefs near modern Phoenix City, Alabama, where he received assurances of friendship. That cleared the way for an attack on St. Augustine, and early the next year he went to Charles Town to seek assistance. South Carolinians, however, were just recovering from an epidemic of yellow fever after suffering the most serious slave uprising of the colonial period only a few months earlier.* Thus they were not in especially good shape to mount an expedition. Nevertheless, they blamed the slave rebellion on Spanish instigation, and the thought of revenge augmented their sense of duty. Although the legislature was slower in making preparations than he would have preferred, Oglethorpe professed to be satisfied with its efforts.

In April, several vessels from the royal navy began a blockade of the Florida coastline, and Oglethorpe captured some posts in northern Florida. In May, perhaps as many as 400 South Carolinians under the command of Colonel Alexander Vander Dussen marched southward with Oglethorpe's Georgians. Taking the overland route proved to be an exhausting mistake, but more were to come. At St. Augustine,

---

*For the Stono Rebellion, see chapter 8.

Oglethorpe intended to storm the fortress from the west with the main army while cannon brought into range by shallow-draft barges bombarded it from the east. However, the Spanish had their own shallow-draft vessels, and they were sufficiently powerful to make that idea impracticable. Oglethorpe settled down to a siege, during which a Spanish party stole out of the castle one night and killed and captured more than 100 of his men encamped at Fort Moosa. About the same time, Oglethorpe began a long-range and ineffectual bombardment, which ended when the naval commanders announced that because of the danger of hurricanes, they would have to remove their ships by July 5. The retreat began July 4. All of this puzzled the Spanish commander who observed that he could not "arrive at a comprehension of the conduct, or rules of this General."

Neither could the Carolinians, and mutual recriminations followed. Oglethorpe blamed the legislature for having been dilatory and excessively frugal. South Carolinians, on the other hand, it was said—and doubtless quoted more often by historians—flew into such a rage at the sound of Oglethorpe's name "as sets the very dogs a barking." The assembly launched an investigation and concluded that his mismanagement had been responsible for the fiasco.

It is therefore understandable that when he again asked for help in 1742, Carolinians were rather dilatory. Some extenuating circumstances help to explain their conduct. Less than six months after Oglethorpe's forces straggled back to Charles Town, the most devastating fire of the colonial period swept the city. Beginning on the afternoon of a windy day in November, 1740, it swept southeastwardly from Broad and Church streets toward the Cooper River. Fighting it was futile until the wind died in the evening, and at one time about a third of the city was aflame, while rum, naval stores, and gunpowder in the warehouses along the water exploded. Few if any died, but many lost all of their possessions. Petitions for relief estimated the damage at more than £250,000 sterling, and Parliament contributed £20,000 to ease the suffering. Given the circumstances, it is perhaps not surprising that "never," as Alexander Hewatt observed, "did the Carolineans make so bad a figure in defense of their country" as during the Spanish invasion of Georgia in 1742. No doubt they were at least partially ignorant of Spanish plans, but Oglethorpe was not crying wolf; the Spaniards had a good-sized fleet and perhaps 2,000 troops (the figures differ). Moreover, they were prepared to offer land and freedom to slaves who would join them. In short, the purpose of the expedition, as Spanish authorities outlined it, was no less than "to raze and destroy Carolina and its plantations," as well as Georgia, and thereby reduce the threat to Florida.

Fortunately for Oglethorpe and the Carolinians, it was the Spanish commander's turn to be enigmatically irresolute. On July 5, 1742, he landed his troops on the southern shore of St. Simon's Island; Oglethorpe, after putting up some resistance, pulled his forces back to Frederica at the north end. Two days of intermittent skirmishing followed, and in the battle of Bloody Marsh on the 7th, Oglethorpe's Indians and Scottish Highlanders drove a substantial Spanish detachment onto the tidal flats and annihilated it. That apparently took most of the fight out of the Spanish commander, and the appearance of unknown vessels on the horizon finished the job. He withdrew— prematurely, it turned out, for reinforcements from Charles Town did not arrive until the end of the month, though at this point the delay seems to have been as much the fault of the naval commander, Captain Charles Hardy, as of the South Carolinians. All of which prompted the *Boston Evening-Post* of October 4, 1742, to observe that,

They both did meet, they both did fight, they both did run away;
They both did strive to meet again, the quite Contrary Way.

Despite such satire, the conflict on the southern frontier had serious ramifications, not the least of which involved the allegiance of various Indian tribes. In general, the Choctaws of the central Gulf Coast were allied with the French; the Creeks pursued a policy of neutrality; and the Cherokees were friendly to the English. Each side attempted to subvert the other's allies, and long-standing enmities among the tribes complicated the picture. In addition, the war disrupted normal trade, which was one of the most important sinews of any alliance. To cope with some of the resulting tensions, early in the 1740s colonial authorities began negotiating a series of agreements intended to bring peace among all the Indians friendly to the English interest. In general, this was the policy pursued by the new governor of South Carolina, James Glen. A Scottish lawyer who had been appointed to the office in 1738, he failed to arrive until 1743, or the same year that Oglethorpe left Georgia never to return. That made Glen the key figure in negotiating with the southern Indians. Despite the delay in his arrival, he was a conscientious individual. Experience made him more adept in dealing with the Indians and comparative success may have contributed to his increasingly proprietary attitude toward them. If that attitude tended to make him shortsighted and resentful of what he took to be meddling by other authorities with "his" Indians, it also made him more protective of them. "We call them Savages," he once observed, but "have we been at any pains to civilize them?" In short, being humane and reasonably pacific, he found the notion of peace and amity among the English Indians congenial. Not all Carolinians saw the matter in the same light. Throughout the history of the colony there were always men who believed, as one succinctly phrased it after the Yamasee War, that in the case of mutually hostile tribes, the proper course was "to hold both as our friends...and assist them in Cutting one another's throats." During the 1740s and 1750s that policy was in abeyance.

Indian affairs occupied much of Glen's attention. In 1746 the Choctaws revolted against the French, and the following year sent a delegation to Charles Town. The ensuing agreement called for the Indians to fight the French; in return South Carolinians would supply arms and commence regular trade with the tribe. Unfortunately, Glen and the South Carolina traders promised more than they could deliver. Some of the difficulties were due to the distance involved and the proximity of French settlements, but Glen made the mistake of relying on a new firm, McNair and Company. He also offered to give it a monopoly of the business if his brother became a partner. Such clandestine arrangements gave the partnership the nickname of the "Sphinx Company" but, under any name, it failed to deliver goods in sufficient quantity to retain the friendship of the Choctaws. Subsequent inconclusive investigations produced chiefly friction between Glen and the council. A scheme to attack the French settlements on the lower Mississippi also came to nought when the governor was unable to induce either the Creek Indians or imperial authorities to support it.

Glen had better luck with the Cherokees. Although he was unable to induce them to raid the French settlements, as he hoped, he was in general able to retain their friendship until the coming of peace in 1748 reduced some of the tensions on the southern frontier. In the meantime, French influence and Indian hostility toward the English had been increasing in the Overhill Towns of modern Tennessee. Partly to counter this trend, the assembly appropriated funds, and in 1753 Glen personally supervised the construction of Fort Prince George near the lower Indian town of Keowee on the eastern side of the mountains. Plans for a similar fort among the Overhills encountered various delays and actual construction did not begin until after a new governor had arrived in 1756. But during the waning months of his incumbency Glen met about 500 Cherokees at Saluda Old Town in western South Carolina. There, ceding all their lands to the crown, the Indians acknowledged the king of England as their sovereign. In return, Glen promised more and improved trade. Despite the impressive sound of the treaty, it is doubtful that the Indians intended it to be much more than an indication of their friendship and current alignment. Suspecting this, the governor of Virginia termed it "a very preposterous, irregular, and inconsistent Step," fearing that the French might exploit it as evidence of English land hunger. His interpretation highlights a basic misunderstanding on Glen's part. Virginians *were* land hungry; Glen, despite the cession, was still thinking in terms of the old trade relationships. Thus he failed to understand events in Pennsylvania and Virginia leading up to the French and Indian War, and he tended to regard calls for help from these quarters as attempts to impede South Carolina's interests. That attitude did not endear him to imperial officials.

Nevertheless, Glen was popular with many South Carolinians. Under him, as one who had reason to know observed, the people were "happy and contented." Receiving such a compliment—even from a fellow Scotsman—was no small achievement, for the latter part of King George's War was as difficult as the first for South Carolinians, though in a different way. There was no further military activity of consequence in the area, but in 1744 France entered the war and the presence of a large and hostile fleet on the high seas crippled the dwindling rice trade. As a result, the war was an economic disaster for the colony. To be sure, privateering contributed to some mercantile fortunes; the search for alternative crops eventually made indigo a commercial success; and recovery quickly followed peace. But as Glen himself later observed, South Carolina "was brought to the Brink of Ruin by the last French War."

Economic dislocations had political repercussions. Because few men could afford the time and expense of serving in the legislature, the Commons frequently had trouble mustering a quorum, and even an attempt to make service less burdensome by shortening the term of election to one year failed to remedy the problem. Steps to provide relief for debtors were not much more successful, for imperial authorities soon disallowed an emission of paper currency as well as an attempt to reestablish local courts with jurisdiction over small sums. By then the war was over and returning prosperity had reduced the need for such measures. What is surprising, though, is the relative ease with which these acts passed, and, indeed, considering the seriousness of the depression, the comparatively superficial impact of economic and social issues in general on politics. In short, despite the war and the attendant economic dislocations, the character of politics changed during the 1730s and 1740s. As a careful student of the subject, Eugene Sirmans, observed, earlier political battles often embodied "social and economic conflicts involving the entire population." By midcentury, however, "a lasting political peace existed in the colony at large, and there were no major internal divisions." This is not to say that conflict disappeared but that, as this scholar also noted, "the frequently violent constitutional struggles in the assembly stood in marked contrast to the general political calm that prevailed outside the legislature."

This striking change demands explanation. Perhaps the most important underlying factor was increasing prosperity which, despite the temporary setbacks of King George's War, knit the community together in several ways. It not only lessened competition among groups for a portion of its benefits but also fostered upward social mobility by individuals. This mobility, in turn, tended to homogenize interest groups as successful merchants purchased plantations and in the process acquired an understanding of the planters' economic interests and problems. Significantly, by the end of the colonial period almost all of the prominent leaders among the professional men and merchants in the assembly owned plantations. Intermarriage between planting and mercantile families also blurred distinctions. In addition, as every planter was well aware, the economic health of the province depended upon the export trade. Thus consanguinity and a consciousness of shared economic interests helped to bind together potentially disparate segments of society. The passage of time and waning religious zeal also contributed to the growing sense of community as dissenters drifted into the Anglican Church, and Anglicans themselves became more tolerant.

Geographic and demographic features of the society also unified it. Over time, Charles Town became the social and cultural as well as the economic and political center of the colony. As a result, urban values permeated the culture of even the most remote lowcountry parishes, giving substance to the common saying that as the town went, so went the country. In addition, the society was remarkably small, and as late as 1790 most of the lowcountry parishes contained fewer than 200 white families; twenty years earlier there were no more than 1,300 houses in Charles Town. The central position of the city in the life of the colony, coupled with the relatively small population, meant that members of the elite had the opportunity to know each other, communicate, and develop a community of shared values. Thus a prominent figure such as the speaker of the house could realistically assert that "I am well acquainted with the Circumstances of most of our Inhabitants." In sum, lowcountry society possessed many of the characteristics of a primary group and its public mores often had the power of those enforced by the family elsewhere. Perhaps this fact helps to account for much of the harmony and politeness which visitors observed in the community.

Furthermore, strategic considerations contributed to community solidarity. Carolinians had good reason for their periodic fears of imminent attack, whether from the Spanish or Indians or both. And what made this possibility all the more frightening was the burgeoning slave population. Huge importations of slaves accompanied the rising prosperity, and by 1730 blacks outnumbered whites 2 to 1 in the colony as a whole and in some lowcountry parishes by much more. As one contemporary observed, their "harsh usage" could be expected to "fire them with desires of liberty and vengeance." They therefore constituted a potentially formidable "Domestic Enemy." The presence of slaves thus meant that any lapse in vigilance, any failure of government, appeared to threaten the white community with annihilation, and South Carolinians became increasingly leery of any disorders. Indeed, the prevailing atmosphere approached that of a beleaguered garrison. Unity among the defenders was essential, divided command dangerous, and a momentary lapse an invitation to disaster. In part this is no doubt why prominent leaders came to regard internal political discord as "more awful and more distressing than Fire[,] Pestilence or Foreign Wars." In short, disruptive factionalism had become a potentially fatal luxury. As a result, by the 1730s the growing fear of blacks, as well as the social and economic changes which contributed to it, began to mute political discord. Merchants who owned plantations cooperated with planters who were dependent on the export trade to end the long disruptive controversy over paper currency, which became the last major factional battle in colonial South Carolina politics. And the controversies over land, though significant at times, did not prove to be permanently divisive, perhaps in part because men of property acquired enough to last them for a while. Given this context, the shocks of the late 1730s and 1740s acted as a catalyst. Thus the crises in Indian affairs, the slave rebellion at Stono, the fire in Charles Town, the possibility of Spanish attack, and the apparent threat to order and stability posed by the Great Awakening combined to produce an unprecedented willingness on the part of local leaders to compromise and cooperate—if not with Oglethorpe—at least with each other. In short, these crises tended to produce political unity at the same time that potentially divisive issues were losing much of their sense of urgency.

Given these changes, continued controversies over constitutional questions can be partly attributed to institutional momentum. Largely as a by-product of other questions, the Commons House had continued the ad hoc, piecemeal acquisition of powers begun under the proprietors. In the 1690s, as has been seen, it acquired the right to sit separately and to initiate legislation, to which it soon added the power of choosing its own speaker and judging the qualifications of its own members. Although Nicholson briefly challenged the latter in 1725, that right was exercised with no serious question until the pre-Revolutionary era. These powers were similar to those exercised by the Virginia House of Burgesses and other assemblies in the southern colonies, but in some areas the Carolina Commons went further. As early as 1694 an ephemeral Election Act, modeled on the parliamentary Triennial Act of the same year, provided for elections to the Commons at least every three years. Although subsequent election acts were disallowed by the proprietors, under Nicholson the assembly enacted the basic regulations which were to prevail—with only a brief intermission in the 1740s—for the rest of the colonial period. Among its

other provisions, the Election Act of 1721 stipulated that the assembly
should be in session at least every six months and that its term could
not exceed three years. The six-months rule was sometimes interpreted
loosely, but the same was not true of the requirement for frequent
elections. Finding his first house to be cooperative, Nicholson tried to
keep it in session beyond the three-year term. Reprimanding him
politely but firmly, the Commons dissolved itself and thereafter without serious challenge controlled the maximum length of its term. The
same act, like its most recent predecessors under the proprietors, also
established election districts, and the legislature subsequently extended
similar representation to newly settled parishes.

In addition, in 1721 the Commons barred the public treasurer and
other revenue officers from membership; twenty-four years later it
sought to extend the same prohibition to those who held royal offices
as well, but the crown disallowed that act. Nevertheless, the passage
of time achieved what the law could not; by the late colonial period
electors usually agreed with "A Native," writing in the *South Carolina
Gazette,* who reminded voters that "men in public employments are
not the properest for your choice." Perhaps more important, by choosing someone acceptable to the governor, the Commons managed to
nominate the public receiver or treasurer in 1707; in 1721 the same
act that excluded revenue officers from the Commons gave the legislature the right to appoint all "civil officers which now do or hereafter
may receive a settled salary out of the publick treasury," and to all
intents and purposes the legislature meant the Commons. In time, it
appointed and controlled not only these officers but almost everyone
and everything involved with the expenditure of public funds. Indeed,
after 1750 the Commons "borrowed" and spent money merely by
ordering the treasurer to make payment, though royal instructions
explicitly stipulated that the governor and the council should concur
in all expenditures. In many of these cases they concurred after the
fact by approving the next tax act which covered the expenditure in
question.

As these activities imply, money was the vehicle of the Common's
aggrandizement. No tax bill ever passed without its consent. The same
of course could be said about the council, which acted as an upper
house of legislature—though the Commons did try to get Glen to
sign legislation that had not been approved by both houses. In England

the House of Commons claimed the sole right to draft money bills on the grounds that it represented the vast majority of the population. By the end of the seventeenth century, it no longer permitted the Lords to amend tax bills. Rationalizing its behavior by that of its namesake, the South Carolina Commons soon sought to restrict the council's role, even though royal instructions stipulated that the upper house have an equal voice in money matters. Indeed, as early as 1725 the Commons was invoking English precedent to object to the council's amendments. Ten years later, as a result of its attempt to withhold the chief justice's salary, the lower house took a stronger stand. When the council attempted to insert that item in a money bill, the Commons refused to accept the amendment on the grounds that its powers in "introducing and passing Laws for imposing Taxes on the People of this Province" were the same as "the House of Commons of Great Britain have in introducing and passing Laws for imposing Taxes on the People of England." The council gave in and the Commons won that round.

In 1739 the upper house attempted to reassert its rights and provoked an even stronger statement of the Commons's position: imposing taxes was the sole prerogative of the representatives of the people assembled in the British House of Commons, and "His Majesty's Subjects coming over to America have no more forfeited this their most valuable Inheritance than they have withdrawn their Allegiance." The upshot of the dispute was a compromise whereby the council did not amend money bills but sent a separate schedule of suggestions to the lower house, which incorporated as many or as few as it wished. That compromise lasted for a decade during which in all but name the Commons became the dominant force in the legislature. Indeed, it even tried to change the nomenclature, arrogating to itself alone the title of "the Assembly," but the new practice was too great a departure from English usage and failed to catch on.

The attempted innovation, of course, implied that the council was not an upper house at all. It naturally thought otherwise, and it, too, was able to invoke parliamentary precedent. There was a fatal weakness in its position, however, for the councilors were not lords; they were wealthy commoners who were chiefly distinguished from members of the Commons by having enough influence to obtain an appointment, which meant that many of them were either merchants with connections in London or planters with ties to the two William Bulls—father and son—who served as lieutenant governors. At least for the first part of the royal period councilors enjoyed great prestige, partly because their tenure seemed to be more secure than that of their predecessors (who had been appointed at the pleasure of the proprietors unlike royal councilors who held their seats during good behavior), and partly because such an appointment was a mark of distinction implying approbation by the crown. Thus, angling for an appointment in 1725, one of the leaders in the Commons could observe that "the next and most Honourable Stepp in these parts is that of a Councellour." And insofar as they were able, members of the council strove to uphold its prestige and prerogatives. They accordingly concurred with the Commons in passing the disallowed act which unequivocally gave each house of the legislature the power to imprison individuals for contempt of its authority. Similarly, in the late 1730s the councilors decided that the governor should sit with them only when they met as his advisory council; when they met as an upper house they should meet alone. Bull acquiesced, but when Glen chose to sit with them, they tolerated his presence for a time (though he was not permitted to speak). In 1750 when the upper house was investigating his handling of the Choctaw revolt, he again appeared and this time business came to a halt while everyone sat around in silence until Glen withdrew. Soon thereafter the upper house met alone.

Despite an occasional victory over the governor, the council was losing the battle with the Commons, which scrapped the separate schedule of amendments and even denied the upper house a part in auditing the accounts covered by the annual tax bills. A large part of the council's weakness stemmed from the fact that, unlike the Commons, it was apt to be hoist on its own petard if it appealed to parliamentary practice, since such comparisons reminded everyone that councilors were in fact not lords. That left the council with two more or less satisfactory ways of justifying its function as an upper house. One was to invoke the instructions issued to the governor by the crown; the other was to stress the inherent utility of an upper house. In part because it was possible to argue that the governor's instructions bound only him, councilors often tried to take the other route. Accordingly, when the council made an elaborate review of "the Constitution, State and Practice of the Legislature of this Province" in response to the

Commons's attempt to change its name in 1744, it argued that, while the Commons represented the people, the upper house represented property. If the council were not strong enough to resist, "Men of *little Estates*" who might serve in the Commons would be able "to oppress the *best.*" The problem with this argument was that there really was not much difference in the composition of the two houses, and, ironically, the council itself helped to undercut the distinction further in the Election Act of 1745 which raised the amount of property required to sit in the lower house. The crown disallowed the act for other reasons, and so the matter rested temporarily, while the council looked back to the late 1730s when the elder Bull had been acting governor. Then, the councilors believed, things were as they should be and the "three Estates in the Legislature were in the Strongest and clearest manner distinguished by every branch of it, and each was generally restrained to its proper Limits."

Governor Glen did not think much of Bull's practice of letting the upper house sit without him, and he was even less enthusiastic about the assertiveness of the Commons. To him, "the whole frame of Government" appeared to be "unhinged"; the "political balance in which consists the strength and beauty of the British Constitution" was "here entirely overturned" because "all the Weights that should trim and poise it" were "by different Laws thrown into the Scale of the People." In particular, he found that the Commons had usurped "much of the executive part of the Government" and given it to "different setts of Commissioners" responsible to itself. "Thus we have Commissioners of the Market, of the Workhouse, of the Pilots, of Fortifications, and so on, without number." That was bad enough, but in some ways even worse from his point of view was the Commons's control of patronage. "Almost all the Places of either profit or trust," he noted, "are disposed of by the General Assembly." Had he added "or by the crown at home," he would have put his finger on one of the fundamental reasons why he and other governors had trouble coping with the lower houses. As one member of parliament later observed in cynical but succinct fashion, American legislatures were independent and public-spirited because "the Governor's power of gratifying them is very limited." Glen himself owed his appointment to a number of connections, including, it was said, the fact that his sister was Walpole's mistress, and he was well aware that patronage greased the wheels of English politics. But the use of American offices for this purpose hampered his ability to do likewise in South Carolina. Thus during the 1730s one Archibald Hutcheson, a relatively minor figure who had influence with George II, was responsible for a number of local appointments, and even the master in chancery (whose office was worth only £20 a year) owed his position to the secretary of state for the southern department. Glen by contrast had trouble getting his candidates appointed to the council (which paid nothing).

Having few ways to influence members of the Commons after they were elected, the governor might have tried to manipulate elections, but that, too, was largely out of his power. In some English districts it was, of course, an established method for obtaining a cooperative House of Commons, and the proprietary faction had experimented with it in South Carolina. But such practices were most effective when the franchise was narrow and voting viva voce. In South Carolina, however, thanks to the Election Law of 1721, virtually any free white man over the age of twenty-one could vote, though many did not bother to go to the polls. Nevertheless, when they did vote they used the secret ballot. Although, Glen observed, "I am not insensible, that some great Men have recommended this practice in all popular elections, but with great deference to them...I think it has a tendency to destroy that noble generous openess that is the characteristick of an Englishman, and to introduce a Vile Venetian Juggle and Cunning" wherein sleight of hand might rule. Despite the specious sound of his argument, Glen was probably at least partially sincere, but the painful fact remained: neither he nor any of the other royal governors had many of the tools with which to fashion a cooperative assembly. Yet they needed its cooperation to run the government. As a result, they frequently wound up cooperating with the Commons, and the lower house made some of its greatest gains when things appeared to be running most smoothly. The biggest controversies often came when governors tried to regain some of the powers their predecessors had lost.

Nevertheless, stridently or quietly, the governor and both houses continued jockeying for position. Clearly something more than institutional momentum was involved in the contest. A later governor, who clashed with a member of his council, identified a key element when he observed that the councilor in question was "a zealous stickler for the rights and priviledges real or imaginery of the body of which he is a member because he derives his own importance from it." In short, though the council might argue that it represented the property of the colony, it had room for only twelve men at a time, and in theory at least they were appointed for life. Thus most wealthy men who sought to make a mark in public life had to be content with sitting in the Commons. It is no accident that the increasing power of the house coincided with the rise of a local social and economic elite in other areas, and that the men who led the Commons tended to dominate other facets of provincial life as well. The "quest for power," on the part of the lower house was, as the historian who has analyzed it most thoroughly, Jack Greene, observed, also a quest for political influence and political identity on the part of the local elite.

Being provincial, this elite patterned its behavior on English models in as many areas of life as possible. Members of the Commons sought to make it as much like the House of Commons as they could, and the crown itself encouraged this tendency by instructing royal governors not to countenance practices which failed to conform to parliamentary precedents. Members of parliament were not paid; neither were members of the lower house in South Carolina (which made them unusual among American legislators). In Parliament, bills were read three times in each house before being sent to the other; South Carolinians tried that in the 1720s but found it awkward and went back to alternate readings in each chamber. The council insisted that if it were going to lose the right of amending money bills it should at least be able to look at them regularly. The House of Commons had a mace symbolizing its authority; in 1756 the Commons had a London silversmith make one for itself. The House of Commons had the power to imprison for contempt of its authority; the Commons House employed that power liberally, if not arbitrarily. The House of Commons had the exclusive right to frame money bills; the Commons claimed it. What the governor and the council recognized by the 1740s, however, was that the South Carolina Commons had extended its powers well beyond those of the House of Commons—that is, it had taken from the governor powers which in England still belonged to the king. This was difficult indeed to justify on the basis of parliamentary precedent unless one wished to turn to the civil wars of the seventeenth century when Parliament had executed a king. Although Nicholson maintained that the "spirit of Common Wealth Principles both in church and in State" was increasing "daily," he was unusually touchy on the subject, and few Carolinians professed to look back on the Interregnum with anything but horror.

A restless quest for power that took the Commons well beyond its model is at first sight a bit puzzling. In all probability members did not always realize how far they had gone, or, being caught up in the struggle, they sometimes went farther than they intended. That, however, was by no means always the case, and a few years later a speaker of the house bluntly observed that "I . . . Love to have a weak Governor," for that helped to cut what seemed to be an overly powerful office down to size. Nominally, at least, the executive's powers were very large, indeed greater than those of the crown itself in the eighteenth century. No English monarch vetoed a bill after Queen Anne's reign; royal governors continued to do so regularly. Triennial and septennial acts limited the power of the crown to prorogue (recess) and dissolve Parliament; if South Carolinians had their own triennial act, governors still prorogued and dissolved the assembly with greater abandon than contemporary sovereigns did Parliament. After 1701 no king or queen had the power arbitrarily to dismiss a judge; after 1750, when imperial authorities disallowed the Act of 1721 preventing it, governors in Carolina had the authority. Moreover, such disallowances helped to remind men that behind the governor, who represented the royal prerogative, stood the influence of the imperial bureaucracy, the authority of the crown itself, and perhaps ultimately the power of Parliament. Given such claims and such support, it is no wonder that the prerogative appeared formidable to South Carolinians. In this context, the governor's largely defensive attempts to protect his powers often appeared to be dangerous attempts to enlarge the prerogative even further. Nicholson was partially correct; the seventeenth century context seemed relevant, and the Commons House fought the battle of the prerogative over again. But Parliament had largely won; the Commons could not. The array of potential power behind the governor meant that no matter how many powers the Commons acquired, they were not enough. As a result, the governor and the Commons saw each other as formidable antagonists. Power against power, weakness against weakness, the contest took on a life of its own that tended to cut it loose from its ostensible moorings in the real powers of the local contestants and made it appear like the struggle of the House of Commons against the

Stuart kings. Long after part of the context had changed almost beyond recognition, members of the Carolina Commons searched the English journals and parliamentary manuals of an earlier age for still useful precedents and guidelines.

The existential character of the contest also partly accounts for the influence of later British writings. Their roots, too, were in the seventeenth century, and specifically in the 1670s and early 1680s when a series of political crises prompted Shaftesbury—or his associates—to modernize many of Harrington's concepts. In this form, these ideas were picked up, fused with others, amplified, and popularized by the political opposition during Walpole's ministry. The resulting "country ideology"—which embodied a profound mistrust of power, and especially of the executive's putative ability to expand its power by corrupt means—quickly spread throughout the empire. Yet its presence in South Carolina is in some ways anomalous, for many of its main themes do not appear at first glance to have been very relevant to local politics. Take, for instance, the following passage in which Henry St. John, Viscount Bolingbroke, purported to describe how Walpole corrupted members of the House of Commons, some of whom were "tied down with *honors, titles,* and *preferments,* of which the *Robinarch* [Walpole] engrosses the disposal to himself, and others with *bribes,* which are called *pensions.*" That such writings would be popular after 1763 is perhaps easy enough to understand, for then increasingly restrictive measures on the part of Parliament as well as the crown appeared to give this literature great explanatory power. But what preferments did Glen have at his disposal, and which of his predecessors had pensions to dispense? Yet Bolingbroke was one of the most frequently quoted opposition writers, and others who rivaled him in this regard made similar charges. An explanation frequently given for the appeal of such ideas in the colonial context—a heightened fear of factional opponents in the turbulent world of local politics—does not work well for South Carolina, since this ideology became popular at a time when factionalism was waning in the colony.

Memories of earlier conditions may have lingered, but other factors appear to have been more important. Considered in the English context, such charges of corruption made the already frightening bogey of the prerogative more frightening. Partly because this process was self-reinforcing, and partly because remoteness from the center of real power tended to make colonials fearful of unpleasant surprises, Carolinians found this literature fascinating and persuasive. Indeed, it had a certain plausibility when considered only in the local context. Did the crown not appoint the council? And did it not usually support the prerogative? In addition, to be familiar with this ideology was to be au courant, and to act on its precepts was to behave like some authoritative figures in England argued that patriotic Englishmen should behave. Among these figures were a number of writers, like Bolingbroke and the most popular poet in the eighteenth century, Alexander Pope, who professed to see the salvation of the nation in the virtue of the gentry. Such a notion was obviously congenial to men who were already attempting to pattern themselves on the English country gentlemen in other areas of life. Writings like the *Freeholder's Political Catechism* by Bolingbroke and *Cato's Letters* by two skillful popularizers, John Trenchard and Thomas Gordon—whose essays dealt with "Publick Spirit," "the encroaching Nature of Power, [which was] ever to be watched and checked," and "the important Duty of Attendance in Parliament"—thus became textbooks of appropriate political behavior. One can therefore almost say that if the parliamentary journals and manuals of the seventeenth century provided guidelines for the collective conduct of the Commons as an institution, the opposition writers of the eighteenth century provided guidance for the political behavior of its members as individuals.

By midcentury politically conscious South Carolinians shared a coherent body of ideals, assumptions, and beliefs concerning politics which embodied the central tenets of country ideology. The foundation of all their political assumptions was their conception of human nature, which they deeply distrusted. Although man was a social being, he was hardly fit for society. The daily experiences of life demonstrated that he was unreliable, subject to his passions, and motivated by self-interest. The central problem of existence was the maintenance of freedom in the face of the manifold threats posed by human frailties; unless limits were placed on the exercise of passions and power, life was chaos and liberty impossible. Obviously, however, the resources of individuals alone were insufficient to secure the social order necessary to freedom. Governments had therefore been established to aid them by protecting their property, freedom, and life from the aggressions of their fellow creatures. When a government discharged its responsibility, its citizens were obligated to support and obey it, but when it threatened liberty by exceeding the limits of its authority, the people had not only the right but also the duty to resist. Frequent recourse to such drastic measures was dangerous because it threatened to create the chaos that governments were instituted to avoid; therefore, continuous effective checks on the power of government were necessary. Under the English system, the constitution performed this function, and South Carolinians invoked the hallowed term frequently but ambiguously. Often they used it to refer to the limits that society placed on its rulers; power and authority were different attributes. The former represented absolute force; the latter was power sanctioned by right, and the authority of government did not include the power to invade fundamental human rights. At other times, the constitution denoted the spirit and principles that ought to animate government; these included the idea that free men were bound only by laws to which they had consented, that private interests ought not to be set in competition with public good, and that the welfare of the whole was the supreme law. Finally, the constitution also referred to the existing composition of government.

To South Carolinians the glory of the British constitutional system was that it included institutional means to limit government and insure—as far as humanly possible—that it would act according to the principles which ought to animate it. Because the freedom of a citizen depended on the security of his property, taxes were considered voluntary though necessary gifts toward the support of government. To facilitate the grant of taxes, property holders of the nation chose representatives whose primary control over the public purse gave them an effective means to check the executive power and obtain redress of grievances. In practice, the chief historical role of the British House of Commons had been the protection of the people. Considering their own Commons House of Assembly to be a small counterpart, South Carolinians looked upon their local representatives as the natural guardians of the liberties and properties of the people.

The discharge of such important responsibilities required ability and the freedom to use it; therefore a member of the Commons was expected to be a relatively free agent. Theoretically he did not solicit but accepted a duty which imposed upon him an almost professional obligation to use his political expertise in behalf of his constituents, the whole people.

He should therefore be able, independent, courageous, virtuous, and public-spirited. Although riches did not insure that a man would exhibit these qualities, it was assumed that they made it more likely. Economic independence promoted courage and material possessions fostered rational behavior. In addition a large stake in society tied a man's interest to the welfare of the whole, while wealth enabled him to acquire the education believed necessary for statecraft. Finally, the influence and prestige of a rich man helped to add stature and effectiveness to government. Thus a series of interrelated assumptions about the virtues thought to be associated with wealth helped to maintain the belief that members of the elite should rule.

Nevertheless, no matter how qualified and how public-spirited an individual seemed, appearances might be deceiving and human nature was prone to corruption. It was therefore necessary for a representative's constituents to retain checks upon him. The most effective means was to harness his own self-interests to theirs. In theory this usually meant that he should hold property where they did. Over a period of time, however, the interests of a representative and his constituents might diverge; to prevent such a development frequent and free elections were necessary, and the secret ballot provided a convenient means to undermine the efficacy of coercion and bribery. In addition, collective bodies of men should be checked against each other. Everyone therefore gave at least habitual allegiance to the ideal of balanced government. Governors prized it as the "palladium" of liberty, and members of the Commons claimed that they no more wished to see the power of the Commons enlarged beyond its proper limits than vice versa. Not surprisingly, however, most local leaders considered those limits very wide.

The efficacy of balanced government, indeed the validity of the whole concept of checks and balances, appeared to be predicated on the discrete identity of each element in the system. Parties or factions, by definition combinations of men acting together for selfish purposes, were dangerous. In the absence of factions, the self-interested politician found himself checkmated at every turn by individuals whose common attributes were personal independence and a concern for the public welfare. Factional politics, however, provided a context which allowed private interests to flourish at the expense of the public and permitted the executive to build centers of support in the other branches of government, thereby weakening their will and subverting their ability to check the encroachments of executive power. Factionalism and corruption, especially when associated with the executive, presaged the demise of freedom.

Elitist in its assumptions, this ideology envisioned the existence of a society in which the clash of economic and class interests played no role. Instead, a struggle between the executive and the united representatives of the people appeared to supply the dynamics of politics. The idealized political figure was therefore the individualistic patriot who exhibited his disinterested concern for the public welfare by rejecting factional ties while remaining ready to join with like-minded individuals in curbing arbitrary exercises of executive power.

By the middle third of the eighteenth century, this political culture filled a void. As will be discussed elsewhere in more detail, increasing prosperity and a growing sense of community blunted the antagonisms of earlier days. It was therefore less appropriate for a member of the Commons to act as the representative of a particular interest group. What was his role and how was he to conduct himself under the new circumstances? Country ideology provided satisfactory answers. In following its precepts, which legitimized their position of leadership, members of the house discharged what they believed to be their duty and acquired all the accompanying satisfactions at the price of foregoing little their predecessors had enjoyed except the pursuit of private gain at public expense. The increasing wealth of assemblymen from other sources and the relative lack of lucrative patronage in the hands of the governor (or even the lower house, for that matter) made it fairly easy to forego the lesser for the greater reward. Moreover, society was small, and service in the Commons was time-consuming. Turnover in membership was therefore relatively high, and a man could satisfy his ambitions without denying the same satisfaction to others. An essentially altruistic political ethic could flourish in such an environment.

Country ideology and the accompanying rivalry among the three branches of government consequently transformed the character of politics. The more attached to the prerogative the governor and council appeared to be, the more concerned the lower house became about preserving the rights and liberties of the people; and the resulting clashes helped to unify the Commons. By the early 1740s, members were finding it politically expedient to join in supporting claims to rights and privileges whether or not they privately considered these claims to be justified. Later governors would note that members who singly disagreed with steps taken by the house would jointly approve them. Indeed, the younger Bull who had had long experience, not only as lieutenant governor but also as a leader in the house himself, observed that because members felt honor-bound to support the Commons, it was practically impossible to induce one house to reverse the actions of another.

The solid front which the Commons was able to present reflected the absence of factions within the house. Because roll call votes are not extant for the colonial period, it is impossible to assign a precise date for the disappearance of factionalism or even to assert categorically that no vestiges remained. Nevertheless, all available evidence indicates that by midcentury, if factions still existed, few contemporaries were aware of them and their influence on political behavior was slight. Needless to say, the absence of factionalism did not mean that local leaders never differed over men and measures; but it did mean that these differences, even when they involved strong personal animosities or clashes of opinion, did not lead to permanent alignments which fractured the unity of the Commons. From the beginning of the century, it had been customary to elect the speaker unanimously; during the last thirty or forty years of the colonial period, what began as a symbol of wished-for unity became the expression of real unanimity.

Paradoxically, however, this unanimity concealed—even in large measure arose from—the personal independence upon which each member of the house prided himself. No man was prepared to surrender his judgment to another, whether an individual or a group. Yet because members of the local elite shared similar interests and a common code of political behavior, such hypertensive individualism did not prevent cooperation with one another. They could take seriously the admonition to remember that although they were elected as the representatives of a particular area, once they took their seats, their responsibility was to the welfare of the whole. Except in matters of unusual importance, it was of no great consequence whether a member actually owned property or resided in the parish that elected him, and prominent individuals frequently represented constituents with whom they had no direct material connection. On the other hand, in matters of more importance or where different geographical areas or interest groups could be presumed to be unequally affected by public measures, equity required that each entity be separately represented. In similar fashion, local representatives consistently discharged most of the business of the Commons affecting their constituents. Ideological consensus and social homogeneity made localism and particularism compatible with the unity of the whole.

Being human, South Carolinians neither created a utopia nor achieved absolute political harmony through universal dedication to the public weal. Enough of them were forced to tend to their private interests during the depression of the 1740s so as to make it difficult to gather a quorum in the Commons. Thereafter, an occasional opportunist continued to find his way into the Commons, and even the most conscientious members were not exempt from the inability of human beings to use power entirely disinterestedly. Nevertheless, by the time that Charles Pinckney sailed for England in 1753, the *South Carolina Gazette* clearly recognized that he and his contemporaries had transformed the character of public life. The ex-speaker of the Commons was, in the words of the *Gazette,* "a true Father of his Country." During the last thirty or so years before the Revolution, most political leaders actually were the independent men of property revered in country ideology, and to an amazing extent, generally accepted ideals, assumptions, and expectations about political conduct governed their behavior. Upholders of the prerogative and some backcountry men excepted, there was considerable agreement that social and political harmony prevailed in what was an unusually well governed colony.

In short, by midcentury, South Carolinians had a stable and effective government; the long-term trend (despite the aberrations of the '40s) was toward greater continuity of membership in the lower house, and in composition and conduct, it came surprisingly close to approximating the prevailing ideal. The Commons was also extraordinarily powerful. To be sure, it lacked the autonomous power of its counterparts in the virtually independent corporate colonies of Connecticut and Rhode Island, and in some ways it was less autonomous than the lower house in Massachusetts. But in other ways it may have been the most powerful of all. Like most other houses, it had trimmed the power of the council and invaded the executive sphere—perhaps, indeed, through its frequent use of commissions, to a greater extent than many of its counterparts—but unlike them, it also maintained an unusually large degree of control over local affairs. From the standpoint of local leaders who sat in the Commons, this had obvious advantages, not the least of which involved the possibility of using general tax revenues for local projects with the concomitant ability to assure one's constituents that their business was being taken care of. Although a number of petitions over the years requesting more local control suggest that not everyone was entirely satisfied with this arrangement, it seems to have worked reasonably well for most purposes. In the absence of obvious incompetence or overt dissatisfaction, degrees of efficiency and popular support are always difficult to judge, but perhaps the acid test for any government is its ability to collect taxes. By that—and many other criteria—the government in South Carolina failed during the late 1720s. But thereafter, it is worth noting, the receivers of the royal quitrents proposed that they be given access to the provincial tax records in order to correct their own rolls.

This is not to imply that many South Carolinians failed to pay quitrents because they were disloyal to the crown—far from it—but rather that the relative effectiveness of provincial and royal government at the local level was such that allegiance to the one called for an active commitment while the other remained more nominal. Nor should royal disallowance of local laws be misconstrued. Imperial authorities disallowed less than 4 percent of the 638 acts passed between 1719 and 1776; and in some cases at least, it could be argued, the disallowance represented a salutary curb on arbitrary action by the assembly (e.g., the denial of habeas corpus). Furthermore, there is little indication that these actions produced a sense of grievance before the 1760s. Nevertheless, the frequent need to mention the relatively few disallowances while describing the characteristics of the Commons suggests that, as might be expected, vetoes clustered around constitutional questions. Yet, even so, imperial authorities largely failed to prevent the Commons from shaping itself in its own image.

That image, however, was an idealized one, which produced some significant discrepancies. To begin with, the South Carolina Commons was not only more powerful in some ways than the British House of Commons, it was also, in effect, a reformed House of Commons. There were no pocket boroughs in South Carolina; representation in the low country was relatively proportional to population; by and large placemen did not sit in the Commons; and virtually any free man could vote using the secret ballot. None of these was true of England at the time, and for some of these reforms Englishmen would have to wait until the nineteenth century. Yet only rarely, as in the case of the secret ballot, which Glen was shocked to be told was "an improvement upon their Mother Country," were South Carolinians aware of their deviations from English practice, let alone approving of them. So powerful was the English model that, in most areas, to be aware of a difference between "the great world" of London and "our little world" of Charles Town was to consider it a badge of provincial inferiority. Imperial authorities naturally perceived such differences in the same light. "If," as Glen observed, "the greatest and wisest Men have said in former times, We will not alter the Laws of England, much less should a Colony be heard to say, that she has improved upon the Constitution." And there, thanks largely to the isolation of the colonies and Walpole's policy of "salutary neglect" the matter rested—temporarily. The situation was inherently unstable, however, for recognition of the discrepancies between what was thought to be or supposed to be, on the one hand, and what was, on the other, would prompt men to try to close the gap. Doing so would require that they either make reality conform to theory, or theory to reality. Beginning about 1748, imperial authorities tried the first approach, but before discussing their program and its consequences, social and economic realities, of which politics was largely an expression, must be examined.

7

THE ECONOMY

By the mid-eighteenth century South Carolina was famed for its prosperity. Visitors constantly remarked about the wealth of the inhabitants around Charles Town and the opulence of their life-style. One even noted that their "enormous estates" would support "Baronies and Lordships" if the British government saw fit to create them there. Local figures believed that there were more rich in proportion to the population than in any of the other colonies, and Eliza Lucas Pinckney went so far as to imply that the living was so easy that anyone who remained poor must be lazy. Though few historians would go quite that far, most have agreed with contemporary assessments in believing that white South Carolinians enjoyed the highest per capita income and wealth of any of the North American colonists. Furthermore, the economic growth rate appears to have been equally impressive. One scholar, George Rogers Taylor, estimated that at midcentury it was the highest not only in the British empire but perhaps in the world, and, although no one has yet really substantiated that claim, it is not altogether unreasonable. On the eve of the Revolution South Carolina was a kind of El Dorado.

It had not always been like that. Like all of the mainland colonies, South Carolina offered land in abundance. "But," as the author of one early promotional pamphlet observed, "a rational man will certainly inquire, When I have Land, what shall I doe with it?" The answer was not immediately apparent, though the proprietors had encouraged a number of experimental plantings in the early days of the colony. The hope, of course, was that South Carolina might produce, if not tropical products, commodities associated with a climate like that of southern Europe and the Near East. Silk, olives, wine, oranges, and lemons might do well, it was thought, but they never worked out. Among other problems, some of the early silkworms hatched and died en route to Carolina and in later years ants attacked their successors; the climate proved too variable for many of the grapes; and periodic cold snaps killed the orange trees. The results with cotton were discouraging, and difficulties in extracting the dyestuff apparently undermined indigo. In addition, many Barbadians arrived with the intention of supplying the West Indies with lumber and foodstuffs.

Provisions therefore proved to be the first profitable export, and local entrepreneurs sent sizable quantities of corn, peas, and salt meat (both beef and pork) to Barbados and the other islands of the Caribbean. Such trade continued to make up a portion of the export market throughout the colonial period, though it was never especially lucrative. But it did stimulate the development of a livestock industry which was ideally suited to local conditions. Hogs foraged on acorns and hickory nuts; soon almost feral, they became aggressive wanderers— the planters' real problem was not feeding but finding them. Cattle too roamed the woods and open savannahs. Spring and fall roundups, cowpens (corrals), branding, and cattle drives foreshadowed techniques later made famous on the western plains. Because so little capital investment was required, men who started with virtually nothing, it was said, might soon have large herds, and throughout the colonial period some men of prominence do in fact seem to have gotten their start in the cattle business. In relative and perhaps absolute terms ranching made its greatest contribution to the economy in the seventeenth century, yet as late as 1751 after a severe epidemic of bovine distemper, the governor still estimated that there were 80,000 head of cattle in the woods of Carolina.

Lucrative as cattle raising might be for a few individuals, it never made fortunes for many. Indeed, nothing did in the seventeenth century, and the relatively few who prospered appear to have done so mainly by the aggressive and simultaneous pursuit of various opportunities. Providing provisions for pirates, pursuing the perquisites of office, and trading with the Indians were perhaps the most lucrative if not the most edifying activities. The seamiest side of the Indian trade was the slave trade, in which South Carolinians were the most heavily involved of all the colonists. A little experience demonstrated that Indian women and children were reasonably tractable and could be retained in the colony; as previously discussed, many of the men were killed or shipped to the Caribbean and elsewhere. As long as there were nearby Indians to enslave, the business appears to have been profitable. But the declining supply, problems with the captives, and proprietary opposition limited the size of the trade.

Other aspects of the Indian trade held more long-term potential. Early hopes for a cornucopia of furs never materialized because there were not enough beaver in the area. Deer, however, were abundant, and the skins were in demand in England. As a result, by the end of the seventeenth century (when reasonably reliable figures begin to be available), thousands of deerskins were collected annually by Indian traders. Between 1699 and 1715 an average of more than 53,000 skins—worth perhaps £30,000 sterling—per year were sent to England by some 200 traders. For a time deerskins constituted the single most valuable export. But the Yamasee War badly disrupted the trade, and the rise of other commodities relegated the Indian trade to a secondary role in the economy, though it never became a negligible factor. During the 1730s and 1740s, 600 to 700 hogsheads of skins worth about £36,750 sterling on the wharf at Charles Town were exported in an average year.

Substantial as these figures are, deerskins had long since been eclipsed by the value of other products. At first, the most important of these was probably naval stores. During the seventeenth century, tar and pitch made from the sap of pine trees greased wagon wheels, water-proofed cordage, and caulked ships. Traditionally, Englishmen got most of their tar and pitch from the Baltic countries, but the wars with France jeopardized the supply and raised the price. British officials and Americans therefore took an increasing interest in the subject, and Carolinians were making pitch and tar in considerable quantities by 1699 when a royal official, who had been investigating the matter, reported that South Carolina was "the only place for such commodities upon the Continent of America." The season for making them was long, the costs low, and raw materials were abundant. Parliament responded in 1705 by restricting the legal market to the empire and granting a subsidy for the production of colonial pitch and tar. In turn, South Carolinians soon made the colony the leading producer of naval stores in America. By 1717 nearly 44,000 barrels a year were being exported, and within the next two or three years the market was glutted.

The reasons for the short boom are not far to seek. The process was relatively simple and, at least for a time, profits were good. Workers scoured the woods for the resinous heartwood and stumps of dead pine trees. Digging a shallow saucer-like depression in the ground and lining it with clay, they ran a pipe from the low point to a barrel set still lower some distance away. They then carefully piled the wood in the saucer, fourteen or fifteen feet high, and covered it with earth. Making air holes as necessary, they ignited the wood at the top and allowed it to smolder downward with very little oxygen. The tar which cooked out ran through the pipe and collected in the barrel, which was changed periodically; what remained of the wood in the kiln became charcoal. For a substantial run of tar, firing the kiln might take four or five days—if it didn't explode sooner, which was the chief danger in the business. When all went well, the returns could be excellent. Twelve laborers working about 2,000 acres, someone estimated in 1705, might produce enough tar and pitch to be worth approximately £500 sterling.

There was, however, a potential problem in all of this which—as much as overproduction—eventually undermined the tar industry in South Carolina. English ropemakers preferred Swedish tar, believing that the Carolina product "scorched" or weakened cordage. The difference, it seemed, arose from the technique employed in making it. Swedes used live or green trees; Americans dead. English authorities tried to convince colonists to adopt the Swedish method, but Carolinians were reluctant to comply because of the cost involved. Dead wood which had not rotted after a few years was all resinous; a living tree might contain very little heartwood and much labor could be wasted in cutting it. Parliament dealt with the problem from its point of view by allowing the bounty to lapse in 1724, and the Carolina naval stores industry collapsed. Lobbying to have the subsidy restored, Americans and British merchants then induced Parliament to pass a new act in 1729 which, being renewed for the rest of the colonial period, provided somewhat lower bounties for ordinary pitch and tar and a higher premium for "green" tar made by the Swedish method. Carolinians, however, had already discovered their own solution to the technical problems of the tar industry. They made pitch. Cooking or burning off the more volatile elements of ordinary tar converted it to pitch of acceptable quality, which was worth more per barrel than tar, though the bounty was less and the market smaller. Accordingly, South Carolinians continued to make and ship more pitch than tar throughout the rest of the colonial period. Though annual exports of each varied widely, neither item normally totaled more than a few thousand barrels. North Carolina took over leadership in the production of naval stores and eventually became known as the "tarheel state." South Carolinians believed that they had better things to do.

One of those was growing rice. It was among the crops tried in the first experimental plantings, but skill and experience were apparently necessary to make it a commercial success. Even after its reintroduction in the late 1680s and early 1690s with improved seed from Madagascar and the East Indies, several years passed before South Carolinians had mastered the techniques. But once having cleared that hurdle, they quickly brought more land under cultivation and began importing thousands of slaves. By 1722 there were 1.16 million acres on the tax rolls; two decades later the amount had approximately doubled. In 1690 there had been only 1,500 slaves in the province; by 1710 there were 4,100. During the next decade the number tripled. And despite a persistent myth among historians of economic chaos in the 1720s, the price of rice remained relatively good, and the rapid acquisition of slaves continued. Indeed, another jump of 66 percent during the decade brought the black population to 20,000 by 1730. Thereafter, rice prices weakened somewhat but remained strong enough to fuel continued expansion of its cultivation. In 1700 slightly under 400,000 pounds were exported; during each of the next two decades exports quadrupled and then nearly tripled again during the 1720s. Although the exponential growth rate slowed in the 1730s—production did not quite double—the larger base for figuring the percent of increase masks the hectic pace of expansion. In all probability, the amount of new land cleared and planted in rice during the 1730s matched the total brought under cultivation during the previous forty years. It was an exceptionally hard decade for slaves.

The 1740s proved to be somewhat easier on blacks and harder for whites. In 1740, approximately 43 million pounds of rice were exported—a figure not consistently matched or exceeded until the 1760s. For in the 1740s the bottom dropped out of the export market for rice. Overproduction and the disruption of European markets in King George's War were the chief problems. Being a bulky item with a relatively low value per unit of volume, rice depended on cheap freight rates for its marketability. But the hazards of war drove freight and insurance up and the price of rice, which varied inversely with such charges, down. Between 1741 and the low in 1746 the average price of rice in Charles Town fell by 70 percent; and in 1749 the amount shipped was down to less than half of the 1740 high. One indication of the impact of these reversals can be seen in the acreage returned for taxes, which fell by about 400,000 acres or 17 percent during the decade. Imports of British goods to both Carolinas, of which South Carolina took the bulk, were down about one-fourth. Thanks in part to a prohibitory duty imposed on new slaves, less than 1,600 Africans appear to have been imported during the ten years.

Hard times made normally conservative planters receptive to experimentation. A wild species of indigo grew naturally in South Carolina, and initial experiments with unknown varieties did reasonably well in the 1670s. Processing the plant was tricky, however, and it did not become a commercial crop until Eliza Lucas Pinckney and other planters experimented successfully with West Indian varieties. Attempts to obtain a British bounty succeeded in 1748, and the crop quickly caught on, partly because in exportable form it shared some of the characteristics of gold bullion. Being not only an essential dyestuff for the English textile industry but also extremely valuable in proportion to its bulk, indigo enjoyed an assured market and comparative immunity to the vagaries of war. Thus planters, who hoped to avoid the economic horrors of the 1740s, increasingly planted it during the French and Indian War; and during the Revolution indigo even became a form of currency for Revolutionary authorities and fleeing loyalists. However, exports varied widely from year to year, though two or three examples give a sense of the rapid increase in production. In 1750 a little over 63,000 pounds were sent to England; by 1760 the figure was over half a million, and for the first half of 1775 it exceeded a million pounds. Truly, as contemporaries remarked, "these [were] the golden days of indigo," in which the indigo planters were "full of money."

For a number of reasons rice planters also did well. In the first place, increased attention to indigo diverted resources from rice and mitigated the problem of overproduction. Secondly, British naval protection was better during the French and Indian War, and consequently freight and insurance rates did not rise as steeply as in the previous war. Moreover, the capture of large French and Spanish islands in the Caribbean opened up markets that remained accessible after the war. Thus the last two decades of the colonial period were in general a period of heady prosperity for South Carolinians, during which, as near as can be estimated, the value of all exports to England climbed nearly 80 percent while imports almost tripled from the depressed level of 1750.* Blacks and whites alike poured into the colony. During the last twenty-five years of the colonial period, in fact, nearly 57,000 Africans were imported while the white population increased by more than 40,000. Most immigrants, to be sure, settled in the backcountry and were therefore involved in the production of export staples to only a limited extent, though by 1770 more than 3,000 wagons carrying wheat, indigo, and some tobacco, as well as other products, traveled the road to Charles Town each year. Per capita exports to England actually declined between 1750 and the 1760s, but the booming 1760s and '70s brought them back up to near record levels, well above those of other colonies.

Because many economic historians believe, as James Shepherd and Gary Walton recently phrased it, that "the commercial sector... provided the initial driving force for economic growth and development in the colonies," it is worth taking a closer look at how all of this came about in South Carolina. The first ingredient was land, and for most of the colonial period acquiring acreage was surprisingly easy. To men who came from areas where land was in short supply, it must have been a heady experience. One can see some of the euphoria in the journal of an Englishman who came to Carolina in the 1730s. Proceeding up the Pee Dee River, the party he was with found "a great deal of good oak and hickory, and the pine land very valuable, and a great deal of good cypress swamp, which is counted the best for rice, and having a surveyor with us"—almost casually, it seems—"one gentleman in company concluded to run some out." Several miles

---

*These figures are based on combined statistics for both Carolinas which were not distinguished in the extant records. But because South Carolina was the more prosperous of the two colonies, the resulting error is on the conservative side.

farther up the river, they camped on Bear Bluff, which seemed to be "the finest [tract] on all the river." So fine, the diarist continued, that if each of them had possessed a warrant, "we should have fell out about the choice of it." No one had the necessary document in hand, so they "were obliged to leave it for some other." He proved to be their host of a few days later, who, having intended to "run out" the bluff himself the following week, had been "very much afraid lest we had been beforehand with him." His anxieties laid to rest on that score, he exuded hospitality. Good to mediocre land prompted scarcely a second thought; only the very best stimulated covetousness. The tone of these accounts is of men who are in on a great bonanza and know it.

Admission was by the warrants mentioned above, and they were almost free. For those who came to South Carolina "under the bounty"— that is, at the inducement of the legislature—even the fees of the issuing officers were paid by the government. All an individual had to do was to petition the governor and council, who then issued a warrant authorizing a surveyor to stake out a tract of so many acres (during most of the colonial period, fifty or 100 for each member of the petitioner's family). The recipient or his surveyor chose an unoccupied site, made a survey, and returned the surveyor's map or plat to the proper office. In turn, a grant was issued in the name of the proprietors or the crown. Additions to his family of children, servants, and slaves qualified an individual for additional grants. To be sure, the procedure usually involved fees for the officers involved, and quitrents—remnants of the feudal past acknowledging the crown or proprietors as the nominal landlords of the tract—remained to be paid. In addition, the system had some built-in inequities, for here, as elsewhere, the old maxim "them that has gets" applied. Men with more servants or slaves got more land. Nevertheless, the system worked remarkably well, albeit some individuals engrossed more land than they could use, some deliberately failed to return the surveyors' plats (thereby keeping the land which they held under warrant off the quitrent books), and some just neglected to pay the quitrents. But for most of the colonial period, grants provided a way for men and women of modest means to acquire land, and most grants were in fact made to them. Thus in February 1749 an ex-indentured servant, John Gable, came before the council, swore that he had served out his time, and "that he had a wife and two children which he had brought with him into this country and that he had one child born since and had never had any land granted to him." He received 250 acres.

Almost certainly his grant was for high land unsuitable for rice since most potential rice land was in private hands by this time, some of it by accident. At least one man with a sense of humor called his plantation "Starve Gut"; someone with a sense of life's contingencies should have named his "Serendipity," for the sites of many later rice plantations were chosen for other reasons, such as the availability of cypress timber and proximity to water transportation. By the 1720s, however, swamps were known to be valuable; but, as we have seen, the supply was restricted by the proprietors as well as by nature. Accordingly, men dusted off and dealt in old claims, and when the royal government began granting land in 1731, there was a rush to grab potential rice lands at the periphery of settlement. In less than two years, for example, the entire area between the Combahee and Coosawhatchie rivers, which would become Prince William's Parish, passed into private hands.

Although only a fraction of the land acquired at this time was suitable for rice, it was enough to satisfy a generation. By the 1750s, however, the quest was on again, and some freebooters established a settlement on the south side of the Altamaha River. Although the area was included within the original boundaries of Carolina, it was still claimed by Spain; moreover, it was now separated from South Carolina by Georgia. Not anxious to antagonize Spain, imperial authorities ordered the settlement removed, and South Carolinians obliged. But the action may have focused attention on the area, and soon after it became apparent that Britain would acquire Florida at the end of the French and Indian War, the governor of South Carolina began granting potential rice lands along the Altamaha River to well-placed South Carolinians. General instructions from the crown against encroaching on Indian lands and vigorous protests from officials in Georgia brought a halt to these grants. Eventually Georgia asserted its jurisdiction over the area, but at least some of the Carolinians involved retained their lands. Such aggressive expansionism suggests what other testimony confirms—those who wanted additional rice land in South Carolina by the mid-eighteenth century almost had to buy, inherit, or marry it.

The same, however, was not true of higher land suitable for naval stores and indigo. During the first two decades of the eighteenth century, the southern part of the province promised to be the center of the naval stores industry. The Yamasee Indians disrupted those plans, and by the time the area had recovered from their attacks, the boom in naval stores was largely over. Consequently, most of the exported tar and pitch came from farther north. Indigo, however, could be grown almost anywhere on moderately good, dry land. Thus high lands on plantations devoted mainly to rice often became indigo fields, and the sea islands—which had hitherto been relatively undeveloped— joined the economic mainstream. At least potentially, so did the back- country, and it soon commanded the attention of lowcountry magnates as well as immigrants from farther north. By the 1760s scattered here and there among the growing numbers of farms in the upcountry were indigo plantations worked by slave labor.

Indigo was relatively easy to grow but difficult to process; rice on the other hand, required considerable expertise in cultivation but pri- marily brawn in preparation for market. At first, rice was sometimes grown on dry land like other crops, but planters soon learned that irrigation could be used to stimulate growth, control weeds, and drown insects. Part of the trick was finding land that could be easily flooded; clearing it and constructing the necessary dams, dikes, ditches, sluices, gates, and reservoirs was also part of the craft, while knowing just when and how long to flood the fields required precise judgment. Inland swamps provided rich soil and plentiful fresh water, but reg- ulating the amount of the latter presented problems. If spring floods did not wipe out everything, their overflow could be impounded and delivered to the fields as needed. But the process was always chancy and often laborious. Beginning at least as early as 1738 some planters therefore used tidal culture and, by the Revolutionary era, the practice appears to have been fairly common, especially in the Georgetown area. As the tide flows into a river, it drives a wedge of heavier salt water underneath the fresh, raising it. Accordingly, with the proper arrange- ment of dikes and gates, the ebb and flow of the tides can be made to flood and drain contiguous lands. But planters on the lower reaches of the rivers needed to exercise extreme care to prevent the intrusion of salt water which would ruin their fields. Nevertheless, the increase in efficiency was worth the risks. During the first half of the eighteenth century, three to four acres of rice per hand was the rule of thumb; after tidal culture became the norm, one man could handle up to seven.

Despite small improvements—including some pounding machines—comparable gains in harvesting and threshing the grain did not come until the nineteenth century. Cutting and threshing were not considered especially arduous, but pounding the grain in a large wooden mortar to remove the inner husk was notoriously backbreaking, and the task continued from early fall until well into the winter.

Although the cultivation of indigo was less demanding physically, it involved much tedious labor in sowing the seed, controlling weeds, and waging relatively futile war on the grasshoppers which, it was estimated, reduced average yields by as much as 30 percent. The real skill was involved in extracting the dyestuff. The process involved three connecting vats of decreasing size. The first, usually of masonry or oak construction, might be sixteen feet across, sixteen long, and two feet deep, though other dimensions were also common. Known as the steeper, this tank was filled with water, into which the cut indigo plants were thrown and allowed to ferment for about twelve hours. At the proper time the liquid was drained off into the second vat, where it was beaten with paddles or a paddle wheel to oxygenate and coagulate the solids. Timing was crucial at this stage for too little or too much beating could diminish output or ruin the batch. Finally, the mixture was allowed to settle and the superfluous liquid drained off into the third and smallest vat (affectionately known as "the young devil"). Workers then scooped up the goo in the bottom of the second vat, and put it into small cloth bags which were hung up to drain. After a short time, these were taken down and their almost black contents spread out on a flat surface to dry for several days in the shade. Cut like a cake into pieces about the size and shape of a thick domino, the result was the blue gold of Carolina. When broken in the hand, the finest grades revealed an iridescent sheen, like burnished metal. The poorer batches tended to be excessively deliquescent, perhaps because lime made from sea shells was often used to speed precipitation during processing. Thus even the best Carolina indigo was usually not up to the finest Guatemalan. (In South Carolina, it is also worth noting, the plant was near the periphery of its range—planters in the tropics were able to make three cuttings a year, Carolinians only two.) Good or bad, the average price per pound in Charles Town was close to 3 shillings sterling (or perhaps the equivalent of $8.00 to $10.00 today).

Such prices make clear why aggressive and ambitious men turned

Cartouche from the Stuart map of South Carolina published in 1780. The imaginative decoration includes some of the steps in processing indigo and a reasonably accurate picture of the finished product. *Courtesy of the South Caroliniana Library*.

to indigo. Many of them, however, were also involved in other ventures. There were planters who merely planted one crop, just as there were specialized merchants; but the number of entrepreneurs with diversified interests is striking. Large planters sometimes provided transportation for their neighbors' crops; some owned grist and sawmills, and a few even kept stores. Individuals in all walks of life speculated in land with considerable success, though more than one elaborately planned town never made it much beyond the surveyor's plat. Radnor, for example, had sites set aside for a church, a school, and the commons. Had it developed as planned, it might have resembled a New England village; as it turned out, Radnor became a small cluster of buildings of almost forgotten name at a ferry crossing on the Combahee River. In the rapidly developing suburbs of Charles Town, on the other hand, real estate appreciated so rapidly during the late colonial period that one visitor reported that the tales he heard about it sounded positively "romantic." But he was assured they were based on fact. No doubt they were; at least one merchant documented a more than tenfold increase in the price of one lot in about eight years.

Of course not all interest in land, even by men who were not primarily planters, was speculative. Much of it in outlying districts as well as in town involved residential use; and merchants and professional men often maintained "country seats" as well as productive plantations. As one might expect, many merchants were also shipowners and moneylenders, but the role of planters in the web of credit is perhaps more interesting. Many were debtors, and to some extent, no doubt, conspicuous consumption and the seasonal planting cycle contributed to their debts. What is more significant though, is the extent to which their borrowing stemmed from aggressive exploitation of economic opportunity. The will of Charles Pinckney, who was both a lawyer and a planter, illustrates the prevailing pattern. "In as much," he observed, "as the Success in the Busyness of my Profession hath hitherto been more than I had any Right to expect; and thereby hath encouraged me, to run greatly in Debt; hoping the better to advance my Estate by such Means, in the Planting Way; which Expectation I think will answer if it Should please God to Spare my Life, with Health for a few years longer." But, he added, these debts might "greatly injure" his estate in the event of his premature death unless he made provision for their repayment from the most easily spared assets. What is perhaps

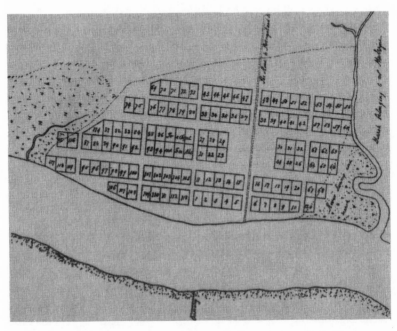

Radnor, an unsuccessful speculative town laid out by William Bull, Sr., in 1734. Note the unnumbered lots to the west of the central square, which were to be reserved for a chapel and a school. Adapted from *South Carolina Historical and Genealogical Magazine. Courtesy of the South Carolina Historical Society.*

most striking of all, though, is that the pursuit of the pound not only led planters to enlarge their planting operations but also frequently made *them* moneylenders.*

Such financial sophistication and aggressiveness are especially intriguing because they bear on questions concerning the source of capital for local development. Did it come primarily from British merchants or from local savings? No one has yet investigated the situation in South Carolina sufficiently to give a definitive answer; in regard to other colonies, however, the opinions of historians have been divided. One might therefore straddle the issue by observing that both sources of capital played a part in South Carolina. It is possible, however, to be somewhat more precise. Based on the claims made after the Revolution, South Carolinians owed British merchants approximately £347,000 sterling in 1776, exclusive of whatever debts may have been paid during the war. In proportion to the white population, this figure—though less than one-third the amount owed by Virginians—was one of the highest of all the thirteen colonies. Yet it was then, and has been since, the subject of much less comment than the famous Virginia debt. Why? Part of the answer arises from the differing distribution of the debts. In Virginia hundreds of small farmers owed relatively small sums to English and Scottish mercantile houses which had established branches in the colony; in South Carolina, however, British firms dealt with the local mercantile community in Charles Town, and relatively large local merchants were therefore the chief debtors. This difference suggests two things: first, why the Carolina debt in Britain was not perceived as a popular grievance and, second, that local merchants and other sources were providing much of the long-term credit in South Carolina.

Changing practices in the slave trade also support these inferences. Early in the eighteenth century local merchants acted as little more than agents for British slave traders, collecting commissions on sales and, when the purchasers made payment (which was usually in installments), forwarding the sums to Britain. By the end of the colonial period, however, British houses frequently demanded full payment for

---

*On the eve of the Revolution Rawlins Lowndes, for example, received annually about £1,500 currency from his rice crops, £3,000 from rental property in Charles Town, and approximately £8,000 in interest on loans.

the entire cargo in twelve to eighteen months. Local merchants with sufficient capital could thus become active middlemen, making payment out of their own funds but extending longer credit to the planters. Late in the colonial period one firm was reputed to have £50,000 sterling outstanding. It therefore seems reasonable to conclude that, as time went on, local sources supplied an increasingly large amount of the capital for internal development.

Precisely how large the amount was is difficult to say, but some rough estimates are possible because the local government taxed "money at interest"; in the last extant tax return of the colonial period (for 1768) the equivalent of £550,593 sterling was listed under this category. Unfortunately that figure—which was a little more than one and a half times the sum known to have been owed to British merchants—is not directly comparable with the external debt. In the first place, an unknown amount due absentees was undoubtedly included in the local debt. Secondly, eight years separated the two figures. However, the local debt doubled between 1760 and 1768. Thus, despite the nonimportation movement of 1769–1770, commercial activity of the early 1770s was sufficiently vigorous that internal debts may well have doubled again before the Revolution. If so, they might have been over three times the amount of the external debt. But even that figure would represent no more than a fraction of local credit. For charitable trusts and institutions were exempt from taxation while merchants' book debts appear to have been lumped under another heading (where it is impossible to sort them out from other assets). And, finally, taxpayers were required to report only sums on which they were earning interest over and above what they themselves paid interest for. Thus £20 on a tax return might indicate that an individual was receiving interest on £120 but owed £100, and a sampling of inventories suggests that such a pattern was common. Thus the use of credit was far more widespread than the tax returns indicate. Nevertheless, it seems safe to conclude that the complex structure of the debt resembled an inverted pyramid. British capital doubtless played an important part is supporting the whole, but local funds almost certainly made up the bulk.

Much of this local capital obviously came from local merchants, but private individuals and charitable societies frequently advertised money "to let." Moreover, wills often stipulated that a portion of the assets be put out at interest for the maintenance of children or widows. Managing such estates, incidentally, became enough of a business so that some merchants and lawyers became quasi-professional executors. One man was even reputed to have made £10,000 sterling "and more" in this fashion. These activities were characteristic of a society that was already wealthy. In the early decades of the eighteenth century, much of the capital must have come from British merchants, but the controversies over paper money suggest that their investments were not always made willingly. That is to say, the depreciation of paper currency—like inflation in the 1970s—transferred assets to those who operated on credit. For example, anyone who bought goods and delayed payment in a rapidly depreciated currency paid less than the goods were worth when he received them, and the same principle governed any investment made with borrowed money. That paper currency ceased to be an issue in the late 1730s and early 1740s is therefore perhaps significant. By that time, one suspects, a depreciating currency no longer appeared to serve a redeeming social purpose, and men who were on balance creditors rather than borrowers controlled its emission.

If this hypothesis is correct, government may have played a greater role in local development than is sometimes realized, though many of its contributions are obvious. Free—or almost free—land represented a huge transfer of capital to private hands, while low rates of taxation prevented reversal of the process. No one, Governor Glen reported in the 1740s, paid more than 5 percent of his income in taxes and some much less. Moreover, the taxpayer received quite a bit for his money in addition to mere protection. Government services ranged from rewards for useful innovations, such as rice pounding machines, to navigational aids. A beacon just east of James Island at Charles Town, as well as pilot boats and pilots at the ports of entry—for which £1,200 to £1,500 currency was spent annually at Georgetown just before the Revolution—and the like came under the local government. Special commissions strove to keep rivers and streams free of obstructions and widened channels. There was even some discussion in the late colonial period of building a canal to connect the Santee and Cooper rivers, though the project did not materialize until the 1790s.

Parish road commissions supervised the maintenance of highroads, for which local residents were required to supply labor. Thus, despite the floods that often washed out bridges, lowcountry roads—many of which, travelers reported, were "level as a bowling-green" and some of which, at least, had markers every mile—were among the best in the colonies. Those in the backcountry were another matter, not only because the sparsely settled population made maintenance difficult but also because the traffic was different. Roads in the lowcountry were used predominately for travel by light carriage and horseback, while broad-wheeled oxcarts moved rice barrels to plantation landings from which most of them went to Charles Town by boat. In the backcountry, however, wagons carried perhaps two tons of freight and the narrow rims of their wheels cut up the roads, producing erosion. As might be expected, fords were the primary river crossings in the backcountry, while ferries predominated in the low. The latter, it should be noted, were operated by individuals who, in return for a monopoly granted by the legislature, were required to maintain certain standards of service at prices set by law.

Though not explicitly regulated, newspapers were also closely tied to the local government. Requiring a vehicle for public notices, the legislature advertised for and obtained a printer, Thomas Whitmarsh, a partner of Benjamin Franklin, who founded the *South Carolina Gazette* in 1732. After his death in the same year, the paper was taken over by another partner of Franklin, Lewis Timothy. Continued by his son Peter, the *Gazette* was the only newspaper in the colony until the late 1750s when a bookseller, Robert Wells, established the *South Carolina and American General Gazette*. Slightly less than a decade later, another newspaper appeared during the Stamp Act crisis when the existing weeklies suspended publication. Designed to be the mouthpiece of the Commons House of Assembly, the *South Carolina Gazette and Country Journal* was published by Charles Crouch, Peter Timothy's ex-apprentice. Thus, after the other printers resumed publication in 1766, three newspapers served Charles Town and its hinterland. No other southern city had as many at the time, and no other southern newspapers carried as much advertising (about 75 to 100 notices per paper, per issue in the 1760s). Moreover, there were subscription agents for the *South Carolina Gazette* in every southern colony from North Carolina to Florida. In short, though primarily organs of government, these newspapers facilitated commerce over a wide area.

Nor was their contribution restricted merely to intra- or intercolonial trade. Most of their news, in fact, was reprinted from British newspapers and much of it dealt with economic as well as political concerns. As one merchant observed, though he was "never very eager in the pursuite of newes" unless it was in his "proper way of business," he was "both watchfull & vigilant to learn what is going forward & to improve upon the earlyest intelligence" relevant to his affairs. To anyone accustomed to modern electronic communications, the "earlyest intelligence" from Britain may seem almost light years old. Even after British authorities established packet-boat service from Falmouth to Charles Town in 1764, two months usually elapsed between an event in Britain and its appearance in a local newspaper. Doubtless a merchant interested in dispatch would have turned first to his own mail, since there could be a week's delay between the arrival of news and its publication. But either way, Carolinians were partly indebted to government for their information, for mail service was under the supervision of the crown, and local postmasters (who were at times also printers) were royal officials.

Important as the role of the crown was in facilitating communications, its other contributions to the local economy were at least equally significant. To a limited extent, direct expenditures for defense as well as the salaries of royal officials brought sterling into the colony, though the amounts were seldom large. No warships were assigned to the colony until 1719; thereafter a twenty-gun vessel was usually stationed at Charles Town, and larger ships sometimes visited. The first army unit to be permanently posted on the southern frontier was the "independent company" garrisoned at Fort King George from 1722 to 1727; Oglethorpe had a regiment and three independent companies; and when they were disbanded in 1748–1749, some of their personnel were shifted to three new companies controlled by the governor and council of South Carolina until these units were abolished in 1763. Although they were replaced by three companies of the Royal American Regiment, with the exception of the troops sent to South Carolina during the Cherokee War in 1760 and 1761, most soldiers in the colony were only passing through. If that made quartering less of a constitutional issue in South Carolina than in some other colonies, it also reduced the economic impact of the military presence. Nevertheless, some men apparently made money supplying these troops. Many more profited because British authorities encouraged indigo production with bounties and preferential access to the British market. The latter, it seems, was the most important factor, since reduction of the bounty in the late colonial period caused relatively little alarm whereas competition from other areas in and outside of the empire after the Revolution ruined the local industry. Most important of all, Britain provided naval protection for vessels carrying the exports on which the prosperity of the colony depended. How much that was worth is difficult to estimate, but the difference between conditions during King George's and the French and Indian wars suggests that adequate protection was essential for the success of the export trade.

There was, of course, a price to pay for all of this. According to the prevailing tenets of mercantilism, colonies were supposed to serve the mother country as a source of raw materials and a market for manufactured goods. Even before Carolina was founded, Parliament began passing a series of acts closing colonial ports to foreign vessels and restricting the purchase of most European products to those handled by English middlemen. Equally important, desirable colonial commodities, like rice and indigo, were placed on an ever-lengthening list of items which could be exported only to England or to other colonies (though, as will be seen, some exceptions were later made in the case of rice). Thus almost all of the marketable indigo as well as approximately 50 percent of the rice was sent directly to Great Britain in the 1760s and an additional 15 percent or so of the latter went to the West Indies, where it was one of the single most valuable commodites imported from the mainland colonies. Overall, rice ranked third by value among colonial exports, and indigo fifth. Together, they constituted about 15 percent of all exports from the thirteen colonies. Conversely, in 1765 for example, South Carolinians may have taken about 17 percent of all colonial imports from England. Moreover, the total trade was such that despite the apparent deficit suggested by these figures, South Carolinians seem normally to have enjoyed a favorable balance of trade—that is, except perhaps in years of unusually heavy slave importations, the value of their exports was greater than the value of their imports (which helps to explain where the capital for local investment originated). Impressive as these figures are, their real significance is apparent only when one realizes that in 1760 white South Carolinians represented less than 3 percent of the free population of the thirteen colonies.

These statistics suggest that the imperial system was no great constraint. Few men, contemporaries assumed, would work for others when they could become planters. Accordingly, because land was plentiful and cheap, while labor was scarce and expensive, South Carolinians were not given to manufacturing of any kind. Nevertheless, attempts were repeatedly made to induce them to produce goods which might be beneficial to England, such as wine, silk, and hemp; none of these proved very successful. Silk, one royal official observed, was a hopeless case unless Indian women or others "who set no great value on their time" could be trained to do the work. If South Carolinians would not manufacture desired products in any quantity, neither did they compete much with English goods. To be sure, home looms were fairly common by the 1760s, especially in the backcountry, and there were also a few local tanneries, brickyards, potteries, rope walks making cordage, and two or three distilleries, as well as two sugar bakeries and, at least temporarily, a brewery. During the Revolutionary era two ironworks were even established in the northern part of the state. But the largest single industry was undoubtedly shipbuilding, though the output remained small compared to that of the New England colonies. In 1768 the *South Carolina Gazette* estimated that there then were 130 locally owned boats and schooners operating in provincial waters, of which three-quarters were decked vessels capable of carrying between ten and fifty tons. Beginning in King George's War when shipping, but little else, was in demand, builders also constructed quite a few larger vessels. Moreover, Carolina-built ships enjoyed an excellent reputation because of the durability of their live oak timbers. In the 1760s and 1770s some British firms were therefore having vessels like the *Countess of Dumfries* built in South Carolina. Designed for the Carolina and Virginia trades and launched at Beaufort in 1773, she was capable of carrying 1,100 barrels of rice.

Had colonial vessels not been considered British for purposes of the navigation acts, neither the *Countess* nor much else but plantation canoes would have been built in the colony. Nevertheless, the failure to develop even encouraged manufactures to any great extent suggests that other considerations were more powerful than the law in shaping local economic behavior. Did this mean that South Carolinians smuggled? Some royal officials thought so, and for approximately the first forty years of the colonial period they were probably correct. But after 1720 theirs was a minority opinion, held mostly by men who either had an ax to grind or let their imaginations run wild over the possibilities of an irregular coastline. Despite some illicit trade during King George's and the French and Indian wars, most South Carolinians found legitimate pursuits lucrative enough to make the rewards of smuggling insufficient to compensate for the risks.

In sum, South Carolinians seem to have been willing to comply with the British commercial system. This does not mean, however, that it did not cost them something or that they were totally happy with it. The economic burdens and benefits of the empire have been the subject of renewed scholarly interest of late, and there have been a number of sophisticated attempts to calculate the figures involved. Doing so is a complex task involving many assumptions, particularly about the elasticity of supply. It is not surprising therefore to find that results vary in detail. More significant, though, is the considerable agreement about the rough outlines of the patterns. In the first place, being part of the imperial system entailed buying and selling at the "company" store and, in the end, this involved Americans in some added expense. The enumerated commodities of the southern colonies, such as rice and tobacco, which were sent to Britain but ultimately sold outside of the empire, were the most heavily burdened. Because tobacco was the single most valuable commodity and because South Carolinians received a bounty on indigo (which was not generally grown in Virginia), Virginians paid the highest price—perhaps 2.5 percent of annual per capita income. However, the burden on Americans in general may have averaged no more than 1 percent. South Carolinians fell somewhere between these two figures. Suffice it to say here that a reasonable estimate places the burden on the rice trade in 1770 at about £120,000 sterling. Though a substantial sum, it obviously did not undermine the prosperity of the colony.

Furthermore, after 1720 South Carolinians exhibited little resentment against imperial economic restraints until the last fifteen years of the colonial period, and even then complaints were frequently directed against restrictive "innovations." Enforcement of regulations requiring that decked vessels clear each voyage with customs officials imposed an impossible requirement on plantation owners; and new bonding procedures governing the shipment of non-enumerated, as well as enumerated, commodities created additional red tape. Being generally innocent of the activities the new procedures were designed to prevent, South Carolinians tended to view them as being unnecessarily burdensome. Worse yet, the new system offered an opportunity for crooked officials to entrap local merchants. In addition, the crown stopped granting land in 1773 while the bureaucrats in London revised policy. Henceforward, it was decided, land would be sold rather than granted gratis. Although the new policy never had a fair trial because of the Revolution, the acting governor reported that Carolinians were much concerned about the temporary closure of the land office.

For the first time in nearly a generation, paper money also became something of an issue when Parliament passed the Currency Act of 1764. Aimed primarily at Virginians and North Carolinians, this legislation forbade the further emission of legal tender paper currency. Perhaps because of their financial sophistication South Carolinians had less trouble adjusting to the restriction than North Carolinians. But, interpretation and enforcement of the act was capricious and unpredictable, and South Carolinians were deeply angered when the crown vetoed their attempt to replace a worn emission already in circulation. Depriving them of it, they believed, was "downright Robbery," the results of which by the early 1770s were compounded by an ongoing dispute with imperial authorities over another matter that prevented the passage of tax acts after 1769 and thereby deprived Carolinians of the annual tax certificates which normally augmented the currency supply.* By this time, they also began to feel that British authorities were jealous of colonial growth and prosperity. The secretary of state, it was reported, even told one South Carolinian, "We must clip your canvas, you increase too fast in shipping. You will soon be too powerful on the water to be governed by the mother country." Relatively petty annoyances also multiplied. British merchandise for the colonial market often seemed to be overpriced and shoddy, whereas colonial indigo in particular, South Carolinians believed, was unjustifiably downgraded in London. Such were the pitfalls of dealing with "the discontented, monopolizing[,] selfish Great Britain," as one merchant-planter termed the mother country. And after the Revolution began, Fourth of July

---

*For the Wilkes Fund controversy see chapter 12; tax certificates are discussed in chapter 6.

orators and others celebrated the fact that vessels from all over the
world could now call at Charles Town. Competition, they predicted,
would lower freight rates to their advantage.

Despite the existence of real grievances as well as the bitterness of
some of these statements, the significance of such concerns should not
be overrated. There were other, more important causes of the Revolution in South Carolina. Furthermore, many of the bitterest comments
came almost as afterthoughts, as if, being angered about something
else, Carolinians added, "and, oh, by the way." Because they con-
gratulated themselves on what might have been an incidental benefit
of the Revolution, it would be wrong to infer that they went to war
to achieve free trade. Nevertheless, historians Joseph Ernst and Marc
Egnal have recently argued that "the time has come to reassert the
essential reasonableness and necessity of the American Revolution in
terms of the overall economic situation of the colonies and of the specific
interests of the actors." More specifically, they maintain that after 1745
the production of British goods increased more rapidly than the capacity
of the colonial market to absorb them. Consequently, British merchants
became more aggressive in pushing their wares, widening their contacts
in the colonies, lowering profit margins, and selling first-class merchandise at auction. American merchants accordingly lost ground,
while colonists generally became more indebted to British suppliers.
In short, to paraphrase John Quincy Adams's famous figure of speech,
in which he later argued that the United States should not be a cockboat
in the wake of the British man of war, the eighteenth-century British
economy had the colonies in tow and was threatening to swamp them.
Although one can raise a number of questions about this interpretation
which are beyond the scope of the present inquiry, the point of view
deserves serious consideration—in part because it is based upon considerable evidence and in part because, as will be discussed later, an
analogous social phenomenon did contribute to the Revolution in South
Carolina.

At first glance, the apparent general prosperity of Carolinians in the
1760s and early 1770s seems to belie this interpretation. Unlike most
Americans to the north, they largely escaped the depression following
the French and Indian War, and despite a rapid rise in imports during
the next decade, exports kept pace. Yet there were significant areas of
concern. Retail trade, for example, was becoming an overcrowded

occupation. As the bookseller-printer, Robert Wells, remarked in the mid-1760s, it was then much harder for a young man to make a start than it had been when he began his career more than a decade earlier. Someone else also jocularly observed that enterprising Scotsmen who came to the colony expecting to become merchants were more apt to wind up as *"shoe-blacks."* Waves of bankruptcies hit even some well established mercantile houses in the mid-1760s and again following a credit crisis in England during 1772. The mounting debt as well as the security problem associated with the importation of new Africans prompted the legislature to impose a prohibitory duty on them which lasted from 1766 to 1768. And then, some scholars would contend, the non-importation movement of the next two years was intended not merely to pressure the British authorities into repealing the Townshend duties but also to protect American merchants from the flood of British goods. Finally, there was a hectic quality to the prosperity of the last few years of the colonial period which at least some Carolinians recognized and deplored. Too much of it, they thought, was based on debt, and too much of it, they feared, represented "luxury" or materialism run amuck. Deciding whether to attribute their resulting posture of resistance primarily to economic or moral concerns involves a difficult distinction.

The most worrisome and pervasive economic concern of South Carolinians involved exports rather than imports. Relatively speaking, the latter affected the livelihood of a comparatively small number of individuals—namely, the merchants who imported and the artisans who competed with them. Others might feel that they had only themselves to blame if their appetites outran their purses. On the other hand, the welfare of the most powerful merchants, as well as of a much larger number of individuals, was more closely tied to the fate of the export sector; and South Carolinians had long been anxious about it. Their anxiety was not merely the result of their experiences during King George's War; it went back to 1704 when Parliament first enumerated rice for the benefit of English merchants. For the next quarter of a century all rice exported from South Carolina had to be shipped within the empire. Most of it went to England, from which it was reexported to the European continent. Although duties were reduced on reexportation and British merchants provided valuable marketing services (such as cleaning the grain), the indirect route increased costs and therefore, to some extent, reduced the size of the market. Carolinians were soon pleading for concessions. In particular, they noted that transshipment through England caused enough delay to make rice arrive in Portugal too late for the Lenten and Easter seasons when it was popular. Bowing to such arguments and the pressure of the British merchants involved, parliament permitted direct shipment to the Iberian Peninsula after 1730.

The ultimate destination of most rice, however, was still the towns of northern Germany and the Low Countries. Lobbying in hopes of widening the market therefore continued, and once again, it partially paid off when in 1763 Parliament allowed South Carolinians and Georgians to retain the Caribbean market captured during the French and Indian War but returned to France and Spain at the Peace of Paris. Yet Carolinians remained nervous about the situation, for as they had so often noted earlier, their production continued to be "sufficient for our present markets," which was a euphemistic way of saying that a bumper crop might be a disaster. Removal of the British duty on Carolina rice in 1772 was a good sign, but hopes that Englishmen would become large consumers proved to be abortive. Most starch-makers, Carolinians discovered, "laugh at the Scheme of making Starch from Rice" which one of them planned to try, and an attempt by an ex-Carolinian acting as an overseer of the poor to induce his charges to eat rice only "loaded [him] with execrations for giving them that *'outlandish Meal.'*" Meanwhile, production in Georgia was increasing even faster than in South Carolina, and rice from Georgia was reputed to be of higher quality. Although that report may have been erroneous, the fear of overproduction was not groundless. As late as 1840—long after South Carolinians were free to ship rice anywhere in the world— exports were less than those of the peak colonial years.

Obviously, colonial South Carolinians could not predict the future, but their anxieties are understandable. To argue that nervousness undermined their allegiance to the empire would be to exaggerate, but they could scarcely have failed to note that the unrestricted trade to the Caribbean grew the most rapidly in the late colonial period. Accordingly, their Delphic pronouncements about the Navigation Acts at the Stamp Act Congress and First Continental Congress make sense. Christopher Gadsden, to be sure, left no doubt that he was opposed to making any but the most minimal concessions to Parliament. But observers, who should have been in a position to know, thought that as late as 1774 most South Carolinians still believed that the Navigation Acts were legitimate exercises of imperial authority. Documenting that belief is difficult. Most articulate individuals, it seems, tried to walk a fine line between making concessions that might deprive them of possible gains and offending Parliament to their future disadvantage. Given the prosperity of the colony, British authorities might well have observed that gratitude had a short memory.

South Carolinians would probably have responded that gratitude was not the issue; economic interest was. In theory, the imperial system was supposed to benefit all of its members, and to a remarkable extent it did—witness the prosperity of most of its constituent parts during the eighteenth century. But the resolution of conflicting interests did not occur automatically; rather it was the product of an intense lobbying effort. Each of the colonial legislatures maintained agents in London who were also sometimes members of Parliament. They spoke at least in part for the colonial assemblies; colonial officials might or might not reflect the local point of view, while a plethora of private individuals frequently demonstrated there was no unified thinking on a given subject. Nor were English interests silent. After 1696 the clearing house for these often conflicting demands was the Board of Trade. Though frequently condemned for its lack of power—it was primarily an advisory body—it performed a necessary function reasonably well until the middle of the eighteenth century. By that time, however, special interest groups became more successful in manipulating government policy for their own ends, and the constitutional quarrel with Americans made imperial authorities increasingly deaf to colonial interests in other matters. Thus South Carolinians correctly concluded that when their interests conflicted with those of others closer to the seat of power, they were apt to lose.

Until its breakdown on the eve of the Revolution, the imperial system was a school for lobbyists, and one of its chief lessons appeared to be that the tenacious pursuit of self-interest abroad was essential. That lesson, it seems, was lost on few colonists, who were in general notorious among imperial officials for devotion to their particularistic interests. South Carolinians, however, took the lesson especially to heart because they were so deeply involved in the British commercial system that even minor alterations might have large consequences.

Moreover, being committed to the production of staples which complemented rather than competed with British products, they appear to have assumed that what was good for Carolina was good for the empire. Besides, if anyone had pressed them hard on the matter, they would doubtless have answered that the checkrein maintained in London licensed the colonial pursuit of self-interest. Imperial authorities, on the other hand, believed that such "irresponsibility" on the part of colonials necessitated even tighter controls. Fears for the integrity of the commercial system upon which the strength of the empire seemed to depend therefore blinded imperial authorities to the political evolution of the colonies. It was no accident that the commonwealth system postdated free trade. Meanwhile, South Carolinians and other Americans demanded the virtual equivalent of a commonwealth system partly because the acts of trade codified a subordinate status which was both galling to their pride and worrisome, for it placed ultimate power in the hands of others who could not be counted on to protect colonial interests.

South Carolinians apparently concluded that if others would not look out for them, they would look out for themselves, and the resulting habit proved hard to break. When the First Continental Congress sought to stop the shipment of colonial products to England, most of the South Carolina delegation threatened to walk out unless rice ultimately destined for northern Europe was exempt from the embargo, and Congress reluctantly approved. At the Constitutional Convention in 1787 when Carolinians demonstrated themselves to be equally tenacious in defending slavery—which, John Rutledge maintained, had nothing to do with morality but was merely a matter of economic interest—other Americans once again bowed to their demands in order to achieve unity. Later, however, federal officials and Yankees became increasingly unwilling to make concessions. The avid pursuit of collective self-interest was one thing, it seems, when weakness prohibited rash action by one side or the other, but it turned into something else when the parties no longer felt constrained to compromise. All this is not to imply that South Carolinians went to war in 1775 and 1861 primarily in the pursuit of economic self-interest, though it was doubtless a consideration in each case; it is rather to suggest that Carolinians appear to have learned some of the lessons of the imperial system too well and forgotten them too slowly.

A view of Charles Town prior to 1768, from a nineteenth century engraving after a painting by T. Mellish. *Courtesy of the South Caroliniana Library.*

One of the most important reasons why South Carolinians pursued a singular course in the nineteenth century was their commitment to what they themselves termed the "peculiar" institution of slavery. To blame that on Great Britain would be to imitate Henry Laurens who observed that he had not enslaved blacks, they had Englishmen to thank for that. Congress perhaps wisely dropped Jefferson's comparable indictment of the crown from the final draft of the Declaration of Independence, and scholars should perhaps follow suit. South Carolina developed naturally along lines approved by mercantile doctrine. Indeed, parliamentary regulation usually lagged behind colonial innovation; it was only after rice caught on that Parliament placed it on the enumerated list. Similarly, indigo production antedated the bounty on it. However, membership in an empire in which colonists were supposed to grow staples encouraged them to do precisely that; and in part because contemporaries believed that rice in particular could not be grown without slave labor, South Carolinians became the most heavily committed to slavery of all North Americans.

Furthermore, because rice and indigo made them rich, Carolinians developed a planting society with characteristics closely related to the production of these crops. To be sure, the backcountry produced almost no rice and a relatively small part of the indigo. The chief inland villages of Camden and Ninety Six developed after 1750 as milling, trading, and, later, courthouse towns. Similarly, Beaufort and George-town were founded to provide export facilities for naval stores and lumber. But the naval stores industry largely fizzled after the 1720s, and lumber was never an especially lucrative commodity. Thus both ports remained small and not very prosperous until rice and indigo became important crops in their vicinities. By this time it was too late for these towns to achieve a major role in the transatlantic trade; and their combined exports may never have exceeded 8 percent of the indigo and 7 percent of the rice shipped annually. Charles Town was therefore the dominant commercial center of the colony, and, as might be expected, it exhibited many characteristics which were scarcely specific to the production of these particular staples. By the end of the colonial period, for instance, Charles Town had become enough of a financial center to offer marine insurance, and to a far greater extent than is often realized, it was a seafaring town. As early as 1720, the governor noted that at the height of the shipping season in February and March more than 500 seamen were ashore; by 1765, his successors reported, the number had almost tripled. The mystery of more than 100 "tippling houses" in a town of 1,300 dwellings five years later seems to be solved. What is not clear at this point, though, is how many of these sailors were Carolinians. One's first reaction is to assume that not very many were, but local vessels played a prominent part in the growing West Indian trade. A contemporary "Account of the Number of Seamen Employed in the Merchant Service at the Several Ports in America" compiled for British authorities gave Charles Town 350 in 1771, and this figure almost certainly did not include slaves, of which there were quite a few. Moreover, Charles Town was a city of boarding houses and rental property for the accommodation of sailors, legislators, and planters' families whose seasonal peregrinations were tied to the shipping, legislative, and social seasons.

Despite all of these qualifications, the fact remains that such seasonal activities were themselves dependent on the agricultural cycle, and even such an ostensibly quintessential urban characteristic as rental housing had roots in the rice fields; for men and women came to Charles Town partly to escape the fevers associated with the lowcountry swamps. The permanent population of the town was relatively small—thanks again partly to the nature of the rice and indigo trades. Because both commodities were processed and packed on the plantation, neither required much more than warehousing facilities in Charles Town. And because so much of the trade in each focused on England, British owners supplied most of the shipping and British merchants performed most of the final market services. Thus as one historian, Jacob Price, has recently observed, perhaps a bit too categorically, Charles Town tended to be "a mere 'shipping point' rather than a real 'commercial center'"; and despite a larger volume of trade than New York (measured by the value of exports and imports as well as the tonnage of shipping), the population of the southern city in 1770 was only about 11,000 or less than half that of its northern counterpart. Compared to New York, the cost of living was reputed to be considerably higher in Charles Town, and craftsmen engaged in the luxury trades made up a conspicuous part of the small permanent population. The explanation appears to rest on the fact that the two staples were the source of a great deal of wealth in the eighteenth century.

Given the importance of these commodities, it is startling to discover that the record rice crop of the colonial period—that of 1770 when approximately 137,400 barrels totaling about 36,000 tons was shipped from South Carolina—was doubtless grown on no more than 110,000 acres by less than 37,000 slaves, or slightly under 50 percent of the black population and 3 percent of the land in private hands. The figures for indigo are even more striking. By the end of the colonial period, at peak production, South Carolinians probably planted about 19,000 acres of indigo, which could have been cultivated by less than 10,000 slaves or about 13 percent of the blacks.* In fact, nearly two-thirds of the total crop exported in 1774 was shipped in two vessels.

Although there are other possibilities which might account for these figures, they suggest that if the average staple-producing plantation worked thirty or so prime field hands, fewer than 2,000 plantations could easily have accounted for most of the rice and indigo production. Because both operations could involve a considerable capital outlay, such a concentration of productive capacity might be expected. To what extent it prevailed will be dealt with during the course of the following two chapters about slavery and white society.

---

*These estimates of the resources employed in the production of rice and indigo are intended to be conservative in the context of the present discussion—that is, if they err, they err on the side of overestimating the number of slaves and acres involved. Thus it is assumed that one-third of the rice crop was consumed locally (which is in the upper range of contemporary guesses), that a full hand could cultivate three acres of rice or two of indigo, and that an acre yielded 1,000 pounds of rice or 50 pounds of indigo. Both the task and yield figures are from the lower range of contemporary estimates. Annual exports of indigo averaged approximately 934,700 pounds during the last two years of the colonial period, and there were about 75,000 slaves in 1770. Nearly 3.3 million acres were returned for taxes in 1769, the last year for which figures are extant. It should also be noted that slaves frequently cultivated rice and indigo simultaneously; given the relatively light tasks per slave employed in the present estimates, one cannot assume that nearly two-thirds of the black population was composed of full hands employed exclusively in cultivating these two crops. Slaves normally also raised "their own provisions," as one contemporary phrased it, and scattered records from individual plantations suggest that the proportion of full hands may not have greatly exceeded 40 percent of the black population.

8

BLACKS, WHITES, AND SLAVERY

More than 40 percent of all blacks who came to North America from 1700 to the end of the colonial period probably came through Charles Town, and Sullivan's Island, where they underwent quarantine, has been aptly termed "the Ellis Island of black Americans." Like the nineteenth and twentieth century immigrants who passed through New York on the way to other destinations, many blacks who landed in Charles Town eventually went to other colonies. Perhaps 75,000 remained in South Carolina, where, for well over the last half of the colonial period, they made up more than one-half of the population. Their story is therefore not just an integral part of the history of the colony; it is one of the most important parts. Until recently, however, historians knew surprisingly little about it, and the depth of our current understanding still by no means matches the significance of the subject. The problem stems from both the elusive nature of the source material and the complexities of a historical situation in some ways paradoxical and anomalous enough to merit Winston Churchill's famous description of the Kremlin: "a riddle, wrapped in a mystery, inside an enigma." Nevertheless, a number of historians have demonstrated recently what ingenuity and patience can do in resolving these problems.

One reason the topic is so complex is that slavery was not the same in the colonial as it was in the antebellum period, nor was it static during the colonial period itself. It was, however, legal in South Carolina from the very beginning in 1670, and it is perhaps significant that one of the first Englishmen to import slaves in any number seems to have been Sir John Yeamans, who embodied the early planters' ethos. Ruthless and tough, he appears to have been out to make a pound at all costs; but no lucrative commercial crop like sugar emerged for more than a generation. Thus the demand for slaves was limited, and most who came to the colony probably arrived, as did Yeamans', in relatively small numbers with their owners. Being comparatively few, they did not inspire fear, and the contrast between the situation in South Carolina and that in Barbados, where blacks out-numbered whites by perhaps two to one at this time, made masters more permissive than they might otherwise have been. Certainly, they felt no need to enact a complete slave code until 1696. Meanwhile, blacks enjoyed a considerable degree of autonomy in the frontier environment where their woodcraft skills were at a premium. Thus, ironically, the cowboy who ranged the woods alone is as much the archetype of the black Carolinian in this era as Yeamans was of the exploitative planter. In fact, as one historian, Peter Wood, has suggested, blacks in Carolina may well have been the source of the term "cowboy" itself.

Although black cowboys existed all through the colonial period, conditions began to change for the majority of slaves in the 1690s as planters developed exports which could be produced on a large scale. Whether rice or naval stores were primarily responsible for the first rapid increase in the slave population is not entirely clear; both appear to have contributed simultaneously. Together their production provided an almost insatiable demand for labor. As an aspiring planter remarked in 1701, merely the timber on his land would yield more than £10,000 sterling, "but I can make little advantage of it till I can compass a good gang of Negroes." If the demand for blacks was there, so was the supply. From 1672 to 1698 the Royal African Company (with which several of the original Carolina proprietors were affiliated) possessed a monopoly on supplying slaves to the colonial market. A combination of rising demand throughout the empire and pressure from aggressive merchants who wanted a share of the market led Parliament to open the trade to all English vessels. As a result, slavery in South Carolina flourished like the proverbial green bay-tree.

By 1708 half of the population, exclusive of Indians, was black; by 1720 the proportion was two-thirds and in several lowcountry parishes there might have been seven or eight slaves to every white person. Thereafter, the situation changed little in the older areas, while new districts in the lowcountry assumed similar demographic profiles. Not until the Revolutionary era was the racial balance again about equal, and then it was because of a heavy influx of white settlers into the upcountry after 1750. The migration did not affect black-white ratios in the lowcountry itself. Much of colonial South Carolina resembled the West Indies more than most of the other mainland colonies, none of which—including Georgia—ever had such a heavy preponderance of blacks.

The great demand and rising percentage of slaves in the population changed the character of slavery. Once most incoming slaves were being purchased rather than brought with their masters, fears developed that South Carolina might become the dumping ground for sick and rebellious slaves from other colonies. The Duty Act of 1703 therefore imposed lower duties on slaves imported directly from Africa, and subsequent acts continued that policy throughout the colonial period. More than 80 percent of all slaves coming to South Carolina came directly from Africa, and because English merchants handled most of the transatlantic trade, they came mainly on English vessels. It may have been small comfort for the blacks to learn that their accommodations were somewhat better than if they had arrived on American ships, for the English slavers were generally larger and more seaworthy; certainly the trade subjected Africans to almost indescribable conditions. Just as Indian traders relied on Indians to provide captives for enslavement, Europeans purchased slaves from Africans who, having kidnapped, captured, or otherwise acquired them, conducted the merchandise to trading posts or "factories" on the western coast of Africa. Such deliveries sometimes involved relatively long treks from the interior during which slaves were tied together with leather thongs around their necks. Those who could not keep up were left to die by the side of the trail; those who made it to the factories waited until sufficient numbers had been assembled to make a cargo.

Cargoes varied in size with the size of the ship and exhibited considerable variation. But during four randomly selected years (1731, 1753, 1760, and 1769) the average ship brought, respectively, 70, 50, 170, and 69 slaves to Charles Town. In most cases, one can be sure that these vessels left Africa with many more individuals aboard. Mortality on the middle passage—the second leg of the round trip voyage from England to Africa to America and home—depended on a number of factors, such as the weather and the time in transit, and was sometimes suprisingly light. Moreover, with increasing experience and better sanitation over the years, the death rate declined during the eighteenth century. In fact, the slaves appear to have benefited more from these changes than the crews, and by the end of the period mortality among the latter was often higher than among the slaves. Yet when all is said and done, the stark fact remains that perhaps one in six slaves died on the middle passage, and for some ships the toll was far worse. Sharks, it was said, followed the wakes of these vessels clear across the Atlantic, waiting for the corpses to be thrown overboard.

That there were not even more deaths is astonishing, considering the conditions. Slave vessels frequently had platforms built between decks on which slaves were stacked like cordwood or "books on a library shelf," as one contemporary observed. Sometimes without room to sit up, much less stand, each man might have floor space measuring as little as 16 inches by 6 feet (women got 5 ft. 10 in.). Toilet facilities, if they existed at all, were open tubs. When dysentery struck, as it frequently did, the result is best described in the words of Alexander Falconbridge who later served as a surgeon aboard a slaving vessel. "The floor of their rooms, was so covered with the blood and mucus which had proceeded from them in consequence of the flux, that it resembled a slaughterhouse. It was not in the power of the human imagination to picture to itself a situation more dreadful or disgusting." In good weather, the slaves were brought on deck, where the men were chained and all were made to exercise to the beat of a cat o' nine tails. In bad weather, all remained below and the hatches were closed. That many who survived such voyages—which frequently took up to six weeks—were so weakened that they died soon after arriving in South Carolina is scarcely astonishing; what is perhaps more surprising is that enough of the dead were thrown overboard in the port of Charles Town in 1769 to prompt the governor to issue a proclamation against the practice. Truly, as one visitor observed, the "Guinea captains" were "a rough set of people."

The reception awaiting newly arrived blacks was also harsh, especially if they came during winter. Finding that many died then, slave traders adjusted their schedules to import most slaves during the summer when there was also a ready demand for labor to help with cultivation and the coming harvest. After undergoing a short quarantine on Sullivan's Island, slaves were sold. Usually an entire cargo was put up for sale on a given date and planters frequently traveled long distances to attend. They were reluctant to leave without purchasing and in most cases, it seems, the entire shipload might be sold during the course of the day. Whether most slaves went by ones and two or in larger lots is not clear. At an average price of about £30 sterling during the mid-eighteenth century, slaves were expensive, yet South Carolina planters were frequently and accurately reputed to be affluent; and there is considerable documentation of sales in lots of ten or twelve. One might therefore guess that most sales involved one or two slaves but that most slaves were sold with several others.

Endured alone or in company, the process was traumatic. Those who survived to be sold in Charles Town might well have seen some of their companions kill themselves rather than go aboard the slave ships; others may have died at sea in revolts; and many who lived to tell about it appear to have believed that they would be eaten upon arrival. Comprehending that this was not the case undoubtedly took some time and may actually have involved a psychological letdown. Not only had these men and women nerved themselves to face impending death but many apparently believed that afterwards they would return to Africa. Instead, shorn of their previous status and material possessions, they faced an alien and demanding world. No wonder that some committed suicide, like the "poor, pining creature" who was so emaciated that she could hang herself with a small vine. This was survival of the fittest with a vengeance, and in all probability for every person who lived to become a slave in the New World, there was one who died along the way. That any survived testifies to the resiliency of the human spirit and the physical stamina of these Africans.

That in actuality many survived also suggests that African cultural traditions supported them in the valley of the shadow of death. How these traditions might have been a source of strength is readily apparent from the words of a survivor. Olaudah Equiano was an Ibo from Benin who spent many years as a slave before the mast, during which he visited Charles Town. Eventually acquiring his freedom, he published a narrative of his life in 1790. Among the Ibo, he noted, ceremonies created a strong communal bond. "We are almost a nation of dancers, musicians, and poets," he wrote. "Thus every great event, such as a triumphant return from battle, or other cause of public rejoicing is celebrated in public dances, which are accompanied with songs and music suited to the occasion." Regarding religion, he continued, "the natives believe that there is one Creator of all things, and that he lives in the sun, and is girded round with a belt that he may never eat or drink.... They believe he governs events, especially our deaths or captivity." Such beliefs and ceremonies gave meaning to life and coherence to the community. Although only a relatively small percentage of slaves in South Carolina came from the same region as Equiano, similar observations apply to many African societies. Despite significant variations in their belief systems, most—like the Indians'—were well integrated internally and therefore self-reinforcing, and in all probability, extremely durable. Certainly, later colonial administrators often described Africans as "this incurably religious people." Thus a newly enslaved individual did not stand entirely naked to his captors.

Precisely how much African culture persisted through the middle passage and the initial years of slavery has been the subject of scholarly controversy, and though it is now conceded to be more than was only recently thought to have been the case, many scholars would still probably agree with Richard Hofstadter's contention that what Africans "had been and known receded rapidly, and the course of their experience tended to reduce their African identity to the withered husks of dead memories." His words are nearly as eloquent as the experiences were tragic, and they may accurately describe the situation in some of the North American colonies. There are reasons to believe, however, that in this, as in so much else, South Carolina was somewhat different. In the first place, the rapid importation of slaves after about 1700 made for an unusually high proportion of Africans in the black population. By the end of the 1730s, in fact, well over half of the slaves were undoubtedly African-born. Although the percentage declined somewhat thereafter, it remained relatively high—thanks largely to the importation of nearly 42,000 Africans between 1760 and 1774. Blacks from the south-western coast of Africa, loosely called Angola, were the largest single group, perhaps partly because planters in the West Indies disliked them and suppliers consequently sent them to South Carolina.

From 1735 to 1740, 70 percent of the imports came from this area of Africa; and despite the prominence of Angolans in the most serious rebellion of the colonial period, South Carolinians continued to purchase them in large numbers. Neary 40 percent of all imports from 1733 to the end of the slave trade in 1807 were still Angolans. During the later period, the next largest contingents were from Senegambia (19.5 percent), the Windward Coast (16.3 percent), and the Gold Coast (13.3 percent). The slave trade through each of these West African areas drew from a considerable hinterland, but the fact that the African origins of most slaves in South Carolina were not randomly distributed increased the chance of a black encountering his own countrymen. So too did the distribution of slaveholdings within the colony.

Although the evidence is sparse, it suggests that, from the 1720s on, more than half of the slaves were owned by the largest planters. In some areas of the lowcountry there might be more than twenty slaves for every white adult male; at times more than 50 percent of them were African-born; most of them were owned by planters who probably purchased them in sizable lots and held relatively large numbers; and, finally, most Africans came from fairly localized areas. Given the demographic situation, there was probably a greater chance, in some cases, that a slave would be among his own tribesmen than that he would encounter his master after arriving at a plantation.

Nor is this supposition as preposterous as it may appear at first sight. That new Africans frequently ran away in groups of their own countrymen and that ethnic cleavages affected the dynamics of some revolts suggest that tribal identity did at times achieve the level of a critical mass. Moreover, many slaves undoubtedly had masters who kept a low profile on the plantation. Among wealthier planters, absenteeism was frequent, partly because of extended visits to Charles Town and elsewhere and partly because many of them owned several plantations. Moreover, sufficiently large single tracts were usually broken up into distinct "settlements" of about thirty slaves each. Given the difficulties of travel in a region interspersed with swamps, these satellite settlements were often quite isolated.

Even resident planters probably had no more contact with the slaves than necessary. Certainly most of their recorded comments betray little knowledge of African customs and life. (Even their preferences for

blacks from certain areas were often based on stereotypes and phy-
sique.)* "Familiarity breeds contempt" was the saying then as now;
and the main purpose of the enterprise was production. Anything which
might interfere with that was to be avoided if possible. In many ways
the situation was analogous to that of a vessel at sea, where in theory
the captain possessed virtually unlimited power, yet in practice, as
countless seafaring tales make clear, he overstepped certain customary
bounds only at the risk of jeopardizing the efficiency of the crew and
his own safety. Similarly, more than one planter who overworked his
slaves found his barn mysteriously burned down. Why take such risks
when the issue was of less consequence to a master than to his slaves?
A prudent planter did not meddle much with the private lives of his
slaves. Thus the colonial authorities refused to send 130 women slaves
to Virginia in return for help in fighting the Yamasee Indians. To
have done so, they sagely observed, was "impracticable" because of
"the Discontent such Usage would have given their husbands . . . which
might have occasioned a Revolt."

As this episode illustrates, the relationship between masters and
slaves involved something akin to negotiation, and blacks did much
to shape the conditions of their own lives. One would therefore like
to know more about the origins of two institutions that enabled a
planter to keep his distance, on the one hand, and slaves to maintain
considerable autonomy, on the other. Though not exclusively confined
to South Carolina, each was considerably more common there than in
other mainland colonies (though both became widespread in the antebellum period). One was the task system; the other was the use of
a driver. Under the task system, each slave worked at a job usually
assigned daily by the driver. Although slaves themselves, drivers occupied posts of considerable respect and authority. In many cases, they
knew more about the day-to-day operation of the plantation than the
owner, and planters often recognized this. Not a few masters, in fact,
ignored the law stipulating that no plantation was to be operated
without a white man on the premises, and, for all practical purposes,

---

*A preference for Senegambians, who came from a region of Africa in which rice
was cultivated, suggests the possibility—as Daniel Littlefield has recently argued—
that planters may have been more knowledgeable about such matters than the literary
evidence reveals.

blacks served as overseers in these cases. Indeed, even when an overseer was present, drivers or other skilled slaves, such as those who were expert in the making of indigo, might have a decisive voice, for just a slight miscalculation in timing could ruin the better part of a crop. Incidentally, the same principle applied with still greater force to the operation of plantation schooners. Nothing inverted the "normal" master-slave relationship so clearly and so regularly, especially when women and children were involved, for the technical skill of the patroons who commanded these vessels gave them effective as well as nominal authority. Many a white therefore waited for wind and tide—and the boatman.

These inherently interesting anomalies in the system are especially significant in the present context because they provide clues to how the task system and the use of drivers in South Carolina may have originated. At least four plausible explanations come to mind: West Indian precedent, geography, early practice, and African skills. Drivers were employed on the sugar plantations of the Caribbean, and South Carolinians might simply have carried over the practice. But there slaves worked primarily in gangs, and fields tended to be fairly large. In South Carolina, on the other hand, the activities associated with the first large importations of slaves dispersed workers over wide areas, especially in the naval stores industry which required that workers range through the woods. Even many of the early rice fields were relatively small and scattered. Thus masters who could not be everywhere at once may have found it convenient to delegate authority to drivers, whose job was in turn simplified by assigning tasks to individual slaves. If so, the widespread adoption of these practices on plantations may have represented merely slight modifications of an already established pattern. As previously discussed, when slaves were few their work had not been highly regimented. Moreover, it often involved traditional skills. Africans from pastoral societies would have made "natural" cowboys, and the best way to benefit from their expertise would have been to let them go about their business. Later the same was true of rice, which was widely cultivated in some areas of Africa. As Peter Wood has also plausibly suggested, blacks may have played a crucial role in helping to introduce the crop. Undoubtedly, however, the subsequent rapid increase in the number of slaves, many of whom spoke no English, vastly complicated the problem of tapping their skills and familiarizing them with developing plantation routines. If there were no natural leaders among the blacks who could act as intermediaries, planters would have been obliged to try to create them. It is scarcely an exaggeration to observe that the situation was in some ways roughly similar to that which prevailed in the late nineteenth and early twentieth centuries with European laborers, large numbers of whom immigrated to the United States speaking no English. In that case, the intermediary was the *padrone* or boss who marshaled his countrymen; in this, his counterpart may often have been the driver.

Who were the early drivers and whence came their authority? Neither question has an easy answer. Clearly they had to have the support of the master. Thus a standing rule on many antebellum plantations was that any disciplinary action against a driver implying loss of confidence was to be accompanied by removal from his post. By that time, however, generations of slaves had been born and reared in slavery and the master loomed large in countless subtle as well as obvious ways. In the colonial period his ancestors often dealt with new Africans who had little reason to be impressed with anything about him except his power. Though sheer force may be more effective in bending one man to the will of another than one would prefer to believe, there are frequently more efficient ways of doing it. Thus a driver who could lead as well as drive would have been an invaluable, if perhaps dangerous, man. Like his descendants in the antebellum period, who have been aptly described as "men between," a driver stood between the master and the other slaves. In the early eighteenth century, especially, he also stood between white South Carolinians and Africans and that, one suspects, gave him a considerably stronger position vis-à-vis the master. Surely, he was a key man. That scholars still know relatively little about these individuals in a personal sense is therefore especially frustrating. Logic suggests that many of them were experienced slaves; some of them may have been Indians and perhaps even in some cases Indian women. But logic also suggests that someone with more immediate ties to blacks might have been more effective, and it is not surprising to discover that preliminary research by other historians indicates that the drivers' authority may have been in part patrilineal. They often appear on the inventories of estates as the men with the largest families. Despite questions about which was cause and which was effect and possible biases in the records (drivers' families may not necessarily have been larger but only more consistently and completely recorded), the hypothesis is plausible.

At this stage perhaps the safest thing to say about the drivers' authority is that, like almost everything else in the system of slavery, it evolved out of the interaction of masters and slaves. If perhaps a few drivers were the natural leaders among relatively recent arrivals, more experienced and Americanized slaves doubtless were the chief transmitters of the Afro-American culture. In all probability, the crucial formative years of this culture were the late seventeenth century, when close contact and a relatively easy familiarity between master and slave characterized the experience of many blacks. As a result, they acquired numerous English cultural characteristics and proceeded to pass these on to those who arrived later. Undoubtedly, language was one of those traits. Quite literally, enslaved Africans spoke dozens of distinct languages and dialects, including Arabic. To facilitate the slave trade a kind of trade jargon or pidgin embodying some Portuguese and Dutch as well as English words developed along the coasts of Africa. (Use of the term "pidgin" by linguistic scholars implies no invidious distinctions; rather, it connotes "any speech evolved from several languages and used by speakers for whom it is not the primary tongue.") The process of "pidginization" then continued during the middle passage and in South Carolina itself, where a few slaves even had French- or German-speaking masters. Out of this veritable Tower of Babel evolved the predecessors of modern black English in general and Gullah in particular. Still spoken on some of the sea islands of South Carolina and Georgia, Gullah is intelligible to white natives but hard for the unpracticed ear to understand. Conversely, blacks, to whom Gullah had become a native tongue, thought that Yankees whom they encountered during the Civil War spoke strangely.

Despite these difficulties in communication, Gullah had predominantly English and African roots. Quantifying the proportion of each is difficult, in part because some African and English words sound alike. Tybee and tabby, for example, are almost certainly borrowed words. The former, which became the name for an island near the mouth of the Savannah River, means "fertile, low-lying farmland"; the latter refers to a kind of masonry construction in which lime from burnt oyster shells and sand are the main ingredients. "Tabax" referred to similarly constructed houses in Africa. That the term should have been applied to a form of construction especially characteristic of the sea island cotton plantations developed in the 1790s and early 1800s proves little, of course, but it suggests the tenacity of the Africanisms in Gullah speech. To perhaps an even greater extent, the same could be said about personal names. Africans frequently named children after the day of birth. That his man was called Friday therefore did not necessarily mean that the master chose the name; nor did the prevalance of names like Cuba and Joe, for the former meant Wednesday and the latter was often a variant of Cudjo, signifying Monday.

The frequent occurrence of such names—along with purely African ones such as Bungey and Cumbo—was doubtless symptomatic of an attempt to retain not only African identities but also patterns of family life. Although some African societies were matrilineal, in most, men were polygamous and patrilinealism prevailed. In South Carolina, however, these characteristics collided with the realities of slavery. Here, the planter, not the immediate head of household, ultimately controlled the fate of the family, and he might or might not choose to recognize slave marriages as binding. Normally, one would assume, he tried to do so. Not only was it prudent not to interfere with such matters, but stable family life tended to promote fertility. Furthermore, the established church as well as more diffuse English cultural traditions considered marriage to be the "normal" thing. Nevertheless, however much a planter might wish to promote it, economic pressures might override other considerations while he was alive, and his executors might divide slaves along with other property after his death. Furthermore, planters were not apt to be interested in promoting polygamy, especially when there were not enough women to go around. Because two out of every three blacks shipped from Africa were men, the sex ratio among imports into South Carolina undoubtedly remained imbalanced, though not as markedly as in the West Indies where planters appear to have been more reluctant to buy women. This difference, incidentally, may help to explain why the rate of natural increase in South Carolina was higher than on the islands. Nevertheless, polygamy could not flourish under the prevailing conditions, and neither could patrilinealism. Enslavement compromised the father's authority, and in the event that separating families became necessary, planters were more apt to keep women and children together. Thus subtle as well as obvious pressures tended to undermine the position of men and elevate that of women.

The presence of hundreds of Indian women in the slave population may also have contributed to this trend. Having enjoyed a comparatively privileged position and virtual immunity from coercion in their own societies, these women were doubtless reluctant to subordinate themselves to men who were also slaves. Equally important, the imbalanced sex ratio gave all women substantial leverage. Ironically, slavery therefore probably represented a kind of partial liberation for black women. Doubtless few would not have said the price was too high.

Traditional religious beliefs may have been more resistant to change. Maintaining the old forms in a polyglot environment under the most adverse conditions was undoubtedly difficult, but preliterate beliefs are often relatively impervious to experience. Indeed, experiences which one might think would weaken them may actually have the opposite effect as threatened peoples reaffirm old values. Furthermore, however much missionaries may have wished to convert slaves, most planters were more interested in profits. Thus religion was the quintessential area in which it would have been folly for a master to risk gratuitous coercion. Even to force slaves to attend church on Sunday was to invite trouble because of the encroachment on an otherwise free day. These considerations, one suspects, had as much to do with the planters' notorious indifference to converting their slaves as the more traditionally cited fear that the tenets of Christianity might make blacks restive or that professing the Christian religion might automatically make them free. There was no real danger of the latter from a legal point of view after passage of an act in 1712 stipulating the contrary, and as some contemporaries clearly recognized, Christianity might be an opiate as well as a stimulant.

In any case, before about 1740 most slaves appear to have been as uninterested in being converted as their masters were in converting them. Anglican missionaries also complicated their own task by insisting that slaves be educated in the beliefs of the Church before being baptised. As a result of all these factors, traditional African practices, including witchcraft and obeah—that is, the use of sorcery to discover and punish personal enemies—persisted. Many Anglican ministers therefore gave up trying to reach adults and, instead, concentrated on children. As Alexander Garden observed, "as 'mong us Religious Instruction usually descends from Parents to Children, so among them it must at first ascend from Children to Parents, or from Young to Old." Believing that there should be a slave on each plantation who could read the Bible and the Book of Common Prayer, Garden persuaded the Society for the Propagation of the Gospel to provide funds, and early in the 1740s he purchased two young men whom he trained to be teachers of other slaves. Although one of the preceptors failed to work out and the other eventually went mad, Garden established a school for blacks in Charles Town which lasted for more than twenty years; and his spadework may have borne some delayed fruit in the Revolutionary era when, for the first time, Christianity made real headway among the slaves. The large number of converts then made by the Baptist and Methodist churches suggests that the evangelical style and message possessed more appeal for slaves, perhaps in part because the conversion experience sometimes appeared to have affinities to traditional forms of spirit "possession" known in Africa.

Although the Great Awakening had relatively little effect among blacks in South Carolina, it was more important than historians sometimes realize, perhaps because its permanent effects tended to be localized while its general impact was temporary. Yet among the Baptists from Delaware who settled on the Pee Dee River in 1737, the Awakening was a vital ideal, and, significantly, their church had a substantial number of black members by the 1770s. Tax returns also indicate that this area contained perhaps the largest number of free blacks.* Realization that religious enthusiasm could pose a real danger to a slave society quickly quenched more widely publicized manifestations of zeal. For in the early 1740s a prominent surveyor and planter, Hugh Bryan, began having mystical experiences which prompted him to speak to large gatherings of blacks in the southern part of the province. At these meetings, it was reputed, he assured slaves that they would someday be free. Dangerous doctrine at any time, this was intolerable to many South Carolinians only shortly after the most serious slave revolt of the century. The legislature investigated, and Bryan, having seen the error of his ways, promised to cease his activities. Rumor also reported that he had attempted to part the waters like Moses and almost drowned. Whether accurate or not, the story served to discredit his efforts.

---

*For the possibility that tax returns may not be an accurate index to the actual number of free blacks, see the subsequent discussion of the topic in this chapter.

Thereafter, attempts at Christian fraternization by men of prominence were rare.

Despite the efforts of Bryan and a few others, blacks remained largely as they had been described twenty years earlier—"a Nation within a Nation," neither wholly African nor more than partly English in culture. The physical conditions under which they lived were often appalling. Clothing was usually scanty and coarse, and, had their diets not been supplemented by their own efforts, food would not have been much better. Rice too small and broken to sell as well as dried peas, beans, and corn were the basic staples. Medical care, on the other hand, was often surprisingly good by the standards of the day as masters sought to protect their investment, and at least one physician advertised that he maintained a hospital for slaves in Charles Town. Given counterproductive seventeenth and eighteenth century treatments such as bleeding, most slaves probably would have preferred to take their chances with their own remedies and practitioners, and they might well have been better off. Quarters varied from hovels to brick cabins which might house two to four families. Work was hard and dangerous. Tar kilns sometimes exploded, and mucking about in the humid rice swamps when the temperature was 95° in the shade was anything but easy. Even processing indigo was unpleasant for it created a stench that drew millions of flies. For white men, it was perhaps conveniently reputed, such work was certain death, and they would not do it in sufficient numbers at low enough rates to make it profitable. So blacks were compelled to labor at it. Malaria and yellow fever might not kill them as swiftly and as surely as whites, but in the 1720s and 1730s, especially, the death rates were high as the workload increased. During these two decades the black population roughly tripled, but the amount of rice land under cultivation may have quintupled.

It is not surprising to find that one historian has found that a black population "which had been increasing at a rate of 5.6 per cent per annum before 1720 appears to have been decreasing at a rate of 1.1 per cent per annum over the next twenty years." How these figures compare with those for the remainder of the colonial period must await the still unpublished work of other researchers, but it is doubtful that their findings will be so grim. By the eighteenth century slaves were increasing naturally around Chesapeake Bay, and if health conditions in South Carolina were worse, there is reason to believe that the sex ratio was nearly as favorable. Moreover, the pell-mell development of new rice land slackened somewhat after 1740. Thus one would expect perhaps a small natural increase to have been the rule in South Carolina from 1740 to 1775. That officials sometimes estimated the size of the black population by merely taking a known figure at a given date and adding subsequent imports suggests that the rate of natural growth was not large. In short, slavery in South Carolina stood somewhere between slavery in Virginia and in the islands of the Caribbean, where the rule of thumb for figuring depreciation assumed a useful life of five to seven years. Slavery there has been aptly described as "physically more cruel and debilitating than Negro bondage in the English main-land settlements, yet psychologically perhaps less traumatic." Appropriately modified to make the comparison with Virginia, that description applies equally well to South Carolina.

Despite the rigors of their lives, blacks in South Carolina possibly enjoyed the most personal autonomy of slaves anywhere in North America. Sunday was a day off everywhere; sometimes part of Saturday was too. In South Carolina, moreover, the task system permitted additional free time during the week. The amount varied with the efficiency of the slave, his relationship with the driver who assigned the work, the season of the year, and numerous other considerations, but it could be considerable. Visitors to the rice districts in the nineteenth century frequently noted that slaves had completed their assigned tasks and were through for the day by 2:00 P.M. By then, more efficient methods of tidal cultivation were widely used, and it is doubtful that their colonial predecessors had as much free time. Nevertheless, it was sufficient in many cases to permit the raising of garden vegetables and sometimes poultry for sale as well as home consumption. Indeed, disgruntled whites complained that blacks threatened to dominate the city market. Boatmen, as one would expect, often had a great deal of latitude in their comings and goings, but the same seems to have been true to a surprising extent of even some plantation slaves who, on occasion, loaned guns to whites. There were laws against such things, to be sure, but they had loopholes and were regularly honored in the breach. Blacks frequently managed plantations in violation of the law, and there were only scattered attempts to enforce the act requiring at least one white for every ten blacks on a plantation.

In town, controls were even looser. Slaves frequently hired out their

"Mulberry Castle," built by Thomas Broughton about 1714, as it appeared nearly one hundred years later in a painting by Thomas Coram. Brick slave quarters were unusual. *Courtesy of the Carolina Art Association.*

own time, and black laborers had a regular stand at which they waited for the day's work, the rates for which were supposedly set by law. In 1763 black chimney sweeps raised their prices and refused to work unless customers met their demands. To the periodic dismay of the grand juries, blacks regularly frequented many of the taverns in Charles Town. To the additional distress of grand juries as well as others, blacks also habitually met and socialized in large numbers—and that, too, in violation of the laws. One author, writing in the *South Carolina Gazette* in 1772, described such a gathering. It was a "Country-Dance, Rout, or Cabal of *Negroes*," held just outside of Charles Town one Saturday night. "It consisted of about 60 people, 5-6th from Town, every one of whom carried something . . . ; as, bottled liquors of all sorts, Rum, Tongues, Hams, Beef, Geese, Turkies and Fowls . . . with many luxuries of the table, as sweetmeats, pickles &c." Entertainment included "the men copying (or *taking off*) the manners of their masters, and the women those of their mistresses, and relating some highly curious anecdotes, to the inexpressible diversion of that company." Dancing and games of chance followed. The author also observed several private conferences, which alarmed him, and he finished his description by asking, "Whenever or wherever such noctural rendezvouses are made, may it not be concluded, that their deliberations are never intended for the advantage of the white people?" As the author clearly saw, the interstices in the system were wide enough to permit what he considered to be far too much de facto freedom, and the slaves obviously knew how to exploit their opportunities to the maximum. What the author did not recognize, though, was that maintenance of the system may have depended partly on its looseness.

The test came during the Revolutionary War when the British invaded the state. Although they offered eventual freedom to slaves who would desert to them from rebel masters, wholesale desertions did not ensue. Nor, despite a scare or two among whites, did insurrections. It is true that, just before the evacuation of Charles Town, in 1782, the British commander noted that there were 4,000 black loyalists among the refugees, and South Carolinians later estimated that they had lost 20,000 to 25,000 slaves during the conflict. But at least 6,000 appear to have been removed from the state by loyalist masters, and others were stolen by Whigs as well as by the British. Many slaves also died from disease and malnutrition. Thus it is almost impossible to estimate how many actually tried to join the British, let alone determine why. Many of those in British hands undoubtedly came from plantations which were in the path of the opposing armies. Even if all who may have fled plantations because their food supply was impressed did so because British authorities promised freedom, and all slave losses represented runaways to freedom, about three-quarters of the blacks in South Carolina still remained with their masters. If they pushed harder at the limitations on their freedom—which they did—most slaves exploited their opportunities within the system in the traditional manner.

Why more did not take radical action is an intriguing question. Answers tend to fall into two main categories. Perhaps the Draconian provisions of the 1740 slave code and the repression that followed were sufficiently harsh to intimidate slaves, and by the 1770s and 1780s most were incapable of taking advantage of their increased opportunities for freedom. It is also possible that, despite the letter of the law, slaves had hammered out enough actual autonomy for themselves to make the attractions and risks of the unknown less desirable than the pains and satisfactions of the known. That this was often the case is suggested by an episode which took place on General William Moultrie's plantation near the end of the war. Having been exchanged after being a prisoner of the British, he stopped by on the way to rejoin the southern army, and was greeted by his slaves singing an African war song. There is no indication that their action was anything but voluntary, and, if Moultrie's memory was accurate, not a single slave had deserted his plantation during the war despite British attempts to lure them away. Anyone who has read Frederick Douglass's autobiography cannot help but recall his statement that slaves were saddest when singing. Being an ex-slave, he knew whereof he spoke. But in this case Olaudah Equiano's words seem to supply the appropriate context, "thus every great event, such as a triumphant return from battle, or other cause of public rejoicing, is celebrated in public dances, which are accompanied with songs."

None of this is meant to imply that slaves were happy about being slaves, or that they did not frequently resist. They did. Like slaves elsewhere, many apparently considered stealing food from a master as merely transferring it from one container to another, both of which belonged to him. Malingering was common, and almost every issue of the newspaper contained advertisements for slaves who had run away. Sometimes they went singly and sometimes in groups. Some went on foot; others took horses or boats. Some returned voluntarily; others did not. Many were recaptured; a few made good their escapes. Generalizing about such variety is difficult, but two points stand out. First, by late in the colonial period, enough runaways were visiting friends and relations to suggest the existence of extended kinship networks and reasonably well developed black communities. Furthermore, many of the slaves who sought freedom by absconding were at the extreme ends of the spectrum of acculturation—that is, they tended to be either newly arrived Africans or skilled and assimilated slaves such as house servants and artisans. For these men, the restraints of slavery were undoubtedly especially galling, and while the first were not in a position to evaluate the possibilities of success, the others had reason to believe that they had a good chance.

More violent acts of resistance included arson and murder. Neither was common, but both were by no means unknown. In some cases, something akin to maroonage also developed. Some of the outlaw bands of whites which roamed the backcountry in the 1760s included runaways, and a mounted band of blacks, led by one Caesar, raided Drayton Plantation near the end of the colonial period. More significantly, a fairly large group of armed ex-slaves who called themselves the "King of England's Soldiers" took refuge during the 1780s in the swamps along the Savannah River, from which they pillaged the surrounding countryside. It took a combined force of militia from both South Carolina and Georgia to rout them out. Yet in the long run maroonage was never a really serious problem for white South Carolinians. Unlike the maroons of Jamaica who found sanctuary in the mountains, runaway blacks in South Carolina had almost no place to go. It was almost 250 miles from the plantations of the lowcountry to the Appalachian Mountains, and they were occupied by the Cherokee Indians, who were rewarded for returning fugitives.

There was, however, one notable exception to the general rule that fugitive slaves could find no haven, and that was St. Augustine. In the same manner that the rival great powers attempted to tamper with Indians in each other's territories, the Spanish, who did not own many slaves, sought to capitalize on the potential weakness of South Carolinians who did. By 1728 the situation had become enough of a problem to prompt an official appeal to London. That the Spanish were "receiving and harbouring all our Runaway Negroes" was bad enough, South Carolinians argued, but worse yet, they were sending not only Indians but "our own slaves against us, to Rob and Plunder us." In all probability, South Carolinians overrated the role of the Spanish in instigating insurrections, for blacks scarcely needed outside mentors in this matter, but the possibility of refuge in Spanish Florida clearly increased the chances of success. It is therefore significant that the first major attempt at insurrection in 1720 apparently ended when the rebels were cut down trying to escape to Florida. More or less scantily documented mini-insurrections and insurrection scares continued through the 1720s and, with increasing frequency, during the 1730s. Conditions then were especially harsh and importations were unusually large. Thus by 1739 a large majority of the blacks were African-born, and more than half had been in the colony for less than a decade. In addition a very substantial proportion were Angolans. The situation became even more volatile in 1738 when Spanish authorities not only publicized a royal edict granting liberty to slaves who fled the English settlements but also established a fortified camp for them, popularly called "Fort Moosa," just outside of St. Augustine. All of this was part of the larger quarrel between England and Spain which reached the flashpoint in 1739. Rumors had been rife for a considerable time, but over the weekend of September 8 and 9, official word of the declaration of war reached Charles Town.

Early Sunday morning, about twenty blacks, apparently Angolans under the leadership of Jemmy, attacked a store at Stono about fifteen miles southwest of Charles Town. Killing the storekeepers, they seized powder and arms and began ravaging the immediate countryside. By a fateful coincidence, they soon collided with the lieutenant governor, William Bull, who was returning to Charles Town along the same road. Being mounted, he and his party escaped—though with some difficulty—and spread the alarm. In all probability the rebels failed to recognize him and therefore underestimated the significance of the encounter. For having proceeded about ten miles, they encamped in a field, raised a banner, and began beating drums—apparently in the belief that other slaves would join them. Many did, and by afternoon their numbers were estimated to be between sixty and 100. Meanwhile, the white militiamen were also assembling, and they had the advantage in training and firepower. As a result the battle was short. About fourteen blacks died in the first volley; those captured were questioned and in most cases summarily executed; but more than thirty escaped. It was nearly a week and thirty miles farther south along the road to St. Augustine before the largest group was wiped out in another encounter. More than twenty whites and an untold number of slaves had been killed by the time the revolt was over.

The Stono Rebellion was the largest slave revolt to occur anywhere on the mainland during the colonial period, and given its magnitude as well as the continuing threat of future insurrections—there were two abortive ones in the first year following the large upheaval—South Carolinians reacted with a remarkable lack of hysteria. Aside from military action against Spanish Florida during King George's War, their chief response was embodied in two acts: a prohibitive duty on the importation of new slaves (which, like the war, lasted for most of the 1740s) and the slave code of 1740, which remained the legal backbone of slavery until 1865. Time and the duty substantially reduced the percentage of new Africans among the slave population, which may have been one of the most important reasons that there were no subsequent revolts comparable to the Stono Rebellion. Undoubtedly the slave code also contributed to the relative calm. But given its generally lax enforcement, its precise role is difficult to determine.

Defining slaves as personal property or "chattels," the act sought to prohibit anyone "having the care and government" of them from "exercising too great rigour and cruelty" in order to reduce the provocation for revolts. Adequate food and clothing were to be provided; field work was not to be required on Sunday, and no slave was to be worked more than fifteen hours per day (a prohibition that speaks volumes about conditions in the 1730s). Anyone who maimed or killed a slave was subject to a stiff fine. (Authorities in London futilely and repeatedly urged that whites convicted of murdering a slave be executed.) To protect whites, owners and overseers were to issue written passes to slaves who were permitted off the premises; no slaves were to be taught to write (this stipulation was relaxed for the Anglican school in Charles Town mentioned earlier); justices of the peace were given blanket authorization to search suspected slave quarters for weapons and stolen goods; and whites were to accompany any group of more than seven male slaves traveling on the highways. For defiance or running away, owners could inflict punishments short of maiming. Finally, additional legislation also sought to improve the patrol system. At each muster of the militia, a "beat company" consisting of a captain and four men was to be chosen from among the slaveholders and overseers; its function was to make periodic rounds of each plantation after working hours to insure that the law was being enforced. Violators received summary "justice"—usually, a whipping.

There is considerable irony here. Slaves were the ones punished, but the slave code was directed mainly at whites. By instructing whites in their behavior toward blacks, the legislature sought not merely to protect masters from slaves and vice versa but society as a whole from both. That there was cause for concern in each case would need no further demonstration, were it not for some intriguing aberrations common enough to be significant. One was the apparent inability of some masters to control their own slaves. William Bartram, who would later become a famous naturalist, was a good example. Financed by his father and tutored in the intricacies of the business by an experienced South Carolinian, Henry Laurens, young Bartram set himself up with seven slaves to become a planter on the frontier in Florida (after it became English in 1763). The slaves refused to take orders, cheerfully telling their master that they would kill him if he did not leave them alone. Despite Laurens's coaching, Bartram had to admit defeat and abandon the venture.

Managing plantations was not an easy task, and a few men seem to have had almost constant trouble with their slaves. But that some men frequently needed some outside help to maintain discipline is less significant than that, in the final analysis, everyone did. Where slaves heavily outnumbered whites no man could feel secure without the backing of law and his neighbors who constituted the militia. Where the law was weak and neighbors too sparse, anyone might become a Bartram. This does not mean, however, that planters always welcomed visits by the patrol. Indeed, the patrol itself was often a problem. Like the town watch in Charles Town, the patrol sometimes harassed innocent blacks, and "beating up of quarters" was a recognized form of amusement for young men. Perhaps here—in the perversion of the laws making every white man a guardian of law and order—lay one of the tangled roots of vigilantism and nineteenth century lynching.

More immediately, grand juries also discovered that the patrols frequently failed to make their rounds at all. Yet even this inefficient system exacted a heavy price, for it weakened the militia as an effective fighting force, and by the end of the colonial period the militia had become little more than a giant patrol.

If the price was high, no one saw an alternative. If Sambo—that incompetent and contented slave of nineteenth century mythology—was anywhere to be found, few individuals recognized him. Rather, most were convinced that, loving liberty as much as other men, blacks harbored "a secret rancor" against whites which made them a "Domestic" or "intestine" enemy. Moreover, they were formidable. Representatives of a "fierce, hardy and strong" race, they were a major military consideration. A source of weakness after they became a majority, some had been armed in earlier crises. For example, troops preparing to resist the impending Spanish invasion in 1708 included "1000 good Negroes that knows the Swamps and Woods, most of them Cattle-hunters." And again, during the Yamasee War, blacks served Carolina as regular fighting men, not merely pioneers or auxiliaries. Despite later proposals for their use, few, if any, blacks served in the front lines after the Yamasee War. In fact, by the time of the Revolution, there was some feeling that to enlist men who had allowed themselves to be enslaved would be to sully the cause of liberty. Whatever rationalizations lay behind that tortured logic, it was an illustration of the intricate and mutually reinforcing relationship between prejudice and slavery. If by this time the perception of blacks was different from what it had once been, it was not nearly so different as it would eventually become. Advertisements for runaway slaves in the antebellum period frequently depicted a domesticated slave, who resembled a tramp carrying a bundle. Pictorial representations in the colonial newspapers often featured a man wearing African dress who carried what appears to be a war club.

Terror therefore lay at the heart of the system as whites, who were potentially terrified at what the large number of slaves might be able to do, attempted to terrorize the slaves into not doing it. Thus punishments could be Draconian. As early as 1698 two blacks caught trying to run away to St. Augustine were castrated. Some planters in particular had a reputation for extreme cruelty, and even men who were otherwise humane could be ruthless in dealing with slaves. J.

Hector St. John de Crevecoeur visited South Carolina, and his *Letters From an American Farmer*, published in 1782, included a harrowing description of a black, whom he claimed to have seen hanging in a cage, left to die in the woods. That scene may have been a figment of Crevecoeur's imagination, but there is no question that similar punishments had in fact been inflicted at a not much earlier date, and it was almost standard procedure to display the corpses of executed slaves by hanging them in chains at prominent points. Similarly, as late as 1769, a slave woman who had been convicted of poisoning her master was publicly burned at the stake on one of the greens in Charles Town. No regular jury and no appeal process protected a slave accused of a capital crime. Instead, a court usually composed of two justices of the peace and three freeholders heard the case and summarily imposed the sentence.* Then, to prevent concealment of crimes by owners fearing the loss of their slave property, the legislature compensated the owner of the executed slave.

In the final analysis the system rested on force. Few persons ever forgot that, and questions of security were never far from anyone's mind. Fires were especially alarming, for they not only suggested the possibility of arson but also provided cover for other activities. Fanned by a high wind, the great fire of November 1740 destroyed more than 300 buildings in the commercial and residential sectors of Charles Town. Execution the next year of an arsonist who reputedly "looked upon every White Man he should meet as his declared Enemy" could not still the nagging fear that, if the great fire had not been the work of slaves, others could be. Accordingly, the militia turned out under arms for fires. Newspapers regularly suppressed news of insurrections— and of anything else that might incite trouble—until the immediate danger appeared to be over. Defeat of the Cherokee Indians in the early 1760s, some Carolinians argued, should not entail their extermination, lest their mountain strongholds be a haven for runaway blacks and South Carolina become another Jamaica plagued by maroons. Similar considerations also made the legislature more conciliatory toward restive backcountrymen who might someday be needed to help suppress a

---

*Appeals became possible in 1833. Under the basic 1740 Act, two justices and one freeholder, or one justice and two freeholders made a quorum; and the conviction or acquittal of any slave by such a quorum was "final in all capital cases."

slave rebellion. To live in colonial South Carolina was to live in fear at least part of the time.

Prudence was a pervasive consideration, but it would be misleading to imply that everyone was always fearful. Newcomers and visitors tended to be the most apprehensive. Frequently, they were afraid to walk the streets of Charles Town after dark; occasionally they were thrown into panic at meeting a group of slaves on a lonely country road; and almost always they grossly overestimated the ratio of blacks to whites. Even individuals who had been in the colony for a considerable length of time sometimes lost their nerve. Pleading ill health, one minister precipitously set sail for England. His superior thought he knew the real reason and reported that the man's chief malady was a fear of being "Knocked o' the Head" by slaves or others. On the other hand, most experienced residents were able to cope. They knew very well in an abstract sense that slaves were dangerous, but on an everyday basis they tended to assume that the dangerous ones belonged to someone else. Thus presentments of the grand juries reveal some almost incredible anomalies. After 1739, the law required men to bring arms to church on Sunday, and the timing of the Stono Rebellion suggested that this stipulation was not entirely unreasonable. So law-abiding men brought their weapons—and gave them to their slaves to keep while they went inside to the services. Similarly, after musters, militiamen sometimes permitted their servants to carry their guns home. Nor was such trust entirely folly. More than one slave helped to put down the Stono Rebellion, and at least one unquestionably saved the life of his master at that time. Such behavior suggests that even during an unusually harsh and tense era like the 1730s, relations between master and slave could be close and at times affectionate. In the eighteenth century as well as the antebellum period, blacks often acted as wet nurses for white children, and the effects of such close contact could be heard as well as felt. One historian, George Rogers, has wittily described the modern Charles Town accent as "high Gullah," and its roots clearly go back to the colonial period.

The results of close contact between the races were visible in other ways, as well. There was a puritanical streak in many South Carolinians, and it is doubtful that miscegenation was widely condoned, at least by the middle of the eighteenth century. Yet young men especially were able to contemplate the possibility of interracial sex with greater equanimity than most Americans. Certainly, jokes about the subject were fairly common in the newspapers. Moreover, enough extant wills with intriguing provisions have survived to suggest that there was some substance beneath the rhetoric. One testator, for example, stipulated that a mulatto boy be freed and apprenticed as a carpenter. When he reached the age of fourteen, two slaves were to be purchased for him and also trained as carpenters. Another man directed that a slave woman be freed and given a house. Occasionally, someone explicitly acknowledged mulatto children. Though significant, all of this is perhaps to be expected. What is more surprising, though, is that colonial South Carolinians appeared to be able to tolerate the notion of a black man consorting with a white woman. Take the case of Gideon Gibson. A free mulatto carpenter, he moved to South Carolina from Virginia in 1731. The governor, who was puzzled over what to do about him, made him take out a personal recognizance bond and then brought the matter up with his council. Observing in Gibson's behalf that he had a trade and a white wife, the governor indicated that he proposed to let him stay in the colony. Apparently no one objected sufficiently to do anything about it. Gibson remained and, nearly twenty years later, a man who was probably his son became a prominent Regulator. That made him the subject of some derogatory remarks by a member of the legislature, but others defended him.

What makes this episode especially significant is the ability of at least some white South Carolinians to look at the Gibsons relatively objectively. Few things have been as apt to produce an irrational reaction from white men as sex between white women and black men. And, as Winthrop Jordan and others have pointed out, such responses would long militate against emancipation and acceptance of free blacks and mulattoes. Thus the Gibsons' reception prompts one to inquire about the condition of free blacks generally in South Carolina.

Estimating precisely how many free blacks there were at any one time during the colonial period is a difficult task. The census of 1790 lists 1,801, after approximately 1,000 had been emancipated during the Revolutionary era. Leaving aside natural increase, these figures suggest that there might have been about 800 free blacks in the colony at the end of the colonial period. The last extant tax return, for 1768, enumerates only 159. Either free blacks were unusually fertile during the Revolution, or the tax returns fail to enumerate them accurately.

Actually both factors probably contributed; certainly free blacks who paid other taxes were exempt from the head tax by which they can be identified. Moreover, under the headright system free men—including blacks—were eligible to receive fifty or 100 acres of land, which was taxable. Furthermore, skills or stock in trade were taxed on the basis of an assessed value. Thus it is probably safe to assume that the tax returns identified only the poorest free blacks—those who were both landless and unskilled—and that they represented only a fraction of the total. Perhaps the proportion was smaller in the rural parishes where land was easier to acquire than in Charles Town, but what correction factor should be applied in each case remains unknown. What is clear is that, in 1790, 1.7 percent of the black population was free and that in 1768 the comparable figure was at least two-tenths of one percent. Even when allowances are made for under-enumeration in the colonial period, the conclusion is inescapable; there were not many free blacks. Indeed, in proportion to the total black population there were less than one-sixth as many in South Carolina as in Virginia in 1790. The tax return of 1768 which listed eighty-eight in the rural parish of St. David's, where Quakers and the Welsh Neck Baptists were especially receptive to them, suggests that a substantial number of free blacks may have been landless. This does not mean that all were poor. In 1731, John Primas paid £100 sterling for 100 acres of land in the Beaufort area, and that was a substantial sum for the time. Similarly, Thomas Jeremiah, a fisherman and harbor pilot in Charles Town during the mid-eighteenth century, was himself a slaveholder reputed to be worth more than £1,000 sterling.

Jeremiah is an enigmatic yet illuminating figure. Known as "Jerry" to contemporaries, he was free, probably since 1748. More than once, it seems, he distinguished himself as a fire fighter. His "Publick services," the governor reported, "were universally acknowledged, particularly in cases of fire, where by his skill and intrepidity he had often been remarkably useful." Nor does it seem that he was entirely averse to capitalizing on his public image, for in 1768 the *South Carolina Gazette* carried the following notice. "The Negro JERRY (well known for his activity in extinguishing of fires) has just compleated a WELL-BOAT, in order to supply the inhabitants of this town with LIVE FISH every day." He had also made the news in less favorable contexts. Thirteen years earlier the same newspaper had carried an account of a

nearly fatal accident which resulted from the "Carelessness of a Negro
Pilot (Jerry)." For reasons unknown, he also got into an altercation
with a white ship captain in 1771, for which he was convicted of assault
and sentenced to an hour in the stocks and ten lashes. But, in view of
his public services, the governor pardoned him. In short, he was a very
prominent black. "A forward fellow, puffed up by prosperity, ruined
by Luxury and debauchery and grown to an amazing pitch of vanity
and ambition," was the assessment of one white contemporary. Nineteenth century Southerners would have used the phrase "an uppity
Nigger."

In late May or early June 1775, Jerry was arrested once again, this
time, it was alleged, for plotting insurrection. But the evidence was
not conclusive. Accordingly, he was confined while more was gathered.
Brought to trial again in August before a "Negro Court" composed of
justices of the peace and freeholders, he was condemned, hanged, and
his body publicly burned. Neither the court nor the chaplain who
visited him after sentencing was able to extract a confession, and Jerry
went to his death courageously telling his executioners that they would
suffer for "shedding his innocent blood." One of the alleged co-con-
spirators later retracted his confession, though another did not. The
royal governor, who believed Jerry to be innocent, termed the trial
judicial murder, and futilely pardoned him. Henry Laurens, who as
president of the Council of Safety had more effective power than the
governor, refused to intervene. Someone—perhaps Laurens—also cautioned the royal governor against interfering, warning him that to do
so would "raise a flame that all the water in the Cooper River would
not put out." On the basis of apparent perjury (Jerry claimed not to
know a slave who, it later turned out, was his brother-in-law) Laurens
believed him to be guilty.

Given the welter of conflicting testimony as well as the paucity of
substantial evidence, it is impossible to sort out truth from falsehood.
Nevertheless, much is known about the context of the trial, and it is
relevant. Early 1775 was a period of rapidly increasing tension between
England and the colonies. War broke out in Massachusetts on April
19. News of the battles at Lexington and Concord reached South
Carolina in early May, about the same time as local Whigs received a
letter from an American in London who maintained that British authorities planned to employ Indians and blacks against the colonists.

Rumor held that the royal governor, who was due to arrive at any time, was bringing arms for this purpose. Jerry was supposed to have told other blacks that "there is a great war coming" which would "help the poor Negroes"; that he, Jerry, was to have "the Chief Command of the said Negroes"; and that "he had Powder enough already, but that he wanted more arms which he would try to get as many as he could." Finally, Jerry—whether innocent or guilty—was not alone. Other blacks were accused and some were executed in similar insurrection scares in all of the southern colonies during 1775 and 1776.

What is to be made of all this? At the time, loyalists thought they knew. Jerry was the victim of a Machiavellian policy having a twofold purpose. The first was to intimidate harbor pilots who might otherwise be willing to guide British warships into the ports of South Carolina; the second was to promote military preparedness. Handbills describing the iniquitous British involvement in the providentially discovered insurrection were circulated at militia musters where, one loyalist dryly observed, they were believed "like Holy Writ." Although it is hard to imagine anything better than a good insurrection scare to justify calling up the militia and put spirit in its training, this interpretation is perhaps a bit too cynical. Jerry may well have planned to take advantage of the conflict between whites to help his fellow blacks, and similar ideas almost certainly influenced some of those accused in other colonies. There is, however, also another possibility.

To use an anachronistic analogy, black resistance to slavery was like static on an older radio. It was always there, but one became accustomed to it. Only a significant increase in its volume or a headache caused the listener to pay much attention. Conflict in the white community doubtless increased the volume of resistance; for rival powers might provide sanctuaries and other assistance, masters would be distracted, and the excitement of the struggle might be contagious. Certainly the last is what South Carolinians later thought had happened during the Stamp Act crisis when a number of blacks paraded through Charles Town crying "Liberty." But at that time whites had a headache, too, since political conflict increased their anxieties and made them more sensitive to signs of restiveness in the black community. It is therefore not surprising to find that slave insurrections and insurrection scares coincided with political upheavals, wars, or rumors of wars, most notably in 1720 (shortly after the revolution against the proprietors and while the issue was still in doubt), in 1739 (coinciding with the outbreak of war with Spain), 1759 (on the eve of the Cherokee War), 1766 (the Stamp Act crisis), and in 1775. What is especially intriguing about the last two abortive incidents is the character of the accused. One man was deported in 1766 because, Laurens later maintained, "in the general course of his life he had been a sad Dog & perhaps it was necessary to save appearances." Jerry, as we have seen, had had prior friction with some whites. Moreover, being black, both men were marginal and relatively powerless figures. If one were to substitute white women for black men and "witchcraft" for "insurrection," the pattern would resemble the dynamics of many witchcraft scares, which frequently appear to have involved demonstrations of solidarity by a threatened community at the expense of its marginal members.

The extent to which witchcraft and insurrection scares generally exhibited similar characteristics can be investigated elsewhere; here the most immediate concern is that Jerry's death illustrates the precarious position of free blacks in colonial South Carolina. The price that he and all blacks paid to make the colony prosperous can hardly be expressed. One measure is the anonymity of so many. Thus, Samuel Wragg's directions for his own funeral are worth noting. Having become wealthy trading in South Carolina produce, he lived much of his life in England, but his burial in 1750 was to be on his estate in South Carolina. His pallbearers were to be four blacks. They were Joe, a wheelwright; Walter, the carpenter; Iron Castel, a cooper; and Stephen, the tradesman. Perhaps Wragg only attempted to exhibit in death the paternalism that masters rarely demonstrated in life, but perhaps he may have understood something of what he owed to these men. In the same vein, another man unconsciously revealed even more of the profit and the price of slavery for white South Carolinians when he observed that he had decided to move to a "less improvable" but "more secure" part of the world.

9

SOCIETY: THE SOCIAL AGGREGATE

The crucial role and numerical preponderance of blacks not only made
South Carolina appear "more like a negro country," as one contemporary
observed, but also affected the composition of the free population as
the government sought to attract whites to help offset the black majority. The result was a heterogeneous population and, to some extent,
a sectionally divided society as most of the newer immigrants settled
in the backcountry. The composition of white society, the nature of
sectional differences, and the question of social stability are therefore
essential topics for an understanding of colonial South Carolina.

The most striking feature of white society throughout most of the
colonial period was its small size. Although early population figures
are notoriously inaccurate and even the best estimates are often wildly
disparate, they are sufficient to provide a reasonably good indication
of the general trend. Perhaps 200 individuals established the first
settlement at Old Town; by the end of the decade in 1680 there may
have been 1,000 in the immediate vicinity of Charles Town. During
the next few years, the proprietors' promotional efforts among English
and Scottish dissenters brought in more than 500, while Louis XIV's
revocation of the Edict of Nantes granting toleration to Huguenots
added perhaps another 500 individuals. Thus, despite the failure of
the Scots' settlement at Stuart Town, these and other immigrants
probably brought the total number of whites up to 6,000 before the
end of the century. Yet partly because of the fears and losses resulting
from the Yamasee War, this figure may have declined by 1720. Slow
increases followed until in 1750 there were about 25,000 whites in

the colony. The population then almost doubled during the next twenty years. Contemporaries were aware of this growth, but they were scarcely prepared for the massive influx in the Revolutionary era. Pushed partly by a desire to escape the war in the middle states through the later 1770s and primarily lured by land and opportunity in the 1780s, enough people streamed in to add more than 90,000 individuals in two decades. Stated slightly differently, fewer than 50,000 white South Carolinians rebelled against Great Britain; nearly three times that many joined the Union in 1788. Though still one of the smallest states, South Carolina was among the most rapidly growing.

In view of this phenomenal population growth in the late eighteenth century, one has to ask why it was so late in coming. A complete answer probably requires a full-scale demographic study of the colony, for which there may not be sufficient data extant. Nevertheless, several scholars are now examining selected parishes and their work promises to be illuminating. In the meantime, it is possible to formulate a working hypothesis. A number of considerations suggest that the rate of natural increase was quite low in the tidewater area. The environment was unhealthy, and whites were less resistant to some of the most prevalent diseases than blacks. Furthermore, the persistence of a higher mortality rate for whites than blacks aboard slave ships suggests the possibility of a similar pattern ashore, and scattered evidence indicates that such may well have been the case. At least, in 1714 the legislature observed that "through the afflicting Providence of God" whites did not increase proportionally to blacks. At first, the imbalanced sex ratio among immigrants and the tendency of newly arrived women to be relatively late in bearing children were among the most important causes for the slow increase of whites. Seventy-six out of ninety-two, or nearly 83 percent, of the passengers aboard one of the first vessels in 1670, the *Carolina*, were men; of the approximately 680 settlers who have been identified as being in South Carolina during the next decade, only about 200 were women. Undoubtedly, the proportion of women among the earliest immigrants who faced the harshest conditions was lower than among those who came in the eighteenth century, and time gradually narrowed the numerical gap between the sexes as more of the population was born in the colony. Yet, in 1708 the governor reported the presence of 1,360 men and 900 women, giving a 1.5 to 1 ratio, and nearly twenty years later, when the rector of St.

George filed an unusually complete report about his rural parish near Charles Town, women still represented only 44 percent of the adult white population.

Because native-born women might have had children earlier in life and creoles possessed more resistance to endemic diseases than immigrants, the emergence of a creole generation should have contributed to a greater rate of natural increase. Custom may have delayed the age of marriage, however, and disease continued to inflict an appalling toll on children. Precise figures are not yet available, but recent scholarship indicates childhood mortality ran about 40 percent in some of the areas around Chesapeake Bay in the seventeenth century, and in regions of the Carolina lowcountry the rate may have been twice as high well into the eighteenth century. Given all of these considerations, it is not surprising to find that in 1726 there were only about 266 children among the 108 families in St. George's Parish—or approximately 2.5 per family. Clearly, the white population in St. George's would have had trouble reproducing itself, and such rural areas often seem to have had higher birth rates than Charles Town. In the city—where a physician who studied vital statistics noted at midcentury that, except during smallpox epidemics, births slightly exceeded deaths—the situation may have been worse, though the omission of epidemics, as well as the seasonal presence of planting families and the deaths of transients, complicates questions about the significance of his figures. Despite these uncertainties, one doubts that there was much natural increase among whites anywhere in South Carolina until the middle third of the eighteenth century, when an appreciable number of immigrants began to settle in the healthier inland areas, away from the crowded conditions of Charles Town and the swamps of the lowcountry. However, the already established reputation of the colony as a dangerous place, exposed to human enemies as well as the ravages of disease, tended to retard such settlement.

Local officials attempted to break the vicious circle after the Yamasee War and the growing preponderance of slaves made the problem of security painfully obvious. Establishing four garrisons on the Savannah and Congaree rivers in 1716 and 1717, the local government actually purchased indentured servants to serve as soldiers. It also made equally unusual provisions to induce settlers to locate near Fort Moore (the most exposed of these posts on the north side of the Savannah River across from modern Augusta, Georgia). An act of the assembly exempted residents of that area from taxes, forbade the seizure of their cattle for debt when driven to market, and protected them from writs issued in legal cases involving small sums. As previously discussed, the legislature also attempted to use the land confiscated from the Yamasee Indians to lure immigrants of military age to the southern frontier, but the proprietors repealed that plan. During the 1720s, while the proprietors refused to make additional land grants, the assembly enacted a series of laws requiring each slaveholder to keep one white male servant for each ten slaves or 2,000 acres. As it turned out, these acts were virtually unenforceable.

Much more effective was the "township scheme" adopted early in the 1730s. Drawing on precedents from New England and elsewhere, local leaders long advocated the establishment of compact settlements on the frontier; and the crown, after acquiring title to the land in Carolina, proved to be cooperative. Governor Robert Johnson received instructions calling for the establishment of eleven townships to be located about sixty miles inland on major rivers from the Waccamaw south to the Altamaha. (The two southernmost settlements became part of Georgia before they were launched; ten were established in South Carolina by 1759; and three more, located farther in-the interior, were added in the 1760s.) Twenty thousand acres, or a square nearly six miles on a side, were to be reserved in each of the areas for immigrants who would settle next to each other. Every family was to receive a town lot as well as fifty acres of outlying land for each member. The assembly agreed not only to pay the costs of the necessary survey and grant but also to assist immigrants with tools, food, and transportation; and the crown waived the payment of quitrents for the first ten years. Appropriately enough for a fund designed to bring in whites to offset the increasing numbers of slaves, import duties—of which the one on slaves was the most important—were appropriated for this purpose; and, coincidentally, by an act of 1751 three-fifths of the proceeds of the slave duty were to be used to help settle Protestant immigrants. A full generation before the famous compromise in the Constitutional Convention whereby three-fifths of the slaves were to be added to the white population of each state in apportioning representation and taxes, South Carolinians were employing the same ratio in a somewhat similar context. Despite some tinkering with the fund—

and its temporary depletion in the late 1730s—the legislature continued to subsidize immigrants throughout most of the colonial period. Indentured servants whose time was up, as well as individuals who came from other colonies and agreed to settle in strategic areas outside of the townships, also frequently received land "on the bounty."

Although the townships never attracted a flood of immigrants like that which settled the backcountry during the Revolutionary era, inducements by the legislature helped to create a considerably different and much more rapidly growing society beyond the older settlements. By 1760 it probably contained about 50 percent of the white population. Ten years later, the acting governor estimated that between two-thirds and three-quarters of the inhabitants lived in the backcountry. And just before the first federal census in 1790, state officials calculated that the white population of the lowcountry was 28,644; the comparable figure for the backcountry was 111,534. Thus nearly 80 percent of the whites lived outside of the lowcountry.

Inland settlers also accounted for a disproportionate share of the non-English stock. An analysis of names appearing in the 1790 census, published in 1931 under the auspices of the American Council of Learned Societies, indicated that 15.1 percent of the total population was of Scottish ancestry; 13.8 percent was Irish (mostly from Ulster, which was heavily Scotch-Irish); 5 percent was German; and 3.9 percent was French. More recently, Forrest and Ellen Shapiro McDonald have revised the figures for the Celtic proportion. If they are correct, nearly a third of the population was Scottish, almost 12 percent Irish, and nearly 9 percent was Welsh; altogether, 63.3 percent of the population was of non-English stock. Whatever figures one accepts, it is clear that South Carolina had the highest proportion of individuals of Scottish ancestry of any state except Georgia and the highest percentage of French. With the exception of a few in the backcountry around New Bordeaux, most Frenchmen lived in Charles Town and along the Santee River to the north, which was a bilingual area as late as the 1730s. In town, there was also a small community of Sephardic Jews, some Germans, and quite a few Scotsmen. In general, however, the larger minority groups settled in the backcountry. Orangeburg was heavily German, and nearly 60 percent of the population in the Camden area was of Celtic ancestry. In the lowcountry, on the other hand, more than 80 percent of the whites may have been of English stock.

Religious diversity accompanied ethnic variety. In 1710, when the population was mostly English, contemporaries believed that about 45 percent was Presbyterian, 10 percent (Regular) Baptist, 2.5 percent Quaker, and 42.5 percent was Anglican. Although a number of Anglican ministers reported that their parishes were between 50 and 100 percent Anglican during the 1720s, Governor Glen apparently still believed the figures from 1710 to be reasonably accurate at midcentury. One is therefore tempted to try to calculate the actual numbers involved, but Glen may merely have borrowed the earlier estimate without giving the matter adequate thought. During the first half of the eighteenth century, many French and some English dissenters converted to Anglicanism, while Germans, who belonged primarily to the Lutheran and Reformed Churches, began to populate the interior; within the next few years, many Presbyterians of Scotch-Irish extraction and large numbers of Separate Baptists would also settle in the backcountry. Some of these newcomers were potential adherents of the Anglican Church, and an itinerant clergyman in the Camden area organized nearly thirty congregations in the 1760s and '70s. However, many of his listeners were Presbyterians without ministers of their own. Perhaps the safest course at this point is therefore merely to observe that during the legislative debates over the status of the churches in 1778, a leading dissenter claimed knowledge of ninety dissenting churches and twenty Anglican. While only one Anglican Church west of the old lowcountry parishes petitioned for incorporation under the arrangement adopted at this time, numerous dissenting congregations took advantage of the opportunity. Although many eligible congregations failed to request incorporation, it is obvious that the dissenters constituted the overwhelming majority of the backcountry population and that Anglicans probably predominated in the tidewater. In short, in religious as well as ethnic composition, the backcountry differed from the low.

As might be expected from the character of the legislative inducements to settlement, the backcountry was also mainly the home of small farmers. Most of the grants made in that area were for relatively small amounts, and the average farm was about 175 acres. During the Revolutionary era, for which there are scattered tax returns, only about 6 percent of the men did not own land, and some of these had a few slaves. Thus, despite its ethnic and religious diversity, the region was relatively homogeneous economically, with the richest 10 percent of the taxpayers owning about 40 percent of the wealth. As this figure also suggests, areas of the backcountry soon began to contain a few plantations and large planters. Some of the larger operations belonged to men who resided on the coast and invested in the backcountry; others, however, were owned by men who immigrated with some capital and by hard work, luck, and occasionally a little chicanery, added to it. Moses Kirkland, for example, moved into the area some-time before 1752 and set up business on the lower Saluda River where he soon operated a sawmill, a gristmill, and a ferry. Amassing grants, he became the owner of at least 3,000 acres and, eventually, a large indigo plantation worked by slaves in the Ninety Six District. Kirkland and men like him were the exceptions, and as late as the end of the 1780s more than 50 percent of the taxpayers in the western portion of the region lacked slaves, though farther to the east (but still in an inland parish) as many as one-third of the landholders were fairly large planters. In the 1760s, however, slaves constituted only about 10 percent of the population in the uplands.

Though fluid and fairly homogeneous in a material sense, this emerg-ing white society was not well integrated during the late colonial period, either within the backcountry itself or with the lowcountry. That does not mean that there were no cohesive communities in the area; indeed, internal cohesiveness sometimes militated against adhe-sion to the wider society. Religious differences frequently reinforced ethnic divisions, while the pursuit of traditional activities, such as wheat farming by the Germans, weaving among the Scotch-Irish, and wine making by the French and Germans, may have helped to per-petuate a sense of group distinctiveness and solidarity. Certainly re-lations between discrete elements of the population were occasionally strained. Undoubtedly, segregation of foreigners southwest of the San-tee River was deliberate, for in the early 1750s the Commons House, alarmed by the large influx of Germans, unsuccessfully attempted to restrict the bounty to settlers of British extraction. Scots, too, it was hoped, would hie themselves to the remotest parts of the province, for they were the butt of much prejudice during the late colonial period. New Light or Separate Baptists did immigrate to the backcountry, and they were perhaps even more unpopular with members of more con-servative denominations who frowned on uneducated preachers, female participation in church services, and some Baptist rituals such as foot washing. Furthermore, "enthusiastic" (a pejorative term in the eighteenth century) meetings and personal religious experiences sometimes—it was rumored—resulted in sexual license. Devout New Lights took an equally dim view of those who condemned them. Whereas the Regular and General Baptists had long been part of the establishment in the lowcountry, the Separate Baptists condemned the materialism and worldliness of the planting elite as unchristian. Richard Furman, a prominent leader who eventually engineered the merger of the Regular and New Light churches in South Carolina, was a backcountryman who, many of the New Lights believed, had been seduced by the glitter of Charles Town.

Nor was any love lost between Presbyterians and the Church of England. To some orthodox Anglicans, Presbyterianism did not qualify as a religion; to many Presbyterians, on the other hand, Anglican clergymen were "black gowned sons of bitches." During the 1760s an itinerant Anglican minister claimed that backcountry men harassed him by hiring "a Band of rude fellows to come to Service who brought with them 57 dogs (for I counted them) which in Time of Service they set fighting." If religious hostilities sometimes resulted in comparatively innocent pranks, religious enthusiasms on at least one occasion got sufficiently out of hand to result in murder. Although that probably represented a unique aberration, it helps to explain why the acting governor later reported that the backcountry was as religiously fragmented "as illiterate enthusiasm or wild imagination can misinterpret the scripture."

Lurid crimes for secular motives were, however, fairly common during the 1760s. Horse thieves and cattle rustlers had been a plague of the backcountry virtually since the beginning of settlement, but perhaps emboldened by the vulnerability of the area following the dislocations of the Cherokee War (which ended in 1761), outlaw gangs increasingly preyed upon individuals. By the summer of 1766, they were raiding plantations with seeming impunity, torturing householders with "red hot Irons," raping women, and not infrequently murdering men. Among these gangs, a contemporary claimed, there were more than a few runaway slaves, mulattoes, and "many Women and Girls . . . very deep in the foulest of Crimes, and Deeds of darkness not to be mention'd" who chose their way of life. Other women "who tho' now bold in Sin—Yet were either Stollen—debauched—trepann'd or forcibly made to take on" with the outlaws. Distinguishing between the two was difficult, however, and some thirty-five "recaptured" girls had "grown too abandon'd ever to be reclaimed."

Believing themselves to be locked in a deadly struggle with "crackers and rebells" who made war upon the values of a civilized society, the rising planters of the backcountry organized themselves into vigilante groups to "regulate" not only the outlaws but also the drifters and hunters who, if they did not aid and abet the outlaws as believed, lived undisciplined lives which were the antithesis of the planters' ideal. Thus, in the interests of law and order, men of property—which not incidentally included slaves—chastised supposed miscreants and, according to their spokesman, achieved their aims. "The Country was purged of all Villains. The Whores were whipped & drove off. . . . Tranquility reigned, Industry was restor'd." Violence in the name of order and lawlessness in behalf of law, scholars have recently become aware, have long been a part of British and American history, but, as might be expected, in this case they eventually produced some misunderstandings with the authorities at Charles Town. Nevertheless, lowcountry men rather quickly came to understand the Regulator movement for what it was—an attempt to "civilize" the backcountry. In short, the Regulators helped to educate the lowcountry elite about the hinterlands of its own province. Thus the episode not only marked the emergence of the sectionalism which was to prove a long-standing feature of South Carolina politics, but also helped to contribute a basis for sectional reconciliation by demonstrating that the values, and, indeed, the society, of the backcountry were not very different from their lowcountry counterparts. In fact, it would be only a slight exaggeration to say that in some ways the lowcountry at this time was merely the backcountry writ small and two generations older.

While the backcountry contained small farmers and a few large planters, the lowcountry was reputed to be made up entirely of big planters and their overseers. That, of course, was not quite true, but because most of the work force was enslaved, there were relatively few white laborers; and because slaves were also a form of capital that earned more for those who had more, the spread between rich and poor was greater. By almost any measure short of counting slaves as potential holders of wealth rather than a form of wealth, lowcountry South

Carolina was the richest society in colonial America. Significantly, a recent study of more than 900 inventories filed in all of the colonies during 1774 reveals that nine of the ten richest men represented were residents of Charles Town or the immediately surrounding area, and during the Revolutionary era at least 50 percent of the wealth in the area was owned by the richest 10 percent of the population. Obviously, if 90 percent of the free population owned less than half of the property, not everyone was rich. Some of the poor were in the city itself which, according to one contemporary in 1775, was overrun with beggars. Indeed, nearly a decade earlier complaints about the cost of poor relief prompted the Commons to launch an investigation which discovered that there were 130 individuals being at least partially supported by public funds. That was slightly over 2.5 percent of the white population and, though not large by modern standards, the figure represented a substantial number in a town renowned for prosperity. Even in the rural parishes, a few women and children received assistance. Self-supporting but "spiritless peasants," as one visitor termed them, also existed. Who they were is not always easy to discover. Extant tax returns frequently listed men with slaves but no land; these individuals, however, were usually overseers. But militia rolls also contain landless men who appear to have constituted at least a small floating population. In addition, there certainly were landholders without slaves who must have lived a marginal existence. Those on Hilton Head Island were described by a naval report as "persons of small circumstances," and on Edisto Island in 1732 nine of the forty-five taxpayers (or 20 percent) who owned land had less than six slaves. Twenty-four years later the inland township of Williamsburg had already become a slaveholding area. Yet four out of sixty-eight individuals whose holdings are legible, or about 6 percent, of the taxpayers on an incomplete return owned land but no slaves, while an additional nineteen or 28 percent held land but no more than five slaves. Thus of those who were sufficiently settled to pay taxes, about one-third were small planters. Governor James Glen, it seems, may have been a bit too optimistic when he estimated in 1751 that about a fifth of the population had only "a bare subsistence."

Many small planters as well as perhaps most of the overseers and artisans belonged among the 40 percent who, Glen believed, possessed "the necessarys of life." Actually, some artisans and even some overseers did somewhat better. The latter varied widely in character, and, despite complaints by contemporaries and similarly unfavorable representations by historians, during the nineteenth century overseers in the rice districts were generally considered to be the most professional. Even in the colonial period some overseers were in effect apprentice planters, while the professionals often contributed a few slaves to the plantation work force and received in return a share of the crop as well as a salary. Artisans, too, ran the gamut from fairly poor men—though it should be noted that wages in South Carolina were among the highest in the colonies—to wealthy individuals who, as one contemporary noted, "bear nothing more of their Trade than the name"—that is, they resembled large modern contractors except that they operated with slave rather than free labor. Seamstresses and tailors had perhaps the most trouble getting by; builders and cabinetmakers were often quite well off.

Perhaps Glen counted some artisans and shopkeepers among the 20 percent of the population which he thought possessed "some of the conveniencys of life," though retail tradesmen and shopkeepers are perhaps the hardest to classify. Studies of probate records suggest that petty shopkeepers were often among the poorest of those having estates large enough to inventory, but a silversmith like Jonathan Sarrazin was sufficiently wealthy to purchase a large rice plantation in 1764. Merchants also came in all shapes and sizes, but the term usually referred to the more affluent overseas operators, though some of the smaller ones probably had only "some of the conveniencys." No doubt the same was true of many clergymen and doctors, since the ministry was usually more prestigious than profitable and medicine was a relatively overcrowded field in colonial South Carolina. Planters with medium-sized estates, say about twenty field hands, might also be in this category.

Large planters, big merchants, and the top professional men, and their families, constituted the 20 percent of the population that according to Glen had "plenty of the good things of life." For the most fashionable physician or two in Charles Town, medicine was a very rewarding pursuit, while the busiest lawyers who were engaged in the most lucrative of all professions probably made ten times the income of the average doctor. The law was like medicine in that the bar, though small, was larger than the available business could support.

Some lawyers did not practice and, as contemporaries recognized, as late as 1770 only about five or six of the leading lawyers made excellent livings; those who did not practice were primarily planters.

Estimating the income of a farmer or planter has always been difficult, partly because it can vary widely from year to year and partly because some domestic expenses should be credited to the proceeds of the plantation. Attempting to resolve the latter problem, one contemporary implied that the returns in planting at midcentury were perhaps 10 to 12 percent a year, together with the planter's living; other observers frequently lumped such incidentals with the total returns which, they sometimes claimed, might be more than 33 percent a year on invested capital. Merchants could do even better, especially in the slave trade where, once again, the largest handful of firms handled the vast majority of the business.

Such figures may be inherently interesting, but they need to be put into perspective. Perhaps the most illuminating comparison arises from the conversion of eighteenth century income and expenditures to current (or nearly current) United States dollars. In 1774 the purchasing power of the pound sterling, Alice Hanson Jones has recently estimated, was the equivalent of approximately $50.52 in 1977. Although this figure should probably be viewed with some skepticism, if it is even approximately correct, a ship carpenter who might make 6 shillings per day received the equivalent of about $15.00; a relatively small planter who cleared £200 a year made about $10,104; and a leading lawyer who, it was reported, earned as much as £1,200, realized the equivalent of approximately $60,624. Wealthy professional men and merchants, it should be noted, also frequently owned productive plantations, so their combined incomes could be considerably larger. What did they spend and what were they worth? A "well-to-do" cabinetmaker, Thomas Elfe, provides an answer to the first question, and a lawyer who did not practice but served as speaker of the Commons House, Peter Manigault, helps with the second. In 1770, the cost of living for Elfe's family, which included two sons in school, was £546 or about $27,583. And when he died in 1773, Manigault, who also owned several plantations, was the wealthiest individual represented in Jones's sample of inventories. His net worth was about $1,653,924 in 1977 dollars, which, as she has remarked, is "hardly a superfortune by today's standards."

Frankly, it is far enough from really great wealth in the twentieth century to suggest that these figures are too low, for they seem incompatible with the fabled wealth of Carolinians. Nevertheless, such estimates are worthwhile if they do no more than illustrate the difficulties of comparing levels of wealth in a modern industrial society with those in an eighteenth century agricultural colony in which unfree labor performed much of the productive work and domestic drudgery. Yet the figures are considerably more useful than that, since they help to clarify the reactions of contemporaries. That Manigault's estate was more than twice as large as that of the next richest man in Jones's sample, who was from Massachusetts, helps to explain why other Americans regarded South Carolinians as extraordinarily wealthy. Englishmen, on the other hand, were impressed but not staggered. The equivalent of $60,000 may have been a large income in South Carolina, but wealthy Englishmen, it has been estimated, might take in three to four times this amount. Not false modesty but a clear perception of the situation caused Lieutenant Governor Bull to write that "our fortunes are moderate" when he addressed the British secretary of state in 1770.

If the Carolina elite was not especially rich when compared to the wealthy in England, it stood at the pinnacle of a small local society with an unusual configuration. Being exceptionally wealthy as mainland colonies went, South Carolina supported a surprisingly large proportion of artisans and men in trade for a predominantly planting society. Planters (with whom he may have intended to include professional men), Governor Glen estimated in 1749, made up more than two-thirds of the population; artisans about a sixth, and traders approximately one-eighth. Applied to contemporary estimates of population, Glen's ratios suggest that there were slightly over 2,000 planters, 500 artisans and nearly 400 merchants in the lowcountry at midcentury. These figures appear to be reasonably compatible with the estimates of other contemporaries who believed, for example, that the total number of rice and indigo planters did not much exceed 2,000 in 1765.

These statistics indicate that lowcountry South Carolina really was what one Carolinian termed it, "our little world." Moreover, despite the fact that contemporaries correctly believed that an unusually large proportion of the population enjoyed a high standard of living, much of the wealth was in the hands of a relatively small minority. And, finally, the concentration of wealth seems to have been increasing toward the end of the colonial period. Certainly in the 1760s, the percentage of the local tax paid by the residents of Charles Town rose faster than its share of the population (from 41 percent of the tax in 1760 to 46 percent in 1767, and from about 11 percent of the white population in 1760 to about 11.8 percent in 1770). Thus the social pyramid was steeply sloped, and its altitude was increasing faster than the width of its base.

How stable was this society? By the mid-eighteenth century the colony possessed a reputation for social peace and harmony. That, however, does not necessarily imply the absence of underlying strains and concealed friction. South Carolinians were known for not "being Overburdened with Sincerity," as well as for their social graces. In such a small society the hypocrisy of common politeness was almost essential for survival, while threats to the security of the colony increased the importance of internal solidarity. The expanding economy also helped to defuse latent hostilities. Despite disparities in wealth, Glen was probably correct in believing that about 80 percent of the white population had at least "the necessarys of life," and contemporaries clearly recognized their good fortune—which is one reason why so many immigrants came to Carolina after 1750. It was, as a physician in Philadelphia observed immediately after the Revolutionary War, the land of opportunity. Men who had not yet climbed the ladder of worldly success could look around them and see others like the merchants of Charles Town who, one of them claimed, "almost to a Man . . . [had] risen from humble and moderate Fortunes to great affluence, from walking upon foot to the command of Conveniences which render their Legs and feet almost useless." Such upward mobility occurred at all levels. Indentured servants were entitled to land upon receiving their freedom. Many who served out their terms in the lowcountry became freeholders and small farmers in the backcountry. Others, like Michael Kalteisen, who became commandant of Fort Johnson at Charles Town, made their mark farther east. Indeed, the origins of not a few prominent men differed little from that of indentured servants except for the latter's temporary servitude. Most members of the Commons House, one critic claimed, "were not worth 20 Shillings" twenty years ago. Not a critic but a close friend of Rawlins Lowndes, speaker of the house

in the late 1760s, observed that he had "hardly a common education."
Clearly, society was still young and fluid enough for wealth to be the
chief criterion for social status. Given the prevailing prosperity, it
seemed to be within the reach of many.

Not the feeling that "there but for the grace of God go I" but its
opposite may help to account for an apparent lack of hauteur on the
part of most men of property, which is rather surprising in the light
of their descendents' posturing. Colonial South Carolinians were conscious of class, and some of them, especially young men educated in
England after midcentury, were occasionally arrogant. William Henry
Drayton revealed their attitude when he took umbrage at the committee
seeking to prevent the importation of British goods in 1769, which
included mechanics. "The *profanum vulgus,* is a species of mankind
which I respect as I ought," he observed, "—it is *humani generis.* —
But, I see no reason, why I should allow my opinion to be controlled
by theirs." An educated man, he continued, "should make a proper
use" of his advantages, and not consult in matters of statecraft "with
men who never were in a way to study, or to advise upon any points,
but rules how to cut up a beast in the market to the best advantage,
to cobble an old shoe in the neatest manner, or to build a necessary
[out] house. Nature never intended that such men should be profound
politicians." Such open snobbery proved to be a serious mistake. Taking
to print themselves, the artisans replied that, though they might lack
education, they at least had *"common sense."* Drayton, on the other
hand—"whether it might have happened from an ill construction of
his sensory, or his upper works being damaged by some rough treatment
of the person who conducted his birth, we know not"—they observed,
seemed "highly defective in this point, whatever exalted notions he
may entertain of his own abilities." Members of the elite also pounced
on Drayton for his arrogance, maintaining that the artisans were "the
bones and sinews of society; and in any general plan, are as much to
be regarded, where their liberties and properties are equally at stake,
as any others whatever." This was good politics and, given the context,
these comments should perhaps be taken at less than face value. Yet
a loyalist historian—whose biases would have made him quick to find
fault with the Carolina elite—reported that "in respect of rank, all
men regarded their neighbour as their equal."

Others bear witness to the fact that a comparable sense of fellowship appeared to exist among religious denominations in the lowcountry. For example, an engineer, William Gerard De Brahm, described the situation in Charles Town at some length in 1773. There were, he noted, two Anglican Churches "and six Meeting Houses, vide, an Independent; a Presbyterian, a french, a German and two Baptists; there is also an assembly for Quakers, and another for Jews" which differed "in religious Principles, and in the Knowledge of Salvation"; yet, he continued, they were "far from being encouraged or even inclining to that Disorder which is so common among Men of contrary religious Sentiments in many other parts of the World, where that pernicious Spirit of Controversy had laid Foundation to Hatred, Persecution and cruel Inquisition." De Brahm was a German which suggests that the failure to capitalize "french" was deliberate, and, if so, he *did* exaggerate. Obviously, all ethnic and religious animosities had not evaporated under the Carolina sun. In addition to the prejudice against Scots, which increased during the Revolutionary era, there was some fleeting anti-Semitism, which a rash of thefts in Charles Town brought out when someone accused Jewish shopkeepers of selling goods stolen by blacks. Nevertheless, considering that the Anglican Church had originally been established by political legerdemain, relations between it and the dissenting denominations were surprisingly amicable during most of the eighteenth century.

There was, however, some friction. As in so many other places, the Great Awakening came to South Carolina in the person of the most famous itinerant evangelist of the eighteenth century, George Whitefield. A great orator and a shrewd operator, Whitefield concentrated his efforts on cities where he reached the maximum number of people and where his criticism of supposedly unregenerate Anglican clergymen appealed to local dissenters who resented the privileged position of the established church. During several visits to Charles Town in the late 1730s and early 1740s, he preached to large and sympathetic audiences; Alexander Garden, the local commissary or representative of the bishop of London, was not impressed. The masses, he believed, had been misled by Whitefield's "fascinating Gibberish." Like his superior, Garden also frowned upon Whitefield's criticism of the established clergy and liturgical deviations from the Book of Common Prayer. Garden's admonitions led to a bitter polemical battle in the local newspaper, and eventually, when Whitefield refused to desist, the calling of an

ecclesiastical court which suspended him from the ministry—all without effect, for he had long since left the colony. Perhaps Garden reacted
strongly because he already believed the established church to be em-
battled, but he was probably unduly concerned. If the Great Awakening
elsewhere resonated with overtones of tension within the local community, in South Carolina fears of its effects on blacks outweighed
other considerations and served as a powerful inhibitor of religious
enthusiasm among whites. Thus the Great Awakening had no permanently divisive effect in the lowcountry.

Indeed, as the eighteenth century wore on, South Carolinians exhibited an increasingly irenic spirit in religious matters. As one leading
merchant observed, though he was an Anglican, if a church of his own
denomination were not at hand, he would be perfectly willing to take
communion in a Congregational meeting. Perhaps Lieutenant Governor
Bull summed up the prevailing spirit as well as anyone when he
observed, that he "charitably" hoped that "every sect of Christians will
find their way to the Kingdom of heaven," although for political reasons
he believed "the Church of England [to be] the best adapted to the
Kingdom of England." In a sense, Bull's sentiments expressed con-
ventional Anglican doctrine. The Church of England was the established church and as such was partly an arm of the state. Its approach
was therefore territorial and inclusive—a subject of the king, Anglicans
believed, should be a member of the Church of England. Moreover,
being linked to the state, the Anglican Church was legally charged
with certain secular responsibilities. In particular, the churchwardens
conducted elections to the Commons House of Assembly and, together
with the vestry, collected taxes and dispensed funds for the relief of
the poor in each parish.

Thus for secular if not religious reasons a cooperative relationship
developed between the established church and leading dissenters in
many parishes. The latter needed the public services provided by the
Church, and the Church in turn relied on their influence and assistance.
In not a few cases dissenters were members of the parish vestry. Unlike
comparable vestries in England where ministers were "seized of their
livings"—that is, had tenure—local vestries also hired ministers on a
trial basis. Furthermore, despite Garden's unusual, and futile, attempt
to discipline Whitefield, the Anglican Church failed to develop a strong
hierarchical organization in America. Local vestries therefore enjoyed

considerable immunity from outside interference as well as much influence over their own ministers. No wonder Anglican laymen in South Carolina were not enthusiastic about British plans for establishing a bishop for America, and no wonder that one disgruntled minister blasted Carolinians for being "independent in Matters of Religion, as well as republican in those of Government." To say that the Anglican Church in South Carolina had become "dissenterized" would be to overstate the case, but the situation was certainly one which made it easier for dissenters to live with the established church. No doubt the arrangement also acclimated Anglicans to the idea that an established church need not be exclusively Anglican and thereby paved the way for the religious settlement of the Revolution.

If the institutional weakness and rather hybrid character of the established church helped to make it relatively acceptable to dissenters, its public functions helped to stabilize society in other ways. For example, church services acted as a kind of theater for displaying and reinforcing the social position of the gentry. When Whitefield preached, he discovered that his audience was not only large "but very polite," by which he meant upper class and sophisticated. "I question," he continued, "whether the court-end of London could exceed them in affected finery [and] gaiety of dress." The silver utensils for the communion service were often donated by one of the local magnates, whose imposing gravestone might stand in the churchyard. After church, one of his descendants, like Stephen Bull of Sheldon, might entertain the local gentry while his overseer kept open house for the common people. And on special occasions, members of the Commons House attended church as a body. Being designed in part to command awe and respect, such ceremonies represented the theater of deference in full panoply.

In more humble ways, too, the Church may have served to subordinate the "lower orders." In other places and at other times, poor relief apparently functioned as a form of social control. Although how, when, and where has been a subject of debate, some scholars have interpreted the relatively large expenditures for poor relief in Charles Town in this manner. It should be noted, however, that most of the individuals receiving relief in Charles Town were the tragic human detritus of a port town—that is, mainly widows and orphans of soldiers and sailors, with only an occasional disabled male. Able-bodied men rarely received assistance, and exceptions to the rule often involved what seems to have been considered the moral equivalent of a loan designed to help an individual through a run of bad luck. In short, poor relief was seldom given to those who might have been a threat to the social order. This does not mean that it was never used as a tool for imposing discipline on individuals who exhibited a penchant for "irregular" lifestyles or that poor but able-bodied men might not have slept easier in the knowledge that when they died their families would receive assistance. But one suspects that public benevolence did as much to promote identification with the community among the benevolent as it did to control the recipients.

Like the poor and poor relief, crime and punishment can be an index to social stability. By definition, penal codes are attempts to control behavior by authority, and violations of them often exhibit collective as well as idiosyncratic roots. Furthermore, court proceedings—perhaps even to a greater extent than church services—possess dramaturgical dimensions which serve to bolster the position of men in authority. Red-robed jurists, the complicated formality of the law and courtroom procedures, the awful solemnity of a death sentence, and the exhibition of mercy in a pardon, constitute theater of a high order. In it one sees the power of the state, the majesty of the law (which stands above the rulers as well as the ruled) and the benevolence of the authorities—all of which legitimize their power. In this sense, the seemingly incongruous proliferation of statutes defining capital crimes in England during the eighteenth century without a concomitant rise in the number of executions is perfectly understandable. Indeed, at least one scholar has contended that "the criminal law, more than any other institution, made it possible to govern eighteenth century England without a police force and without a large army. The ideology of the law was crucial in sustaining the hegemony of the English ruling class."*

In some ways the situation in South Carolina resembled that in England, but there were significant differences. By 1712, when the South Carolina assembly became the first colonial legislature to adopt specific English statutes, the process of making crimes against property capital offenses had progressed far enough in England for South Carolinians to adopt a harsh penal code, which remained the basis of local

*Douglas Hay.

criminal law throughout the first half of the nineteenth century. In addition, as one might expect, South Carolinians do not appear to have been more eager than English authorities to inflict the death penalty. During the last eight years of the colonial period (for which a court journal survives) the court of general sessions imposed sixteen death sentences, of which at most only six were carried out. Whereas in England almost all of the new capital statutes concerned crimes against property, more than half of the cases that came to trial in South Carolina involved crimes against persons, such as rape, murder, and—overwhelmingly—assault.

Certainly, throughout the colonial period random acts of violence in the lowcountry matched anything the backcountry could produce. In the 1720s, a family of Huguenot extraction living slightly north of Charles Town, the Dutartes, began having divine revelations which commanded the son-in-law to "put away" his wife, whom he had married as a widow, and take for his new wife her virgin sister so that the "holy seed" might be preserved in its original purity. Word got around; the local magistrate attempted to curb what he took to be licentious behavior; the Dutartes resisted and, before being captured, killed the captain of the local militia company. For that, three of the family were executed. In the 1730s, a traveler reported that, at the tavern in which he had recently stayed near Georgetown, "two men being in liquor" quarreled "till they came to blows." One threw the other down; "the undermost, finding the other to be too strong for him, bit off his nose, which made the other immediately let him go; upon which the fellow made his escape." Eye gouging was a known, if not commonly accepted, mode of fighting, and some roughnecks, it was said, had perfected the art. Men of property, on the other hand, favored pistols. Late in the colonial period, a royal official and a local doctor had a falling out, supposedly about political matters. They shut themselves up in a room at a tavern in Charles Town and proceeded to fire away at each other. The doctor, being the more accurate marksman, killed the other man, for which he was convicted—and pardoned. During the last eight years of the colonial period, the judicial machinery processed nearly 320 similar crimes of violence, or an average of about forty per year. At the same time, it also dealt with approximately 225 crimes against property, primarily larceny, for an average of about twenty-eight a year.

Although these figures appear to confirm Carl Bridenbaugh's impression that crime was less common in Charles Town than in most other colonial cities—and indeed, one might think, much less prevalent than in modern Charleston—interpreting them presents a number of difficulties. In the first place, the court of general sessions in Charles Town served the whole colony until 1772 when completion of district courthouses and jails permitted compliance with the Circuit Court Act of 1769. Thereafter, the Charles Town court had jurisdiction over the lowcountry parishes between the Santee and Combahee rivers, or approximately the area that would constitute the Charleston District for the census of 1790. At that time its white population was 16,352 which, outside of the city at least, probably reflected little change over the past twenty years; in 1770 the white population of the entire colony was approximately 49,000. Based on these figures, the annual crime rate in the late 1760s and 1770s turns out to have been on the order of 1.6 crimes of violence per 1,000 population; the rate for crimes against property was approximately 1.0. Two centuries later, crimes against persons in South Carolina were about two and a half times as frequent while those against property occurred almost twenty times as often!

Before leaping to conclusions about the modern situation, it is worth recalling that these modern statistics are based on the reported incidence of crime, while the colonial figures represent cases that actually went to trial. There is every reason to believe that then as now only a fraction of the crimes committed resulted in court proceedings. Furthermore, because blacks were subject to the summary jurisdiction of the freeholders' courts for which there are few surviving records, the colonial figures—unlike their modern counterparts—fail to include crimes committed by blacks. This discrepancy, it should be noted, helps to account for a striking difference between the two sets of figures. Crimes against property now outnumber those against persons by about five to one; in the colonial period, however, the court of general sessions tried approximately half again as many crimes against persons as against property. Though figures to test their belief are lacking, these comparisons help to explain why colonial and antebellum South Carolinians perceived crimes against property "almost exclusively as the work of slaves." In contrast, white crime, as Michael Hindus has recently noted, "was seen as the product of passions, not hunger." The latter was considered to be the lesser threat, for it was randomly distributed, episodic in character, and, contemporaries appear to have believed, largely unpreventable. Slave crime, on the other hand, was thought to be endemic—and unless vigorous countermeasures were taken—potentially epidemic. This difference in perception helps to explain an important difference in the legal systems governing blacks and whites. In the one instance, South Carolinians turned the clock backwards and made blacks subject to the summary jurisdiction of a rump court; in the other case, the colony was one of the earliest to provide legal counsel for whites accused of a crime.

All of this suggests that the presence of slaves modified "the ideology" as well as the nuts and bolts of the system of criminal justice imported from England. No doubt the courtroom supported the position of the elite in indirect as well as direct ways, much as in England, but given the sparsely distributed population, the lack of local courts, and the relegation of most cases involving crimes against property to the "negro courts," relatively few white South Carolinians saw the machinery of the criminal law in action against whites. Undoubtedly whites knew that their rights under it were considerably greater than those of blacks. Accordingly what happened in South Carolina may have been something of a mirror image of what Edmund Morgan has argued occurred in Virginia where men of property turned to slaves and prevented the growth of a white proletariat; in South Carolina whites who grew increasingly fearful of their slaves called in more whites to redress the balance and thereby fostered the growth of a class which, in comparison to the majority of the population who were blacks, was privileged. Thus, as in Virginia, black slavery was in some ways the price of white freedom and solidarity.

Certainly, the weight of the evidence reviewed so far suggests that, despite ethnic, denominational, and sectional differences among white South Carolinians, unity—or at least the basis for unity—was the rule rather than the exception by the middle of the eighteenth century. A longer period of development and the presence of more blacks helped to make the lowcountry a crucible in which the fusion of disparate elements had progressed farthest, but the spread of plantations to the backcountry—and indeed the Regulators' attempt to impose middle class values on the "crackers"—suggests that the society developing in the interior was in many ways a younger version of its eastern counterpart. Thus it is not really surprising to find that, after men were able to vote in the backcountry, use of the secret ballot produced results roughly similar to those in the lowcountry. In both sections, the populace turned to men of property for leadership. As has been seen, this propensity can be attributed partly to the effect of the prevailing political culture on the voters. But as will shortly be seen in greater detail, it was also partly the result of the effect of the prevailing culture on the political elite itself.

10

SOCIETY:
ASPIRATIONS AND ACHIEVEMENTS

The South Carolina gentry were not intrinsically the most important part of local society, but men of property were universally recognized as "the leading men," and the abundance of literary evidence about them reveals their aspirations. Comparable knowledge is not yet available for the common people, although it is quite possible that the environment affected them in ways similar to the elite. Accordingly, the conduct of the propertied gentry permits generalizations that disclose much of the character of Carolina society.

As one might expect, these aspirations had roots in the behavior of the English gentry, who valued family. A perceptive historian once observed that in the early modern period, the prospect of immortality in the form of a continuing family is what reconciled members of the English upper classes to mortality. Men who went to Barbados, however, sometimes found that their hopes were blasted by the high mortality rates of the area, while those who had surviving children frequently discovered that the increasingly crowded island limited their chances of providing an adequate patrimony for younger sons. Thus many who immigrated to South Carolina came with the intention of re-creating stable family life. That a substantial proportion of the eighteenth century elite was composed of descendants of these early settlers suggests that these hopes were not entirely unrealistic, but achieving them turned out to be more difficult than expected, for South Carolina proved to be more unhealthy than anticipated. As a result, some of the important families of the eighteenth century partly owed their contemporary position to the survival of their ancestors. Other once prominent names died out entirely, and more than one man without male heirs sought to perpetuate his name by devising his estate on the condition that the legatee assume the family surname.

Such demographic considerations had several important implications. In the first place, they made more difficult attempts to link the family name with a specific piece of real estate and thus augmented a trend common throughout the colonies—namely the abandonment of entail and primogeniture. A legal device whereby each generation in effect held land in trust for the next, entail sheltered the family estate from adverse economic circumstances; whether practiced by law or custom, primogeniture provided that the estate would descend to the eldest son. The propensity of early settlers to think of South Carolina as but a means to the end of returning "home" to England in style contributed to the tendency to see land as just another commodity, and the continuing commercial orientation of many South Carolinians helped to perpetuate that attitude. Moreover, increasing prosperity and wealth made it relatively easy for South Carolinians to provide equal inheritances for their sons and daughters. Under these circumstances primogeniture and entail became superfluous encumbrances rather than useful devices for perpetuating the family's economic base. Entail was apparently deliberately rejected as part of the legal system in 1712, and primogeniture—though embodied in the statute of distributions governing interstate estates—was rare among testators. The statute of 1791 dictating partible inheritance in the case of intestate estátes merely recognized prevailing practice. Nevertheless, testators often left the home plantation to the eldest son. More important, however, they seem to have tried to give all children—including girls—equal shares.

In part because their brothers sometimes failed to live long enough to receive their inheritances, women became important conduits of family wealth. How this affected their status is not entirely clear. In the seventeenth century, one might assume, when society was relatively fluid and the colonial economies comparatively unsophisticated, women occupied essential economic roles, were frequently well informed about financial matters, and enjoyed reasonably high status. At first sight, this supposition appears to be inherently plausible, and some peripheral evidence seems to support it. The relatively informal law of early

Virginia and New York, for example, accorded women greater equality of rights than more formalized later practice. All of which suggests, but of course does not prove, that if the economic importance of women in the seventeenth century did in fact give them higher status, the wealth of Carolina heiresses may have helped them to preserve their position. Certainly, marriage was in large measure an economic arrangement. The *South Carolina Gazette* reported marriage "treaties" and discussed family "alliances," and, like the groom, the press was often as interested in the lady's fortune ("£30,000 sterling," or whatever it might be) as in her other "amiable" qualities. It is also possible, however, that the wealth of the elite may indirectly have reduced a wife's leverage, for it enabled her to have slaves. And as historians of the Chesapeake Bay area have suggested, relegating domestic drudgery to blacks reduced the economic value of white women. Furthermore, blacks symbolized sexuality, and racism made them the image of all that a "pure" white woman should not be. These associations suggest that Victorian women did not invent the notion that sex was a chore and that, in fact, the circumference of a pedestal was already beginning to circumscribe the sphere of white women in eighteenth century South Carolina.

That these considerations involved much substantive change in the position of women is at least questionable. One of the leading authorities on the history of women in the colonial and Revolutionary periods, Mary Beth Norton, has recently argued—quite convincingly—that neither the seventeenth nor the eighteenth centuries produced much improvement in the status of American women generally until the Revolution. Although some of her data was drawn from South Carolina, no one has made a comprehensive study of the local situation. The scattered bits of readily available evidence remain tantalizingly discrete entities, difficult to fit into neat patterns. About 1700, for example, Elizabeth Hyrne, the wife of a planter, was apparently well informed about—and, one suspects, the source of—some of her husband's schemes for making them rich. Similarly, Sarah Rhett, the wife of the prominent politician and customs collector, William Rhett, was not only a merchant in her own right but also apparently an unusually able business person. Fifty years later, however, loyalist women (including a number of South Carolinians) were often patently ignorant of their husbands' financial affairs. Yet in the 1740s, as virtually everyone knows, Eliza Lucas Pinckney managed plantations with exceptional success. Thus whether the general position of women in colonial South Carolina was rising, falling, or remaining the same is a question awaiting a definitive answer. In the meantime, it is possible to observe that, whatever the trend may have been, the fact that one of the most liberal South Carolinians of the late eighteenth century, David Ramsay, had great respect for his wife's intellectual abilities but thought it appropriate to praise her for her dutiful "submissiveness" speaks volumes about the condition of married women at the end of the colonial period.

Women may, however, have been slightly better off legally in South Carolina than elsewhere. In the eyes of the law, a woman became a "feme covert" when she married—that is, she was literally "hidden" behind her husband who normally assumed control of her property, but other arrangements could be made. In particular, equity courts recognized marriage settlements, which often took one of two forms: in some cases, a husband agreed to compensate his wife or her heirs with certain property in return for her assets; more commonly, however, a bride and her male relatives drew up an agreement whereby they acted as trustees of her property during her marriage. As the latter arrangement suggests, marriage settlements were often as much in the interests of the bride's family as her own, but they could protect her as well. Thus it is not surprising to find that some women, like the young widow who after the Revolution refused to marry a suitor because he would not agree to a marriage settlement, were tenacious in seeking them. As this case suggests, in many of the colonies widows were the most apt to have substantial property and were therefore more likely to demand the safeguard of a settlement. Only further research will tell whether the unusual wealth of maiden heiresses in South Carolina had a similar effect, but marriage settlements became common enough in the Revolutionary era to warrant the establishment of a separate series of records for them, Paradoxically, in this case, the pervasive legal conservatism of South Carolinians may have had something of a "progressive" result; for in seeking to curb some of the ancient anomalies and discretionary powers of the equity courts, other states soon undermined some of the protection previously afforded women. South Carolinians, on the other hand, were slow to reform and therefore

probably left women in a slightly stronger position. During the eighteenth century, another long-standing custom also provided additional
protection for some women in commercial cities like Charles Town,
where it was possible for a married woman in trade to control her own
property and business as a "feme sole." Again, until someone makes a
systematic study of the subject, how common the arrangement was
remains uncertain. More frequent with small shopkeepers than among
the elite, it was probably always relatively rare. Nevertheless, even
among the elite, it could sometimes prompt intriguing notices like
the advertisement that Ann Gailliard placed in the *South Carolina
Gazette* of July 11, 1761, stating that she traded independently of her
husband.

Such a notice might or might not indicate trouble in the marriage.
What is clear is that divorce required an act of the legislature and for
all practical purposes was unobtainable in South Carolina, not only
throughout the colonial period but until after the Civil War. As Eliza
Lucas Pinckney sardonically observed, marriage was "a nice affair for
if we happen to judge wrong and are unequally matched there is an
end of all human felicity." She was devoted to her husband and theirs
was obviously a happy marriage, but others were not always so lucky.
One newcomer to the area, who heard many tales of domestic strife
shortly after the Revolution, considered such difficulties to be expected
in a society where marriages were frequently contracted "for sinister
views." Although the disruptions of the war may have contributed to
marital problems at that time, scattered indications of them appear
earlier. One prominent man sued another in the 1750s for the "rape"
and alienation of his wife's affections; and the scion of one of the
proprietary families, whose wife tricked him into marriage thinking
that she was pregnant with his child, later came to believe that he was
not the father. Royal officials also had their scandals. Early in the
1760s, the wife of a well-known local merchant ran away with a
departing governor, and a few years later, Egerton Leigh, who was the
attorney general and judge of the vice-admiralty court, had an affair
with his wife's sister, who was a ward in his own household. Although
his conduct was universally condemned, sexual morality among upper
class Englishmen was lax in the eighteenth century, and Carolinians
might have imitated them in this regard as in so much else. But despite

some obvious aberrations like those recounted above, the elite in South Carolina by and large seem to have retained what were later to be called middle class standards of morality.

Clearly, stable family life was the prevailing ideal, but such an ideal does not necessarily reveal much about the emotional bonds of real families. Some historians, working mostly but not exclusively on other colonies, have suggested that high infant mortality rates were associated with a low emotional investment in children on the part of parents during the seventeenth century. And some scholars have contended that fathers in South Carolina generally continued to neglect their children throughout the eighteenth century, as one might expect in an area where the death rate was high. Yet there is no question that in many cases where the documentation is good, such as those of Henry Laurens and Eliza Lucas Pinckney, parents not only perceived their children as unique individuals but virtually doted on them. Such evidence, though too scattered to be conclusive, suggests that the apparently increasing emotional density of the family may have had more to do with a rather broad transformation in western culture than death rates at a specific time and place.

Nevertheless, early parental death in South Carolina almost certainly affected both the speed with which children matured and the nature of the family itself. Recent scholarship dealing with New England and the Chesapeake Bay colonies suggests that in the case of the former the longevity of parents contributed to an extended period of economic dependence on the part of children who had become adults but had not yet inherited the family property; farther south where parents frequently died young, children often inherited as soon as they legally came of age, and sometimes earlier. There is as yet no systematic study of the situation in South Carolina, but there is every reason to believe that in this regard it resembled the Chesapeake. In fact, the death of adults at a relatively young age seems to have been frequent enough in South Carolina to create problems for the state as well as families. Lands belonging to individuals who died without heirs theoretically reverted to the crown, but escheat procedures were handled in England by the Court of Exchequer, which also tried cases involving the royal revenue. The assembly was leery of such proceedings and neglected to pass legislation which would have provided juries for the court, thereby complicating matters for the royal governors.

Government and established residents were more successful in dealing with the problem of orphans. The court of chancery, which was
merely the royal council sitting as a court, considered itself to be the
"Supreme Guardian of all Orphans and Minors," and in fact most of
its business concerned them. Families coped too, in the cases of widows
and widowers, by a kind of serial monogamy which helped to create
strangely convoluted and interrelated families in which one man might
be both the uncle and brother-in-law of another, and which are now
the bane of genealogists. But the widening ties of kin and "quasi-kin"
served an important function, for relatives, semi-relatives, godparents
and the like might care for minor children if both parents died.

Here, it would seem, was one of the roots of the extended network
of kinship which has long characterized the South, though recent
findings for colonial Virginia cast doubt on the supposition that this
pattern necessarily militated against the development of nuclear house-
holds. The same may prove to have been true for South Carolina. No
one doubts, however, that the South Carolina elite, like the Virginia
gentry, was in Bernard Bailyn's words, "one great tangled cousinry."
To cite just one example, the avuncular progenitor of the Middleton
family, Arthur, was a merchant who came to South Carolina from
London in 1679 by way of Barbados. By the time his collateral de-
scendant Arthur signed the Declaration of Independence, the latter's
father, both grandfathers, brother, father-in-law, and six brothers-in-
law were or had been members of the legislature, and the family was
related by marriage to at least sixteen families prominent in South
Carolina, including the Bulls, Draytons, Manigaults, and Rutledges,
not to mention the British aristocracy. Although the Middleton family
can scarcely be considered typical, what was unusual about it was not
so much the multitude of advantageous local marriages but the tie to
the British aristocracy. (Henry, who died in 1784, married a daughter
of the Third Earl of Cromartie.)

Given the small size of local society, the central role of Charles
Town, and the prudential element in marriages, it would be surprising
if the local elite had not been closely interrelated. The result in the
political sphere, however, was not always what one might expect. To
be sure, family ties have probably been relevant to local politics
throughout the history of South Carolina. Yet at the end of the colonial
period their influence seems to have been at a low ebb. Condemned

by the prevailing ideology which elevated the public welfare above partial interests, family influence also encountered obstacles posed by the plethora of relationships among leading families. When everyone was related to nearly everyone else, kinship often proved to be an ineffective way to discriminate among individuals; personal qualities such as ability and compatibility therefore tended to assume more important roles. Not until the Revolution when members of the elite found themselves challenged by new (and unrelated) men from the backcountry did family once again become a major political force. Furthermore, the chaos and hardships of the war often caused individuals to turn to their families for material and emotional support. Thus the augmented sense of family displayed by members of the South Carolina elite during the 1780s and 1790s is a rather misleading guide to its role in politics a generation earlier.

Another common assumption about the Carolina elite, namely, that its members were unusually materialistic, is more accurate. After all, as they were well aware, establishing a family meant providing it with a material base. For early Carolinians, the errand into the wilderness involved primarily the pursuit of wealth, and it was thus perhaps natural that visitors found their grand and great-grandchildren still talking mainly about "negroes, and the price of indigo and rice." What has been termed "the Carolina paradox: the unacquisitive spending standards of an acquisitive society" may, however, seem more anomalous. Yet those who observed Carolinians after they began to grow rich were certain that they had few inhibitions about spending money. As early as 1700 one traveler noted that they had "rais'd themselves to Considerable Fortunes." Within another generation, their dress would not have been out of place in the "court end of London"; and on the eve of the Revolution visitors from less affluent colonies were astonished at local munificence. "State, magnificence and ostentation, the natural attendants of riches," one observer noted, "are conspicuous, among this people." To a new arrival Charles Town was "a very gay place" in which he met merchants whose side tables were furnished with silver "in such a manner as wou'd not disgrace a nobleman['s] dining room." In short, the latest fashions, the best wines, the richest furnishings were to be found in almost every rich man's home, and even small shopkeepers dressed like gentlemen. Such behavior bespoke "the familiar story of the plutocratic stage of any rising people."

Carolinians may nevertheless not have been *that* much more materialistic than many other wealthy Americans. Recent examinations of extant inventories suggest that South Carolinians spent proportionally about the same amount of their wealth on clothing and household furnishings as their counterparts elsewhere. Being generally richer, the sum was larger in absolute terms and thus made a considerably bigger splash. Furthermore, Carolinians rarely appear to have had conscience qualms about enjoying their wealth. Ministers and a few laymen did occasionally lament that "We eat, we drink, we play, and shall continue to until everlasting flames surprise us" because, as another observed, "we have hardened under the Sun-shine" in the "bounteous Dispensations of his Providence." Such warnings tended to be fleeting and intermittent; they were most common during the Great Awakening and on the eve of the Revolution when disasters like the Stono Rebellion and the great fire of 1740, or apparent repression from Britain, followed a period of rapid economic expansion which had seemed to produce an orgy of materialism. At these times, some dissenters in particular seem to have believed that God was scourging Carolinians for their sins, and if they did not promptly mend their ways but continued to wallow in "luxury" they would become incapable of meeting current and future challenges. But this was the voice of a minority. Early on, a shocked minister found that when he asked dying men if their consciences reproached them with any "Evil done by them & which ought to be remedied," they "commonly" answered "No!" Nothing could more clearly reveal the prevailing attitude.

This should not be construed to mean that the Carolina elite was irreligious, though some observers believed that to be the case, and more than one visitor was appalled at the casualness with which Charlestonians attended church services. Visiting St. Philip's one Sunday morning in 1773, a New Englander discovered that the members of the small congregation continued their conversations throughout the sermon, which lasted less than eighteen minutes. An Anglican minister, on the other hand, gave the wealthy credit for considerable outward piety but not much inward belief. "Great Regard to Decency and proper Deference is observ'd by these Provincials, as to Externals," he observed, but "as to Internal Righteousness, Holiness, and Purity, it lyes in small Compass." Yet these observers overlooked or chose to ignore a quiet but nonetheless pervasive religious commitment in the lowcountry. Most persons were of "a religious turn of mind," one woman remarked in 1742. That, to be sure, was during the Great Awakening, but more than thirty years later a delegate to the Continental Congress from New England described a colleague from South Carolina, Christopher Gadsden, as "one of the most regularly religious men I have ever met." Religion, for most of the elite, was largely a matter of morality and ethics, and "enthusiasm," by which they meant uncontrolled emotion, was to be avoided. In this, of course, Carolinians shared the dominant mood of most Anglicans in England during the period. In their religion, South Carolinians were once again emulating the English gentry.

In fact, in almost every area of life (including even their materialism) English standards governed the behavior of Carolinians. They were, observers believed, "more attached to the Mother Country" than residents of the northern colonies, and, as one contemporary admitted, "fond almost to excess of British manners and customs" in everything from recreation to education and politics. No wonder South Carolinians enjoyed their wealth, for in spending it they saw themselves as bringing civilization to the wilderness. If some manifestations of this civilization appear a bit crude to us, some upper class Carolinians undoubtedly felt the same way. Bear-baiting was popular in England and Carolinians who cared to could watch it at Ashley Ferry; or if a gentleman preferred, he might attend the cockfights and races. Although both were held in hamlets throughout the colony, the races outside of Charles Town during February—first at the Old York Track and then, after 1760, at the New Market Course—were the climax of the racing season. There, large sums changed hands as men wagered and, not incidentally, engaged in a conspicuous casualness that demonstrated them to be gentlemen of wealth and nerve.

The theater too was a seasonal thing, primarily confined to the late winter. Beginning in 1703 with Anthony Aston, visiting players presented performances of both recent and classic works of the English stage. A generation later, local subscriptions helped to build a theater on Queen Street which burned in the great fire of 1740. Hard times then put a further damper on the stage until 1754 when, because of the French and Indian War, its revival seems to have been limited to a single season. But in the 1760s and early 1770s the American Company under David Douglass repeatedly visited Charles Town, and in

1773 subscriptions were used to construct another theater. The ensuing season has been called "incomparably the most brilliant" in the history of the colonial theater; it included eleven of Shakespeare's best-known works and more than 100 performances.

Charles Town was equally noted for music. Certainly by the 1730s, and probably earlier, there were public concerts, and after 1767 one might attend performances at Vauxhall (which was named after the famous pleasure garden in London). The best music was that presented by the St. Cecilia Society. Founded in 1762 and now the oldest musical society in the United States, it sponsored regular concerts by both amateur and professional musicians. Attendance was limited to members and their guests and, though impressed by the music, some visitors appear to have found the restrictiveness and formality of the admission procedures a bit much. Perhaps they would have preferred some of the early balls, which were open by public subscription for the support of local dancing teachers. Later, such affairs became increasingly private.

Like the dances and the music, many of the numerous private clubs in South Carolina had English antecedents. In the rural areas, especially by the time of the Revolution, there were various hunting clubs whose purpose was as much wining and dining as hunting. In Charles Town, it seems, clubs of more varied nature began quite early. Some, like the Candlestick Club which claimed to meet every night in a different tavern and advertised that it had £3,550 to lend in 1759, probably restricted their functions to spending their earnings on conviviality. Others, like the St. George's Society, though catering primarily to members of particular ethnic groups (in this case English), may have been predominantly social in character from the very beginning. But still other groups, like the St. Andrew's Society (Scots) and the German Friendly Society, at first resembled the burial societies of later immigrant groups—that is, they were partly designed to help care for widows and orphans. With increasing prosperity, most of these associations dropped the exclusively ethnic identifications, took on more catholic benevolent purposes, and became more socially exclusive. Ironically, the South Carolina Society which started out as a Huguenot artisans' group illustrated the trend as well as any, for by the last decade of the colonial period it had become an elitist benevolent organization with more than £7,500 sterling lent out at interest.

A few societies were founded primarily for intellectual purposes. The most famous of these was the Charles Town Library Society established in 1748 by seventeen individuals, mostly merchants and professional men, who hoped that "access to good and useful libraries might, in some measure," compensate for the lack of other education resulting from the "remoteness" of the colony and thereby "save their descendants from sinking into savagery." Thereafter, the Library Society was the center of much of the local intellectual activity, and by the time its library was destroyed by fire in 1778, the society owned more than 6,000 volumes. Although its members failed to establish a local college (despite vigorous efforts), in 1773 they did manage to found the first museum in North America. Meanwhile, the leading physician in South Carolina, Alexander Garden, became sufficiently renowned for collecting and writing about botanical and zoological subjects to be the only Carolinian elected to the Royal Society. As many know, the gardenia was also named after him. Other physicians, most notably John Lining and Lionel Chalmers, sought to establish links between the distinctive climate and endemic local diseases. Outside of Charles Town a number of individuals around Georgetown founded the Winyah Indigo Society in 1757, not only to gather and disseminate information about the new crop but also to support a local school.

To point out, as several scholars have done, that most of these efforts involved the consumption rather than the production of culture is scarcely an indictment. To expect much more from a small provincial society of recent origin would be unrealistic; yet it is worth noting that this intellectual activity was largely urban and that recent investigations of the libraries held by individuals have found that on the average South Carolinians owned fewer books than other Americans. Perhaps the most charitable interpretation would be that the presence of the Library Society obviated the need for private copies. In the closing decades of the colonial period, South Carolinians certainly had access to the largest bookstore south of Philadelphia in the form of Robert Wells's "Great Stationery and Book-Store on the Bay." Wells also supplied the Library Society before he fled to England during the Revolution, and the Society reestablished the relationship across the Atlantic after the war.

Clearly, even if most South Carolinians failed to maintain personal libraries commensurate with their wealth, they were willing to go to considerable lengths to keep abreast of the latest English publications;

"Mr. Peter Manigault and his Friends" as drawn by George Roupell in the 1750s. Manigault was later speaker of the Commons House of Assembly. From a nineteenth century copy. *Courtesy of the Carolina Art Association.*

furthermore, they read them. One of the more striking features of the locally written essays and poetry which frequently appeared in the newspapers was the relative speed with which authors alluded to recent English works. Thus, for example, a local essayist writing in 1769 quoted extensively from Blackstone's *Commentaries on the Laws of England* published four years earlier, and echoes from the *Letters of Junius* (1768–1772) appeared soon after their inception. As the use of the master satirist's work suggests, much local prose—like that published in other colonies—was polemical and often concerned political matters. Disagreement over the wisdom and legitimacy of the nonimportation movement, for example, touched off an unusually significant exchange. That debate is noteworthy not only because of the importance of the issue but also since one of the participants, William Henry Drayton, who opposed the measure as an infringement on his personal independence, considered his ideas worth preserving in book form. Perhaps appropriately for someone who also hoped to bring himself to the favorable attention of the ministry, Drayton republished all of the essays in London. Bringing them out in Charles Town would probably not have been feasible even if his point of view had been popular—which it was not. Local printers rarely had the opportunity or the capacity to undertake such extensive projects. Instead, they usually confined themselves to handbills and other miscellaneous items, short pamphlets, and almanacs, in addition to their newspapers. The latter, though mainly filled with material reprinted from English papers, provided a continuing forum for local men (and women) who wished to try their hand at the graceful essay or heroic couplet in the manner of English literary giants of the age.

The influence of the London magazines extended to the visual arts as well, for in the 1750s George Roupell made a delightful sketch of "Mr. Peter Manigault and his Friends" modeled on the cartoons carried by English publications. Roupell, who was both a minor crown official (searcher of the customs) and a member of the assembly at times, also did botanical illustrations for Garden's scientific papers. While in England as a young man Manigault himself revealed a more typical artistic interest by having his portrait painted. The work by Allan Ramsay—"one of the best Hands in England"—Manigault reported, was "not only an Exceedingly good Likeness, but a very good Piece of Painting." Because it depicted his own clothing, Manigault especially

Marie DuBose (Mrs. Samuel Wragg) as she appeared in a pastel portrait by Henrietta Johnston, done sometime after 1707. *Courtesy of the Carolina Art Association.*

hoped "Mr. Theus may see it." Jeremiah Theus, who worked in Charles Town from 1739 to the eve of the Revolution, painted many of the wealthy South Carolinians not lucky enough to sit for celebrated English artists—which, contrary to family tradition, was most of them. Accordingly, Manigault's words were carefully chosen, for Theus relied on stock props (including one necklace which appears in numerous paintings) to which he added an individual's face. Despite such devices and a weakness in depicting hands which often caused him to hide them, Theus's pictures were generally competent likenesses in the aristocratic manner, which made local men of property and their families resemble members of the British upper classes. Much the same could be said about the work of other portrait painters and miniaturists, of whom the most notable were probably Henrietta Johnston, who worked in Charles Town from about 1707 to 1729; John Wollaston, who was there in the middle 1760s; and Henry Benbridge, who arrived about 1771.

Their work graced the walls of houses that increasingly resembled English country estates and town houses. With a few exceptions, such as Mulberry which was built by a leading Indian trader in the first two decades of the eighteenth century, most early plantation dwellings were not especially imposing. With increasing wealth, men began to develop "country seats" in the immediate environs of Charles Town and along the main roads running north and south. The latter were usually working plantations, while many of the estates in Goose Creek and St. Andrew's parishes became largely show places. Formal and informal gardens ordered the landscape; imposing tree-lined drives led up to the houses from the landward side, while windows facing the rivers often commanded magnificent vistas. In town, the fire of 1740 contributed to a kind of urban renewal as buildings seemingly more appropriate to the rising level of affluence replaced destroyed structures. Two styles dominated both the old and new residences. Some dwellings were laid out symmetrically around a central hallway in a design that came to be known as the "double house"; others were the so-called "single house," which was only a single room deep. In these, a gable end faced the street, and the hallway might become a piazza entered through a false door. This arrangement, which produced a maximum amount of ventilation and privacy on a minimum amount of land, gave the city a West Indian look that it retains to this day. In reality,

Jeremiah Theus painted this portrait of Barnard Elliott, Jr., about 1766. Elliott later served in the Commons House of Assembly and the Royal Council before being commissioned in the Revolutionary armed forces. *Courtesy of the Carolina Art Association.*

however, both the single and double houses were adaptations of English styles, often constructed from published builders' manuals. Significantly, because stone was not readily available, wood and brick were sometimes finished to look like it. Furniture, too, though most of it was built locally, was based on English prototypes, and despite an occasional rice-plant motif, concessions to the local environment remained as minimal as possible. Mirrors, glass, and the like were usually imported from England. In fact, some gentlemen appear to have brought coaches, horses, and accompanying servants directly from the mother country.

Rising prosperity also encouraged a spate of public building similarly patterned on British models. Thus the parish church of St. Andrew's was remodeled in the 1720s; a new St. Philip's Church followed during the next decade. Ten years later a renewed spurt of building produced a number of impressive structures. The most beautiful was probably St. Michael's Church built after the old St. Philip's parish was split in two in 1751 to accommodate the growth of Charles Town. Under construction for ten years, St. Michael's not only resembled St. Martin's in the Fields in London but also had a rack of bells cast in England. The white spire in which they were housed became one of the chief landmarks used by harbor pilots. As the British prepared to attack the city in 1780, the American naval commander ordered the spire painted black, which—it turned out—made it even more visible. St. Michael's still stands at the southeast corner of Broad and Meeting streets in the heart of the historic district, but the other buildings at this intersection during the late colonial period have long since disappeared. One, quite out of keeping with the others, was the public meat market. Across the street from it was the headquarters of the town watch and, on the second floor, the public treasurer's office. On the fourth corner was the colonial state house constructed in the early 1750s, prior to which the assembly had met in private houses and the courts in taverns. The courtroom was on the first floor of the new building; the house and council chambers were upstairs, and the latter, which was frequently used for ceremonial purposes, had a balcony from which new governors were proclaimed. In 1788, after the legislature had voted to move the capital to Columbia, the state house accidentally—but in the interests of sectional peace perhaps providentially—burned down. Finally, the most imposing public building of all was the Exchange. Built during

Mrs. Barnard Elliott, Jr., by Jeremiah Theus, probably about 1766. *Courtesy of the Carolina Art Association.*

the late 1760s and early 1770s of brick and imported stone, it resembled its counterparts in London, Bristol, and Liverpool, with a large meeting room suitable for public functions above and storage areas below. Recently restored, it is now open to the public. Nowhere among this array of public buildings, it should be noted, was there a house for the governor. Having to rent various private residences, the governors were victims of the private character of so much of the city life.

Education, too, suffered from being predominantly private, despite more provision for public schooling than has sometimes been realized. Once again, English practice provided the prevailing models, though at least one Englishman professed not to recognize the affinity. Seeking a post as tutor to a planter's family late in the eighteenth century, he encountered a prospective employer who sought to discover his qualifications as a disciplinarian by asking if he could "*drive* well." No doubt many planters did know more about managing slaves than educating children, but after 1712 their sons had access to free schools in some of the outlying parishes as well as in Charles Town. Despite the name, these schools were not really free, for parents who could afford it paid tuition, and children whose education was underwritten by the parish or private benevolence—whether by individuals or associations such as the Winyah Indigo Society—appear to have always been in the minority. In addition, over the years a large number of specialized teachers advertised in the *South Carolina Gazette*. Thus it is clear that a combination of public and private facilities provided reasonably adequate opportunities for a local education through grammar school (or roughly the equivalent of modern high school), though some students, especially after the 1730s, attended English public (private) schools such as Westminster.

After grammar school, local opportunities for further training were limited. One possibility was an apprenticeship with a local merchant or professional man; another involved college elsewhere. No invidious social distinctions stigmatized merchandising if it was done on a sufficient scale, and the sons of some very rich planters served as clerks to local merchants. Similarly, a number of prominent lawyers received all or most of their training by reading law with local attorneys, though, toward the end of the colonial period, an increasing number of aspiring lawyers attended the Inns of Court and a few young men graduated from Oxford and Cambridge. In fact, as Lieutenant Governor Bull

Governors' chair, attributed to the local firm of Thomas Elfe and Thomas Hutchinson, made during the late 1750s for use in the first State House. *Courtesy of the South Caroliniana Library.*

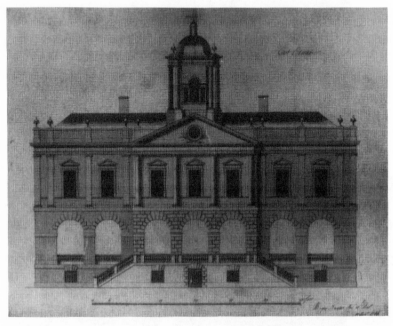

The Exchange as depicted in plans drawn in 1766 by William Rigby Naylor, a local architect and builder. *Courtesy of the South Carolina Department of Archives and History.*

observed, all those in the colony who had a "learned education" received it in England. And there were enough of them—if one includes lawyers—so that Carolinians represented the largest contingent of American students in England during the late colonial period. Not all South Carolinians thought this was something to brag about; lack of a local college made their behavior almost as much a matter of necessity as choice. The more parents heard about the "Relaxed state of Education" in the mother country, the more they feared that a sojourn there was apt to make a young man "adept in every thing which Wise Men wish to be ignorant of." More than one parent "trembled" to put his son at either Oxford or Cambridge, and a few sent them to Geneva instead. By the end of the 1760s, as the pre-Revolutionary controversy intensified, some South Carolinians began attending the College of Philadelphia.

Interest in establishing a local college also increased. Earlier discussions of the matter never progressed very far, but during the late 1760s and early 1770s the project came close to fruition. Fund raising drives for other colleges—to which South Carolinians responded generously—helped to stimulate interest, and perhaps the Regulators' demands for local educational facilities indirectly increased the awareness of problems caused by the absence of local institutions of higher learning. Friction with the mother country was undoubtedly the crucial factor, however, not only in directing the attention of prominent men to the need for a college but also in subverting their attempts to establish one. Ironically, the lieutenant governor, who was a strong supporter of the idea, may also have helped to undermine the project by attempting to use it as a means of diverting the Commons House from its intensifying quarrel with imperial authorities. The house refused to be sidetracked and establishment of the college had to wait until after the Revolution. Yet some local figures gave money toward it, and one local planter and member of the assembly, John Mackenzie—who, not incidentally, had been educated in England himself— willed his large library to the college, when established.

Despite such widespread and undeniably enthusiastic support by some individuals, there was also significant opposition. Part of it was the result of excessive frugality and mere inertia, but some appears to have been associated with the notion that one's education should be appropriate to one's station in life and the belief that parents who could legitimately expect to send their sons to college would be able to finance an education abroad. As one newspaper essayist implied in the early 1730s, better a good cobbler than a poor scholar; not every shopkeeper's son should aspire to be a gentleman. Similar assumptions circumscribed a girl's future, and most women—even among the daughters of the wealthy—received educations designed for the "domestic sphere" where a woman was supposed to be "a notable house wife." Her training was therefore in reading, writing, arithmetic, and perhaps French and embroidery, as well as other "genteel employments." Yet this was also the age of the English blue stocking, women intellectuals who not only kept "salons" but were often also writers of stature in their own right. Thus an alternative role model existed, and at least a few colonial women were well educated. Eliza Lucas Pinckney, who was probably born in the West Indies, and Martha Laurens Ramsay provide striking examples. Among other accomplishments, Eliza Lucas was quite capable of drafting wills for dying neighbors, while Martha Laurens sought to master such traditionally masculine subjects as geography. Alarmed when she requested globes, her father provided them but cautioned, "when you are measuring the surface of this world, remember you are to act a part on it, and think of a plumb pudding and other domestic duties."

Boys faced wider choices and, contemporaries believed, more arduous roles. In particular, the sons of the elite were destined, in the current vernacular, to be "the Ornaments of their Country." These youths were to be the leaders of the society, and their training involved the highest aspirations of contemporaries. The prerequisite for such a station— indeed, for political participation or manly competence in any walk of life—was personal freedom. To be free in the most general yet most immediate sense was to be subject to one's own reason, not one's passions or the will of another, for it was possible to be a slave to either. The possession of sufficient property to keep one above dependence was therefore essential. As a planter, William Wragg, stated in 1775, that if he had "no other resources than what a plantation afforded," he would "endure everything, rather than have the freedom" of his "will or understanding limited or directed" by men without authority. His declaration was courageous and almost categorical— but it began with a conditional clause. Like Franklin who observed that it was difficult for an empty bag to stand upright, eighteenth century Carolinians were realistic. Economic independence, though seldom an immediate concern for men of property, was never taken for granted, and the education of youths was partly designed to provide them with skills necessary to safeguard the material base of freedom.

But if the external conditions of freedom had become largely a matter of inheritance for the sons of the elite, the internal required more active effort on their part. Remember, Eliza Lucas Pinckney wrote her brother, "the greatest conquest is a Victory over your own irregular passions." By greatest she meant not only the most difficult but also the most essential for, as she noted, a man who had not learned regular habits and self-control in childhood was a "burthen to Society and himself." Thus she urged him to "lay down betimes a plan" for his "conduct in life." Similarly, a relatively minor Revolutionary leader, Thomas Ferguson, directed the executors of his will to be especially careful in keeping his sons busy until they were twenty-one, "so as to give a true Relish for Industry," for he was "well convinced that the Habit of Idleness is productive of the most fatal Consequences to Youth." Every man, Locke observed, "must some time or other be trusted to himself, and his own conduct; and he that is a good, a virtuous, and able man, must be made so within." Freedom and self-discipline were the hallmarks of an autonomous man.

As the quotation from Locke suggests, in committing themselves to these values, South Carolinians were once again following English standards, and that fact alone would have been enough to make them take these ideals seriously, since personal independence and disciplined order were highly valued in the culture of eighteenth century England. It was, as one acute student of English political culture, J. G. A. Pocock, has observed, "the most classical-minded of English centuries"; order and regularity in everything from architecture to zoology were considered to be cardinal virtues; and the favorite maxims of the age were those of the ancient poets extolling the benefits of calm rationality. Yet, as Pocock has also noted, there was one subject on which contemporary Englishmen "allowed" themselves "to become fanatical." It was personal independence. However powerful the English model was in this case, conditions in South Carolina augmented its effect. In the first place, coping in a new and fluid environment required the flexibility of personal freedom, while relatively weak institutional support made self-discipline socially and psychologically more important. So,

too, did the presence of slaves, since racism augmented the commitment
to personal freedom on the part of white Carolinians who thereby sought
to distinguish themselves from blacks. What has been perhaps less
well recognized, though, is that racism similarly enhanced the importance of self-discipline. If whites tended to believe that blacks
deserved their conditions because they permitted themselves to be
enslaved, masters also justified slavery on the grounds that it disciplined
an otherwise savage being. Thus a white man demonstrated that he
merited freedom not only by his willingness to fight for it but also by
his ability to discipline himself. Personal independence and self-control
were considered to be attributes of the civilized man, and Carolinians
strove to make their plantations and their minds islands of good order
and regularity in a potentially chaotic world.

Part of the process involved inculcating succeeding generations, and
the depth of the Carolinians' commitment to certain core values stands
out in letters and testamentary injunctions to their children. Consider
the following passage from a letter of Henry Laurens to his eldest son
concerning his children. "You may all of you[,] for aught I know[,]
come to be Learned, Smart, & what the World calls sensible," he
noted. "But as much as I love you which is so much as to induce me
to exercise very great self denials for your sakes, if I did not hope that
you would be truly Wise, that is to say, that you will cultivate in your
Hearts, the Love of Truth & Justice & the Love of Mankind which is
the Love of God & which will lead you on to be useful Members of
Society I would rather wish you all taken from this Life before you
could experience more of those Pains & Sorrows which are the Inheritance of the Sons of Men." Though seldom stated so starkly, similar
passages can be found in the letters and wills of other parents. It would
be a rare member of the Carolina elite, one suspects, who could have
grown up without believing that there were values more important
than self and without understanding that to reject them was to forfeit
a parent's love. If Laurens expressed the importance of these values
more baldly than most parents, Charles Pinckney spelled them out
more explicitly. His will filed after his death in 1758 merits quoting
at length:

> to the end that my beloved son Charles Cotesworth may the
> better be enabled to become the head of his family and prove

not only of service and advantage to his country, but also an Honour to his Stock and kindred, my order and direction is that my said son be virtuously, religiously and liberally brought up and Educated in the Study and practice of the Laws of England; and from my said son I hope, as he would have the blessings of Almighty God, and deserve the Countenance and favour of all good men, and answer my expectations of him, that he will employ all his future abilities in the service of God, and his Country, in the Cause of virtuous liberty as well religious as Civil; and in support of private right and Justice between Man and Man; and that he do by no means debase the dignity of his human nature, nor the honour of his profession, by giving countenance to, or ever appearing in favour of irreligion, injustice or wrong, oppression or tyranny of any sort, public or private; but that he make the glory of God and the good of mankind, the relief of the poor and distressed, the widow and the fatherless, and such as have none else to help them, his principal aim and study.

Neither the example of the father's life—which his wife described as one continuous course of "active Virtue"—nor his words were lost on Charles Cotesworth. To him, his biographer has recently observed, "duty, honor, service—all were sacred words." Though more prominent than most of his contemporaries, Charles Cotesworth did not stand alone in espousing these ideals. His great popularity, in fact, was probably partly due to the degree to which he exemplified values held by all.

Charles Pinckney the elder may or may not have been aware of what scholars have recently rediscovered, namely that the ideology of the law—including its putative commitment to justice—played an important part in legitimizing the rule of the aristocracy in eighteenth century England, but he certainly knew that the law was in high esteem there. Furthermore, as his will implied, he also knew that a knowledge of the law was a useful adjunct to public service on the part of the English gentry as well as the Carolina elite. This did not mean that every man of property should be a lawyer—despite Pinckney's wish for his son—but that every gentleman could profit from some knowledge of the law, not only to protect his own property but also to qualify him for his station in life. As the great English systemizer of the law William Blackstone argued, those "on whom nature and fortune have bestowed more abilities and greater leisure" had a greater responsibility. "These advantages are given them, not for the benefit of themselves only, but also of the public: and yet they cannot, in any scene of life, discharge properly their duty either to the public or themselves, without some degree of knowledge in the laws." Called upon to act as justices of the peace, members of the grand and petty juries, and in many cases of the Commons House, wealthy South Carolinians took these words to heart. Thus, they often perused editions of Michael Dalton's *The Country Justice,* one of the more frequently owned law books designed to provide guidance for a man who might be required to act without benefit of professional assistance and who therefore needed to be able to "resolve, and satisfie himselfe what hee ought to doe in every particular." In short, the law was central to the public position and self-image of the Carolina elite, and its administration therefore reveals much about the elite and their society.

Carolina, like other colonies, had a long tradition of lay justice which had roots in the seventeenth century hostility to lawyers. The Fundamental Constitutions forbade anyone to plead for pay, and though the Constitutions were unacceptable on other grounds, this provision was compatible with the feelings of most of the inhabitants. In the relatively simple economy, legal complexities were apt to appear like traps for the unwary, and lawyers were often regarded as leeches of the law. For the first twenty years there seem to have been no professional attorneys in the colony, and throughout the remainder of the colonial period the vast majority of justices of the peace and, indeed, most of the assistant judges—not to mention the councilors who constituted the Court of Chancery and who would have acted as an appellate court in the event of appeals from the common law courts—were laymen. Not surprisingly, their knowledge of the law was often rudimentary; nor was their ignorance entirely their own fault. For one thing, much of the work of the J.P.s involved offenses committed by slaves, and nothing in the English manuals like Dalton's gave them much help with these matters. Lieutenant Governor William Bull the younger in 1761 therefore prevailed upon William Simpson to publish a guide for justices of the peace that would be more adapted to the local situation. But that work could scarcely be much of a guide to the common law which had evolved through thousands of English judicial decisions or to the voluminous British statutory law that was at least relevant if not necessarily in force in the colony. By the eighteenth century English law was in fact complex enough to give even the brightest and most energetic students serious trouble. As one young Carolinian admitted, he spent three terms at the Inns of Court in a London fog before "the divine light of the law began to shine upon me with its benign rays."

In England, however, lawyers at least had access to published statutes and printed decisions; in South Carolina the only collection was Nicholas Trott's *Laws of the Province of South Carolina* published in 1736 as an outgrowth of his work in preparing the Act of 1712 which had adopted specific English statutes. Thereafter, nothing more was done, though members of several grand juries and others repeatedly pointed out the need. No doubt the sheer magnitude of the task intimidated some who might have attempted it; for, as commissioners who undertook it after the Revolution reported, the problem involved not only ascertaining the laws in force but also clearing away "a stupendous pile of old and new law rubbish." In 1768, John Rutledge was willing to make the attempt, but a sufficient number of subscribers failed to agree to purchase the collection, and the project was dropped as unfeasible. Sir William Blackstone's *Commentaries on the Laws of England* published in London in 1765 thus proved to be something of a godsend, for it provided an extraordinarily systematic and accessible textbook of English law, and Carolinians who rejected his conservative bias were soon quoting him for their own purposes. Like Coke's famous *Institutes,* Blackstone provided a body of general principles which could be adapted to many situations. Nothing could have been more appropriate for lay justices who had access to few other volumes.

Yet overlaying the prevailing substratum of amateur justice was a professional tradition. In South Carolina, unlike some of the other colonies, nearly all the chief justices were lawyers, and, as elsewhere, the increasing complexity of the local economy increased the usefulness and, accordingly, the status of skilled attorneys. In the generation after 1750 no less than fifty-one natives of South Carolina attended the Inns of Court. Similar professionalization of the bar in other colonies occasionally led to friction with men who represented the older tradition and frequently produced a resurgence of hostility to lawyers on the part of laymen reminiscent of the seventeenth century. Yet, as some scholars have noted, attorneys in the southern colonies and states appear to have been more successful in retaining popular trust, perhaps because they were often plantation owners whose interests thereby seemed to be identified with their local communities. There was, to be sure, some friction in South Carolina. In the 1720s the ignorance of lay judges, the acting governor reported, "became a ridicule to the lawyers," and similar problems appear to have plagued the county courts established after the Revolution. Conversely, some laymen among the Regulators and politicians of the Revolutionary era professed to see a "Junto" of lawyers manipulating public affairs in order to "palm immense sums." But displays of such hostility seem to have been, comparatively speaking, rare and muted.

Among the many possible explanations for the relatively harmonious state of affairs may be the tendency of local conditions to reduce the distance between the extreme ends of the spectrum of legal knowledge. District courts failed to flourish because the judges were too ignorant and the tools of the trade in the form of books and statutes too scarce in outlying areas. Conversely, the pretensions of more sophisticated members of the bar tripped on limited libraries and the lack of adequate works dealing with the local law. As one chief justice implied, it was impossible for anyone to have a thorough knowledge of South Carolina law, and this included the professionals. Perhaps because the situation had some advantages for them—cynics, for example, professed to see a correlation between the high income of the leading lawyers and the popular ignorance of the laws resulting from the lack of a published compilation—potential young Turks seldom made themselves obnoxious by attempts to professionalize the practice of law. Rutledge dropped his plan to publish a codification, and his attitude toward Blackstone's text is revealing; he considered it "useful." In contrast, Jefferson was contemptuous of its products, instant "Blackstone lawyers," whom he termed "ephemeral insects of the law." Even he probably protested too much, for the Declaration of Independence appears to echo Blackstone's assertion that the All Mighty had "reduced the rule of obedience for humans" to this one paternal precept, "that man should pursue his own true and substantial happiness."

Nevertheless, Jefferson would probably have been shocked at legal proceedings in South Carolina; professional lawyers from elsewhere certainly were. The bar was small, justice highly personal, and procedure informal if not irregular. The chief justice signed blank warrants which were then filled out by the lawyers; in times of crisis, the attorneys and the chief justice huddled to decide how to conduct themselves; opposing lawyers "compounded"—that is, negotiated settlements before a case went to trial—and then conducted the whole business so informally that a newly arrived attorney, who took a dim view of such laxness, believed that the general sloppiness made appeals on procedural points virtually impossible. Few lawyers—or even judges—appear to have regularly cited statutes, let alone prior judicial decisions, in support of an argument or a decision; the distinctions between law and equity were, according to Rutledge, often blended "very ridiculously" and unknown to many of his colleagues, while proceedings in the court of equity itself were "extremely relaxed." More significant, a judge's role in the common law courts was at one and the same time narrower in scope and more active than that of his English counterpart. In England, judges were supposed to counsel defendants on points of law in criminal cases. In South Carolina, the accused was allowed an attorney because the lay judges were not considered competent to provide the same protection. On the other hand, local judges like Rawlins Lowndes not only weighed general considerations such as the defendant's character in rendering decisions but also offered testimony about the man. Needless to say, this homespun justice appalled the English lawyers who became judges after passage of the Circuit Court Act of 1769. That act and the role of the English judges will be dealt with more fully in the next chapter; suffice it to say here that the jurists were extremely unpopular. Their attempts to tighten up procedures had a counter-productive effect and may have served as a warning to others who might have been overly zealous in attempting it. Furthermore, circuit courts, though viable with trained judges and lawyers, tended to perpetuate earlier conditions. Thus, it was said that after the Revolution Charles Cotesworth Pinckney in giving advice to clients while on the circuit always noted the location to indicate that he acted without benefit of a library.

In some ways the bar was emblematic of the elite as a whole. Much in the same manner as the bar became increasingly (albeit partially) professionalized, the elite increasingly (albeit with less than complete success) sought to set itself apart from the rest of society. More interest in genealogy, private schooling, especially in England, membership in increasingly exclusive clubs and associations—even an attempt of the Commons to raise the property qualifications of its own membership— were all part of the same pattern. Such a trend possessed potentially contradictory effects; whether it would consolidate or undermine the position of the group depended on how far the pattern progressed and, more critically, to what extent others considered the pretensions of the elite to be justified.

As might be expected, the Carolina gentry did not completely live up to its own ideals. Laziness and dissipation constituted perhaps the most common indictments. The wealthy planters especially, according to one local professional man, were "above every occupation but eating, drinking, lolling, smoking, and sleeping, which five modes constitute the essence of their life and existence." A traveler charitably offered an explanation: "The rays of their sun," he theorized, seem "to urge them irresistibly to dissipation and pleasure." Whatever the cause, the amount of drinking literally and figuratively staggered those not accustomed to it. One man who visited Charleston shortly after the Revolution noted that "Carolina would be for many a toper a loved country; it is the doctrine here that during the warm months one should think and work little, and drink much." Not being willing to let go "untasted any of the pleasures of life," the residents of Charleston, he thought, lived "rapidly" and burned themselves out early; few reached "a great age" and many died "in the bloom of their years." About the same time, an immigrant from New Jersey found the men to be generally "very dissipated, little inclined to study and less to business." Another observer was certain that "cards, dice, the bottle and horses engross prodigious portions of time and attention: the gentlemen (planters and merchants) are mostly men of the turf and gamesters." Even the members of the Commons House, he believed, lacked all ambition "to shine and blaze in the forum or a senate." And, indeed, an assemblyman once noted that his colleagues had suspended legislative activities so they could attend a round of balls. Historian Carl Bridenbaugh has concluded that the Carolina aristocracy exhibited a "callous social irresponsibility."

There was also another side to this image of the aristocracy. Even some visitors who were on balance harsh in their assessment noted that its members were personable or, as one phrased it, "as agreeable as any

I have ever seen." Perhaps the Carolina charm affords an explanation of the widely recognized ability of the local society to co-opt Yankees and others at least up until the Civil War. Nor were the virtues of colonial Carolinians limited to the social graces. Punctual in paying debts, they had a reputation for being men of honor whose word was as good as their bond. "A great many of 'em," an Englishman observed in the 1760s, were "very carefull and thrifty"; and he encountered "severall eminent merchants, who transact their business very quick and discreet." Many, another Englishman remarked, were "very clever in business." What is perhaps most surprising in this supposedly dissipated society, one Quaker even reported that the conversation of Carolinians was remarkably free from "Scandal." Moreover, as several historians have noted, the Commons was not only an effective body but also, to judge from the amount of time it was in session, one of the hardest working assemblies in the colonies. Perhaps a break to attend balls was not unjustified.

Reconciling these conflicting reports and opinions presents a difficult problem because none was without foundation. Perhaps the most exaggerated is the notion that the elite was callously irresponsible. With the possible exception of the failure promptly to extend representation to the backcountry (which was a more complicated matter than it might initially seem) and the issue of slavery (which was no problem to most contemporaries)—both of which have probably blackened Carolinians in the eyes of some historians—there can be little doubt that, in general, men of property were public-spirited in intent by the middle third of the eighteenth century. Their performance is open to more question, but even in this regard they have occasionally been maligned unfairly, perhaps because their failure to establish highly visible institutions of local government has produced some misunderstanding.

Local government was actually considerably more effective than has commonly been realized. At the provincial level, a practice analogous to senatorial courtesy enabled men with knowledge of local affairs to sit on the appropriate legislative committees, while at the local level itself members of the elite regularly served on ad hoc commissions for building bridges, and the like, as well as on the standing road commissions. In addition, acting as churchwardens and vestrymen, men of property not only handled church affairs but also dispensed poor relief. Additionally, in Charles Town numerous local commissioners—

of the streets, pilotage, market, workhouse, and so forth—regulated commercial life. All of them were elected in a kind of town meeting each Easter Monday.

The belief that Carolinians completely neglected local government is untrue, but the number of presentments by the grand jury indicating that certain commissioners had not fulfilled their responsibilities suggests that the charge of laziness may have had more substance. Even such a local booster as the younger Bull implied as much when he observed that in winter "we are often invigorated with purifying cold winds from the Cherokee Mountains, which recovers us from the languid habit acquired in the warm months." Endemic fevers constituted another extenuating circumstance, and no doubt some observers received misleading impressions because many of the planters seen in Charles Town were on a holiday. There was not only wide individual variation, as might be expected, but different norms sometimes governed the behavior of subgroups within the elite. Members of the Commons House were, for example, theroretically supposed to be paragons of virtue. But the treasurers who reported to the house regularly mixed public with private funds and pocketed the interest on both. Despite periodic charades designed to suggest the contrary, this practice was widely recognized to be one of the perquisites of the office. Similarly, other posts were frequently bestowed on disabled or bankrupt members of the elite, and a candidate could unabashedly observe that, having a large family to support, he was especially well qualified for a particular job.

Yet when all is said, the impressions remain contradictory. What, then, is finally to be made of them? Perhaps Bull summed up part of the matter as well as anyone. "A gratuitous execution of many branches of power"—that is, voluntary public service—was, he believed, more common in South Carolina than in any of the other colonies because of the relatively large number of men who were "under a desire of shewing a public spirit and easing the public expenses." But then, he noted, "this laudable spirit is attended with its inconveniences, for when a man receives no compensation for his service, there is a tenderness and reluctance shewn to call him to account for his neglect of duty, whereby the public often receives detriment." In the increasingly cozy world of the eighteenth century elite, the intent and the gesture, it appears, were sometimes able to satisfy one's colleagues.

Nor does it seem that the populace was generally unhappy with the conduct and performance of its leading men. Certainly, their constituents were willing to reelect them to the Commons House with greater frequency as the eighteenth century progressed and, in the absence of contrary indications, the trend suggests that men of property were succeeding in their attempts to consolidate their social and political role. Being the ornaments of what the *South Carolina Gazette* termed "this polite and Rich Colony," members of the elite were in some ways both the architects and the beneficiaries of a highly visible collective achievement which was a source of increasing pride for individuals in all walks of life. Angered by British restrictive measures, one of the assistant judges, Robert Pringle, gave a charge to the grand jury in 1769 which reveals the prevailing feeling. "Some of your progenitures," he observed, "arrived in this country when it was a dreary wilderness; inhabited only by wild beasts, and great numbers of savages . . . ; and not withstanding the great hazard they ran of losing their lives, and the many hardships and disadvantages they labored under . . . yet they bravely maintained their ground, and withstood and defended themselves against the frequent assaults and attacks of the savages, though attended with a great effusion of blood." Since then, Pringle observed, they have "by their great industry, improved and cultivated the colony to so great maturity, that it is become the land of plenty, as well as of liberty, and fruitful, like the land of Egypt"; and, he pointedly added, "all this done without one farthing expense or charge to the mother country." It is now, he concluded "the most opulent and flourishing colony on the British Continent of America."

The increasingly strident pride of Carolinians in their own achievement reveals the extent to which Anglicanization of the colony involved not only an attraction to things English but also a commitment to South Carolina. In all probability, most of the early settlers hoped to be birds of passage: they would go to the wilderness, make money as quickly as possible and, like many West Indian planters, return to England. But it took more than a generation for the leading families to acquire sufficient wealth, and by the time they could retire to England many no longer wished to. They were born in South Carolina and possessed a sense of gratitude to the land that had made them rich. It was the sepulchre of their fathers and the home of their relations, while by this time many Carolinians had lost earlier contacts in England. Though they still figuratively spoke of England as "home," they called South Carolina "my country," and out of their love for both proceeded to make the one as much like the other as they possibly could. With considerable reason they thought they had done a good job. To them, the increasingly impressive skyline of Charles Town evoked, if ever so remotely, images of London or Bristol. Thus to discover that Englishmen were more apt to notice that vultures provided perhaps the most effective means of keeping the unpaved streets clean was an unsettling and threatening experience.

11

THE CHEROKEE WAR
AND THE INDIRECT CHALLENGE
TO THE CAROLINA GENTRY

Convinced that they had transformed "a dreary wilderness" into a "polite and Rich Colony" by the mid-eighteenth century, South Carolinians expected to receive credit for their achievements. Instead, when the French and Indian War brought them into closer contact with Englishmen, Carolinians found that British authorities frequently operated on the assumption that Americans were still backward colonials. How that belief complicated efforts to defend the colony during the war and subsequently to deal with the problems of the rapidly growing backcountry is the theme of this chapter.

For a brief time following King George's War in 1748, a number of developments led imperial authorities to reverse Walpole's policy of salutary neglect. Rapid growth made America more important to Britain, yet, a new ministry feared, more uncontrollable. Insubordination and disorder bordering on anarchy seemed to prevail in some of the provinces where the "frame of Government" appeared to be not merely "unhinged," as Governor Glen reported from South Carolina, but dismantled. Yet, as Glen also observed, "these evils" seemed to be "too bigg for correction during the War." Peace provided an opportunity to tighten things up. George Dunk, the forceful Earl of Halifax, who was appointed to head the Board of Trade at this juncture, infused that agency with some of his own energy and ambition. Governors like Glen, who in Halifax's estimation was incompetent, had to go, and early in 1755 William Henry Lyttelton was named to replace him. But once again, war intervened. In 1754 hostilities broke out in America and, two years later, in Europe. During the Seven Years War — the French and Indian War or the Great War for the Empire, as it has been variously called — imperial authorities were generally forced to defer plans for bringing the colonies under tighter control. That Lyttelton was captured by a French squadron while en route to America and, after his release, had to return to England for a fresh copy of his instructions is perhaps symptomatic of the difficulties encountered in carrying out the new policy. That the new instructions not only represented the first thoroughly revised version since 1720 but also specifically directed the governor to roll back some of the assembly's powers also suggests the depth of the British resolve to bring the colonies under closer control. When peace returned in 1763, imperial authorities would redouble their efforts.

In the meantime, however, Lyttelton had to make some compromises. Although he managed to reassert the prerogative in a number of relatively minor areas, he was for the most part not able to undertake a full-scale assault on the powers of the Commons; instead, he inadvertently augmented them. When he arrived, the two houses of the legislature were locked in a struggle over the appointment of a colonial agent in Britain; and because his salary was involved, the question of the council's role in amending money bills became part of the controversy. It had reached the point where a member of the Commons writing in the *Gazette* flatly asserted that councilors who were appointed by the crown lacked the independence necessary to constitute an upper house. In reply, the council shifted the grounds of the argument and for the first time unequivocally based its claim to equal status on the governors' instructions which, it argued, were binding on all branches of the government. "This province, and the legislature of it," the upper house maintained, are "entirely subordinate and dependent. Its powers are *derivative* and not *original*. . . . The whole power of legislation here springs from the crown." That is to say, the constitution was what the crown said it was, and neither the people of South Carolina nor their representatives enjoyed inherent political rights. This was precisely what most imperial officials believed, and it is not surprising that the man responsible for voicing the point of view was a new — and singularly forthright—member of the council who had spent most of his life in England, though he had been born in South Carolina.

William Wragg's outspokenness put the council in a precarious position, for any failure of support on the part of imperial authorities at this point might undercut the upper house's argument of last resort. What Lyttelton did was even more damaging. Arriving in the middle of the controversy, he wanted to get on with the main business at hand—the war against France—with which, he thought, a dispute about *"trivial points of privilege"* was interfering. Thus, when Wragg challenged him on a number of less important matters, Lyttelton responded by suspending him from the council, and having perhaps the greatest influence in London of all the royal governors, he was able to make the suspension stick. The Board of Trade then further diminished the already dwindling prestige of the council by adopting a deliberate policy of appointing placemen in the hope of obtaining a more pliant upper house. Later, after the ministry belatedly realized that the council needed strengthening, it could find few South Carolinians of stature who would accept appointments; obviously a position held by so precarious a tenure was not compatible with the status of an independent country gentleman. Thus, by the end of the colonial period the council had become a cipher, its real power practically nonexistent, and most of its members virtual incompetents, not only in the estimation of many South Carolinians but also in that of some capable crown officials.

Although more serious than most, Lyttelton's blunder in regard to the council was only one of a number of misunderstandings and mistakes that occurred during his administration, though not all of them were his fault. Another miscue inadvertently precipitated a quartering controversy during the winter of 1757–1758 when the assembly, which feared a French invasion, requested the assistance of British troops, and independently of each other both the secretary of state and the commander in chief in North America sent forces. More than 1,700 regulars descended on the colony which was unable to provide adequately for so many. In America the shortage of barracks led commanders to adopt methods for housing troops previously restricted to Scotland and Ireland where soldiers could be quartered in private houses irrespective of the inhabitants' wishes. To avoid that eventuality the Commons agreed to construct new barracks but like other colonial assemblies believed itself under no obligation to provide supplies requested by the British commanders. By the time the troops withdrew in 1758, the constitutional questions had not been settled, and the dispute insured that future cooperation between South Carolinians and royal officers would be more difficult to achieve. Despite the Common's partial cooperation, the commanding officer's initial reaction expressed his feelings about South Carolinians who were, he reported, very happy to have soldiers around to protect their plantations, but would not trouble themselves to accommodate them, for they saw "no great difference between a soldier and a Negro."

Since the beginning of the war, South Carolinians had been equally critical of regular troops. Even Henry Laurens, who was later to prove exceptionally fair in his judgments, exploded at the news of Braddock's defeat in the Pennsylvania wilderness. "Our Ministry would do well to prosecute a War in America with Americans. Only they are not frightened out of their wits at the sight of Indians which by our Accounts was the case with your English Veterans." Laurens fulminated, "we wish they had staid at home as the advantage the Enemy have gain'd by their shamefull behaviour will put us to ten times the inconveniency in this part of the World that their coming has been of service." Fear that the defeat would undermine British influence with the Indians everywhere on the continent was the immediate cause of Laurens's harsh words. Yet he was also voicing a typical reaction to reports of the contempt which regular British officers often exhibited toward colonial troops. Perhaps an anonymous New Englander best expressed American feelings when he protested against British accounts of the expedition against Fort Duquesne: "Unhappy *provincials!* If *success* attends where you are joined with the regulars, they claim all the honour, tho' not a tenth part of your number; If *disgrace,* it shall be yours, though you happen to be but a small part of the whole, and have not the command."

Recognizing that such rivalry contributed to the friction between colonial and regular troops, Lyttelton sought to overcome the problem in formulating his own plans. Hoping to lead an expedition against Fort Toulouse, near present-day Montgomery, Alabama, he proposed in 1759 to assemble a force of 2,000 men composed of the South Carolina Provincial Regiment, the local militia, and about 100 soldiers from the Independent companies already in the colony. The latter, he noted, "might be of much use to me & yet wou'd not be likely to produce the same ill effects... [of] a more considerable body of His Majesty's Regular Troops in exciting the Jealousy of the Provincials and robbing the Province of a part at least of that honour in the Enterprize, the idea of which I believe will be a principal Motive to the Inhabitants... to engage in it." Although British operations in Canada precluded approval of his southern expedition, Lyttelton found another field for the pursuit of glory. During 1758 and 1759 the Cherokee Indians, who numbered about 3,000 men at this time, became increasingly unhappy with the British. Intruders encroached on their lands, while misunderstandings developed between the British commander and Indians who had accompanied his forces against the French in western Pennsylvania. On the way home, some warriors encountered Virginia frontiersmen who, perhaps correctly, considered them to be horse thieves, and a number of Indians were killed. Pro-French Indians were thus able to exploit legitimate grievances. Meanwhile Lyttelton attempted to mollify the Cherokees with presents, though existing treaties as well as Indian custom required retribution in blood. Later he placed an embargo on all trade with the tribe. These steps failed, and during the late summer of 1759 the Indians attacked outlying settlements in North and South Carolina. Despite serious reservations on the part of the Commons, Lyttelton prepared for war, and by the time a delegation of Cherokee chiefs arrived in Charles Town seeking peace, these preparations had acquired considerable momentum. Nevertheless, some of the council suggested that Lyttelton hold the chiefs hostage until the Indians made "satisfaction" for their raids; at this point Lyttelton refused to substitute duplicity for war.

The prospect of military action, coupled with news of the British capture of Quebec, evoked a martial spirit, and more than thirty young men of means, including some from Christopher Gadsden's recently formed artillery company, volunteered to serve without pay. Private individuals contributed money to help defray the cost of the expedition, and more than 1,300 men, most of them militia, marched westward in mid-November. Morale and whatever fighting effectiveness the force ever had quickly dissolved in the winter rains as first measles and then smallpox swept through the ranks. To avert a fiasco, Lyttelton fell back on the use of hostages and signed a treaty calling for the Indians to surrender those who had raided the settlements in return for the release of the negotiators whom he now held as hostages. His men deserting in droves, Lyttelton and the remnants of his force then straggled back to their homes in what the veteran Indian trader, James Adair, termed a "wild ridiculous parade." Lyttelton received a hero's welcome. Stranger still, some South Carolinians retained fond memories of him and his expedition long after it became apparent that his efforts had been misguided.

As might have been expected, the peace soon broke down. In February 1760 the Indians attacked Fort Prince George where the hostages were held, and in the ensuing melee all twenty-one were butchered by the soldiers. The "Unlucky affair" of the hostages, as it came to be known, seriously impeded future negotiations. Lyttelton requested aid from the British commander in chief, and he dispatched a unit with orders to expedite the business and return as quickly as possible. Its commander was Colonel Archibald Montgomery, who had been involved in the quartering controversy, and he came prepared to believe, not without reason, that the Indians were more sinned against than sinning. Moreover, in part because Lyttelton had been promoted to the governorship of Jamaica and did little but prepare for the move, Montgomery believed that "the Shameful backwardness of this Province" in providing assistance put all kinds of impediments in the way of the expedition. Pushing into the mountains, Montgomery was awed at what he saw: "So difficult and Strong a Country" would be "completely impenetrable," he observed, "if the enemy attempted to defend it rigorously." That is precisely what they did at the end of June near the town of Etchoe. After the skirmish, Montgomery's forces held the field and burned the town but, as he observed, the victory "Rather Cost us too Dear." Encumbered by his wounded, he soon arrived at the decision for which he had been seeking an excuse since coming to South Carolina. His mission was accomplished and it was time to return northward. Then, as he described it, he "Stole A March upon them [the Indians] in the Night in order to get Clear" of the dangerous mountain passes. Montgomery might call it a "strategic withdrawal," but the South Carolinians as well as the Indians knew a retreat when they saw one. What it meant was only too clear. Being a past master at letting facts speak for themselves, the new lieutenant (and now acting) governor, William Bull, Jr., reported that, on the same day the army left Fort Prince George for the coast, a soldier of the remaining garrison "was scalped, and his belly ripped open by the Savages, not one hundred yards from the Fort" during broad daylight.

Fearing that Montgomery's expedition had, in Bull's words, "rather inflamed, than extinguished" the war, the Commons House prepared to raise another military force; Bull preferred to try negotiations. But the Cherokees had surrounded Fort Loudoun in eastern Tennessee, and Montgomery's failure to relieve it forced the garrison to capitulate. The Cherokees then took revenge for the "affair of the hostages" at Fort Prince George in a second massacre that made Bull reverse course. Requesting aid from the British commander in chief and other southern governors, he raised the newly authorized provincial regiment. After the first choice for its colonel turned down the position, Bull appointed a merchant-planter, Thomas Middleton; another merchant, Henry Laurens, became lieutenant colonel. The soldiers spent the winter of 1761–1762 at a training camp near modern Columbia, where, Laurens later observed, they "died Like Dogs" from inadequate supplies and exposure to inclement weather. Middleton, who was an amateur soldier, spent most of his time in Charles Town. Such mismanagement makes one understand why the Scottish lieutenant colonel, James Grant, who commanded the regulars sent to aid the province, bore a special commission giving him control of the expedition, though Middleton, being a full colonel, technically outranked him. Similar arrangements were standard procedure in operations involving both regular and provincial troops. However, Middleton, who seems to have been concerned about it, obtained permission from Bull to resign if his position became "irksome."

For his part, Grant found himself becoming less irritated with South Carolinians. Having served on Montgomery's expedition the previous year, he too came expecting the worst, and soon after his arrival reported that the colony was in "as helpless a State as ever." Worse yet, he found that Bull was on the verge of proclaiming the accession of George III, which would dissolve the Commons before it could make necessary preparations for the expedition. Discovering that Bull's information came through unofficial channels, Grant resorted to subterfuge, quietly telling local leaders that it was normal procedure to carry on all business until notified of the sovereign's death by the secretary of state. "As I intended," Grant reported, "these conversations were repeated and believed. The Assembly was called, met and did Business in *Mourning.*"

Gulling the provincials was risky, but in this case it produced results. Some South Carolinians, Grant began to see, also knew how to get things done. The assembly proved to be "pretty diligent," and he soon reported that "we agree extremely well." Even the training of the provincial troops pleased him, and, as his adjutant noted, he "resolved to put them as they deserved, on a higher Footing than provincial Regiments had ever been on the Continent." They were to march and camp as part of the line and "do every Duty with the Regulars in their Turn." In fact, after the expedition moved out, Grant went so far as to place a separate detachment of regulars and provincials under the command of a provincial officer. He did not, however, consult much with provincials—or with anyone, for that matter. "An Officer who commands should think for himself" was one of his maxims; "If he succeeds 'tis well, & if he fails, the sanction of the advice & opinion of a hundred people is not worth a shilling."

Like Montgomery, Grant pushed into the mountains in June 1761, and at almost the same place where Montgomery had been ambushed, the expedition encountered resistance and suffered substantial casualties. But unlike Montgomery, Grant moved on, destroying the Indians' cornfields and villages. By the time his forces returned to Fort Prince George, Grant estimated that he had driven 5,000 Indians into the woods where they faced starvation. "Luckily," he added, "nothing was left to be done. . . . It would have been impossible for us to proceed further. Our provisions were almost expended and our men wore out and unable to act." Veterans familiar with western Pennsylvania agreed "that no such march was ever made by Troops," and Grant himself told his men that they had been through country worse than some Alpine passes he had seen. Even the provincials about whom Grant had been doubtful "behaved well," and, he was candid enough to admit, proved to be "very usefull." Most important, it appeared that he had achieved his objectives. Where the luckless soldier had been disemboweled only a few months before, "waggoners and even soldiers, contrary to orders," the adjutant noted, now "cross the River and ramble all Round the opposite Hills picking strawberrys unarm'd" while they waited for the Indians to sue for peace.

At this point, things began to unravel. An Indian delegation did eventually go to Charles Town, where it signed a preliminary peace treaty in September 1761. There was some temporary confusion over the terms, which got Bull in trouble with both Grant and the Commons House. More significantly, the Cherokees refused to agree to the first article, which demanded that four warriors be executed. Realizing how difficult it would be to compel acceptance, Grant and Bull were willing to drop that stipulation. The Commons, however, was not. Bull had once made the mistake of terming the first article a sine qua non, for by agreeing to the executions the Cherokees would acknowledge defeat. Now the treaty appeared without that stipulation. Unfortunately, the logic involved seemed inescapable: no Article I, no victory. Few members of the house could see much reason to argue against that logic. Moreover, Grant had killed fewer Indians than Montgomery who mostly burned villages among the lower towns; Grant had merely extended these operations to the middle settlements. A committee—including Middleton—to which the house referred the proposed treaty believed that both men had botched the job. Observing that a treaty without Article I would be "useless and Dishonorable," the committee recommended that the Commons insist upon its reinsertion. Most of the members were more realistic. Grudgingly, believing themselves compelled "by the Necessities and particular Circumstances" of the colony, they eventually agreed with very poor grace to approve the treaty as it stood. No Americans, the house maintained, could have "exerted themselves more vigorously," but it obviously believed, and came very close to officially stating, that Grant had robbed Carolinians of victory.

Consequently, when Grant marched his troops through Charles Town to board the waiting transports, his reception was scarcely that of a conquering hero. People insulted him on the streets and Middleton met him on the dueling field. To understand Middleton's action as well as the intensity of popular feeling, it is necessary to look at the origins of what Laurens later described as a "serious Quarrel upon a very silly subject." As soon as the troops had returned to Fort Prince George, Middleton had availed himself of Bull's permission to return to Charles Town. Middleton's initial statements—and much of the other evidence bearing on the question—suggest that personal considerations relating to business and family matters may have had as much to do with his departure as irritation over Grant's failure to consult him about tactics and strategy. Whatever the reason for it, his behavior was a poor example to the men, who soon began to desert in large numbers. Grant was understandably outraged, and there was even some talk of a court-martial. Middleton's escape from an increasingly tight situation proved to be surprisingly easy. Grant's imperious style of command, the similarity of his operations to Montgomery's, and the latent jealousy toward regular troops predisposed many South Carolinians to believe that differences over policy were the main issue. Obviously Middleton must have called for more aggressive tactics and Grant had ignored his advice. Middleton easily and probably honestly assumed the role of the patriotic but ignored provincial. His needs and the expectations of his fellow South Carolinians coincided so perfectly that it would have taken an unusually self-critical individual not to rationalize his motives for what had probably been at least in part the hasty act of an exhausted man.

Attacking Grant in the newspaper, Middleton soon made himself the hero of all those who believed that Grant had been too soft on the Indians. Among the latter, Christopher Gadsden was one of the most vociferous. Publishing two long essays over the pen name "Philopatrios"—a lover of his country—he damned Montgomery and especially Grant who should have been more aggressive in permitting his men "to go upon the backs of these Indian murderers, to whom he was in every way superior, to cut the throats of as many as they could have come up with." Now the British troops were being withdrawn, and having "been brought into this scrape," Gadsden observed, we are "left to get out . . . in the best manner we can." Laurens wrote an effective reply but, being a prudent man, apparently decided not to publish it. Grant took more decisive action. "With great reason," as one contemporary observed, he "considered such treatment . . . as a base recompence for his services." Grant apparently challenged Middleton to a duel and was later able to report that "tho he has used me worse than any man ever did another, I gave him his life, when it was absolutely in my power"—which redeemed the Scotsman somewhat in the eyes of Carolinians. He, on the other hand, with all the conviction of a man who has strayed but once again seen the light, reverted to his earlier opinion of the province where, he observed, "the Spirit of Prejudice & Party has run higher, than it ever did in any part of the World." No doubt in 1775, when Grant arose in the British House of Commons to declare that he "would undertake to march from one end of America to the other wth 5,000 men," he remembered his last campaign in South Carolina.

Meanwhile, South Carolinians enjoyed the fruits of the victory which they believed had been denied to them. Although they were correct in believing that Grant had not completely broken the power of the Cherokees, the Indians were in no position to offer concerted opposition to white expansion. Thus they agreed in the treaty of 1761 to surrender some land. Nearly a year and a half later, representatives of all the major southern tribes, and governors of the southern colonies, and the British superintendent of Indian affairs for the southern district of North America met at Augusta and approved plans to have the boundary line between Indian and settlers' lands surveyed.* Subsequent negotiations at Fort Prince George in 1765 established its location, and surveying parties, accompanied by Indians, soon marked the line by blazing trees from the Savannah to the Reedy rivers; much of the present boundary between Anderson and Abbeville counties coincides with the line laid out in 1767. Lying east of the Royal Proclamation Line of 1763 that limited colonial settlement to the seaward side of the Appalachian Mountains, the negotiated boundary was compatible with imperial policy and did much to alleviate Indian concern about white expansion. Thereafter, most of the Carolina backcountry was open to white settlement, and the relative security from Indian attack augmented the flow of settlers into the area. By the late 1760s the backcountry contained almost three-quarters of the population of South Carolina, including numerous drifters and outlaws who found the dislocations produced by the Cherokee War a fertile field for their operations.

So matters continued until the summer of 1767 when a rash of housebreaking and horsethievery led to the arrest and conviction of a number of culprits. Their pardoning by the newly arrived governor, Lord Charles Montagu, who wished to inaugurate his administration with clemency, then prompted men of property in the backcountry to move on two fronts. In the west, armed bands calling themselves Regulators pursued criminals and inflicted summary justice; in the east, four leading Regulators, said to represent 4,000 of their followers who had threatened to march on Charles Town, presented a petition

---

*The conference at Augusta also confirmed the establishment of a 225-square-mile reservation for the Catawba Indians, to be located in the vicinity of modern Rock Hill, South Carolina.

or "remonstrance" to the legislature demanding assistance in solving their problems. In particular, they wanted the appurtenances of law and order: jails, courts, churches, schools, and the regulation of taverns. Other demands called for the taxation of land in proportion to its value, modification in the procedures for granting land so as to make trips to Charles Town unnecessary, and more adequate representation in the assembly. The problems were real and the requests legitimate, but the Regulators' penman was an Anglican cleric who seems to have fancied himself another Jonathan Swift, championing the cause of the back-country as Swift had defended Ireland. The documents written by Charles Woodmason were filled with exaggerated statements and satiric jibes which now make entertaining reading but which then offended members of the assembly. As a result, the Commons tabled the re-monstrance, whereupon those who presented it apologized, and the house moved to redress their grievances.

In fact, as early as 1754 the Commons had been willing to consider a bill to establish courts at Beaufort, Georgetown, and the Congarees (modern Columbia), but it had died after the first reading. In 1765, the lieutenant governor advocated a similar measure, and the Commons passed it. The council took no action. In the same year, the legislature established a backcountry parish, St. Matthew's, but, for reasons to be considered shortly, the crown disallowed it. In 1768 the assembly reestablished it and added another interior parish, St. David's. In addition, during the 1767–1768 session, the legislature passed an act establishing circuit courts. Partly because of the need to replace the single provost marshal (who served the whole colony) with sheriffs for each of the new court districts, enacting the bill proved to be a fairly lengthy process. At this time, the marshal's office was held by a patentee, the playwright Richard Cumberland, who resided in England and discharged his responsibilities by employing a deputy, Roger Pinckney (no relation to the Charles Pinckney family). Such patents were a species of property that generated income, and Cumberland was naturally unwilling to surrender his rights without compensation. Cap-italizing future as well as present earnings, he believed the office to be worth £6,000 sterling; the assembly thought £4,000 was enough. After some hard bargaining, they split the difference. The negotiations were straightforward, and there is no indication that South Carolinians saw anything amiss in his claims. Those of the local attorney general, Egerton Leigh, were another matter; his demands for increased compensation for the additional time and trouble attendant on the circuits seemed exorbitant. Yet he had sufficient influence to block approval of the act in England if he were not satisfied, so the house eventually met his figure. Other local officers were more cooperative. The act, which in compliance with royal instructions contained a suspending clause delaying implementation until the crown approved it, was on the way to England by late summer of 1768.

Meanwhile, as a first step in meeting the needs of the backcountry, the legislature had established two companies of rangers for use against the outlaws. This step in effect legitimized the Regulators and facilitated their work. Subsequent operations during the winter of 1767–1768 when Rangers pursued gangs of outlaws across the backcountry of both Carolinas, virtually eliminated the gangs. The Regulators then turned their attention to disciplining marginal members of society whom they accused of aiding and abetting the outlaws or, in many cases, of being merely shiftless and lazy. Bennet Dozier, for example, failed to provide adequately for his wife and children; she complained to a leading Regulator, and he and two other men appeared at Dozier's house where they applied "39 lashes well laid on." Dozier, it was said, reformed, but others—including a few substantial men who had run afoul of the Regulators for one reason or another—were less compliant; some sued. The Regulators countered by resolving to block the service of all warrants and writs issuing from the courts at Charles Town except those involving debts. This put the movement on a collision course with the duly constituted authorities. In June 1768 a deputy of the provost marshal who tried to serve legal documents in the western part of the colony was stopped, held captive for several days, beaten, and before he escaped told that he would be made to "eat the process." A few weeks later, a complicated incident at Marrs Bluff in the northeastern part of the province led to a confrontation between Provost Marshal Pinckney and the colonel of the local militia regiment, George Gabriel Powell, on the one hand, and the rank and file on the other. The authorities intended to use the militia to arrest a leading Regulator; the men refused to cooperate and instead harangued the officials about their grievances. The officers retired to the coast empty-handed. Powell, mortified by his inability to command obedience, then resigned his commission.

Still, most of the authorities in Charles Town retained their composure. Lieutenant Governor William Bull promptly issued two proclamations, one calling for the suppression of the Regulators and the other pardoning most of them who would thereafter keep the peace. When rumors began to circulate a few weeks later that westerners planned an armed march on the lowcountry to exercise the franchise during the upcoming election, there was some alarm but no panic. Despite a bit of confusion, the election went relatively smoothly. The Regulators, as the *Gazette* reported, "behaved every where with decency and propriety," and at least some of the churchwardens who ran the polls reciprocated by allowing those of doubtful residence to vote on the grounds that it was better to err on the side that "favoured the Liberty of the Subject and the right of voting." As a result, the Regulators elected at least six of their choices to the Commons. In short, local officials had acquiesced in the Regulators' de facto control of the backcountry, and the Regulators had acquired substantial representation in the assembly. Thus the *Gazette* was able to report that the "very appearance of tumult subsided."

Unfortunately, however, the calm did not last. For reasons not connected with the Regulation but with the mounting pre-Revolutionary controversy over constitutional issues, Governor Montagu dissolved the new house after a session lasting only four days. Furthermore, within the backcountry itself a serious challenge to the Regulators developed when some influential men sought to curb the Regulators' excesses by organizing a counter or "Moderator" movement, for which they obtained sanction from the governor and council. Joseph Coffell and a band of ruffians, some of whom seem to have been seeking revenge for having been "regulated" themselves, took care of the rough stuff. The result was almost a pitched battle when in March 1769 opposing forces numbering perhaps as many as 600 or 700 on a side confronted each other in what is now Newberry County. Meanwhile, however, reports of the Moderators' activities led to their repudiation by the authorities, and just when it appeared that bloodshed was inevitable, three leading men appeared with orders for the Moderators to disperse. Thanks as much to the courage and influence of the three as to the substance of their message, the immediate crisis passed. The Moderators soon disbanded, and a reasonable semblance of calm prevailed in the backcountry.

There were still difficulties to be surmounted since the crown disallowed the acts establishing both the new parishes and the circuit courts. The problem with the new parishes, from the royal point of view, was that their representatives enlarged the Commons House, which conflicted with recently issued instructions limiting the colonial assemblies to their current size in the hope of checking their growing power. The churchwarden who had been responsible for allowing the Regulators to vote at Goose Creek, John Mackenzie, termed the instruction perhaps the most "peculiar" ever issued, and Henry Laurens considered the disallowance of the new parishes to be "tyrannical." The only effective action the assembly could take was to reapportion itself. Given the difficulties that legislative bodies commonly have in doing this, the fact that the house reestablished these parishes by giving them two representatives from existing lowcountry districts is perhaps as significant as that the backcountry nevertheless remained under-represented.

In the case of the court act, the crown objected mainly to clauses governing the judges' tenure of office. In England, since the reign of Queen Anne early in the eighteenth century, judges were appointed during "good behaviour"—that is, they could be removed only for causes more substantial than decisions displeasing to royal authorities. In the colonies, however, the ministry insisted that judges be appointed "during pleasure"—that is, be removable at the will of the crown. There were several valid reasons for the position taken by imperial authorities, not the least of which was an unwillingness to be stuck with a layman when it might be possible to replace him with a trained jurist. Even more important to the ministry was the fact that local assemblies appropriated funds for the judges' salaries on an annual basis. If judges were given tenure, crown officials believed, they would become too responsive to the legislatures. Colonials, on the other hand, demanded equal rights in this, as in other areas. Attempts to appoint local judges during good behavior led to controversies in other colonies, most notably in New York and New Jersey during the early 1760s. In South Carolina the issue arose not only because the Circuit Court

Act appeared to provide an opportunity to establish a desirable principle but also because stipulating that judges would hold tenure during good behavior might offer security to the incumbents, who were local men. Consequently, the act proved unacceptable to the crown. Once again, the legislature faced an unpalatable choice: retreat on a constitutional issue or risk increasingly serious difficulties in the backcountry. It took the prudent course and quickly passed substantially the same court act without the provisions governing judicial tenure.

Even that did not close the matter; there was an unpleasant sequel. Knowing that the leading professional lawyers made more in private practice than they could as associate judges, Bull predicted that none would accept the new positions. He was equally sure that laymen "whose best qualifications were their integrity and common understanding and leisure to attend the Courts; tho' sufficient" in the past would not "be equal to the trust reposed in them by this Act"—that is, on the circuit. Consequently, he hoped that "from among the many Gentlemen in London regularly bred to the Law who have arrived at a time of life, when the sanguine hopes of rising to eminence or a comfortable share of practice in the profession are extinguished by a very moderate employment therein, some could be prevailed upon to accept of such commission in this Province." Though sensible in many ways, Bull's suggestion led to trouble when British jurists replaced the South Carolinians on the bench, and their presence produced resentment.

Not all the newcomers arrived at once, and the chief justice in particular served for a while with American assistants, one of whom was Rawlins Lowndes who had himself hoped to be chief justice. Moreover, the docket included a number of cases involving Regulators. Lowndes, who knew the history of the movement, regarded these cases primarily as a political matter over which it would be wise "to draw a Vail." The chief justice, Thomas Knox Gordon, approached the matter from a more legalistic point of view. As a result, the courtroom was occasionally enlivened by exchanges between the two judges such as the one in which Lowndes told the senior man that his point of view "might be law but he was Sure it was not Reason." Similar animosities also affected behavior outside of the courts, and the British judges later charged—perhaps correctly—that the commissioners responsible for constructing the new courthouses delayed their work to prevent the judges from receiving salaries for as long as possible. On the other hand, imperial officials disallowed the emission of governmental certificates with which to construct the buildings.* However, by the time notification reached Carolina, the public orders had been issued and spent, so the disallowance was simply ignored.

Looking back on all of this, one may perhaps see a little humor in some of it, but it is doubtful that many contemporaries did. Two of the charges against the crown in the Declaration of Independence arose out of these and similar developments in other colonies. Among George III's sins, one recalls, were his refusal "to pass... laws for the accommodation of large districts of people, unless those people would relinquish the right of Representation in the Legislature" and his persistence in making "Judges dependent on his Will alone, for the tenure of their offices." To observe that these charges appear—as Jefferson intended they should—to build a prima facie case against the crown's concern for the rights and welfare of its people is not to make the king a scapegoat for the mistakes and oversights of the South Carolina elite, whose members did not always respond as quickly and fully to the needs of the backcountry as they might have. Ignorance was part of the cause. Though given to exaggeration, Woodmason related a plausible tale to the effect that "a Gentleman (now one of the Assistant Judges) being chosen Member for [the Assembly] for P.[rince] Frederick Parish (only 60 miles from Charlestown)" took another man "aside... and privately ask'd, Where the Parish lay?" Furthermore, local lawyers as well as royal officials were undoubtedly reluctant to ride the circuit if they could avoid it, and there is no question that the Commons was in no hurry to change the tax system. Reform of the latter did not come until after the Revolution.

But the elite was neither totally ignorant about the backcountry, nor heedless of its needs. In particular, those who served in the campaigns of the Cherokee War got a glimpse of western growth and potential, and some acquired land in the area for speculative purposes. Such men were quite well aware that the establishment of law and order, the provision of government services, and adequate representation in the assembly would make the region more attractive to immigrants and thereby increase the value of their own holdings.

---

*As a violation of the Currency Act of 1764.

Furthermore, the Regulator movement continued the education of the lowcountry about the backcountry, for it revealed that a substantial number of its residents were men of property who shared the values and goals of their counterparts farther east. The willingness of the South Carolina Regulators to permit the service of writs for debt helped authorities to distinguish the indigenous movement from the contemporaneous phenomenon in North Carolina. Although there is now considerable scholarly disagreement about the basic nature of the Regulator movement in North Carolina, it was obvious to contemporaries that whereas North Carolinians objected to the abuses of the law, South Carolinians complained mostly about the lack of it. Finally, even if they were misinformed about these matters, few men in the lowcountry could be oblivious to the fact that they might need to rely on the backcountrymen for assistance in the event of a serious slave insurrection; to alienate them unnecessarily would have been the height of folly, and everyone knew it.

Thus, Woodmason was in error when he implied that members of the Commons House opposed the creation of both the interior parishes and courts. He, in fact, went so far as to suggest that men from the lowcountry somehow clandestinely worked to obtain the disallowance of the acts establishing the new parishes. Had he maintained that the lowcountry was not willing to surrender control of the province to the majority in the backcountry, he would undoubtedly have been correct. (In fact, the creation of two new lowcountry parishes in 1767 may have been intended in part to offset the anticipated additional representation from the backcountry.) In reality, however, the royal disallowances caught the Commons by surprise. The limitation on its size was unexpected and, according to the reports of its agent, there was good reason to believe that imperial authorities would accept the provisions regarding judicial tenure until a ministerial change produced an unanticipated hard line.

British measures were not playing into the hands of lowcountry leaders, as Woodmason suggested, but making life difficult for them. Not only were their economic interests linked to the backcountry, but their own security also depended in part on their ability to satisfy men who, after all, constituted a majority of the white population. At its height the Regulator movement may have included as many as 6,000 armed men who, as the lieutenant governor noted, were not "idle vagabonds, the canaille, the mere dregs of mankind" but "landholders" with a stake in the local society. There was no way, he observed, that "a Military Force" from the lowcountry, "where white inhabitants are few and a numerous domestic Enemy" of slaves demanded the "utmost attention," could suppress the insurgents. The "surest and only method of quieting their minds," he observed, was to treat them "with moderation and their complaints with attention, and their Grievances with reasonable redress." To do otherwise might make the militiamen's refusal to obey their colonel at Marrs Bluff look like a very minor incident. Clearly worried, Powell privately noted that "these disturbances seem to have so dismal a tendency that I am at a loss to guess where they may terminate." Scores of armed men coming down to vote at lowcountry polling places did nothing to reassure him, but their message was clear enough. In short, though the Regulators' challenge to the establishment was by and large a limited product of their unmet demands, it was nevertheless a serious challenge; and the only way to meet it successfully, local authorities knew, was to be responsive to those demands. Yet imperial authorities seemed to be bent on hindering their efforts.

Furthermore, the pre-Revolutionary debate over constitutional issues spawned its own internal challenges to established leaders. On the one hand were men who considered resistance to ministerial measures to be unjustified; on the other, there were perhaps more who believed current actions to be insufficient. The attendant popular disorders might also undermine deference. During the Stamp Act crisis, for example, Laurens received a visit from a mob which mistrusted him because he "held way" with Grant during the Cherokee War. A number of "Jacks . . . not knowing me & dreading no body," Laurens reported, "were zealous to execute the business . . . & would for some time admit of no 'Parleys' nor 'Palabres'" and "not only menaced very loudly but now & then handled me pretty uncouthly." Later, in an apparently conscious effort to contrast his own experience with the widely reported damage to Thomas Hutchinson's house in Massachusetts during a similar disturbance, Laurens suggested how "amazing" it was "that such a number of men [,] many of them heated with Liquor & all armed with Cutlasses & Clubbs [,] did not do one penny damage to my Garden nor even to walk over a Bed and not 15 [shillings] damage to my Fence, Gate or House." If he was not exactly whistling in the dark,

Laurens was clearly trying to assure himself—and others—that he could still command deference. That there might be some doubt was the result not only of his personal experiences but also of a widespread belief that every society contained the "idle, the dissolute and abandoned" who found disorder to be an avenue for personal advancement. Thus the elite feared that those who had been "made men of consequence" by leading protest movements would be unwilling to have "their consequence...sunk into nothing." Given this assumption, established leaders could scarcely view the election of 1768 with equanimity; for, in addition to the Regulators, the mechanics of Charles Town turned out in force and, for the first time, nominated their own slate of candidates. Their choices were all men of property, a fact that was reassuring to the elite, but the organized participation of artisans, many believed, was an ominous sign.

This context makes understandable the reaction of South Carolinians to official and unofficial British snubs. The relative neglect of the local elite in making royal appointments was a grievance in many colonies, and one historian, James Kirby Martin, has gone so far as to imply that lust for executive offices fueled Revolutionary ardour. Although he may have overstated the case, South Carolinians were extraordinarily disappointed by their failure to achieve preferment. In fact, it has been said that they might never have revolted if their native and popular lieutenant governor, William Bull, Jr., had been made governor. This is undoubtedly an exaggeration, but that someone would have considered it a realistic possibility indicates how important the issue was to Carolinians. In part, their concern was the result of a conspicuous record of painful experiences. In 1752, after a long career of distinguished public service, Charles Pinckney received a temporary appointment as chief justice. It lasted only a few months before Peter Leigh replaced him. Leigh was a qualified jurist, but South Carolinians believed that he had been given the post as a reward for rigging an election in London. Only a few years later, Wragg was removed from the council; no misconduct on his part was ever charged and no public explanation given. Later the native assistant judges gave way to British replacements. No wonder Carolinians believed that "none of us, when we grow old, can expect the honours of the State—they are all given away to worthless poor rascals."

At one level, such treatment was merely insulting. To find oneself subordinate to a junior officer or to be replaced by a British judge was a little like what one proto-loyalist claimed happened "when any of our great men go over" to England. There they expected to be "as important upon the Royal Exchange as they have been under our Vendue House," but, he continued, "a little experience shows them their mistake; and after having run out something more than their income in supporting their ideal importance, they find England to be a land of slaves, and betake themselves in high dudgeon to their native swamps." Though perhaps a bit unfair, this writer may well have hit upon one of the reasons that many of the men educated in England proved to be, in John Adams's fine phrase, "high Americans." It is worth noting, however, that those who returned to Carolina on the eve of the Revolution also needed to demonstrate that they had not been corrupted by their English education. But the reaction of many Americans in London was not merely a matter of wounded egos, as Charles Pinckney's experience demonstrates. After losing his post as chief justice, he and his wife went to London to oversee the education of their sons. While she reveled in the life of the city, he was unhappy. In Carolina, he had been at the center of power where he had been able to make a real contribution to his community. In England, though he served for a while as an agent for the Carolina council, he had relatively little influence; he was just another American at loose ends without a real function. The result was not only a painful blow to pride but also a threat to his deepest aspirations.

Furthermore, British hauteur, whether encountered in England or in Carolina, was especially disturbing because it evoked synchronous vibrations in the colonial psyche. South Carolinians lived with the knowledge that they were provincials. Underneath their pride lay something akin to a colonial inferiority complex, which frequently revealed itself when they implicitly compared themselves to Englishmen: "Our moderate fortunes"; "the few who have a learned education, have acquired it in England"; "our small world." This self-doubt sometimes affected performance; thus the lay judges, Bull reported, were often reluctant to exert their authority because they felt "great mortification and timidity from a sense of their being not well acquainted with their power and their duty." Their specific fear, of course, was of displaying their ignorance; in a more general sense, however, they feared that their ignorance would reveal them to be not as English as they thought they were, and that was exactly what being snubbed by Britons told them.

Undoubtedly, Scotch arrogance was the most galling, for it came from men who were essentially provincials themselves. Samuel Johnson, Carolinians would have believed, summed the matter up perfectly when he observed that "the noblest prospect which a Scotchman ever sees, is the high road that leads him to England." That many of them took not only it but also the low road to the colonies made them most unpopular with many South Carolinians. In part, hatred of Scots arose from a widespread belief that John Stuart, Earl of Bute, and his Scottish cohorts wielded an insidious influence at court which contributed to the restrictive measures aimed at Americans. Equally to the point, in the colonies the Scots seemed to be both clannish and ubiquitous. *"Scratch me, Countryman!—and I'll scratch thee"* was, according to the *South Carolina Gazette,* their prevailing syndrome. Regarded as slavish, fawning, miserly tools of oppressive ministries, Scotsmen were often considered to be beyond the pale. Thus, for example, a local planter, Adam Daniel, partially disinherited his daughter in the event that she married a Scotsman. To have the likes of such look down on Carolinians was, to many, intolerable.

If Scottish hauteur was disturbing, English arrogance was frightening. For the failure of men from the wider world, who presumably knew its ways, to recognize the claims and pretensions of the South Carolina elite threatened to emasculate them on their own turf. To make a provincial officer subject to the commands of a regular whom he outranked was to suggest that the colonial was a counterfeit colonel; and to gull the gullible regarding procedural matters was to seem to expose their naïveté (though many of the members of the Commons may not have been as naïve as Grant believed). Similarly, the unwillingness of British authorities to appoint colonial judges during good behavior suggested that they were fit only to keep the bench warm until a qualified incumbent could be found. Such things, local leaders realized, could undermine their position with their own constituents. Nor were their anxieties without basis. British-born officeholders and other recent immigrants frequently took pains to remind South Carolinians that their leaders deserved little respect when measured against British standards. Thus Woodmason, contemptuously (and somewhat inaccurately) outlined Lowndes's career. "He was originally a Parish

Orphan Boy, nor knows his own Origin—Taken from the Dunghill by our late Provost Marshal—Made his Valet—then learn'd to read and write—Then became Gaoler—Then Provost Marshal—Got Money—Married Well—Settled Plantations—became a Planter—A Magistrate—A Senator—Speaker of the House and now Chief Judge." What was true for Lowndes was also true for most other local leaders, Woodmason noted. And by the standards of the day, the "illegitimate" character of their origins called into question their capacity to govern. As the Scotch newspaper publisher and bookseller, Robert Wells, declared in 1765, "I wish to be under the direction of the British Parliament and not our little Provincial Senate aping the grandest Assembly in the World without Knowledge, skill, power or any other requisite almost."

All of this is important because it suggests that, from the late 1750s on, the local leadership was in a quandary. Beginning with the Cherokee War and continuing with the increased official interest in the colonies during the next decade, men of property in South Carolina were, for perhaps the first time since the seventeenth century, being closely measured against British standards, and by and large they were found wanting. From the British point of view, the leadership was too new, too much like its own constituents to command respect or merit its position. From the point of view of the Carolina elite, such an attitude might be positively subversive, for, if it spread widely among their constituents, it could turn the clock back to an earlier period when election riots and the like suggested that men of (relatively little) property had trouble commanding deference on the part of the people. Given pervasive British attitudes, local leaders could therefore feel that they were damned if they did and damned if they didn't resist restrictive imperial measures. That their role as champions of liberty would help to legitimize their position is something for which they might hope but could not know.

This is not to imply that local leaders eventually waged a revolution solely—or even primarily—to preserve their own positions; rather it is to suggest that the result of their dilemma may have been somewhat analogous to the effect of the French and Indian War elsewhere. Historians and contemporaries alike have speculated that Americans might not have dared to resist imperial measures so vigorously if they had remained dependent upon Britain for protection against a powerful

French presence in the Mississippi Valley and Canada. Acquisition of these territories at the Peace of Paris in 1763, this argument suggests, gave the colonists sufficient security to reduce their inhibitions in dealing with imperial authorities. Whatever may have been the case elsewhere, South Carolinians scarcely emerged from the war with a greater sense of security. It was reassuring to have the French out of Louisiana and the Spanish removed from Florida, even if the latter did take over Louisiana; and relief contributed to the great surge of British patriotism felt by Carolinians as well as other Americans who gloried in the British triumph at the end of the war. Few Carolinians, however, believed that the Cherokee Indians were really humbled, and many knew that the primary threat from France to the lowcountry was still what it had always been—French seapower. More important, war had not reduced the preponderance of slaves in the rice-producing areas. Thus from a military point of view, South Carolina and Georgia remained what Laurens accurately, if ungallantly, termed them in the late 1760s, "weakest Sisters." Nevertheless, given sufficient provocation and no acceptable alternatives, even those who are most conscious of their weakness may decide that a gesture of defiance is better than meek submission.

Though it would be a mistake to imply that all Carolinians emerged from the French and Indian War disenchanted with British authorities—or vice versa, for that matter—the cooperative war effort not only left an emotionally turbulent wake but also produced some significant areas of misunderstanding. As early as 1757, Lyttelton reported that South Carolinians raised nearly five times as much in the annual revenue bill as had been customary in peacetime, and, before the war was over, their tax per adult, white male was the highest of any colony. With considerable justification, Carolinians accordingly felt that they had done more than their fair share. Officials in London, on the other hand, tended to believe that they had not pulled their own weight. In part, this assumption arose from Glen's failure to understand events in Virginia during the early years of the war; and to a greater extent, their critical attitude stemmed from the apparent unwillingness of Carolinians to meet recruiting goals. Parliament, in order to stimulate American cooperation during the war, agreed to compensate the colonies for some of their expenses; to promote recruiting, authorities made the size of the reimbursement proportional to a colony's success in raising troops. South Carolina failed miserably in this regard, not because its inhabitants were unique in being reluctant to enlist but because local conditions made it especially difficult—and even imprudent—to overcome their unwillingness. While prosperity and a high standard of living rendered low pay in the ranks unattractive, the threat of Indian attacks and slave insurrections seemed to demand the presence of men at home. South Carolina therefore received only a fraction of the sum to which it might have been entitled. Furthermore, though smuggling was not a big business in Carolina, some South Carolinians appear to have found that supplying provisions to the enemy along the Gulf Coast was profitable during the war. Nor were South Carolinians alone in engaging in such activities; comparatively speaking, they were minor offenders. Thus, with some reason, British authorities emerged from the war with something like a sense of grievance of their own. At the very least, they believed, Americans had demonstrated that they needed to be brought under tighter control. Carolinians, on the other hand—like many other Americans—were sure that no one, in the words of the Commons House, "could have exerted themselves more vigorously." Thus they expected praise and recognition of the status to which they assumed their efforts entitled them; instead, they encountered criticism and new attempts to restrict their scope. The apparent unfairness of it all rankled.

12

THE OVERT CHALLENGE AND THE COMING OF THE REVOLUTION

Peace and the removal of the French from North America also, in a sense, removed some of the inhibitions of imperial authorities in dealing with Americans, since the need for colonial cooperation against the common enemy seemed to be less pressing. More convinced than ever by recent experience that the colonists needed to be curbed, they embarked upon the policy initiated in 1748 but shelved during the war. Furthermore, they added at least one important new ingredient— a substantial number of British troops in North America. The decision to keep them there seems to have been the result of a number of considerations, including a not very carefully examined assumption that the newly acquired territory required soldiers to defend it. Their presence, however, after the French threat had been substantially reduced, if not eliminated, prompted colonial fears that the forces might be intended to coerce Americans, and perhaps the possibility of so using them made British authorities less willing to be conciliatory.

Equally important, the need to support the troops contributed to the ministry's resolve to tax Americans. Although that decision proved to be a fateful step, the first of the new revenue measures, the Sugar or Plantation Act of 1764, initially commanded relatively little attention in South Carolina. Its preamble indicated that its purpose was to raise revenue in America; but it was a long and complicated act, and accompanying legislation provided concessions to the Carolina rice trade. Thus Carolinians at first perceived the Sugar Act in the context of the older acts of trade, attempted to figure out how it would affect them and, as the speaker of the Commons admitted privately, were not immediately able to come to a conclusion.

A major reason for the delay was that local leaders had not been able to give the matter much thought because the Commons was then locked in controversy with the new governor, Thomas Boone. By most criteria, Boone should have been a popular and successful governor. He was the nephew of a prominent dissenter-politician from the early decades of the century; he had just been promoted from the governorship of New Jersey, where he had had a rather uneventful administration; and his later career as a customs commissioner in England suggests that he was an able man. Yet he soon ran into trouble with the Commons in a way which even the Board of Trade was later to observe displayed "more Zeal than Prudence." An explanation for his strange behavior may lie partly in his predecessor's reputation. In the eyes of the imperial authorities it seemed that Lyttelton could do no wrong; yet he had been unable to obtain a satisfactory revision of the Election Act of 1721, as he had been instructed to do. Boone seems to have resolved to succeed where "the great" Lyttelton failed, but when he suggested that the Commons revise the act, it refused. He therefore pounced on the first opportunity to demonstrate the error of its ways. That opportunity, it turned out, was the election of Christopher Gadsden by the voters of St. Paul's parish in 1762. No doubt Gadsden was correct in believing that his polemical attacks on Montgomery and Grant had made sharp-eyed enemies; certainly someone noticed that his election involved an irregularity. The churchwardens who managed the poll, it seems, had forgotten to take the special oath stipulated by the Election Act of 1721, though they had taken the general oath of office required when they assumed their positions. To the Commons, which investigated and discovered that Gadsden was the overwhelming choice of the voters, that was sufficient, and it voted to seat him. Boone, however, refused to administer the necessary oath of office and precipitously dissolved the house for declaring him elected. No governor under the crown had ever challenged the Commons's right to judge the qualifications of its own members in such a blatant fashion. The newly elected house therefore censured Boone, and the dispute soon widened into a controversy involving the right of representation itself, which the Commons maintained was one of the natural rights of freemen. In December 1762 the Commons refused to do any further business with the governor until he apologized for attempting to infringe upon its privileges. Meanwhile the controversy spilled over into the press.

Boone then ordered the printers to publish nothing derogatory about the government, which indicates that, by the spring of 1763, he was becoming increasingly concerned about the public attacks on him, though he still refused to make overt concessions. Instead, it appears, he tried an indirect approach. The proprietary charter gave South Carolina a claim to land as far south as St. Augustine, yet during the 1750s imperial authorities attempted to keep Spain neutral by forbidding settlements south of the Altamaha River. The Peace of Paris in 1763 turned Florida over to England, and in April, Boone—with unseemly haste—began granting land in this area. Recipients were, by and large, prominent Carolinians, not a few of whom were members of the Commons House. The carrot worked no better than the stick, and the impasse between the governor and the house continued while both sides appealed to London. In 1764 Boone gave up the struggle and sailed for England. Having successfully resisted Boone's challenge, a new generation of politicians who would lead the house through the remainder of the colonial period won their spurs; the Commons collectively emerged as more self-confident and tenacious of rights than ever before; and most important, the controversy forced its members to clarify what they believed representation was all about. Like Gadsden, they overwhelmingly concluded that South Carolinians could have no freedom unless they possessed a *"free* assembly, *freely* representing a *free* people."

They soon faced a tougher test. Informed that the ministry was planning a stamp tax for Americans, the Commons directed its agent in London, Charles Garth, to oppose it "or any other tax [imposed] by act of Parliament on the colonies," including the Sugar Act. Such taxation, Garth was informed in no uncertain terms, was inconsistent with the inherent right of every British subject, "not to be taxed but by his own consent, or that of his representative." Despite the strong words, South Carolinians had probably not yet fully made up their minds about the act. Direct taxation of the colonies by Parliament was new, certainly unwelcome, probably burdensome, and possibly unconstitutional; but Carolinians were not yet prepared to take an uncompromisable position. They would, the house added, "submit most dutifully at all times to Acts of Parliament."

Neither the tact nor the tough talk of Americans made sufficient impression to prevent Parliament from passing the Stamp Act. Effective on November 1, 1765, it imposed taxes of varying size upon a wide variety of official and unofficial papers—including playing cards, legal papers, and newspaper advertisements. During the interim, South Carolinians—along with other Americans—resolved the constitutional question to their own satisfaction. Daniel Dulany of Maryland exploded the British contention that Americans enjoyed "virtual representation" in Parliament by demonstrating that members of the House of Commons failed to share the interests of Americans and therefore could not be considered to be their representatives. The Virginia House of Burgesses added strong resolutions denouncing the act, and the Massachusetts House of Representatives invited all American colonies to send representatives to a meeting to be held in New York the following October. News of these developments reached South Carolinians by way of the *South Carolina Gazette,* Peter Timothy's weekly published in Charles Town. Most colonial printers, as one stamp distributor noted, *"stuffed* their papers with the *most inflamatory* Pieces they could procure." Timothy was no exception. Lieutenant Governor William Bull termed the *Gazette* the "conduit Pipe" for propaganda which, he believed, "poisoned" the minds of South Carolinians with "principles . . . imbibed and propagated from Boston and Rhode Island." Bull doubtless exaggerated. What seems to have come from the north was not so much principles as examples of violent resistance.

For the time being, however, South Carolinians preferred peaceful protest, and the Commons named three delegates to attend the Stamp Act Congress. John Rutledge, at twenty-six the youngest of the delegates, was well on the way to being the principal lawyer in Charles Town; Thomas Lynch was a planter with the reputation of being a "solid, firm, judicious man," and Gadsden, as we have seen, was an indefatigable, public-spirited zealot who later would be able to boast with pardonable pride that "no man in American strove more (and more successfully) first to bring about a Congress in 1765, and then to support it afterwards than myself." The Congress met and adopted fourteen declarations "respecting the most Essential Rights and Liberties of the Colonists, and of the Grievances under which they labour, by Reason of several late Acts of Parliament," as well as an address to the king and petitions to both houses of Parliament.

The effect of all this would not be known for some time, and the effective date of the act was imminent. Not surprisingly, during the triennial election for the Carolina Commons held in October, "the minds of the freeholders were inflamed," as one observer noted, "by many a hearty damn of the Stamp act over bottles, bowls and glasses." South Carolinians were well prepared for the arrival of the *Planters Adventure* with stamps aboard when it anchored under the protecting guns of Fort Johnson on the 18th. Early the following morning a gallows forty feet high appeared in the center of the city; hanging from it was an effigy of a stamp distributor. Powerless to maintain order, royal officials could only stand aside that evening as a crowd of about 2,000 persons carried the figure eastward along Broad Street to the bay, where it burned the effigy and buried a coffin labeled "American Liberty." Before dispersing, the mob broke into and searched the houses of the men who were to supervise distribution of the stamps. Similar disorders occurred the following day, so Bull had the stamps secretly transferred to Fort Johnson and then later to the HMS *Speedwell* for still greater security. Meanwhile, emissaries of the mob located the two officials and "invited" them to resign. Their hesitation before complying was brief. Thus the nascent Sons of Liberty had insured that no stamps would be available on the first of November. On the day the act was to go into effect the customs house and the civil courts closed down.

The port presented the most serious problem, for the next three or four months were the period in which most of the rice crop was normally exported. Vessels therefore continued to arrive expecting to load, only to be trapped in the harbor because they could not leave without legal clearances, which could not be obtained without the stamps. In time, the economic impact would be severe; in the interim, more than 1,400 idle sailors presented a serious threat to public order. The Sons of Liberty were therefore under considerable pressure to permit use of the stamps, but they remained firm. Even the backsliders, Gadsden declared, would be "made happy in the preservation of their and our just rights and privileges, whether they will or no."

Meanwhile the newly elected Commons met, approved the actions of the Stamp Act Congress, and passed a series of resolutions similar to the declarations adopted at New York. Significantly, however, these resolutions omitted the ambiguous phrase by which the Stamp Act Congress acknowledged "due subordination" to Parliament. Instead, the house told Garth that "in taxing ourselves and making Laws for our own internal government or police we can by no means allow our Provincial legislatures to be subordinate to any legislative power on earth." In all probability the members also privately arranged to support a newspaper to take the place of the *South Carolina Gazette* because Timothy had suspended publication for fear of incurring the penalties for violating the act. At any rate, the house resolved to publish its proceedings so that its members' "Sense of Liberty" and loyalty might "be known to their Constituents, and transmitted to Posterity." Their resolutions appeared in the first issue of the *South Carolina Gazette and Country Journal* published by Charles Crouch.

In addition, the Commons put pressure on Bull. Incredible as it may seem, he had yet to receive a copy of the Stamp Act through official channels, and the house attempted to turn the tables on British officialdom by adopting Grant's ploy from the Cherokee War. Certainly Bull was under no obligation to enforce the act, the Commons argued, until he had received an official copy, but Bull refused to play the game. By January widespread violence seemed inevitable unless the impatient sailors left town. Bull and the Sons of Liberty appear to have thereupon reached a tacit compromise, for a number of the largest vessels in the harbor from British home ports quietly cleared and sailed, in all probability using stamped paper acquired in Georgia (where it was available). The Sons of Liberty, as Gadsden later implied, feared that the sailors might be able to compel the general use of stamps and therefore made a tactical retreat to save a strategic victory. Bull also did his part and early in February began issuing special certificates stating that no stamped paper was available. Protected by these documents, customs officials then issued regular clearances on unstamped paper. Any more vigorous attempts to enforce the act before the king had responded to the petitions against it, Bull informed imperial authorities, would have caused "much confusion and some bloodshed, and will not in all human probability establish the regular Execution of the Act."

Violence obviously had its uses, but it was not well suited for opening

the courts where the resumption of business depended as much upon
the willingness of local lawyers to violate the letter of the law as it did
the cooperativeness of royal officials. Lawyers being conservative by
training, if not by temperament, this willingness developed slowly.
Nevertheless, by the end of January, a delegation from the local bar
asked the chief justice, Charles Shinner, to resume business in the court
of common pleas. A well-meaning but slow-witted placeman, Shinner
was thrown into a quandary by the request since the lawyers had
previously advised him to close the court. Eventually he decided that
he would not be a party to any violation of the act and clung to that
decision with monumental stubbornness. Bull tried to circumvent him
by appointing three new assistant judges, and when the court met for
what would have been its normal spring term, Rawlins Lowndes spoke
for them. Could Parliament, he asked rhetorically, have intended "by
this Law . . . to unhinge the Constitution of the Colonies, to unloose
the hands of Violence and Oppression, to introduce Anarchy and Confusion amongst us, and to reduce us to a State of Outlawry?" Of course
not, yet that might be the result of closing the court. Thus the act
should not be construed to require the suspension of all legal business
merely because stamped paper was unavailable. Whatever the cause,
"impossibilities," he declared, "are still impossibilities." The present
situation was "as much to be attributed to the Act of God, as if the
Ship which brought them [the stamped papers] . . . had been cast away
in a Storm, for nothing less than his immediate and irresistable influence could have as it were in a Moment united all America and made
them as the heart of one Man." Shinner was unimpressed by such
ingenious reasoning and refused to proceed with business, even after
unofficial word was received that the act had been repealed. The Commons then turned its attention to removing him. A rather pitiable
man, Shinner was incompetent, and the house had little difficulty
assembling a damning indictment. Suspended by the governor, Shinner
died while his case was being appealed to London.

     To contemporary South Carolinians, all of this was mere trivia com-
pared to their joy at the repeal of the Stamp Act. Although colonial
unrest, pressure by British merchants, and a new ministry combined
to bring about repeal in mid-March 1766, preliminary news of it did
not reach Charles Town until May 3, and the official report took a

month longer. As a result, South Carolinians had two celebrations instead of one, and the Commons commemorated the occasion by commissioning a statue of William Pitt as a tribute "for his noble, Disinterested, and Generous Assistance" in obtaining the repeal. Equally significant, it also asked its own delegates to the Stamp Act Congress to sit for portraits to hang in the State House "as a memorial of the high esteem this House have for their Persons and merit, and the great service they have done their Country."

All these festivities and tributes simultaneously reflected and almost obscured the seriousness of the crisis, which had brought many of the American colonies, including South Carolina, to the brink of rebellion. Faced with direct internal taxation by Parliament, Carolinians believed that submitting would establish a precedent which might place their property at the mercy of men beyond their control. In the future, it seemed reasonable to suppose, imperial authorities would find it expedient to shift the burden of taxation from their own constituents to those who had no recourse. As one South Carolinian summed up the matter, Americans were like unbroken donkeys; if they accepted this measure, *"more Sacks, more Sacks"* were coming. The concern was not merely over what the sacks might contain but, more important, over the fact that the British ability to impose taxes without the consent of the Carolina Commons threatened to deprive South Carolinians of the traditional first line of defense against tyranny.

Unable to prevent enforcement of the act in other ways, Americans resorted to violence. That it proved successful had significant ramifications. In the first place, it made resistance to British authority an apparently viable option thereafter. Realizing that this might well be the case, many British politicians considered repeal of the act to be a mistake. Partly to placate them, Parliament simultaneously adopted the Declaratory Act stating that it had the right to legislate for the colonies "in all cases whatsoever." Although it is difficult to imagine a more explicit refutation of the Commons's declaration that Carolinians could permit their assembly to be "subordinate to no power on earth," many Americans believed—because they wanted to believe—that repeal of the Stamp Act meant that British authorities had accepted their point of view. Thus the Declaratory Act seemed, in the words of Henry Laurens, to be "the last feeble struggle of the Grenvillian party" which had been responsible for the Stamp Act. This belief was wrong and, as Laurens later realized, the principles of the Declaratory Act would make a "platform for the Invincible Reasoning from the mouths of four and twenty pounders."

Cannon would eventually decide the issue, but in 1766 only a few die-hards like Gadsden, who harangued the Sons of Liberty in the shade of the Liberty Tree, recognized the dangers. Nevertheless, the crisis had seriously jeopardized the connection between Britain and the colonies. Thereafter each side became increasingly suspicious of the other. Americans also learned that there was safety in numbers. As Gadsden observed, there should be "no New England men, no New Yorker, etc., known on the Continent, but all of us Americans." Corresponding and meeting with each other, especially in the Stamp Act Congress, Americans had laid the foundations of the American union. Indeed, the Stamp Act even provided them with a national holiday before they were a nation, for throughout the rest of the colonial period they celebrated March 18 as the day on which the act was repealed.

Scarcely a year intervened before South Carolinians faced the next crisis, which began with the arrival of a new customs collector in the spring of 1767. Having been a member of Parliament, Daniel Moore may have been imbued with patriotic zeal to tighten up the customs service, but the evidence suggests that he was equally interested in making his fortune at the expense of South Carolinians. At any rate, he enforced trade regulations so strictly and venally that he himself violated the spirit, if not the letter, of the law; he also had the help of the royal navy. Enraged local merchants and seamen responded on two fronts. When the captain of the HMS *Sardoine,* James Hawker, sent a boarding party to inspect a schooner's papers, the crew, accompanied by the cheers of a waterfront crowd, repelled it. Then Hawker himself "with the British flag in my hand," as he later reported, led the boarding party. "But sorry I am to say it," he observed, "that instead of having that respect paid which was due it . . . , it received the highest insults," and he was welcomed with "cutlasses, axes, stones, clubs, etc." In addition, he was horrified to find that the local militia drummers "beat to arms, not to quell the mob . . . but to collect them together." This, he added, "is hardly credible, but it is really fact." Nevertheless, Hawker accomplished his immediate errand. Moore was less successful in the long run, for in less than six months he was forced to flee to England to escape an avalanche of suits and complaints filed by local merchants.

In the interim, however, his actions precipitated one of the most notorious local incidents of the pre-Revolutionary period. Technically, coasting vessels were required to clear each voyage at a customs house; normally, however, this provision was waived in cases where compliance was clearly impracticable. Apparently wishing to make an example of a leading local merchant, Moore unexpectedly ordered his underlings to seize two plantation schooners belonging to Henry Laurens, and a trial ensued in the court of vice-admiralty, which operated without a jury. At this time, the judge was Egerton Leigh who was not only related to Laurens by marriage but also a personal friend. Leigh attempted to arrange a compromise by ordering one of the vessels forfeited and the other returned to Laurens. In addition, he neglected to declare that reasonable grounds existed for believing the discharged schooner had been operating in violation of the law, and this omission permitted Laurens to recover his losses on the one vessel by suing for damages in the case of the other.

Leigh's attempt at compromise only compounded the difficulties. Laurens sued George Roupell, the customs searcher who had made the actual seizure, and the jury awarded a judgment which Roupell was unable to pay. To rescue himself from this predicament he then conspired with the new customs collector to seize another vessel belonging partly to Laurens. Roupell then offered to release the ship if Laurens would surrender his demand for damages. Laurens refused, and the case went before the court of vice-admiralty, where Judge Leigh found himself upon the horns of a real dilemma. On the one hand, because local customs officials had been filing a steady stream of complaints against him, he could not hope to retain his office unless he protected Roupell. On the other hand, because the customs officers had resorted to subterfuge, it was extremely difficult to shield them from another suit. Leigh solved the problem by forcing Roupell to take the seldom used oath of calumny, a declaration that his actions had not been motivated by malice. Using this statement as a basis for his action, Leigh then certified that there had been probable cause for seizure but discharged the vessel, noting that he had a "Strong Suspicion that there was more of design and Surprise on the part of some officers than of any intention to commit fraud on the part of the Claimant."

Considering the pressures upon him, Leigh's decision was reasonably fair, but it made him vulnerable. Roupell complained to his superiors that "no Judge of Admiralty can make a Court of Equity of it upon all occasions, which for this year past has been the case." Laurens, who was understandably filled with righteous rage at the treatment he had received, pilloried Leigh in a pamphlet entitled *Extracts from the Proceedings of the Court of Vice-Admiralty*. Leigh defended himself with *The Man Unmasked*. Leigh's polemics were largely a personal attack; Laurens was able to give his pamphlet wide distribution and broader significance by showing that the customs officials had been guilty of a gross abuse of their powers. He also clearly demonstrated that Leigh had put his own self-interest above his duty to curb them. Finally, Laurens attacked the composition of the admiralty court itself for permitting men like Leigh to render such decisions, unchecked by a jury or other judges.

Ever since passage of the Sugar and Stamp Acts—revenue acts that were enforceable in the vice-admiralty courts—these courts had become increasingly unpopular with Americans who attacked their jurisdiction on the grounds that it deprived colonials of the basic right to trial by a jury of their peers. Coincidentally, at almost the same time as Laurens was undergoing his ordeal, another merchant, John Hancock, was having similar and widely publicized experiences in Boston. Although Hancock may not have been entirely innocent, there is evidence to indicate that by the 1760s some customs officials did attempt a kind of racketeering at the expense of Americans. Laurens's pamphlet therefore found a receptive audience. As a result of the controversy, Leigh lost his position as judge of vice-admiralty and a good deal of prestige. Laurens, who had been rather lukewarm before, became an ardent champion of American rights and a popular figure throughout the colonies. Many Americans came to take a more jaundiced view of the customs service and the admiralty courts. Perhaps equally important in the short run, South Carolinians began to grow increasingly impatient with the caliber of royal placemen.

Meanwhile, yet another controversy was brewing. In the spring of 1767, Parliament imposed the Townshend Duties on all glass, lead, paint, paper, and tea imported into America. The proceeds, expected to be about £40,000 per year, were to be applied to the costs of not only defending but also governing the colonies. In other words, the intention was to make royal officials as financially independent of the local assemblies as possible. Moreover, in an attempt to insure efficient collection of these duties, the act established new vice-admiralty courts and a special board of American customs commissioners with headquarters at Boston. Opposition to the measure first developed in Massachusetts. On October 28, the Boston town meeting attempted to pressure British merchants into working for repeal of the new duties by urging individuals not to import dutied items and other luxury goods. The nonimportation movement soon spread to other cities in New England and the middle colonies, where John Dickinson composed his famous series of essays, "Letters From a Farmer in Pennsylvania to the Inhabitants of the British Colonies." Widely circulated and reprinted throughout the colonies, including South Carolina, these essays argued that a tax was a tax though it might be disguised as a duty. Duties to regulate trade within the empire were perfectly permissible; taxation without representation was unconstitutional. Sharing this point of view, the Massachusetts House of Representatives addressed a circular letter to the assemblies of the other American colonies urging joint action to oppose the Townshend Act. The governor of Massachusetts responded by dissolving the house, and the secretary of state directed other colonial governors to do the same if necessary to prevent their own assemblies from considering the circular letter. Meanwhile Hancock's difficulties with the customs officials led to violence; the officials fled to the fort in the harbor; and by October 1, 1768, British troops moved into Boston to maintain order and support royal authority.

When the Commons met in November 1768 the new governor, Lord Charles Montagu, told its members that he hoped they would treat with the "contempt it deserved" any letter they might receive advocating unwarranted combinations against the authority of the king and Parliament. During the summer, the speaker, Peter Manigault, had received the Massachusetts circular, which he now referred to the consideration of the house. Unanimously endorsing the circular as "replete with duty and Loyalty to His Majesty," the Commons solemnly assured Montagu that it had received no communication challenging the just authority of Parliament. Montagu dissolved it. The secretary of state's instructions thus helped to prevent another meeting like the Stamp Act Congress, but narrowing the options made Americans more willing to adopt nonimportation.

Whatever may have been the case with their colleagues elsewhere, most merchants in South Carolina were reluctant to cut off imports. By and large, they were making money on them, and a boycott would call for a disproportionate sacrifice on their part. Indeed, the reasonably self-sufficient planters might scarcely feel an embargo, and the mechanics, whose handicraft work competed with British products, could well benefit. Naturally, these two groups were more enthusiastic about adopting a nonimportation association, and during the summer of 1769 they were able to force the merchants into line by threatening not to patronize any who continued to import British goods. Gadsden led the charge by publishing a tentative draft of an appropriate agreement. Shortly thereafter the *Gazette* printed another form that had been signed by most of the members of the Commons. The following week, on July 4, the mechanics met under the Liberty Tree, amended, and signed this agreement. The merchants attempted to build a backfire by adopting an agreement of their own, more to their liking. The problem then became one of reconciling the conflicting provisions of the various agreements. That was the work of a large meeting under the Liberty Tree on July 22, 1769, when a compromise was approved. Neither slaves nor most manufactured British products were to be imported; permissible exceptions were such necessary items as writing paper, hardware, and cloth for clothing slaves. Sanctions to insure compliance included a commercial boycott of all individuals who failed to sign within the month; those who reneged upon the agreement after signing were to merit "the utmost Contempt." Finally, a commmittee composed of thirteen merchants, thirteen artisans, and thirteen planters was to oversee enforcement of these provisions.

The initial wave of enthusiasm, augmented by some coercion, was sufficient to induce most persons to cooperate. Within a few weeks, Timothy, who was particularly fond of self-fulfilling prophesies, reported that in addition to the royal officials in town only thirty-one persons had failed to sign the agreement; and most of them, as the *Gazette* assured its readers, were "*little* Scotch *Shop-keepers* of no consequence." Even the royal naval officer for the port of Charles Town, who also acted as an attorney for a local estate, signed. To Bull's intense annoyance, he "judiciously and casuistically" distinguished the roles and claimed to sign in the one capacity but not the other. At the other extreme, a few equally important individuals refused to cooperate at all. Among them was John Gordon, a leading importer of goods for the Indian trade who had signed the agreement drafted by the merchants. Pressured to sign the other forms, he lost patience and would not, as he put it, "be bandyed about from Resolutions to Resolutions." The confrontation between the committee and the two planters, William Wragg and William Henry Drayton, was more dramatic. A fiercely independent individual, Wragg was no more willing to bow to the committee than he had been to Lyttelton, while Drayton was a flamboyant political fledgling who refused to have his personal freedom circumscribed by an extralegal organization. The result of the attempt to coerce them was a display of verbal pyrotechnics in the local newspapers. Wragg remained in South Carolina for the time being but Drayton eventually retreated to London where he republished most of the polemics under the title, *The Letters of Freeman, etc.*, his pseudonym in the controversy. A position on the council rewarded his efforts and he returned to assume his seat in April 1772, only to change sides as the pre-Revolutionary controversy intensified.

As long as the majority signed or cooperated, an occasional maverick like Wragg or Drayton represented only a minor threat to the success of the embargo, but as the restrictions began to pinch merchants who had signed and hitherto cooperated, the problem of enforcement became more serious. Carefully avoiding challenges to individuals powerful enough to present serious problems, the committee attempted to keep backsliders in line by the threat of economic reprisal and violence. Consequently, nonimportation worked. Imports from Great Britain dropped by more than 50 percent, making this one of the most effective embargoes on the continent. At the time, South Carolinians estimated that non-importation saved them more than £300,000 in payments to Great Britain. Impressive as these figures were, the immediate results were disappointing. The British economy was doing better than at the time of the Stamp Act crisis, and trade with the rest of the world was able to take up much of the slack produced by the American embargo. Nevertheless, British merchants did request repeal of the Townshend Duties and Lord North, who had taken Townshend's place at the exchequer, eventually persuaded his colleagues to make concessions.

The retreat by British authorities did not signify that they had accepted the colonial position. North urged repeal of the duties not because he believed them to be unconstitutional but because he was willing to concede that they failed to promote British trade. To maintain the right to levy such taxes, he retained the duty on tea. Thinking that their goals had largely been achieved and generally ignoring the tax on tea—just as they had ignored the Declaratory Act—most Americans began to abandon nonimportation. Carolinians, however, had demanded repeal not only of the Townshend Duties but also of all obnoxious measures adopted since 1763. They therefore made an effort to continue the embargo but found that to be impossible. So, on December 13, 1770, Laurens presided over a meeting which voted to discontinue the boycott on everything but tea.

For South Carolinians, perhaps the most important result of the crisis over the Townshend Acts was a growing belief that arguments based solely on reason would change few minds in London. As John Mackenzie noted, "it is not the head, but the heart" that needed to be set right. If imperial authorities willfully refused to see the colonial point of view, Carolinians had nothing to depend on but their own firmness and virtue.

Once again, there was scarcely a respite before their resolve was put to another test. This time, however, the Commons was at least partly the aggressor. Throughout most of the 1760s, a demagogic Englishman by the name of John Wilkes bedeviled ministries. Returning from France where he had fled to escape a charge of seditious libel, he was elected to Parliament in 1768, but was sent to prison where he seemed symbolically to represent everyone throughout the empire who felt oppressed by the ministry. The Society of Gentlemen Supporters of the Bill of Rights, a group formed in London to offer him political and financial support, therefore solicited funds from Americans as well as Englishmen. Gadsden brought the matter to the attention of the house, and on December 8, 1769, it ordered the treasurer to send £1,500 sterling to the society. Whatever else can be said about this action, it was rash. Harassed at home and abroad, imperial authorities were sure to be outraged, and as Laurens correctly predicted, the house would get "a rap o' the knuckles" for it. That many members later had reservations about what they had done suggests that they did not fully consider the possible consequences of their gift. Nevertheless, their action is understandable. Hitherto, other colonies had taken the lead in resisting the Sugar Act, the Stamp Act, and the Townshend Duties. A token of official support for Wilkes provided a way for South Carolinians to take the initiative in a manner that seemed to be particularly in character. They possessed a reputation for largess of which they were proud, and South Carolina shared with New York the distinction of being the only colonies to thank Pitt for his part in the repeal of the Stamp Act by erecting a statue at public expense. The grant to Wilkes was an action similar in kind, though different in degree. Furthermore, only a few months earlier, Drayton and other dissidents had charged that the committee overseeing nonimportation had become the de facto government of the colony. Though exaggerated, this contention was sufficiently close to the mark to make one suspect that the Commons made the grant to Wilkes partly to regain the initiative on the domestic scene as well. If so, the step worked.

News of the grant produced a violent reaction in London, not only because the ministry perceived it as an insult but also because it called attention to the Commons's ability to spend public funds without the concurrence of the governor and council, which was expressly forbidden by royal instructions. Resolved to end the practice, the ministry dispatched an additional instruction to Bull on April 14, 1770. Under threat of being removed from office, the governor was to veto any revenue bill that did not contain specific restrictions on the expenditure of funds raised by the act. All revenue measures were to include provisions inflicting severe penalties upon colonial treasurers who executed any order of the house lacking the concurrence of the governor and council. If the Commons blundered in making the original grant, the ministry blundered in issuing an instruction that no house could accept, for it not only barred repayment of the funds already borrowed from the colonial treasurer but it also—and much more important—seriously compromised the power of the lower house over money bills. Laurens expressed the prevailing feeling when he observed that he "would rather have no Tax Bill for seven Years" or "forfeit my whole Estate" than surrender "the very Essence of True Liberty," the *"Right* of the People to give and grant [funds] voluntarily in mode and in Quantity free from the fetters of ministerial Instructions." Conversely, the ministry was equally adamant in maintaining that spending—or borrowing—money from the treasury on the sole authority of the house violated the governor's instructions and was therefore not "warranted by the modern practice of a few years, irregularly introduced, and improvidently acquiesced in." As the deadlock lengthened into years, a compromise might have been worked out had it not been for the least fundamental of the issues raised by the instruction of April 1770, namely the borrowed sum itself.

The ministry was determined to make the Commons repudiate the gift to Wilkes, and the house was equally determined not to do so. Each tax bill thereafter contained provisions to raise the necessary funds, and each time they considered the matter the governor and council felt obligated to block the measure. As a result, Governor Montagu was soon embroiled in a serious dispute with the Commons. Although he had been absent much of the time since assuming his position in 1766, he was no longer a novice and should have been able to exercise some judgment; but for reasons unknown, he did not. A story about him claimed that during the Revolution he offered to fight for the Americans. Although probably apocryphal, the tale is consistent with his character. Immature and unstable, he prompted Speaker of the House Peter Manigault to observe that Montagu convinced him that "it was not impossible for a Man to be too great a Fool to make a good Governor." When Montagu returned to the colony in 1771, he soon clashed with the Commons, which had jailed two treasurers who had refused to disburse funds pursuant to its order. Montagu rescued them by dissolving the house, but when a newly elected one met in the spring of 1772, it refused to conduct any other business until permitted to pass a tax bill of its own devising. Impatiently dissolving it, Montagu conceived a dangerously bright idea.

Why not move the meeting place of the assembly to Beaufort? He had that prerogative; Bull had met the legislature at Ashley Ferry (about ten miles from Charles Town) during a yellow fever scare in 1761; and Governor Hutchinson of Massachusetts had recently moved the General Court from Boston to Cambridge. In all probability, Montagu intended the move to be no more than a temporary tactical maneuver. The representatives from Charles Town and its immediate vicinity, who represented the core of his opposition, might be late in arriving, and in their absence it might be possible to push through a tax bill more to his liking. Or, at the very least, the fear that Beaufort might become the permanent capital could make the Charlestonians more cooperative. Certainly that fear existed, and perhaps with good reason. The capital of North Carolina had been peripatetic for most of the eighteenth century, and not until the legislature agreed to build Governor Tryon a magnificent palace at New Bern was its meeting place firmly fixed. Tryon had recently visited South Carolina, which was as well known for its wealth as North Carolina was for its poverty. Moreover, Montagu was embarrassed and irritated by his own difficulty in finding satisfactory quarters in Charles Town. Worse yet, the assembly did little to remedy the situation. In all probability, among the unstated reasons for its failure to build a house for the governor was the knowledge that the Regulators of North Carolina considered the expense of Tryon's palace a grievance, and the South Carolina Commons had no desire to antagonize its own already restive back-countrymen unnecessarily. Montagu took up quarters in Fort Johnson and assuaged his wounded vanity by salutes and ceremonies at his every coming and going, which prompted local wits to enliven the newspapers with essays and poems thanking him for purifying the air with so much gunpowder, etc. Ambitious men from Beaufort might be more considerate, for Montagu later claimed that they had promised to build him a house if he moved the legislature there.

At any rate, against the advice of Bull and others, he summoned the newly elected assembly to meet at Beaufort. The result was a disaster. "No measure of any Governor," a contemporary observed, "was ever more freely and generally condemned." Worse yet, when, to his surprise, most of the members promptly turned up at Beaufort, Montagu kept them waiting for three days and then sent them back to Charles Town. Unknown to them, his strange behavior was the result of a letter he had recently received from the secretary of state directing him to be more conciliatory. Montagu therefore found himself far out on an embarrassing limb, and the return to Charles Town was a futile attempt at retreat.

Thereafter, the more he struggled to extricate himself, the deeper he sank. Upon reconvening in Charles Town, a committee of the Commons recommended resolutions charging him with "an Unwarrantable Abuse of a Royal Prerogative." Expecting action of this kind, Montagu tried to head it off by examining the journals of the Commons every evening, but Rawlins Lowndes, who had replaced Manigault as speaker, took them home the night after the committee made its report.

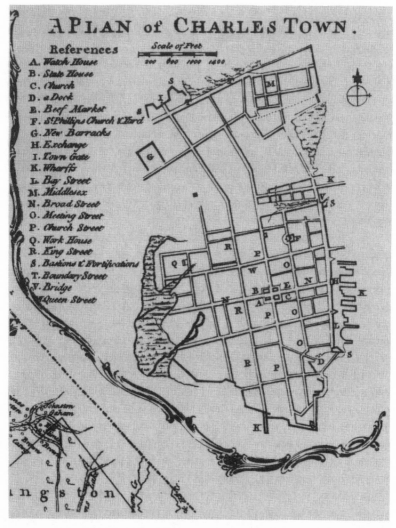

A plan of Charles Town. Inset from "A Map of the Province of South Carolina..." by James Cook (London, 1773). *Courtesy of the South Caroliniana Library.*

The next morning Montagu summoned the house to prorogue it, but, before obeying, it debated and approved the recommendations. Then, after the prorogation, the committee of correspondence directed its agent, Garth, to obtain Montagu's removal. Enraged and thoroughly frightened, Montagu countered by again dissolving the Commons. New elections again returned most of the old members, who promptly reelected Lowndes as speaker. Montagu ordered them to make another choice. They unanimously refused. He prorogued them, but in the process made a minor procedural error which, he feared, might subject him to further censure. So he again attempted to protect himself by dissolving the house. It was the fourth dissolution in less than fifteen months. Clearly, Montagu had lost control of the situation, and without waiting for official permission to leave his post, he retreated to England. Aware that imperial authorities were disgusted with him, he soon resigned.

The chief stumbling block to the resumption of normal business then proved to be the council, which considered the gift to Wilkes to have been neither "fit, or decent." In August 1773 it also conceived a dangerous idea. In the hope of putting pressure on the Commons to pass a tax act acceptable to the crown, the council investigated the state of the treasury, found it nearly empty because no tax bill had passed since 1769, and recommended that merchants be sued for all unpaid duties. In the hope of putting pressure on the crown to resolve the impasse by dropping the unacceptable instruction regarding money bills, the Commons countered the council's strategy by refusing to extend legislation providing salaries for the Anglican clergy. In turn, the council resolved to pass no legislation whatsoever until the lower house renewed the act. At this point, two councilors, John and William Henry Drayton (father and son), who believed that their colleagues had gone too far, formally protested their action.

On August 31, 1773, that protest appeared in the *South Carolina Gazette,* currently being printed by Timothy's partner, Thomas Powell. The council promptly jailed Powell for "a high Breach of Privilege and a Contempt of this House"; William Henry Drayton, who had been responsible for transmitting the protest to Powell, maintained that it was useless unless known to the public and that his own role in the matter absolved the printer. The two Draytons therefore registered another formal protest, this time against the commitment of Powell. The man most responsible for that action appears to have been the president of the council, Sir Egerton Leigh, who had just returned from England in possession of a new baronetcy and a firm resolve to uphold the authority of the council. Like his predecessors in the 1730s, he seems to have reasoned that the power to punish for contempt of its authority would help to establish the council's claim to status as an upper house.

In committing Powell to jail, however, Leigh and his colleagues made a serious mistake. Powell immediately applied for a writ of habeas corpus before two justices of the peace, who were members of the Commons. "Persuaded" by the now familiar argument that, lacking the independence of the House of Lords, the council was without the power to jail persons for contempt of its authority, the two justices set Powell free. Shortly thereafter, the Commons examined the whole case and resolved that the actions of the council were unprecedented, unconstitutional, and "a Dangerous Violation of the Liberty of the Subject." Orders followed to the agent directing him to obtain the removal of the councilors who had engineered Powell's commitment. Meanwhile, the printer sued Leigh for damages arising from his arrest. Chief Justice Thomas Knox Gordon—himself a member of the council—now reversed the opinion of the two justices and dismissed the suit on the grounds that, being an upper house of the legislature, the council exercised legitimate powers in arresting Powell. Many South Carolinians remained unimpressed by Gordon's judicial pronouncement. Leigh's attempt to strengthen the council thus actually weakened it further. So he attempted to redeem matters by publishing a pamphlet entitled *Considerations on Certain Political Transactions of the Province of South Carolina* which was printed in London in January 1774. Revolving around the notion that the Commons had become "the vortex of power," Leigh's *Considerations* were a perceptive analysis of the situation from the perspective of a heavily involved crown official. Seeking to present the other side of the story, Laurens and Ralph Izard induced the Virginian Arthur Lee to compose an *Answer to Considerations on Certain Political Transactions of the Province of South Carolina*. By this time, however, the Commons had broken the deadlock over the tax bill by issuing certificates to public creditors on its own authority without the concurrence of the governor and council, and the aftermath of the Boston Tea Party had so engrossed the attention of nearly everyone that neither pamphlet made much of a stir.

The dispute over the Wilkes Fund was nevertheless immensely important, perhaps most of all because it revealed, more clearly than any previous controversy, a fundamental point at issue between imperial authorities and local leaders. Unlike Wragg who had argued the same thing in the 1750s, Leigh unmistakably reflected the opinion of his superiors when he maintained that the constitution of the colony was completely *"derivative"* from the crown. In other words, the rights and privileges of the Commons House were solely those permitted by the crown. Thus, no matter how many precedents the house might be able to cite to justify the exercise of rights, privileges, and powers acquired over the years, these could be wiped out by royal fiat. Arthur Lee spoke for South Carolina's leaders: "The Rights and Privileges of the Commons House spring from the Rights and Privileges of British Subjects, and are coeval with the Constitution. They were neither created, nor can they be abolished by the Crown." Furthermore, "what has prevailed from the Beginning of the Colony, without Question or Controul is Part of the Constitution." That is, local practice and precedent were integral parts of the colonial constitution which ought to be respected by imperial authorities.

Thanks to the dispute over the Wilkes Fund, royal government came to a standstill during the last six years of the colonial period in South Carolina; but thanks in part to the controversy over the tax on tea, new machinery evolved to replace it. For South Carolinians, as well as for other Americans, the Boston Tea Party was a final turning point on the road to revolution. In 1773 the British government sought to rescue the East India Company from dire financial straits by permitting it to ship tea directly to the American colonies. Although this measure would reduce the price, many Americans failed to appreciate their new advantage. Merchants involved in the tea trade were concerned about the competition from consignees of the East India Company. Many colonists also correctly believed that the apparent concession was partly designed to induce them to buy the tea and thereby give de facto recognition to the legitimacy of the duty on it. Being realists, patriot leaders concluded that the way to prevent Americans from falling prey to temptation was to deliver them from it.

Throughout the colonies men therefore made plans to send the dutied tea back to England without allowing it to be landed. In some ports, such as Philadelphia, the plan worked; in others, such as Charles Town and Boston, it did not. Within a specified period after arrival, the tea would become legally liable to seizure for nonpayment of duties. How to prevent its being seized, landed, and later sold therefore became a more urgent question as time went on. South Carolinians debated the matter too long. Early on December 22 Lieutenant Governor Bull and the customs officers surprised them by unloading the tea and storing it under the Exchange, where it remained until sold during the Revolution to help finance the patriot war effort. Events were more violent in Massachusetts, where well-organized crews boarded the tea ship and heaved the cargo overboard.

Parliament responded with a law closing the port of Boston until the East India Company and the customs service received compensation for the lost tea and duties. Later in the spring, Parliament added other acts modifying the Massachusetts charter and permitting royal officials who were charged with committing crimes in America while performing their duties to be tried in England. The Intolerable Acts, as Americans termed them, were designed to make an example of Massachusetts and thereby divide and cow Americans, but the result was exactly the opposite. Upon hearing of these acts, most South Carolinians forgot their initial horror at the violence of the tea party in their outrage over what they considered to be nothing less than tyrannical measures. In their overwrought imaginations, the Administration of Justice Act became the "Murder Act," designed to give British soldiers an open hunting season on Americans. By preventing the use of all wharves and vessels, the Boston Port Act appeared to be the equivalent of arbitrarily confiscating the property of every merchant in Boston, innocent and guilty alike. By the same reasoning, a minister argued, "All in Charles Town might be laid in Ashes" if "a few ill-minded Persons were to take upon them to make Water against the door of a Customs-house Officer." Somewhat less graphically, Laurens saw the Coercive Acts as precedents for Laws to "Cram down . . . every Mandate which Ministers Shall think proper for keeping us in Subjection to the Task Master who Shall be put over us." Fear of what lay in store for them prepared South Carolinians to aid Boston. The question was how. The Boston town meeting asked for another general boycott of British goods; New Yorkers wished to defer nonimportation until the colonies could concert measures in another meeting similar to the Stamp Act Congress. The Massachusetts House of Representatives had to go along, and on June 17, 1774, called for a general colonial congress to be held in Philadelphia the following September.

Meanwhile South Carolinians began to establish extralegal machinery to enforce the boycott on tea. A mass meeting on January 20 appointed a large steering committee to prepare and call future meetings. News of the Boston Port Act brought another meeting which authorized the general committee to call elections for representatives to a gathering on July 6. When they met, 104 delegates from virtually all areas of the colony joined anyone in Charles Town who wished to participate in what a contemporary noted became "the most general meeting that has ever been known" and which, he observed, was attended by "almost every man of consequence." After adopting resolutions condemning the most recent British measures, the gathering considered the calls to join the nonimportation movement and attend the Continental Congress. It soon appeared that there was widespread support for participating in the latter, but the former proved to be a more divisive issue. The meeting did, however, vote to give its delegates to the Continental Congress power to commit South Carolinians to whatever the colonies jointly decided.

Choosing a reliable delegation therefore became a matter of some importance to various interest groups, and the traditional unanimity of South Carolinians began to show signs of breaking down. Remembering their difficulties during the crisis over the Townshend Duties, merchants had responded to harbingers of trouble over tea by organizing the Charles Town Chamber of Commerce, and, spurred by the new organization, they now mobilized the votes of their clerks. Mechanics and others countered by canvassing the town in behalf of their own candidates. The result was the choice of Henry Middleton (a planter who had resigned from the council), John and Edward Rutledge, Christopher Gadsden, and Thomas Lynch. Instead of the last three, the merchants would have preferred Charles Pinckney and Rawlins Lowndes, as well as Miles Brewton (who was a merchant). There was really not much difference in their preferences, which suggests that the division between interest groups was still not very sharp. Nevertheless, it was sufficient to produce a significant difference in the composition of a new general committee. The committee that operated during the first nonimportation movement included thirteen merchants, thirteen artisans, and thirteen planters. This pattern may have originated in the practice of the Commons, where committees often included spokesmen for concerned interests but seldom in numerical proportion to their strength in the population at large. However, representation on the new general committee was a reasonably accurate reflection of the white, adult, male population. It was composed of fifteen merchants, fifteen mechanics, and sixty-nine planters, with one of the latter—Charles Pinckney (who was also a lawyer)—serving as chairman. Empowered to act as the executive agent of the general meeting, this committee became in fact the temporary government of South Carolina.

Meeting from September 5 to October 26, 1774, the First Continental Congress rejected Joseph Galloway's "Plan of a Proposed Union between Great Britain and the Colonies," which would have established an American legislature to have concurrent jurisdiction with Parliament over colonial affairs. Declarations and resolves followed, enumerating colonial rights and denouncing recent British measures as unconstitutional and oppressive. Congress then adopted a "Continental Association," pledging Americans to embargo most trade with Great Britain. Enforcement would be up to committees to be elected in every city, town, and county throughout America. Adding addresses to the people of both Great Britain and America, as well as to the king, before adjourning, Congress resolved that, barring prior redress of colonial grievances, another congress would assemble on May 10, 1775.

Throughout the meeting Gadsden and Lynch played especially conspicuous roles. Gadsden, impulsive and impassioned as ever, left "all New England Sons of Liberty far behind," as one delegate from Connecticut reported. Since the South Carolinian apparently moved that a preventive attack be immediately launched against British forces in Boston, the estimate seems accurate. Thomas Lynch, who later reported from the Second Continental Congress that business "now goes on Swimmingly, for Why? my Colleague Gadsden is gone home, to Command our troops, God save them," was a more stable individual. Invariably, he impressed men as being a plain "man of sense" who "carries with him more force in his very appearance than most powdered folks in their conversation." Nevertheless, he was as deeply committed to the defense of American rights as Gadsden. On the opening day,

Lynch made three successful motions which represented victories for those who favored vigorous measures: that Congress meet in Carpenters' Hall, that Peyton Randolph preside, and that Charles Thomson be secretary.

The most dramatic incident involving members of the South Carolina delegation developed over the question of nonexportation. On October 20, just when the association appeared ready for signing, all of the South Carolinians except Gadsden threatened to walk out, announcing that unless the colony was permitted to continue exporting rice and indigo, they would not be a party to the agreement. Gadsden, as usual, was willing to make drastic sacrifices to obtain unified action. The others led by John Rutledge believed that unless the exemption was granted, South Carolina would be saddled with a disproportionately heavy burden. Being enumerated products, most rice and all indigo could be shipped only within the empire. The agreement therefore threatened to cut South Carolinians off from their major market. Neither the middle nor New England colonies were as dependent upon enumerated products as South Carolina. Eventually, Rutledge and his colleagues proved willing to compromise. In return for permission to export rice, they agreed to accept an embargo on indigo. Rather than break up the Congress, delegates from other colonies approved this arrangement.

On November 6, the returning South Carolinians arrived in Charles Town, and the general committee promptly called elections for a Provincial Congress to meet on January 11, 1775. When the congress met, trouble quickly developed over the provision regarding rice. Gadsden thought it unfair and recommended that South Carolinians go beyond the letter of the association by agreeing not to export the grain. Again reciting his reasons, Rutledge argued that the exemption should be retained. The argument was sound, but it also applied to indigo. Those who grew indigo but not rice naturally felt themselves to be the victims of an invidious distinction. To placate them, a rather cumbersome plan was devised by which a third of the rice crop would be used to compensate those who produced other products. Committees to enforce the association were also established in each area. More ominously, provisions were made for a secret committee charged with the responsibility of gathering arms and gunpowder. Finally, the congress reelected the same delegation to the Second Continental Congress.

As soon as the provisions of the association were known, South Carolinians began to carry them out. At first the chief effort appears to have been directed toward erecting and oiling the machinery of enforcement. Goods imported from Great Britain were confiscated and put up for sale at public auction. In theory the proceeds were to go for relief of suffering Bostonians. South Carolinians did contribute generously to the relief of Boston but by donation. Because the process of confiscation and auction initially was intended to be only a dress rehearsal, there were no profits. The owner of the goods was allowed to bid for them at their original cost; since this was refunded to him, he kept his property at the price of a little inconvenience.

On February 1, all of this changed radically as rigorous enforcement replaced early leniency. How rigid that enforcement might be soon became apparent. Robert Smythe, a Charles Town merchant, returned from England late in March bringing with him personal property used in England. It included two thoroughbred English horses. Could they be landed? On the grounds that they represented personal property previously acquired and not intended for sale, the Charles Town committee decided that they could be. But the populace at large believed that this decision violated the terms of the association. If enforced, they argued, it would destroy the entire nonimportation movement— which it might well have, once the notion that Smythe received special treatment became prevalent. The hubbub forced the committee to reconsider the matter and by a close vote to rescind its earlier decision. Lieutenant Governor Bull wryly observed that "the many headed power of the people" was not now so easily controlled by its former leaders. Interestingly enough, those leaders had gained an unexpected recruit, William Henry Drayton, who now demanded that the committee listen to the voice of the people.

Drayton's conversion from one of the loudest supporters of the prerogative to one of the most demagogic leaders of the Revolution is puzzling. Because he was clearly a volatile and ambitious man, historians have sometimes ascribed his actions to resentment at having had his personal and economic ambitions thwarted by royal officials. Furthermore, like many of the younger revolutionary leaders in South Carolina, he had recently been to England and may have resented some of the attitudes he encountered. Perhaps all of these elements contributed to his change of heart, and none precludes a sincere change of opinion about the locus of the threat to liberty. At any rate, like many converts, Drayton became a zealous champion of the new cause. His flair for publicity made each step in his progress from proto-loyalist to flaming revolutionary a step toward Revolution for South Carolina as well. After the Powell affair, he repeatedly clashed with his colleagues on the council. He also composed another pamphlet addressed to the Continental Congress in which he advocated a plan for an American legislature resembling Galloway's. In addition, in his role as an assistant judge he made a memorable circuit on which he charged the grand juries of the backcountry to maintain the constitution inviolate "even at the Hazard of your Lives and Fortunes." Most of the juries—including the one at Ninety Six of which Alexander Cameron was foreman—responded by presenting as a great grievance Parliament's attempt to tax America. Because Cameron was the deputy of John Stuart, the royal superintendent of Indian affairs, the action of the Ninety Six jury was a source of great glee to American patriots and of embarrassment to royal officials, who attempted to comfort themselves with a rumor that Cameron was drunk at the time.

Activities of this kind soon produced a request from Stuart and the chief justice that Drayton be removed from the council. On March 1, 1775, Lieutenant Governor Bull complied and suspended his nephew. Six weeks later, Drayton headed the secret committee which descended upon the public powder magazines and armory to remove the arms and ammunition. In response to Bull's inquiry, the Commons reported that it was unable to discover the perpetrators of the crime but found "reason to suppose that some of the Inhabitants of the Colony may have been induced to take so extraordinary and uncommon a step in consequence of the late alarming Accounts from Great Britain."

The news was indeed alarming. On February 27, 1775, the British House of Commons approved the ministry's plan for conciliating the American colonies. Parliament would "forebear" to tax any American colony that made adequate contributions toward paying for the common defense and civil government. As Americans realized, nothing in these provisions recognized the American claim of the right to tax themselves, and imperial officials remained judges of what contribution would be deemed adequate. Moreover, on the same day that the Commons approved this unsatisfactory plan, the ministry introduced a bill to prohibit inhabitants of New England from trading outside of the empire and to bar them from their usual fishing grounds in the North Atlantic. The bill passed and became law on March 30; two weeks later its provisions were extended to four more colonies, including South Carolina. By mid-April, Carolinians could not yet know all that was in store for them, but, early in May, letters from London reported that the British planned to incite Indian attacks and slave rebellions in South Carolina. The report was not true but, given the heated atmosphere and the traditional fear of insurrection, it made a plausible rumor. And almost immediately on top of this report came accounts of the battles of Lexington and Concord.

13

THE REVOLUTION

The outbreak of fighting in Massachusetts prompted the general committee to call the Provincial Congress into session on June 1, 1775. Moving with great alacrity, the Congress raised troops, authorized paper currency to pay for them, and called for the election of a new congress to meet on December 1. Basing its action on seventeenth century English precedents, it also established a council of safety composed of thirteen members to act as an interim executive. And perhaps most indicative of the climate of opinion, members of the Congress adopted and signed "an association"—also with British roots—pledging to "UNITE ourselves, under every tie of religion and of honor" to defend America and, if necessary, "to sacrifice our lives and fortunes to secure her freedom and safety." Henry Laurens, who had replaced Charles Pinckney* as president of the Congress, vigorously opposed attempts to stigmatize men who would not sign the association, but was overruled. As one loyalist discovered as early as six months before, it was considered "even culpable to be passive."

Despite the efforts of moderate men like Laurens, hysteria—and perhaps the need to rouse and unite the people—led to violence. When Lord William Campbell, the new royal governor, arrived on June 18 he found nearly everyone to be greatly excited by a rumor that he brought with him arms for slaves and Indians. "The cruelty and savage barbarity of the scheme," he reported, "was the conversation of all

---

*Charles Pinckney (1732–1782) was a nephew of the Charles Pinckney (1699–1758) who had been speaker of the Commons House in the 1730s.

Companies." And, as previously recounted, Thomas Jeremiah died, allegedly for inciting an insurrection. Three months earlier, in May, John Stuart read the handwriting on the wall and fled southward, first to Savannah and then St. Augustine. Although he would try to prevent indiscriminate attacks upon the frontier settlements, he was unable to convince many South Carolinians that he would not incite the Indians. Other royal officials and intrepid loyalists were hauled before the general committee, disarmed, and confined to the city. William Wragg, the most important native South Carolinian among the group and long a thorn in the side of American patriots, courageously told the tribunal that he would abhor himself if he "was capable, upon any consideration, of subscribing to an opinion contrary to the dictates" of his own judgment. His outspokenness made him dangerous, particularly in Charles Town. He was therefore ordered to be confined to his plantation near Dorchester. Meanwhile, vessels sent out by the council of safety seized gunpowder from ships off the Georgia and Florida coasts. As the members of the Commons told Campbell during its last session, "every Pacific Measure which human Wisdom could devise has been used." Leaving "the justice of our Cause to the Great Sovereign of the Universe, upon whom the fate of Kingdoms and Empires depend," they prepared for war.

More immediately, however, the fate of South Carolina depended on the unity of its people, and the backcountry became something like a diplomatic prize as imperial and local authorities contended for the allegiance of its inhabitants. Contemporaries did not find it easy to predict their responses, and historians have not found it easier to account for them. Ethnic and religious divisions help to explain the neutralism of the pacific Quakers and perhaps the loyalism of Germans, who believed that they owed their land in Orangeburg and the Dutch Forks (modern Lexington County) to a Hanoverian king. Englishmen, Scotch-Irish, Anglicans, and Presbyterians, who together constituted most of the population, were divided among themselves. Most of them seem at first not to have been engaged—that is, they were not necessarily apathetic, but having recently migrated into the backcountry from colonies farther north, they were not closely tied to the lowcountry and, given the assumptions of the prevailing political culture, considered their business to be making a living, not politics. Thus the position of leading local men—the rising planters, storekeepers, mill owners, and militia officers—was critical, for each of them might influence the allegiance of scores of other men in his area. Knowing this, and recalling how a contrary policy on the part of the British had affected them, Revolutionary authorities attempted to conciliate as many back-country leaders as possible by recognizing their status and offering them commissions in the Revolutionary forces.

Because most of the Regulators prominent enough to be identified eventually became Whigs, it appears that lowcountry Revolutionaries were successful in coopting many of the natural leaders of the back-country. As a result, Tories were forced to turn to ex-Coffelites and other marginal members of society for support. British use of such "banditti," as well as Indians and blacks, then in turn helped to confirm the association between ex-Regulators and Whigs. Although the circularity of these developments gives a misleading appearance of inevitability, one should note that the record contains a built-in bias. The rising men of the backcountry who were both Regulators and prescient enough to back the winning side are the ones more readily identified. In the spring and summer of 1775, however, the situation was fluid. No one could predict the future with certainty, and not everyone could be conciliated. Consequently, it seemed that jealousies, pique, and principle would divide the leading men of the backcountry.

Certainly, some backcountry men soon showed that they could not be counted on to support the Revolution. On July 12, 1775, Whigs obeyed the order of the Council of Safety to seize the arms and ammunition at Fort Charlotte, located on the Savannah River some thirty miles southwest of the settlement at Ninety Six. Major James Mayson (who was in charge of the operation) then moved a portion of the stores to Ninety Six, but Moses Kirkland, a thorough-going opportunist who had helped to take the ammunition, suspected that a majority in the backcountry was unhappy about the trend of events in Charles Town. He therefore sent an emissary to Colonel Thomas Fletchall of the Upper Saluda Militia Regiment to suggest that Fletchall recapture the powder on behalf of the crown. Though sympathetic to the idea, Fletchall was not a decisive man. He therefore refused to take an active part in the scheme. His immediate subordinates were men of more resolution. Leading 200 militia, they retook the ammunition and arrested Mayson for having stolen it.

Alarmed at events in the backcountry, the Council of Safety sent two German-speaking men, George Wagner and Felix Long, and two ministers—Oliver Hart, a Baptist, and William Tennent, a Congregationalist—as well as William Henry Drayton, to attempt to sway the Germans and dissenters in the area. Tennent and Drayton went the farthest and expended the most energy. After a long, hot day in August which ended in a ride through pouring rain, Tennent noted in his diary, "if we can stand this we need fear nothing"—to which he added, but the storm "was not to be compared to the fury of the little Inhabitants of the Bed. After a sleepless and wet Night I was shocked by the Blood and Slaughter of [sic] my Callicoed Shirt and Sheets in the morning." Despite these and greater sacrifices, the mission was not a complete success. Meeting effective opposition from Thomas Brown, one of the ablest and most persistent champions of the crown in the backcountry, and others, Drayton concluded that the Council of Safety should arrest its leading opponents. He therefore established headquarters at Ninety Six and sent out parties to capture suspected individuals. In turn, the Tories raised a large number of men. Drayton then prudently offered to negotiate with Fletchall who had now taken over command of the loyalist force. Meanwhile, Drayton issued calls for help to trustworthy militia. By the second week in September Fletchall and Drayton, each with about 1,000 men, faced each other across the Saluda River. Negotiations followed, and on September 16, 1775, Fletchall, over the objections of his chief subordinates, agreed to a treaty of neutrality. Drayton then headed back to the fork of the Congaree River, near modern Columbia, where on September 25, he conferred with a number of Cherokee chiefs who were upset because few trading goods had lately reached them. Drayton explained why and promised to send them as much as could be spared.

In the interim, a loyalist, Patrick Cunningham, raised a number of men to rescue his brother Robert who had been jailed on charges of sedition. On November 3, he captured a wagon train carrying gunpowder to the Cherokees. Claiming that the Provincial Congress intended the ammunition for a general Indian raid on the frontier, the loyalists recruited a force that soon outnumbered that of Andrew Williamson, a Whig major, who had called out his men at news of the capture. Williamson therefore retreated from Long Canes to Ninety Six. On November 19 Major Joseph Robinson led a group of Tories against him. The battle which ensued lasted for three days and drew blood on both sides, the first blood of the Revolution in South Carolina. On the 22nd both sides were ready for a truce—Williamson's because they had only two cartridges per man remaining and, for most of the time, no water except what they could scoop out of hog troughs; Robinson's because they wished to escape before Whig reinforcements arrived.

Having received word of Cunningham's capture of the powder train, the Provincial Congress directed Colonel Richard Richardson of the Camden militia to call up his men, recapture the powder, and seize those who had taken it. The truce arranged by Robinson and Williamson did not, Richardson believed, apply to his own forces which soon numbered nearly 2,500 men, including units from North Carolina. By December 12 he had captured Fletchall and many other leading loyalists. Adding men as he went, Richardson's formidable force moved southwest from the Enoree River toward Ninety Six. Badly outnumbered but uncowed, about 130 of the loyalists fled into the Cherokee country, established a camp on the Reedy River, and tried without success to rouse the Cherokees in their behalf. Here Richardson's expeditionary force surprised them, killed a number, and captured most of the remainder, who were later released by the Council of Safety. As Richardson's army turned back, it began to snow, and from then until they were disbanded on January 1, 1776, the men, unprepared for bad weather, suffered through two weeks of snow, sleet, and rain. Nevertheless, the "snow campaign" was a great success. Not until the British capture of Charles Town were the Tories again to be a serious problem in the backcountry.

Meanwhile, equally important developments were occurring in Charles Town. Suspecting that Governor Campbell maintained communications with the loyalists, a Whig, who claimed to be one of the king's friends, tricked Campbell into revealing their plans. The next night Campbell quietly moved his powerless office from Charles Town to a British vessel in the harbor. Thus on September 15, 1775, the last vestige of royal government finally collapsed.

The Second Provincial Congress, which remained in session from November 1 until the 29th, replaced the colonial assembly. William Henry Drayton, who had just returned from the backcountry, was chosen to preside. If, as has sometimes been assumed, his election was intended to silence him, it failed. Before appointing a new Council of

Safety which included most of the old members, Congress also directed that some of the channels into the harbor be blocked. When on November 11 a vessel attempting to execute this order drew fire from the *Tamar,* a British sloop, war came to Charles Town.

A week prior to this encounter, the Continental Congress advised the South Carolinians to "establish such form of Government as in their judgment will best produce the happiness of the people, and most effectually secure peace and good order" during the dispute with Great Britain. Thus the temporary government was to be, in a sense, the direct successor of the Sons of Liberty, the general committees, and the various public meetings that had organized the boycotts of British manufactured goods and tea. The dual purpose in each case was effective resistance and public order, which experience had shown went together. Early in the spring of 1776, the Provincial Congress appointed a committee composed of such influential men as John Rutledge, Christopher Gadsden, and Henry Laurens to draft a constitution. At this time, John Adams was writing *Thoughts on Government* for similar occasions; in all probability, however, South Carolinians relied mainly on local experience. Indeed, the very idea of a written constitution evolved, at least in part, from the colonial charters and governors' instructions. Moreover, like the British constitution which developed partly through legislative enactment, the new state constitutions would be merely an act of the legislature—though everyone agreed that one of the most important functions of a constitution was to limit the power of government. Here was the anomaly which eventually led to the idea of a constitutional convention. South Carolina, however, was the first colony in the south and only the second in the nation to draft a new state constitution. At this stage, it was not unusual to utilize legislatures for this purpose.

More unusual were some of the provisions of the new constitution. Unlike most of the first American governors, the president possessed a veto over legislation. Furthermore, he was eligible for reelection. Undoubtedly, political considerations and the relative scarcity of qualified men to fill positions influenced these provisions. It is equally probable that the confidence South Carolinians developed in their political leaders during the late colonial period prompted them to trust these men with unusually wide powers. Years of contending that the Royal Council was not an upper house bore fruit in provisions separating

the Privy Council, the governor's advisory body, from the Legislative
Council, the upper house of the legislature. Similarly, judges acquired
tenure in their offices during good behavior, and the lower house
received a clear acknowledgment of its exclusive right to draft money
bills. The backcountry, which contained more than 60 percent of the
population, was allocated approximately one-third of the seats in the
general assembly. The proportion was considerably larger than it possessed under royal government but less than a perfectly equitable ap-
portionment would call for. All in all, the constitution of 1776
substantiated the claim made by the First Provincial Congress that "no
love of innovation—no desire of altering the constitution of government—no lust of independence has had the least influence upon our
Counsels." Following reconciliation with Great Britian, most individuals hoped to retain the reforms contained in the constitution of 1776.
Beyond this, however, almost no one among the established colonial
elite—including John Rutledge who was elected president by the
Provincial Congress at the end of March—wished to go. Significantly,
though he acted as governor, the constitution still gave him the title
of president. Under British rule, it should be noted, the president of
the council served as the acting governor in the absence of the governor
and lieutenant governor. The goal, clearly, was acceptable terms of
reconciliation with Britain, not independence.

Yet, as British authorities proved to be intransigent, the logic of
the situation seemed to make independence the only alternative to
capitulation. In February 1776 Gadsden arrived in Charles Town from
the Continental Congress bringing a superb piece of propaganda in
behalf of separation from the empire, Thomas Paine's *Common Sense*.
Henry Laurens and most of his colleagues in the Provincial Congress
found it full of "indecent" expressions toward the crown. Nevertheless,
on March 23 they empowered their delegates in the Continental Congress to agree to whatever measures Congress thought necessary for the
general welfare. When the time came, Edward Rutledge, Thomas
Heyward, Jr., Thomas Lynch, Jr., and Arthur Middleton, with varying
degrees of reluctance, would construe this authorization to permit them
to sign the Declaration of Independence. Of the few men who seemed
to welcome the drift toward independence, one of the most conspicuous
was William Henry Drayton. Elected chief justice of the state, perhaps
once again in an unsuccessful attempt to silence him, he delivered a

widely circulated charge to the Charles Town grand jury on April 23 in which he contrasted the advantages of the new constitution with the disadvantages of British rule. "The almighty created America to be independent of Britain," he concluded. "Let us beware of the impiety of being backward to act as instruments in the Almighty hand, now extended to accomplish his purpose."

If Drayton's analysis was correct, among the Lord's instruments for making South Carolinians willing to accept independence was the British attack on Charles Town at the end of June 1776. Planning for the expedition was long and involved, and by the time the British forces, commanded by Sir Henry Clinton and Sir Peter Parker, arrived off Charles Town, delays, mismanagement, and bad luck had warped the original purpose beyond recognition. Thus what began as an attempt to rally and support loyalists, especially in North Carolina, ended as a demonstration against Charles Town.

Aware that the city might be the focus of attack, South Carolinians prepared to defend it. Buildings along the Cooper River were leveled and cannon mounted to sweep the area. Men poured into the city, nearly 4,000 South Carolinians—regulars and militia—and another 200 continentals from North Carolina and Virginia. With them came Major General Charles Lee, a professional soldier, formerly with the British army and now with the American. Lee's presence was a tonic for the morale of South Carolinians, though he himself was unimpressed by their efforts. Two months later he wrote from Georgia, "the people here are if possible more harum skarum than [in] their sister colony [South Carolina]." They suggest, he continued, all kinds of schemes without considering their practicability. "I shou'd not be surpris'd if they were to propose mounting a body of Mermaids on Alligators." Lacking mermaids to oppose the British, South Carolinians relied on the garrison in two forts. Though in disrepair, Fort Johnson on James Island was a sturdy structure. Gadsden and the First South Carolina Infantry manned it. About four miles to the east on Sullivan's Island, commanding the main channel, was an unfinished fort being constructed of palmetto logs. General Lee took one look and termed it a slaughter pen, but Governor Rutledge vetoed its abandonment. Colonel William Moultrie and the Second South Carolina Infantry had the unenviable task of manning this fort. At the northern end of Sullivan's

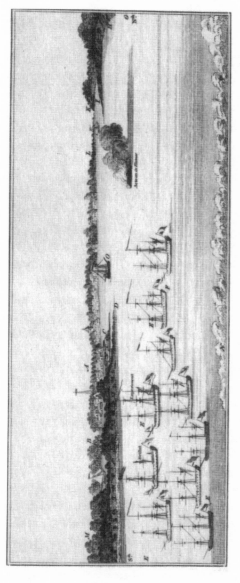

A view of Charles Town on June 29, 1776, the day after the unsuccessful British attack on Sullivan's Island. Engraving after a sketch by Lt. Colonel Thomas James. *Courtesy of the Henry E. Huntington Library and Art Gallery.*

Island Colonel William Thomson with a force of about 800 men protected Moultrie from an attack on the landward side.

The battle took place on June 28. The British plan of attack called
for Clinton's men, already ashore on what is now the Isle of Palms, to
cross the small tidal creek between it and Sullivan's Island and to attack
Moultrie in the rear. Three of Parker's frigates were to run past Fort
Sullivan and take position to its southwest where they would be well
out of the range of Fort Johnson's guns but still able to bring their
own cannon to bear on the unfinished side of Fort Sullivan. Unfortunately for the British, the creek at the north end of Sullivan's Island
was too deep and the shoals at the south end were too shallow. As a
contemporary noted, troops attempting to cross in the face of Thomson's men would have been "pretty well melted down." As a result,
the navy was forced to attack without support from the army. Three
of Parker's vessels then managed to pass the fort—only to run hard
aground. Impotent sitting ducks, they took a terrific pounding from
Moultrie's cannon, while the rest of the fleet was able to do little
damage to the fort's spongy palmetto logs, which absorbed shot like
sand bags. By nightfall Moultrie had sustained less than forty casualties,
Parker more than four times as many. One frigate which had run
aground, the *Actaeon,* was destroyed to prevent capture; several other
vessels were heavily damaged. "Thus," as one British army officer
reported, were "2 fifty Gunn Ships 5 frigates and a Bomb of the
Invincible British Navy defeated by a Battery which it was supposed
would not have stood one Broadside." Thus ended the first British
attack on Charles Town.

Shortly thereafter, a full-scale Indian war broke out on the frontier.
Williamson raised the militia as rapidly as he could and by the end of
July had nearly 1,200 men. Marching to attack the Cherokees, he was
ambushed early on the morning of August 1 as his force crossed the
Keowee River, but he pushed on to devastate the Indian settlements
east of the Appalachian Mountains. Meanwhile, General Griffith Rutherford and Colonel William Christian led North Carolinians and Virginians, respectively, in laying waste the more remote Indian towns.
Badly battered, the Indians in 1777 agreed to the treaty of Dewitt's
Corner ceding the area that was to become the four westernmost counties of South Carolina.

The battle of Fort Moultrie and the fighting on the frontier made it easier for many South Carolinians to accept independence, but many others remained reluctant. At least for the lowcountry elite, mid-eighteenth century South Carolina had been a very comfortable place, prosperous and well-governed. To exchange the known for the unknown, that which had proved capable of providing the good life for the opportunities and dangers of independence, hardly seemed an attractive prospect. Henry Laurens wept at the thought of independence, and he undoubtedly expressed the feelings of many of his friends when he wrote that he felt like a dutiful son driven "by the hand of violence" from his father's house. Though the ties of sentiment and economic interest helped to bind South Carolinians to the empire, other considerations prevailed.

"A Free British American" from Charles Town posed the crucial question, "Is the selfish Nature of Man so much mended, is his Lust for Power so far satiated, that we may resign ourselves, with unsuspecting Confidence, into the Hands of the Fox Hunters and Gamblers of St. Stephen's Chapel?" Neither the fox hunters of Parliament nor the ministry intended to establish despotic rule over the colonies. At first, they merely attempted to bring the colonies under closer control and make Americans pay what Englishmen considered to be a fair share of the cost of defending and governing the empire. When that attempt elicited a challenge to the power of Parliament, they resolved, above all, to uphold the sovereignty of Parliament over the entire empire. For to them, it seemed that to compromise the one was to shatter the other. South Carolinians, as well as other Americans, believed just as firmly that, human nature being what it was, to resign themselves into the hands of Parliament would be the utmost folly. To protect themselves they therefore turned to their own Commons House of Assembly, over which they had the requisite controls, and tried to mark out for it the widest possible area free from the interference of outside authorities. In particular, they attempted to insure that it possessed exclusive jurisdiction over the crucial area of public finance.

To support their claims, Americans invoked two constitutions, the provincial and the imperial. Tennyson later spoke of England, the land "where Freedom slowly broadens down from precedent to precedent." South Carolinians, believing that they shared all the rights of Englishmen, attributed a similar quality of organic growth to their own provincial constitution. They found that imperial authorities disagreed.

Similarly, Carolinians eventually contended that the only link between themselves and their fellow subjects in Great Britain was the king, that their own Commons was a small equivalent of the British House of Commons, to which they were not subject. This, too, they found to be an unacceptable argument in London. Ultimately, therefore, they came to the reluctant conclusion that William Henry Drayton was right, that "Americans can have no safety but by the Divine favor, their own virtue, and their being so prudent as *not to leave it in the power of the British rulers to injure them.*"

On August 5, 1776, the independence of the United States of America was proclaimed in Charles Town. At twelve noon the town regiment of militia was drawn up under arms in Broad Street. Forty-five minutes later President John Rutledge, Major General Charles Lee and his chief subordinates, members of the privy and legislative councils, members of the lower house, and officers of the army appeared in a procession which halted at the front of the regiment. The Declaration of Independence was read. The procession then moved slowly east on Broad Street to the Exchange where the Declaration was read a second time. The multitude responded with cheers; the cannon at the bastions along the Cooper River with salutes. That evening the Declaration was read to the army encamped on the plain north of Charles Town and on the following day to the troops at forts Johnson and Moultrie. "No Event," William Tennent noted, "has seemed to diffuse more general Satisfaction among the People. This seems to be designed as a most important Epocha in the History of South Carolina, and from this Day it is no longer to be considered as a colony but as a State."

Independence itself of course marked a major break with the past, but in many other respects the Revolution in South Carolina remained a remarkably conservative movement. Begun as an attempt to resist what Carolinians believed to be unwarranted political innovations on the part of British authorities, it did, to be sure, make politics more relevant to the concerns of men in all walks of life and thereby opened up the possibility of extensive change. Given the assumptions of eighteenth century political culture, however, the first tendency of a politicized people was not to demand that their leaders be common men but that the leadership provided by the elite be responsive to popular needs. Because men of property responded reasonably satisfactorily, most of the populace failed to demand more. Institutional change during the Revolution was therefore relatively small.

Faced with the need to conciliate backcountry men and freed from the restriction on the size of the assembly imposed by imperial authorities, lowcountry leaders granted the western districts significant representation; and the constitution of 1778, the first for the independent state, continued the practice of giving the backcountry substantial representation, in this case about 40 percent of the representatives in the legislature. In 1785 and each fourteen years thereafter, representation was to be reapportioned "in the most equal and just manner according to the particular and comparative strength and taxable property of the different parts of the same, regard being always had to the number of white inhabitants and such taxable property." Although it took another thirty years, another constitution (of 1790), and an amendment (of 1808), as well as considerable controversy, before such reapportionment actually gave the majority of the population in the west a majority in both houses of the legislature, the Revolution unequivocally made backcountry men part of the political community.

Equally important, changes in the constitution made the dissenting religious groups part of the established church. No sooner had the Revolution broken out than dissenters began petitioning the Provincial Congresses and general assembly to remove the invidious distinctions which set them apart from members of the Anglican Church. In January 1777 the Reverend William Tennent, himself a dissenter and a member of the general assembly, made an eloquent speech in their behalf, reminding his collegues of the prudence and justice of recognizing the force of numbers. Although the vote was close, they saw the light of reason and in the constitution of 1778 provided that virtually any group of fifteen male Protestants might incorporate themselves and be considered part of the established church. The stipulation that such Protestants must believe in one God, that he was to be publicly worshipped, and that there was a future state of rewards and punishments echoed the Fundamental Constitutions so closely as to suggest deliberate copying. Furthermore, the constitution of 1778 substituted the term "seat of government" for Charles Town; consciously implicit here was the notion that the capital might someday move westward. Eight years later, the legislature did in fact vote to move it to the center of the state.

By 1778 backcountry men, a majority of whom were dissenters, had a substantial stake in the Revolution, and the Whig militia gave an able account of itself in keeping the remaining loyalists under control. In fact, by this time many upcountry men may have become more enthusiastic about the Revolution than some of their counterparts in the lowcountry, whose initial unanimity had been somewhat in the spirit of Bolingbroke's ringing declaration of fifty years earlier to the effect that "the friends of liberty" would "rather choose, no doubt, to die than bear to live the first of British slaves." In a militarily weak colony, it was hoped that a vigorous gesture of resistance would be sufficient to force British authorities to reverse course, something South Carolinians believed had frequently happened in British history. South Carolina in fact proved to be the scene of relatively little military action from 1776 to 1778, and the war seemed to drag on. The currency depreciated, economic concerns became more pressing, and some men lost their enthusiasm for the struggle. Others were unhappy with the constitution of 1778. John Rutledge, who was governor at the time of its adoption, resigned rather than sign it, partly because it was too "democratic" and partly because it abandoned the notion of reconciliation with the mother country. In addition, the French alliance early in 1778 aligned South Carolinians with their ancient popish enemy and thereby displeased many. Later in the year, latent hostility erupted in a riot between French and American sailors in which several men were killed. Thus when the prospect of the French alliance induced British authorities in 1778 to offer Americans virtually everything they had demanded short of independence, local authorities rejected the offer not, it seems reasonable to suppose, because no prominent figures were interested in the proposition but because its prior rejection by the Continental Congress meant that they could not honorably accept it.

Soon thereafter, French involvement prompted the British to attack the southern colonies in the hope of enlisting the assistance of the numerous loyalists believed to be in the area. By the spring of 1779, British forces had captured Savannah and began to restore civil government. Meanwhile, the Continental Congress admitted that it could do little to defend South Carolina and recommended that it arm slaves. Although John Laurens, a young American officer whose father, Henry, had been president of the Continental Congress, saw military service

by blacks as a stepping stone toward their freedom and strongly supported the plan, most South Carolinians were horrified at the idea.
The legislature voted it down, and when General Augustine Prevost
led British units up through the southern part of the state to the very
gates of Charles Town in May 1779, some Carolinians welcomed him.
Governor Rutledge (who was once again in office) even went so far as
to offer to surrender the town if South Carolinians would be permitted
to remain neutral for the rest of the war. Rutledge may have been
stalling for time, but many of the men around him believed the offer
to be in earnest. Prevost, however, refused to negotiate and withdrew
to escape entrapment by approaching Continental forces.

Although looting and burning by Prevost's men helped to stiffen
American resistance the following year, Sir Henry Clinton's attack
proved to be well-planned and methodical. Charles Town fell on May
12, 1780, whereupon most of the militia of the backcountry also
capitulated. At this point Clinton over-reached himself. Believing that
he held South Carolina in the hollow of his hand, he revoked the paroles
given to the captured Whig militiamen and called upon them to resume
the duties of British citizenship—which meant service in the loyalist
militia. Many men who might have been willing to accept neutrality
were not prepared to fight against their erstwhile comrades; some
therefore rejoined the American side when Continental forces under
General Horatio Gates approached Camden. After routing this army,
British authorities, who had hitherto vacillated between attempting to
conciliate or terrorize South Carolinians, responded by adopting a policy
of calculated severity. In turn, many Carolinians in the lowcountry
who were under the British thumb "took protection" or resumed their
allegiance.

Backcountry men who could resist and run had more options. A
sufficient number of them became partisans so that the British soon
had trouble distinguishing combatant from noncombatant as well as
friend from foe. British authorities therefore became less discriminating
in the use of violence and less determined to restrain loyalists who
sought to inflict what one termed "retributive justice" on their enemies.
The result was an increasingly ugly war, perhaps best summed up in
the tale of two atrocities related by a British officer. "A few days ago,"
he noted in 1781, "after Genl. Sumter had taken some waggons on
the other side of the Santee, and the escort of them had laid down

their arms, a party of his horse [men] who said they had not discharged their pieces came up, fired upon the prisoners and killed seven of them. A few days after we took six of his people. Enquire how they were treated." Who bore primary responsibility for this kind of thing is less important than that the brutalization of the war threatened to make every man his own vigilante. Under such circumstances even a commander as popular as Francis Marion had to spirit a loyalist prisoner off to keep his own men from killing him.

Restoring law and order turned out to be the victorious Americans' problem. Between October 1780, when a party of backwoodsmen defeated a large loyalist force at King's Mountain, to the battle of Eutaw Springs in September 1781, when a bloody draw worked to the Americans' advantage, units of the Continental Army under Nathanael Greene and the Carolina militia under Marion, Andrew Pickens, and Thomas Sumter forced the British to withdraw virtually within the confines of Charles Town. A minister who had fled the Port Royal area and returned at the end of the war left a vivid description of conditions. "All was desolation.... Every field, every plantation, showed marks of ruin and devastation. Not a person was to be met with in the roads. All was Gloomy." All society, he continued "seems to be at an end. Every person keeps close on his own plantation. Robberies and murders are often committed on the public roads. The people that remain have been peeled, pillaged, and plundered. Poverty, want, and hardship appear in almost every countenance. A dark melancholy gloom appears everywhere, and the morals of the people are almost entirely extirpated." Revolutionary authorities had recovered most of the state, but portions of it were a wasteland, and whether they would be able to control the populace remained for some time an open question.

To reassert the authority of the Revolutionary government, restore order, and facilitate the continuing war effort, a newly elected assembly met at the little town of Jacksonborough about thirty miles from occupied Charles Town during the first two months of 1782. Its most important measures were a series of acts to amerce or confiscate the estates of several hundred specified and unspecified individuals among the most conspicuous loyalists. Coupled with offers of pardon to most other Tories, these acts were intended to pressure them into abandoning the sinking British ship in the hope of saving their property, to raise money from the confiscated estates for carrying on the war, and, perhaps most important, to provide an outlet for Whig bitterness and thereby forestall continuing private vengeance. Local leaders had taken to heart the lessons of the 1760s when Regulators did what the royal government failed to do. Equally significant, the enactment of punitive legislation helped to legitimize the Revolutionary elite which thereby demonstrated its militant patriotism while disassociating itself from "the protection gentry" who had succumbed to British pressure. Subsequent mercy to most loyalists who petitioned for relief after the British evacuated Charles Town in December 1782 caused some popular opposition, but by then the debate had largely been moved indoors, and mercy tended to conciliate the ex-loyalists.

The peace treaty with Britain ending the war in 1783 called for restoration of the loyalists' property. Some Americans might be able to ignore these provisions with impunity, but South Carolinians were still too dependent on British commerce and credit to do so. Despite attempts to broaden trade with France and other countries, the common language, familiar procedures, and the willingness of British merchants to extend credit contributed to the reestablishment of pre-war commercial patterns. Seeking to restock their plantations and enjoy some of the things they had missed during the war, many South Carolinians were soon deeply in debt to their recent enemies. The combined effect of too much credit, too little trade, and wartime damage, as well as partial crop failures in 1783 and 1784, was a sharp depression. In part because men of property were not immune to its effects, the legislature adopted a number of measures which helped to minimize suffering and allay popular discontent, including tax reform, the emission of paper money, and the adoption of stay laws. Thus, despite some disorder, local leaders managed to prevent a serious upheaval like Shays's Rebellion in Massachusetts. What they could not do alone, however, was to put relations with their chief trading partner on a more satisfactory footing. Indeed, the confiscation acts, stay laws, and other measures taken to cope with internal problems complicated dealings with Great Britain. Moreover, the war was extremely expensive and by 1789 the state of South Carolina owed its own citizens and others approximately $5,386,588, which in per capita terms was by far the largest debt of any state. Carolinians believed, however, that, when accounts with Congress were balanced, South Carolina would be the creditor rather than the debtor. Accordingly, a stronger national government might be useful, not so much for handling internal problems—local leaders had demonstrated that they were capable of doing that—but relieving the state of a mountain of debt and restoring its trade.

Nothing in all of this is meant to imply that calculations of public and private interest were the sole, or even in all cases the predominant, consideration among those who favored a stronger central government. Several leading South Carolinians served in the Continental Congress or the Continental Army and had strong emotional ties to the concept of a United States; and, as a generous gift to Greene from the confiscated estates by the Jacksonborough legislature testified, many Carolinians recognized that they owed their liberation in large measure to the army. With a few relatively minor exceptions and hiatuses, however, local leaders had consistently favored attempts to strengthen the authority of Congress. Because this pattern began well before one could expect much emotional attachment to the Union to have developed, it seems reasonable to assume that the attitude had more to do with perceptions of local military weakness than American patriotism. In short, South Carolinians viewed the Continental Congress or an alternative national government primarily as an instrument for accomplishing state ends. Lowcountry men who were vulnerable to attack from hostile seapowers or their own slaves and dependent upon the export trade could see the potential virtues of a strong central government. Four lowcountry men—John Rutledge, Charles Pinckney,* Charles Cotesworth Pinckney, and Pierce Butler—who went to the Constitutional Convention therefore worked out with like-minded men from other sections of the country a series of explicit and implicit compromises which they believed advanced the interests of all of the states individually as well as collectively. Of immediate interest to South Carolinians, the Constitution offered Britain a carrot and a stick. In forbidding the states to pass bills of attainder, impair obligations of contract, or make anything but gold and silver legal tender, the Constitution assured Britains that South Carolinians had foresworn the practices which had impeded commercial relations between them; by erecting a stronger union empowered to pass navigation acts and other commercial measures, the Constitution also served notice that the

---

*The third prominent South Carolinian to bear that name, this Charles was the son of the man who had been president of the Provincial Congress.

United States was prepared to retaliate against damaging trade restrictions. Accordingly, the four delegates to the convention came home to advocate adoption of the Constitution as a fair, equitable, and useful document.

Most lowcountry men in the state legislature and ratifying convention agreed with them and supported the Constitution. Most backcountry men were more skeptical about it. Being numerous and having relatively few slaves, they were less conscious of military weakness; and, in many cases, those who had served in the militia rather than the Continental Army were emotionally tied to the state. In addition, the Constitution appeared at this time to offer relatively few economic advantages for farmers who did not export rice and other staples. Thus they perceived more dangers than benefits in the augumented power of the central government. But though they might be a majority of the population, they were a minority in both the legislature and the ratifying convention. As a result, South Carolina ratified the Constitution; and those who opposed it were forced to take it, as one of them ruefully observed, "as we take our wives, 'for better, for worse.'" That they did so with good grace probably had something to do with their understanding of what the local tax burden might be if the central government could not pay its debt to the state.

14

EPILOGUE:
TOWARD THE NINETEENTH CENTURY

Shortly after South Carolina became the eighth state to ratify the United States Constitution, a Carolinian observed that "we are getting back fast to the system we destroyed some years ago." When his words are applied to the national scene, as he intended them to be, this statement seems to be almost self-evident. When applied to politics at the local level in South Carolina, however, it is a bit incongruous; for the destruction of the prewar system was most incomplete. In fact, South Carolinians carried so many of the assumptions and so much of the style of eighteenth century political life into the nineteenth century that historians have frequently considered local politics to have been "anachronistic." Given the anomalous character of local political behavior and the fateful role of the state in the antebellum period, it seems appropriate to close a history of colonial South Carolina with a few words concerning some of the reasons for this unusual continuity and its implications.

During the late eighteenth and early nineteenth centuries, South Carolinians frequently exhibited a pervasive conservatism that retarded change in many areas of life, including the legal system and politics. Part of the explanation, of course, is that slavery and the commitment to its defense inhibited change. In addition, some members of the established leadership reacted to the popular challenge of the Revolutionary period by becoming more socially exclusive and politically conservative. Yet most individuals appear to have responded with a reasonable degree of flexibility. What is more remarkable, however, is the limited amount of flexibility that was required. In sum, the popular challenge to men of property during the Revolutionary period proved to be relatively weak and ephemeral. Thus, as historian George Rogers has observed, "the same elite guided the destinies of the state from the Revolution to the Civil War."

Full accounts of why the challenge to this elite was not more powerful and how men of property maintained their political position are obviously well beyond the scope of the present inquiry. It is possible, however, to suggest several considerations associated with developments in the colonial period. In the first place, the political culture of the mid-eighteenth century embodied a number of popular features, such as the secret ballot and a broad suffrage. If this political system was "aristocratic," as historians have sometimes termed it, it also involved the possibility of considerable "democratic" participation, and, in the lowcountry at least, local leaders proved to be quite responsive to constituents. In all probability, prevailing practices not only decreased the pressure for change but also acclimated men of property to the idea that the populace had a legitimate interest in politics. It is therefore not really surprising to find that South Carolina was among the first of the southern seaboard states to grant universal white manhood suffrage (in 1810). The history of the colonial period suggests that this concession resulted more from the confidence of the elite than from the pressure of a restive populace.

Moreover, despite the upheavals of the Revolutionary era, men of property in South Carolina had some grounds to feel more secure about their political position after independence than before it. Compared to the English aristocracy, they had been sufficiently middle class to raise questions in the minds of some of their own constituents, as well as of British authorities, about their qualifications for leadership; compared to other Americans, however, they were sufficiently wealthy to be considered, as one European observed, "truly . . . the Nobility of the American States." Under some circumstances and in some quarters, this fact might have undermined their position. However, the social distinctions that set them apart were, as the same visitor noted, typically "cherished under a disguise, to accord with the principles of their government." The worldly success of the wealthy therefore tended to make them emulated rather than envied. At least equally important, during the Revolutionary era, men of property in general had done what, according to prevailing assumptions, a political elite was supposed to do—namely, defend liberty. Their Revolutionary role therefore did much to legitimize the position of the elite in the postwar period.

In similar fashion, the degree to which political practices in the late colonial period conformed to prevailing ideals helped to insure that the Revolution would produce no sharp break with the past. Even men like the historian David Ramsay who participated and gloried in the Revolution could nevertheless look back on the late colonial period and declare that "no colony was ever better governed." Characterized by prosperity and a comparative absence of factionalism, the late colonial period often appeared in retrospect more like a golden age to be treasured than a dark past to be abandoned. The British, of course, had not been impressed, but their attempt to bend reality to their theories had failed; South Carolinians were therefore at liberty to make their theories conform to what they perceived reality to be. Later in the antebellum period, it could be argued, their efforts produced a closed and ossified system. At first, however, their attempts to make the reality and the ideal coincide helped to carry the political culture of the eighteenth century over into the nineteenth century with remarkably little change.

Accordingly, not only the relatively "aristocratic" nature of local leadership but also other unusual features of Carolina politics in the antebellum period appear to have been related to colonial practice. Nowhere else, for example, was so much power concentrated in the legislature at the expense of local governments as well as the governor, and nowhere else were political parties so slow to develop. As a student of the American party system, Richard P. McCormick, has observed, "the conduct of politics in South Carolina was so distinctive as to be markedly different from any other state." No one would doubt that nineteenth century developments were primarily responsible for this state of affairs, but one should recall that local politics in the late colonial period were also exceptional—not so much in the condemnation of partisanship, which was common, but in the degree to which current ideals governed actual behavior. It is equally probable that the power of the legislature in the antebellum period derived in part from its unusually active and powerful colonial predecessor. More important, these two characteristic features of South Carolina politics—the extraordinary power of the legislature and the absence of parties—contributed significantly to the singular course of the state during the antebellum period, for both removed potential brakes on extreme action.

Weak institutional checks on political extremism proved to be crucial because the political imperatives inherited from the eighteenth century themselves produced a tendency toward extremism. The prevailing country ideology of the late colonial period, one should remember, depicted political life as an arena in which public-spirited members of the social and economic elite preserved freedom by combating incipient tyranny. Furthermore, because liberty could be undermined by seemingly innocuous steps, all threats to it—even the apparently trivial—demanded the most vigorous countermeasures. Ordinary political action, popular violence, and revolt were therefore merely different stages of the eternal battle in behalf of freedom. These conceptions meant that prudence was the chief if not the only restraint upon violent political behavior. The very fact, however, that men conceived of politics as the life-and-death struggle of liberty tended to render prudential considerations irrelevant. Thus during the controversy with Governor Thomas Boone in the early 1760s over who was going to control the composition of the Commons House, Christopher Gadsden could declare that "he would rather submit to the distruction of one half of the Country than to give up the point in dispute"; and thus, when the stakes seemed higher on the eve of the Revolution, Carolinians could state that they would rather "die the *last of American Freemen,* than *live the first of American Slaves."* Given this political heritage, it is not surprising that South Carolinians defined the issues of the antebellum period, such as the tariff and slavery, in equally stark terms and responded accordingly. The Carolina fire-eater was a legitimate heir of the colonial political tradition, and Congressman George McDuffie's declaration during the Nullification Crisis of the 1830s that he "would infinitely prefer that the territory of the State should be the cemetery of freemen than the habitation of slaves" clearly paraphrased the ringing declarations of his Revolutionary predecessors. However McDuffie's failure to catch the incongruity in his last three words—to forget, as it were, that South Carolina was the home of over three hundred thousand slaves in 1830—was something that his forbears probably would not have done. His oversight suggests that the fears of slave insurrections which had given them pause no longer inhibited his contemporaries very much. Under these circumstances, the colonial political tradition proved to be an extraordinarily volatile heritage.

To recall that antebellum South Carolinians saw the sectional controversy in much the same way that their colonial forefathers perceived the Revolutionary struggle is to evoke Raimondo Luraghi's observation that "the meaning of life, both to individuals and to nations, is summarized and symbolized by the way they choose to die." It is also to close the story that began three centuries earlier with Renaissance figures like Ribault.

BIBLIOGRAPHY

Although most basic primary sources and standard secondary works are mentioned in this bibliography, no attempt has been made to duplicate listings readily available in published bibliographies. Numerous older items have therefore been omitted to make room for as many recent studies as possible.

After opening sections dealing with bibliographical guides, primary sources, and secondary works of a general nature, items are organized under topical headings corresponding to chapters in the book. Unless there are special reasons for doing so, general works are not repeated under the topical headings, though they may contain pertinent information. Full bibliographical details are given only at the first mention of a title.

BIBLIOGRAPHICAL GUIDES, SOURCES, AND GENERAL WORKS

For guidance to the primary and secondary sources of South Carolina history one can begin with Robert J. Turnbull, *Bibliography of South Carolina, 1563–1950*, 6 vols. (Charlottesville, 1956–1960). An attempt to describe all imprints relevant to South Carolina, Turnbull's work is incomplete but useful. James H. Easterby, *Guide to the Study and Reading of South Carolina History: A General Classified Bibliography* lists published primary and secondary materials. The first edition (Columbia, 1950) was remarkably comprehensive; the supplement by Noel Polk attached to the reprinted edition (Spartanburg, S. C., 1975) is disappointingly incomplete. Lewis P. Jones, *Books and Articles on South Carolina History: A List for Laymen* (Columbia, 1970) provides a selective, annotated list, while James H. O'Donnell, III, *Southeastern Frontiers: Europeans, Africans, and American Indians, 1513–1840: A Critical Bibliography*

(Bloomington, Ind., 1982) is up to date and judicious. Richard N. Côté, *Local and Family History in South Carolina: A Bibliography* (Charleston, 1981) is broader in coverage than its title indicates since it lists other bibliographies, guides to manuscript collections, and the contents of the *Yearbooks of the City of Charleston*, the *South Carolina Historical and Genealogical Magazine* (hereafter abbreviated *SCH & GM*) and its successor, the *South Carolina Historical Magazine* (hereafter abbreviated *SCHM*), as well as the *Collections of the South Carolina Historical Society*, the *Proceedings of the South Carolina Historical Association*, and the *Transactions of the Huguenot Society of South Carolina*—most of which contain much primary source material as well as numerous articles relevant to the colonial period. E. L. Inabinett has compiled a useful guide, *South Carolina: A Dissertation Bibliography* (Ann Arbor, 1980) available through University Microfilms International; Warren F. Kuehl, ed., *Dissertations in History: An Index to Dissertations Completed in History Departments of the United States and Canadian Universities, 1873–1970*, 2 vols. (Lexington, Ky., 1965–1972) lists a few additional works.

The most important collection of manuscript sources pertaining to the colonial period is at the South Carolina Department of Archives and History, Columbia, South Carolina. The basic guide to its holdings is Marion C. Chandler and Earl W. Wade, *The South Carolina Archives: A Temporary Summary Guide* (Columbia, 1976) which is now being revised. In addition, an increasingly comprehensive computer indexing system facilitates access to many of the records of the colonial period, including land plats, grants, conveyances, renunciations of dower, petitions to practice law, judgment rolls of the Court of Common Pleas, and the accounts audited of the Revolutionary period. For an introduction to this indexing system consult "Claims, Committee Reports, and the Consolidated Computer Output Index; a Revolution in Access," *SCHM*, LXXIX (October 1978), 313–318. Fundamental to any study of the colonial period are the legislative and executive journals; guidance to the various versions is provided by Charles E. Lee and Ruth S. Green, "A Guide to the Commons House Journals of the South Carolina General Assembly, 1692–1721," *SCHM*, LXVIII (April 1967), 85–96; "A Guide to the Commons House Journals of the South Carolina General Assembly, 1721–1775," *SCHM*, LXVIII (July 1967), 165–183; "A Guide to the Upper House Journals of the South Carolina General Assembly, 1721–1775," *SCHM*, LXVII (October 1966), 187–202; and "A Guide to South Carolina Council Journals, 1671–1775," *SCHM*, LXVIII (January 1967), 1–13. In addition, the Archives holds the colonial probate records, including wills and inventories of estates.

The Archives has also sought to acquire copies of records filed with counties (after their establishment in 1785) and other repositories, in and out of the state. In particular, beginning with the thirty-six volume set of transcripts of "Records in the British Public Record Office Relating to South Carolina, 1663–1782," made late in the nineteenth century, the Archives has assembled much relevant material from the Public Record Office. Thus, for example, all items listed under South Carolina in Lester K. Born, comp., *British Manuscripts Project: A Checklist of the Microfilms Prepared in England and Wales for the American Council of Learned Societies, 1941–1945* (Washington, D. C., 1955) are available on film at the Archives. These and other microfilm copies will be itemized in the forthcoming guide to the South Carolina Department of Archives and History.

It should be noted that the South Carolina Archives has also made a number of its own holdings available on microfilm. These now include the convenient compilation of "Records in the British Public Record Office Relating to South Carolina, 1663–1782," mentioned above, and the "Records of the Public Treasurers of South Carolina, 1725–1776," both of which have introductory pamphlets. In addition, there is a wealth of South Carolina material available in the collection of early state records assembled by the Library of Congress and the University of North Carolina; these items are listed in Lillian A. Hamrick, ed., and William S. Jenkins, comp., *A Guide to the Microfilm Collection of Early State Records* (Washington, D. C., 1950) with a supplement edited by Jenkins in 1951.

Much primary material is also held by the South Carolina Historical Society in Charleston and the South Caroliniana Library of the University of South Carolina in Columbia. David Moltke-Hansen and Sallie Doscher, *South Carolina Historical Society, A Manuscript Guide* (Charleston, 1979) and Allen Stokes and E. L. Inabinett, *A Guide to the Manuscript Collection of the South Caroliniana Library* (Columbia, 1982) facilitate access. (Both have been published as supplements to the *SCHM* as well as separately.) The Historical Society is also issuing microfiche editions of some collections in its own and other hands; see the announcement of the program in *SCHM*, LXXXII (July 1981), 280. For other repositories in the state—few of which outside of Charleston contain much relevant to the colonial period—one can consult John Hammond Moore, ed., *Research Materials in South Carolina, A Guide* (Columbia, 1967). Additional information about South Carolina in the colonial and Revolutionary periods is also scattered among the holdings of the William L. Clements Library in Ann Arbor, Michigan, the New York Public Library, the Library of Congress, the British Public Record Office, and the British National Library, each of which has its own guide or guides.

Special mention should also be made of the papers of the Bishop of London, who headed the Anglican Church in the colonies, and of the papers of the Society for the Propagation of the Gospel, which supplied missionaries for

South Carolina; relevant sections of each collection are available on microfilm at various repositories. Their character can be seen in the calendars compiled by William W. Manross, *The Fulham Papers in the Lambeth Palace Library: American Colonial Section, Calendar and Indexes* (Oxford, 1965) and *The S. P. G. Papers in the Lambeth Palace Library: Calendar and Indexes* (Oxford, 1974). In addition, the correspondence of two of the most important SPG missionaries can be sampled in Frank J. Klingberg, ed., *Carolina Chronicle: The Papers of Commissary Gideon Johnston, 1707–1716*, University of California Publications in History, XXXV (1946), and *The Carolina Chronicle of Dr. Francis LeJau, 1706–1717, ibid.*, LIII (1956).

Other published primary sources include most of the journals of the Commons House of Assembly. The twenty-one volume series covering 1692–1735, edited by A. S. Salley, Jr., does not meet modern editorial standards, but the more recently published journals of the Commons House (from 1736 to 1752) edited by J. H. Easterby and others are meticulously edited. Less satisfactory is the nevertheless extremely useful work of Thomas Cooper and David J. McCord, eds., *The Statutes at Large of South Carolina*, 10 vols. (Columbia, 1836–1841) which omits some important acts that can be consulted in manuscript at the South Carolina Archives. Francis N. Thorpe, ed., *Federal and State Constitutions, Colonial Charters, and Other Organic Laws of the States, Territories, and Colonies Now or Heretofore Forming the United States of America*, 7 vols. (Washington, D. C., 1909) and Anne King Gregorie and J. N. Frierson, eds., *Records of the Court of Chancery of South Carolina, 1671–1779* (1950; reprinted New York, 1975) are convenient compilations.

Several published collections of British records are also helpful; these include W. Noel Sainsbury et al., eds., *Calendar of State Papers, Colonial Series, America and the West Indies, 1574– (London, 1862–); Journal of the Commissioners for Trade and Plantations, 1704–1782*, 14 vols. (London, 1920–1938); Joseph Redlington, ed., *Calendar of Treasury Papers, 1557–1728*, 6 vols. (London, 1868–1889); William A. Shaw, ed., *Calendar of Treasury Books and Papers, 1729–1745*, 5 vols. (London, 1897–1903); W. L. Grant and James Munro, eds., *Acts of the Privy Council of England, Colonial Series, 1613–1783*, 6 vols. (Hereford and London, 1908–1912); Leo F. Stock, ed., *Proceedings and Debates of the British Parliaments Respecting North America, 1542–1754*, 5 vols. (Washington, D. C., 1924–1941); Leonard W. Labaree, ed., *Royal Instructions to British Colonial Governors, 1670–1776*, 2 vols. (New York, 1935); and, more recently, *Documents of the American Revolution, 1770–1783*, 21 vols. (Shannon and Dublin, Ireland, 1972–1981) edited by Kenneth G. Davies.

Furthermore, the published records of North Carolina and Georgia contain much information about South Carolina. For Georgia, see Allen D. Candler, ed., *The Colonial Records of Georgia*, 26 vols. (Atlanta, 1904–1916) and Candler, ed., *The Revolutionary Records of Georgia*, 3 vols. (Atlanta, 1908). Since 1977 Kenneth Coleman and Milton Ready have been bringing out additional volumes of the colonial records. William L. Saunders, ed., *The Colonial Records of North Carolina*, 10 vols. (Raleigh, 1886–1890) and Walter Clark, ed., *The State Records of North Carolina, 1777–1790*, 16 vols. (Winston and Goldsboro, 1895–1905) are still standard, though the editorial policies are outdated. The first volume in a second series of *The Colonial Records of North Carolina*— Mattie E. E. Parker, ed., *North Carolina Charters and Constitutions, 1578–1698* (Raleigh, 1963)—is especially relevant to both Carolinas.

Contemporary imprints can usually be located in the microcard edition of *Early American Imprints, 1639–1800* compiled by Clifford K. Shipton and issued under the auspices of the American Antiquarian Society. Shipton and James E. Mooney provide guidance to the collection in *The National Index of American Imprints Through 1800: The Short Title Evans*, 2 vols. (Worcester, 1969). Though not indexed, almost all of the extant issues of the newspapers published in colonial South Carolina are available on microfilm from the Charleston Library Society.

Several miscellaneous items are especially useful. Among them are A. S. Salley, Jr., and R. Nicholas Olsberg, eds., *Warrants for Lands in South Carolina, 1672–1711* (Columbia, 1973) and a number of published vestry minutes and parish registers, guidance to which can be found in the bibliographies mentioned above. B. R. Carroll, *Historical Collections of South Carolina*, 2 vols. (New York, 1836) and A. S. Salley, Jr., *Narratives of Early Carolina, 1650–1708* (New York, 1911) contain important material, including promotional pamphlets. Chapman J. Milling, ed., *Colonial South Carolina* (Columbia, 1951) prints two invaluable descriptions of the colony from the middle of the eighteenth century by Governor James Glen and George Milligen-Johnston, a local physician. William Gerard DeBrahm, *General Survey in the Southern District of North America* was completed in the early 1770s but not published in full until 1971 when it was edited by Louis DeVorsey, Jr. (Columbia). John Drayton, *A View of South Carolina as Respects Her Natural and Civil Concerns* (1802; reprinted Spartanburg, S.C., 1972) was Governor Drayton's counterpart to Thomas Jefferson's *Notes on the State of Virginia*. Robert W. Gibbes, *Documentary History of the American Revolution*, 3 vols. (1855; reprinted Spartanburg, S. C., 1972) really deals with South Carolina; unlike the original edition, the reprint contains an index. *The Colonial South Carolina Scene, 1697–1774* (Columbia, 1977) edited by H. Roy Merrens is relatively strong on economic and environmental information. Shorter than the above but nevertheless exceptionally informative are the remarks of a German pastor from the mid-eighteenth century edited by Klaus G. Loewald and others in "Johann Martin Bolzius Answers a Questionnaire on Carolina and Georgia," *William and Mary Quarterly* (hereafter abbreviated *WMQ*), XIV (April 1957), 218–261, and XV (April 1958), 228–252.

The most important collection of private papers is that of Henry Laurens, the definitive edition of which is now projected to approximate fifteen volumes. It has been edited successively by Philip M. Hamer, George C. Rogers, Jr., and David R. Chesnutt (Columbia, 1968–   ). *The Writings of Christopher Gadsden, 1746–1805* edited by Richard Walsh (Columbia, 1966) omits some material but is still most useful. *The Letterbook of Eliza Lucas Pinckney, 1739–1762* edited by Elise Pinckney and Marvin R. Zahniser (Chapel Hill, 1972) is fascinating; being primarily routine mercantile correspondence, *The Letterbook of Robert Pringle*, 2 vols. (Columbia, 1972) edited by Walter B. Edgar is duller but well worth consulting.

Travelers' accounts, a number of which have been printed, sometimes contain a wealth of information. Among the more valuable and frequently cited are two from opposite ends of the chronological spectrum covered by this book: John Lawson, *A New Voyage to Carolina* edited by Hugh T. Lefler (Chapel Hill, 1967) and the "Journal of Josiah Quincy, Junior, 1773," *Massachusetts Historical Society Proceedings*, XLIX (1916), 424–481, edited by Mark A. DeWolfe Howe, but there are numerous other accounts. The first two volumes of Thomas D. Clark, ed., *Travels in the Old South: A Bibliography*, 3 vols. (Norman, 1956) provide guidance. Additional information about visitors and their activities is contained in Frank W. Ryan, Jr., "Travelers in South Carolina in the Eighteenth Century" (unpublished M.A. thesis, University of North Carolina, 1943) which is printed without the bibliography in the *Yearbook of the City of Charleston* (1945).

Standard statistical compilations and reference works include *Historical Statistics of the United States: Colonial Times to 1970* compiled by the Bureau of the Census, 2 vols. (Washington, D. C., 1975) of which chapter Z covers the colonial period, and Robert Mills's two works, *Statistics of South Carolina* (1826, reprinted Spartanburg, S. C., 1972) and *Atlas of the State of South Carolina, 1825*, reprinted in 1980 with an introduction by Gene Waddell (Easley, S.C.). A fine modern atlas with several plates depicting South Carolina is Lester J. Cappon et al., *Atlas of Early American History: The Revolutionary Era, 1760–1790* (Princeton, 1976). *South Carolina, A Guide to the Palmetto State* compiled by the Work Projects Administration (New York, 1941) and *Names in South Carolina*, a periodical edited by Claude H. Neuffer and sponsored by the Department of English, University of South Carolina, contain much interesting lore.

The earliest general histories of the colony and state were those by Alexander Hewatt and David Ramsay. Hewatt's *Historical Account of the Rise and Progress of the Colonies of South Carolina and Georgia*, 2 vols. (London, 1779) reprinted in *Historical Collections of South Carolina*, vol. I, edited by Carroll, was the work of a Scottish Presbyterian clergyman who became a loyalist; Ramsay, a Whig whose *History of the Revolution of South Carolina*, 2 vols. (Trenton, 1785) was in some ways a remarkably judicious work, borrowed heavily from Hewatt in *The History of South Carolina, From the First Settlement in 1670 to the Year 1808*, 2 vols. (Charleston, 1809 and Newberry, S.C., 1858; reprinted Spartanburg, S.C., 1959, 1968). Elmer D. Johnson, "Alexander Hewat: South Carolina's First Historian," *Journal of Southern History* (hereafter abbreviated *JSH*), XX (February 1954), 50–62, and "David Ramsay: Historian or Plagiarist?" *SCHM*, LVII (October 1956), 189–198, suggest the degree to which their works must be used with caution. More favorable evaluations of each can be found in Page Smith, "David Ramsay and the Causes of the American Revolution," *WMQ*, XVII (January 1960), 51–77, and Geraldine M. Meroney, "Alexander Hewat's Historical Account" in Lawrence H. Leder, ed., *The Colonial Legacy*: vol. I, *The Loyalist Historians* (New York, 1971), 135–163. Both Hewatt and Ramsay remain valuable.

William J. Rivers, *A Sketch of the History of South Carolina to the Close of the Proprietary Government by the Revolution of 1719* (Charleston, 1856) was the first scholarly study. At the end of the nineteenth century, Edward McCrady, a local lawyer who had served as a Confederate officer, provided a detailed history of South Carolina in four volumes (1897–1902; reprinted New York, 1969). Primarily a political narrative, McCrady's volumes contain some verbatim transcriptions from the works of earlier historians, such as Hewatt. The next major study, David Duncan Wallace's four volume *History of South Carolina* (New York, 1934–1935), includes considerably more information about social and economic matters. Well-researched, though awkwardly organized and sometimes difficult to read, this work was at one time among the best of the state histories. A one-volume condensation published in 1951 (Chapel Hill) accentuates the weakness of the longer version but is more convenient to use. W. Roy Smith, *South Carolina as a Royal Province, 1719–1776* (New York, 1903) is an institutional study, useful for procedural details. The standard political history is M. Eugene Sirmans, *Colonial South Carolina: A Political History, 1663–1763* (Chapel Hill, 1966), which includes a good bibliographical essay. George C. Rogers, Jr., *A South Carolina Chronology, 1497–1970* (Columbia, 1973) is a brief handbook of important dates.

More specialized studies covering several topics or extended chronological periods include two model works by George C. Rogers, Jr., *Charleston in the Age of the Pinckneys* (Norman, 1969), a readable essay, and *The History of Georgetown County, South Carolina* (Columbia, 1970), an awesome and well-controlled compilation of detail. Many of the other counties also have histories; though some of these are antiquarian in character, Thomas H. Pope, *History*

of *Newberry County, South Carolina, 1749–1860* (Columbia, 1973) represents
a relatively recent example of good scholarship by a nonprofessional historian.
In addition, the tricentennial celebration of the founding of the colony led
to the publication of a number of monographs, including Robert K. Ackerman, *South Carolina Colonial Land Policies* (Columbia, 1977) and Maurice
A. Crouse, *The Public Treasury of Colonial South Carolina* (Columbia, 1977);
both are primarily institutional studies. A series of booklets sponsored by the
Tricentennial Commission also sought to provide sound scholarship for the
general reader. Most of these items will be mentioned later under other
headings; relevant here, however, are Bradley D. Bargar, *Royal South Carolina,
1719–1763* (Columbia, 1970); Larry E. Ivers, *Colonial Forts of South Carolina,
1670–1775* (Columbia, 1970); and Fitzhugh McMaster, *Soldiers and Uniforms:
South Carolina Military Affairs, 1670–1775* (Columbia, 1971).

Biographies can often provide easy access to more general historical topics,
but there are surprisingly few good studies of South Carolinians whose lives
illuminate the subjects of more than one chapter in the present volume. Works
of topical interest are listed later under the appropriate headings. Here, the
following items of wider scope deserve mention. Richard P. Sherman, *Robert
Johnson: Proprietary and Royal Governor of South Carolina* (Columbia, 1966);
Carl J. Vipperman, *The Rise of Rawlins Lowndes, 1721–1800* (Columbia,
1978); and George C. Rogers, Jr., *Evolution of a Federalist: William Loughton
Smith of Charleston, 1758–1812* (Columbia, 1962), only the initial chapters
of which are relevant to the colonial period. David Duncan Wallace, *The Life
of Henry Laurens* (New York, 1915) is useful but now somewhat dated, while
Marvin R. Zahniser, *Charles Cotesworth Pinckney, Founding Father* (Chapel Hill,
1967) is sound. E. Stanly Godbold, Jr., and Robert H. Woody, *Christopher
Gadsden and the American Revolution* will be published by the University of
Tennessee Press late in 1982. Edmund and Dorothy S. Berkeley, *Dr. Alexander
Garden of Charles Town* (Chapel Hill, 1969) supplies much detail; Richard
Barry, *Mr. [John] Rutledge of South Carolina* (New York, 1942) is unreliable.
Studies of individual families include Francis L. Williams, *A Founding Family:
The Pinckneys of South Carolina* (New York, 1978) and two unpublished Ph.D.
dissertations, one on the Manigault family by Maurice Crouse (Northwestern
University, 1964) and another about the Bulls by M. Eugene Sirmans (Prince-
ton University, 1959). A brief sketch of the Bull family, also by Sirmans,
appears in the *Proceedings of the South Carolina Historical Association* (1962).
Emily B. Reynolds and Joan R. Faunt, *Biographical Directory of the Senate of
the State of South Carolina, 1776–1964* (Columbia, 1964) does not include
members of the colonial upper house. However, the second volume of the
Biographical Directory of the South Carolina House of Representatives (Columbia,

1977) edited by Walter B. Edgar and N. Louise Bailey covers the Commons House. John W. Raimo, *Biographical Directory of American Colonial and Revolutionary Governors, 1607–1789* (Westport, Conn., 1980) includes biographical sketches of men who served in South Carolina.

Popular general accounts dealing at least partly with the colonial period are Lewis P. Jones, *South Carolina, A Synoptic History for Laymen* (Columbia, 1971); Henry Savage, Jr., *River of the Carolinas: The Santee* (1956; reprinted Chapel Hill, 1968), a readable and more inclusive history than the title indicates; and Louis B. Wright, *South Carolina: A Bicentennial History* (New York, 1976).

Among the innumerable general studies which might be mentioned, the following are especially useful for putting developments in South Carolina in a broader perspective: Charles M. Andrews, *The Colonial Period of American History*, 4 vols. (New Haven, 1934–1938); Wesley Frank Craven, *The Southern Colonies in the Seventeenth Century, 1607–1689* (Baton Rouge, 1949); and John R. Alden, *The South in the Revolution, 1763–1789* (Baton Rouge, 1957). The latter two are part of the standard multivolume *History of the South* being published by the Louisiana State University Press; volume two covering the eighteenth century is in progress at this time. Douglas E. Leach, *Arms for Empire: A Military History of the British Colonies in North America, 1607–1763* (New York, 1973) gives a good overview of the colonial wars from the viewpoint of the British and the American colonists. Gary B. Nash, *Red, White, and Black: The Peoples of Early America* (2d ed., Englewood Cliffs, N. J., 1982) is an innovative synthesis, while W. Stitt Robinson, *The Southern Colonial Frontier, 1607–1763* (Albuquerque, 1979) is more traditional in its approach but helpful on what it covers.

TOPICAL WORKS

1. *Prologue to Settlement*

The basic documents dealing with the Spanish and the French on the southeastern coast of North America appear in English translations in volumes one, two, and five of *New American World: A Documentary History of North America to 1612*, 5 vols. (New York, 1979), a magnificent collection edited by David B. Quinn. A convenient facsimile edition of Jean Ribault, *The Whole and True Discoverye of Terra Florida* (1563) has been issued with a short biography of Ribault by Jeannette T. Connor (Gainesville, 1964). René Laudonnière's *Three*

Voyages has also recently been retranslated by Charles E. Bennett (Gainesville, 1975), whose work sometimes errs on specifics but seeks to keep the spirit of the original.

David B. Quinn, *North America from Earliest Discovery to First Settlements: The Norse Voyages to 1612* (New York, 1977) is a comprehensive recent account dealing with both the Spanish and the French; it includes a substantial bibliography. Samuel E. Morison, *The European Discovery of America*, 2 vols. (New York, 1971–1974) treats Ayllón and his successors more briefly. The question of where Ayllón attempted to plant his settlement is still open. Paul Quattlebaum, an amateur local historian, made the case for the Georgetown area in *The Land Called Chicora: The Carolinas Under Spanish Rule with French Intrusions, 1520–1670* (Gainesville, 1956); a conference held at Georgetown in 1982 reviewed current scholarly opinion, and a report of its proceedings issued by the Georgetown, South Carolina, Education Center under the direction of John Gordon, III, is available in mimeographed form. The now standard account of Menéndez's activities is Eugene Lyon, *The Enterprise of Florida: Pedro Menéndez de Avilés and the Spanish Conquest of 1565–1568* (Gainesville, 1976). The recent discovery of archaeological evidence regarding the Spanish forts and settlement at Santa Elena is described in two booklets by Stanley South, *The Search for Santa Elena* and *The Discovery of Santa Elena* (Institute of Archaeology and Anthropology, University of South Carolina, Columbia, 1979, 1980). Though stronger in the later part of its coverage, J. Leitch Wright, Jr., gives a good account from the local perspective of *Anglo-Spanish Rivalry in North America* (Athens, Ga., 1971). John J. TePaske, *The Governorship of Spanish Florida, 1700–1763* (Durham, N.C., 1964) is a succinct work which depicts the military situation well from the Spanish side. Howard Mumford Jones, *O Strange New World, American Culture: The Formative Years* (New York, 1964) is stimulating and suggestive regarding the influence of medieval legend and Renaissance ideals on perceptions of the New World and its settlement, while Raimondo Luraghi makes a similar point in provocative fashion from a Marxian point of view in *The Rise and Fall of the Plantation South* (New York, 1978).

2. The Indians

Though frequently dealing more with Indian-white relations than with the Indians themselves, the most comprehensive collection of original documents can be found in the so-called "Indian Books" kept during the eighteenth century by the commissioners of the Indian trade and the secretary of the province. William L. McDowell, Jr., has scrupulously edited the *Journals of* the Commissioners of the Indian Trade, 1710–1718 (Columbia, 1955) and Documents Relating to Indian Affairs, 1750–1765, 2 vols. (Columbia, 1958, 1970). Wilbur Jacobs, ed., The Appalachian Frontier: The Edmund Atkin Report and Plan of 1755 (1954; Lincoln, 1967) not only discusses the influence of Atkin's proposals but reprints the report which includes considerable information about the Indians. James Adair, History of the American Indians (London, 1775) edited by Samuel Cole Williams (1930; New York, 1966) is a notable contemporary attempt at a comprehensive account; for sympathetic evaluations of Adair and his work, see Wilcomb E. Washburn, "James Adair's 'Noble Savages,'" in Leder, ed., The Colonial Legacy: vols. III and IV in one, Historians of Nature and Man's Nature and Early Nationalist Historians (New York, 1973), 91–120; and Richard Beale Davis, Intellectual Life in the Colonial South, 1585–1763, 3 vols. (Knoxville, 1978).

The native Americans have recently become the subject of much scholarship; general guidance to the new work can be found in James Axtell, "The Ethnohistory of Early America: A Review Essay," WMQ, XXXV (January 1978), 110–144. At this time, the Smithsonian Institution's Handbook of North American Indians: vol. XIV, The Southeast, under the general editorship of William C. Sturtevant, is in progress, but the preliminary findings of contributors are discussed in Douglas H. Ubelaker, "Prehistoric New World Population Size: Historical Review and Current Appraisal of North American Estimates," American Journal of Physical Anthropology, XLV (November 1976), 661–665. Charles Hudson, The Southeastern Indians (Knoxville, 1976) is a most valuable survey, primarily from an anthropological point of view. J. Leitch Wright, Jr., The Only Land They Knew: The Tragic Story of the American Indians in the Old South (New York, 1981) covers much of the same ground from the perspective of a historian; his work is especially suggestive in regard to the relationships between native Americans and blacks. Narrower in scope and now somewhat dated but still readable and generally reliable on matters of fact is Chapman J. Milling, Red Carolinians (1940; reprinted Columbia, 1969). Gene Waddell, Indians of the South Carolina Lowcountry (Spartanburg, S.C., 1980) compiles a great deal of evidentiary material.

Specific tribes are treated in Douglas S. Brown, The Catawba Indians: The People of the River (Columbia, 1966) which is more detailed on the eighteenth century but less analytical than Charles Hudson's short but broadly conceived The Catawba Nation (Athens, Ga., 1970). David Corkran deals at length with both The Creek Frontier, 1540–1783 (Norman, 1967) and The Cherokee Frontier: Conflict and Survival, 1740–1762 (Norman, 1962) and summarizes his findings for a popular audience in The Carolina Indian Frontier (Columbia, 1970). John Phillip Reid's two studies, A Law of Blood: The Primitive Law of the Cherokee Nation (New York, 1970) and A Better Kind of Hatchet: Law, Trade, *and Diplomacy in the Cherokee Nation During the Early Years of European Contact* (University Park, Pa., 1976) are unusually successful in treating matters from the perspective of the Indians. Gary C. Goodwin, *Cherokees in Transition: A Study of Changing Culture and Environment Prior to 1775* (Chicago, 1977) takes a relatively narrow view of culture but is helpful on ecological matters. The first three essays in Duane H. King, ed., *The Cherokee Indian Nation: A Troubled History* (Knoxville, 1979) and parts of Theda Perdue, *Slavery and the Evolution of Cherokee Society, 1540–1866* (Knoxville, 1979) are also relevant to the colonial period.

Gary B. Nash traces the changing "Image of the Indian in the Southern Colonial Mind," *WMQ*, **XXIX** (April 1972), 197–230, and puts his findings in wider perspective in *Red, White, and Black*. J. Ralph Randolph, *British Travelers Among the Southern Indians, 1660–1763* (Norman, 1973) is a good guide to the sources but disappointingly restricted in its approach. Almon W. Lauber's dated study of "Indian Slavery in Colonial Times within the Present Limits of the United States," *Columbia University Studies in History, Economics, and Public Law*, LIV (1913), 254–604, should be supplemented by reference to William R. Snell, "Indian Slavery in Colonial South Carolina, 1671–1795" (unpublished Ph.D. dissertation, University of Alabama, 1972). Anthony F. C. Wallace, "Revitalization Movements: Some Theoretical Considerations for their Comparative Study," *American Anthropologist*, LVIII (1956), 264–281, is a classic article on the subject.

For a general study of "The Indian Policy of Colonial South Carolina, 1670–1763," see the unpublished dissertation by David K. Eliades (University of South Carolina, 1981). Additional works dealing primarily with the relationship between Indians and whites from the perspective of the latter are listed under other headings.

3. The Land

Julian J. Petty, *A Bibliography of the Geography of the State of South Carolina* (Columbia, 1952) and Allen D. Bushong, "Research on the Southeast by Geographers, 1946–1967," *Southeastern Geographer*, IX (April 1969), 48–89, are badly out-of-date but still useful. Being the work of a geographer, Petty's own study of *The Growth and Distribution of Population in South Carolina* (Columbia, 1943) contains considerable information about the physical geography of the colony. For a standard work on the early cartography of the area, one can consult William P. Cumming, *The Southeast in Early Maps* (Chapel Hill, 1962). H. Roy Merrens, "The Physical Environment of Early America: Images and Image Makers in Colonial South Carolina," *Geographical Review*, LIX

(October 1969), 530–556, evaluates the observations of different observers, while Merrens, "Historical Geography and Early American History," *WMQ*, XXII (October 1965), 529–548, assesses the importance of the fall line, among other things. Both William S. Powell, "Carolina in the Seventeenth Century: An Annotated Bibliography of Contemporary Publications," *North Carolina Historical Review*, XLI (Winter 1964), 74–104, and Hugh T. Lefler, "Promotional Literature of the Southern Colonies," *JSH, XXXIII* (February 1967), 3–25, list and discuss these promotional publications. A close study of early perceptions of a particular region is Charles F. Kovacik and Lawrence S. Rowland, "Images of Colonial Port Royal, South Carolina," *Annals of the Association of American Geographers*, LXIII (September 1973), 331–340. David M. Ludlum, *Early American Hurricanes, 1492–1870* (Boston, 1963) is a useful compilation, while Elias B. Bull, "Storm Towers of the Santee Delta," *SCHM*, LXXXI (April 1980), 95–101, describes a little-known attempt to provide shelter.

St. Julien R. Childs, *Malaria and Colonization in the Carolina Low Country, 1526–1696* (Baltimore, 1940) and John Duffy, "Eighteenth Century Carolina Health Conditions," *JSH*, XVIII (August 1952), 289–302, treat the fabled unhealthiness of Carolina; Peter Wood, *Black Majority; Negroes in Colonial South Carolina from 1670 through the Stono Rebellion* (New York, 1974) adds some judicious observations about the relative susceptibility of whites and blacks to diseases prevalent in the area. The first volume of Joseph I. Waring, *History of Medicine in South Carolina, 1670–1825* (Columbia, 1964), though heavily indebted to the biographical tradition of medical history, is also helpful on local conditions. Carl Bridenbaugh, "Charlestonians at Newport, 1767–1775," *SCH & GM*, XLI (April 1940), 43–47, deals with those who seasonally departed South Carolina, largely to escape the fevers. For a popular introduction to American flora and fauna that originated abroad, see Robert Froman, "Our Fellow Immigrants," *American Heritage*, XIV (February 1963), 60–63, 94–96. "Governor Drayton's Contribution to Geography" is evaluated by Ralph H. Brown in *SCH & GM*, XXXIX (April 1938), 68–71. Two books by Henry Savage, Jr., offer introductions to the Carolina environment and the early naturalists who studied it: *Lost Heritage* (New York, 1970) and *Discovering America, 1700–1875* (New York, 1979), both of which also direct the reader to additional literature.

4. The Seventeenth Century

Relatively detailed accounts of the attempts to settle Carolina appear in general works discussed earlier. In addition, Converse D. Clowse, *Economic Beginnings in Colonial South Carolina, 1670–1730* (Columbia, 1971) defines its subject broadly, while Wesley Frank Craven, *The Colonies in Transition, 1660–1713* (New York, 1968) adds some interpretive detail. Much of the basic source material has been printed in Parker, ed., *North Carolina Charters and Constitutions, 1578–1698*, which includes successive versions of the Fundamental Constitutions; Langdon Cheves, ed., "The Shaftesbury Papers and Other Records Relating to Carolina...prior to 1676," *Collections of the South Carolina Historical Society*, V (1897); A. S. Salley, Jr., ed., *Journal of the Grand Council of South Carolina, August 25, 1671–June 24, 1680* (Columbia, 1907); and Salley, ed., *Commissions and Instructions from the Lords Proprietors of Carolina to Public Officials of South Carolina, 1685–1715* (Columbia, 1916.)

The most complete treatments of the early, generally unsuccessful, English attempts to settle Carolina are Paul E. Kopperman, "Profile of a Failure: The Carolana Project, 1629–1640," *North Carolina Historical Review*, LIX (January 1982), 1–23, and William S. Powell, "Carolana and the Incomparable Roanoke: Explorations and Attempted Settlements, 1620–1663," *ibid.*, LI (Winter 1974), 1–21.

William S. Powell, *The Proprietors of Carolina* (Raleigh, 1963) provides brief sketches of the original group. K. H. D. Haley, *The First Earl of Shaftesbury* (New York, 1968) has replaced the earlier study by Louise N. Brown as the standard biography of Anthony Ashley Cooper. For the intellectual background of the Constitutions, readers can consult Hugh F. Russell-Smith, *Harrington and His Oceana, a Study of a Seventeenth Century Utopia and Its Influence in America* (1914; reprinted New York, 1971) as well as the introduction by Peter Laslett to John Locke's *Two Treatises of Government* (rev. ed., New York, 1965), and *The Political Works of James Harrington* edited by J. G. A. Pocock (Cambridge, Eng., 1977). Pocock's "Machiavelli, Harrington, and English Political Ideologies in the Eighteenth Century," *WMQ*, XXII (October 1965), 549–583, *The Machiavellian Moment* (Princeton, 1975), and *Politics, Language and Time: Essays on Political Thought and History* (New York, 1971) are suggestive regarding the influence of Renaissance civic humanism on seventeenth century Englishmen like Shaftesbury.

Carl and Roberta Bridenbaugh, *No Peace Beyond the Line: The English in the Caribbean, 1624–1690* (New York, 1972) and Richard S. Dunn, *Sugar and Slaves: The Rise of the Planter Class in the English West Indies, 1624–1713* (New York, 1972) depict conditions in the West Indies that influenced the proprietors' thinking. Dunn, "The English Sugar Islands and the Founding of South Carolina," *SCHM*, LXXII (April 1971), 81–93, and Richard Waterhouse, "England, the Caribbean, and the Settlement of Carolina," *Journal of American Studies*, IX (December 1975), 259–281, are more specific about the impact of these conditions on prospective settlers. Daniel W. Fagg, Jr.,

"Sleeping not with the King's Grant: A Rereading of Some Proprietary Documents, 1663–1667," *North Carolina Historical Review*, XLVIII (Spring 1971), 171–185, treats the groping preliminaries to a successful settlement, while Fagg's unpublished dissertation, "Carolina, 1663–1683: The Founding of a Proprietary" (Emory University, 1970) gives a good general, predominantly favorable, assessment of the proprietors' continuing efforts. Joseph I. Waring, *The First Voyage and Settlement at Charles Town, 1670–1680* (Columbia, 1970) provides a chronicle, while St. Julien R. Childs, "The First South Carolinians," *SCHM*, LXXI (April 1970), 101–108, and Agnes L. Baldwin, *First Settlers of South Carolina, 1670–1680* (Columbia, 1969) supply lists of names.

Other specialized topics receive attention in Daniel W. Fagg, Jr., "St. Giles' Seigniory: The Earl of Shaftesbury's Carolina Plantation," *SCHM*, LXXI (April 1970), 117–123, and John Juricek, "Indian Policy in Proprietary South Carolina, 1670–1693" (unpublished MA thesis, University of Chicago, 1962). Stanley South reviews archaeological evidence regarding the first settlement at Old Town in *Exploratory Archaeology at the Site of 1670–1680 Charles Towne on Albermarle Point in South Carolina* (Institute of Archaeology and Anthropology, University of South Carolina, Columbia, 1969), and John W. Reps puts the move to White Point in a wider context in *The Making of Urban America: A History of City Planning in the United States* (Princeton, 1965). Readers can also consult Henry A. M. Smith, "Charleston—the Original Plan and the Earliest Settlers," *SCH & GM*, IX (January 1908), 12–27. George P. Insh, ed., "Arrival of the Cardross Settlers: *The Carolina Merchant*; Advice of Arrival," *SCH & GM*, XXX (April 1929), 69–80, and Mabel L. Webber, ed., "Spanish Depradations, 1686," *ibid.*, 81–89, print relevant letters, while Peter Karsten, "Plotters and Proprietors, 1682–1683: The 'Council of Six' and the Colonies: Plan for Colonization or Front for Revolution?" *Historian*, XXXVIII (May 1976), 474–484, argues that the Scottish settlement may have been a cover for more devious schemes. "Letters from John Stewart to William Dunlop" edited by Mabel L. Webber, *SCH & GM*, XXXII (January 1931), 1–33, gives colorful contemporary commentary, while Clarence L. VerSteeg, *Origins of a Southern Mosaic: Studies in Early Carolina and Georgia* (Athens, Ga., 1975) and Newton B. Jones, "The Role of the Commons House of Assembly in Proprietary South Carolina," *Proceedings of the South Carolina Historical Association* (1976), 5–13, add significant detail about local political battles during the seventeenth century. Though not definitive, Henry G. Hood, Jr., *The Public Career of John Archdale (1642–1717)* (Greensboro, N. C., 1976) provides an introduction to this important figure. For the failure to perpetuate entail, see James W. Ely, Jr., "Patterns of Statutory Enactment in South Carolina, 1720–1770," in Herbert A. Johnson, ed., *South Carolina Legal History* (Columbia, 1980), 65–80. Robert J. Dinkin, *Voting in Provincial*

America (Westport, Conn., 1977) reveals the degree to which practices in South Carolina were distinctive.

5. *Twilight of Proprietary Government,*
1700–1719

The controversies surrounding the establishment of the Anglican Church receive special attention in S. Charles Bolton, *Southern Anglicanism: The Church of England in Colonial South Carolina* (Westport, Conn., 1982) and VerSteeg, *Origins of a Southern Mosaic.* John W. Brinsfield briefly discusses Defoe's role in "Daniel Defoe: Writer, Statesman, and Advocate of Religious Liberty in South Carolina," *SCHM,* LXXVI (July 1975), 107–111. One of Defoe's pamphlets, "Party-Tyranny or, An Occasional Bill in Miniature; As Now Practiced in Carolina," is reprinted in Salley, *Narratives of Early Carolina,* 221–264, which also contains relevant material from *The History of the British Empire in America* (London, 1708) by John Oldmixon, who had connections with some of the South Carolina dissenters.

The classic study of international rivalry in this area is Verner W. Crane's *The Southern Frontier, 1670–1732* (Ann Arbor, 1929). James Moore's attacks on St. Augustine and Apalachee can be followed from the Spanish side in Charles Arnade, *The Siege of St. Augustine in 1702* (Gainesville, 1959) and Mark F. Boyd et al., *Here Once They Stood: The Tragic End of the Apalachee Missions* (Gainesville, 1951) which includes documentary material in translation. The role of the Yamasee Indians in the expedition against the Tuscaroras appears clearly in "The Tuscarora Expedition: Letters of Col. John Barnwell," *SCH & GM,* IX (January 1908), 28–54. For the Yamasee War itself, see Crane, *Southern Frontier,* Milling, *Red Carolinians,* Wright, *The Only Land They Ever Knew,* and David L. Johnson, "The Yamassee War" (unpublished M.A. thesis, University of South Carolina, 1980).

One of the first—and still basic—accounts of piracy on the Carolina coast is to be found in Daniel Defoe, *A General History of the Pyrates* edited by Manuel Schonhorn (Columbia, 1972) but originally published under a pseudonym in 1724. The most readable and reliable general work is Hugh F. Rankin's popularly written *The Golden Age of Piracy* (Williamsburg, 1969) which has largely supplanted Shirley C. Hughson, "The Carolina Pirates and Colonial Commerce, 1670–1740," *Johns Hopkins University Studies in Historical and Political Science,* ser, 12, V, VI, and VII (1894). More analytical approaches to the subject can be found in B. R. Burg, "Legitimacy and Authority: A Case Study of Pirate Commanders in the Seventeenth and Eighteenth Centuries," *American Neptune*, XXXVII (January 1977), 40–49, and Marcus Rediker, "'Under the Banner of King Death': The Social World of Anglo-American Pirates," *WMQ*, XXXVIII (April 1981), 203–227.

A number of studies treat the attempts of imperial authorities to curb illegal trade and protect the colonies. Especially helpful for understanding the situation in South Carolina are: Andrews, *Colonial Period in American History*, vol. III; Thomas C. Barrow, *Trade and Empire: The British Customs Service in Colonial America, 1660–1775* (Cambridge, Mass., 1967); Philip S. Haffenden, "The Crown and the Colonial Charters, 1675–1688," *WMQ*, XV (July and October 1958), 297–311, 452–466; Michael G. Hall, *Edward Randolph and the American Colonies, 1676–1703* (Chapel Hill, 1960); and, despite somewhat less concern with the local situation, J. M. Sosin, *English America and the Restoration Monarchy of Charles II: Transatlantic Politics, Commerce, and Kinship* (Lincoln, Neb., 1980), which is the first installment of a projected three-volume study. Stuart O. Stumpf supplies additional detail in "Edward Randolph's Attack on Proprietary Government in South Carolina," *SCHM*, LXXIX (January 1978), 6–18. Trevor R. Reese, ed., *The Most Delightful Country of the Universe: Promotional Literature of the Colony of Georgia, 1717–1734* (Savannah, 1972) prints Sir Robert Montgomery's promotional tract for Azilia. The most extensive discussion of the jurisdictional disputes over the Vice-Admiralty Court in South Carolina is R. Randall Bridwell, "Mr. Nicholas Trott and the South Carolina Vice Admiralty Court: An Essay on Procedural Reform and Colonial Politics," *South Carolina Law Review*, XXVIII (1976), 181–218; a condensed and more opaque version appears in Johnson, ed., *South Carolina Legal History*, 39–52. Recent treatments of the disputes over paper currency can be found in Clowse, *Economic Beginnings*, and Richard M. Jellison, "Paper Currency in Colonial South Carolina: A Reappraisal," *SCHM*, LXII (July 1961), 134–147; Leslie V. Brock, *The Currency of the American Colonies, 1700–1764* (New York, 1975) is helpful for the wider context.

The local political background to the revolt against the proprietors can be followed in *A Narrative of the Proceedings of the People of South Carolina in the Year 1719* (London, 1726) by Francis Yonge, who was involved. Reprinted in Carroll's *Collections*, vol. II, 141–192, Yonge's pamphlet has influenced most general accounts of the period. Perhaps partly as a result, Nicholas Trott and William Rhett have not received much sympathetic attention from historians. See, however, L. Lynn Hogue, "Nicholas Trott: Man of Law and Letters," *SCHM*, LXXVI (January 1975), 25–34. Sherman, *Robert Johnson*, stresses the popularity of the governor, which seems to be documented in "A Humble Address to Governor Robert Johnson," reprinted in *SCHM*, LXXIX (October 1978), 325–328. For rosters of leading Carolinians who opposed the proprietors, one can consult this document and "Petitioners to the Crown Against the Proprietors, 1716–1717," *SCHM*, LXII (April 1961), 88–95, compiled by David M. Wright.

6. *The Transformation of Politics, 1720–1748*

Although the crown treated the colonies with "salutary neglect" after the early 1720s, two articles by Stephen S. Webb suggest that Francis Nicholson's appointment was not originally intended to herald a new policy; see Webb's "The Strange Career of Francis Nicholson," *WMQ*, XXIII (October 1966), 513–548, and "Army and Empire: English Garrison Government in Britain and America, 1569 to 1763," *WMQ*, XXXIV (January 1977), 1–31. Bruce T. McCully gives additional information in "Governor Francis Nicholson, Patron *Par Excellence* of Religion and Learning in Colonial America," *WMQ*, XXXIX (April 1982), 310–333.

Peter Coclanis, "Rice Prices in the 1720s and the Evolution of the South Carolina Economy," *JSH* forthcoming, shows that economic conditions in the late 1720s were not as universally disastrous as has frequently been thought.

Robert Johnson's appointment as governor and the land controversies of his administration receive considerable attention in the following: Sherman's biography; Ackerman, *South Carolina Colonial Land Policies*; Robert L. Meriwether, *The Expansion of South Carolina, 1729–1765* (Kingsport, Tenn., 1940); and Smith, *South Carolina as a Royal Province*, as well as in the more general political histories. More critical of Johnson and the assembly than most recent scholarship, Alan D. Watson's two articles on the subject, "The Quitrent System in Royal South Carolina," *WMQ*, XXXIII (April 1976), 193–211, and "Henry McCulloh: Royal Commissioner in South Carolina," *SCHM*, LXXV (January 1974), 33–48, supercede Beverly W. Bond, Jr., *The Quit-Rent System in the American Colonies* (New Haven, 1919) in regard to local matters.

For the role of strategic considerations and Carolinians in the settlement of Georgia, one can consult Crane, *Southern Frontier*, and Kenneth Coleman, "The Southern Frontier: Georgia's Founding and the Expansion of South Carolina," *Georgia Historical Quarterly*, LVI (Summer 1972), 163–174, as well as Phinizy Spalding, "South Carolina and Georgia: The Early Days," *SCHM*, LXIX (April 1968), 83–96. Spalding's *Oglethorpe in America* (Chicago, 1977) is a concise, readable study, while Larry E. Ivers, *British Drums on the Southern Frontier, 1733–1749* (Chapel Hill, 1974) is a detailed military history. "The Report of the Committee Appointed by the General Assembly of South Carolina in 1740 on the St. Augustine Expedition under General Oglethorpe" printed in the *Collections of the South Carolina Historical Society*, IV (1887), 3–177, is inaccurate; however, students may consult either J. H. Easterby, ed., *The Journals of the Commons House of Assembly, May 18, 1741–July 10, 1742* (Columbia, 1953) or John T. Lanning, ed., *The St. Augustine Expedition of 1740* (Columbia, 1954). Governor Glen's Indian policy may be followed in Mary F. Carter, "James Glen, Governor of Colonial South Carolina: A Study in British Administrative Policies" (unpublished Ph.D. dissertation, University of California at Los Angeles, 1951), as well as in Corkran, *Cherokee Frontier* and *Creek Frontier*.

The rise of the Commons House of Assembly, the decline of the council, and the waning of factionalism within the lower house are treated in Jack P. Greene, *The Quest for Power: The Lower Houses of Assembly in the Southern Royal Colonies, 1689–1776* (Chapel Hill, 1963); M. Eugene Sirmans, "The South Carolina Royal Council, 1720–1763," *WMQ*, XVIII (July 1961), 373–392; and Robert M. Weir, "'The Harmony We Were Famous For': An Interpretation of Pre-Revolutionary South Carolina Politics," *WMQ*, XXVI (October 1969), 473–501. George E. Frakes, *Laboratory for Liberty: The South Carolina Legislative Committee System, 1719–1776* (Lexington, Ky., 1970) adds little to Greene's work. For the sources of the prevailing political culture, consult Bernard Bailyn, *The Ideological Origins of the American Revolution* (Cambridge, Mass., 1967) and *The Origins of American Politics* (New York, 1968); Jack P. Greene, "Political Mimesis: A Consideration of the Historical and Cultural Roots of Legislative Behavior in the British Colonies in the Eighteenth Century," *American Historical Review*, LXXV (December 1969), 337–360, as well as the interchange between Bailyn and Greene in the same issue, and the previously mentioned works by J. G. A. Pocock. Francis H. Porcher, "Royal Review of South Carolina Law, 1719–1776" (unpublished M.A. thesis, University of South Carolina, 1962) is thorough.

7. The Economy

General discussions of economic developments and tabulations of data can be found in the following: Clowse, *Economic Beginnings*, and the same author's *Measuring Charleston's Overseas Commerce, 1717–1767* (Lanham, Md., 1981), which is a statistical compilation. Chapter Z of the *Historical Statistics of the United States* is especially useful for Lawrence Harper's figures on the export of rice from South Carolina and Georgia, while the first volume of Lewis C. Gray, *The History of Agriculture in the Southern United States to 1860*, 2 vols. (1933; reprinted Gloucester, Mass., 1958) remains an indispensable mine of information. Arthur H. Cole, *Wholesale Commodity Prices in the United States,*

1700–1861 (Cambridge, Mass., 1938) and John J. McCusker, *Money and Exchange in Europe and America, 1600–1775: A Handbook* (Chapel Hill, 1978) are standard references.

In addition to the above, readers can consult Gary S. Dunbar, "Colonial Carolina Cowpens," *Agricultural History*, XXXV (July 1961), 125–130; William Snell, "Indian Slavery in Colonial South Carolina" (unpublished Ph.D. dissertation, University of Alabama, 1972); W. O. Moore, Jr., "The Largest Exporters of Deerskins from Charleston, 1735–1775," *SCHM*, LXXIV (July 1973), 144–150; and Justin Williams, "English Mercantilism and Carolina Naval Stores, 1705–1776," *JSH*, I (May 1935), 169–185. A good, short discussion of rice production, citing much of the older literature and including considerable information about the colonial period, is Sam B. Hilliard, "Antebellum Tidewater Rice Culture in South Carolina and Georgia," in James R. Gibson, ed., *European Settlement and Development in North America: Essays on Geographical Change in Honour and Memory of Andrew Hill Clark* (Toronto, 1978), 91–115.

David L. Coon, "Eliza Lucas Pinckney and the Reintroduction of Indigo Culture in South Carolina," *JSH*, XLII (February 1976), 61–76, is a spin-off from Coon's useful unpublished Ph.D. dissertation, "The Development of Market Agriculture in South Carolina, 1670–1785" (University of Illinois, 1972). G. Terry Sharrer has two overlapping articles on "The Indigo Bonanza in South Carolina, 1740–1790," *Technology and Culture*, XII (July 1971), 447–455, and "Indigo in Carolina, 1671–1796," *SCHM*, LXXII (April 1971), 94–103. John J. Winberry, "Reputation of Carolina Indigo," *SCHM*, LXXX (July 1979), 242–250, differs from Sharrer regarding imperial incentives. David H. Rembert, Jr., identifies "The Indigo of Commerce in Colonial North America," *Economic Botany*, XXXIII (April-June 1979), 128–134.

For the stimulus to the colonial economy provided by export earnings, see James F. Shepherd and Gary M. Walton, *Shipping, Maritime Trade, and the Economic Development of Colonial North America* (Cambridge, Eng., 1972); a more general and readable version of the authors' argument appears in Walton and Shepherd, *The Economic Rise of Early America* (Cambridge, Eng., 1979), which can also be compared to Edwin J. Perkins, *The Economy of Colonial America* (New York, 1980). The exceptional prosperity of lowcountry South Carolina is briefly described in George R. Taylor, "American Economic Growth Before 1840: An Exploratory Essay," *Journal of Economic History*, XXIV (December 1964), 427–444, while the expansion of agricultural holdings can be seen in Ackerman, *South Carolina Colonial Land Policies*, and John R. Todd and Francis M. Hutson, *Prince William Parish and Plantations* (Richmond, 1935). Henry A. M. Smith deals with speculative ventures in "Radnor, Ed-

mundsbury and Jacksonborough," *SCH & GM*, XI (January 1910), 39–49.
Rogers, *Charleston in the Age of the Pinckneys*, covers the expansion of the city,
while David R. Chesnutt describes the "South Carolina Penetration of Georgia
in the 1760s: Henry Laurens as a Case Study," *SCHM*, LXXIII (October
1972), 194–208.

For differing views on the general question of debt and capital formation
in the colonies, one might begin by consulting the work of Shepherd and
Walton, on the one hand, and that of Marc Egnal and Joseph A. Ernst, on
the other. See in particular Egnal, "The Economic Development of the Thirteen
Continental Colonies, 1720–1775," *WMQ*, XXXII (April 1975), 191–222,
and Egnal and Ernst, "An Economic Interpretation of the American Revolution," *WMQ*, XXIX (January 1972), 3–32. A relatively recent discussion
of postwar attempts to settle the colonial debt to Britain appears in Charles
R. Ritcheson, *Aftermath of Revolution: British Policy Toward the United States,
1783–1795* (Dallas, 1969). Additional information about the character of
internal and external debt in Carolina can be gleaned from the records of the
colonial public treasurers, South Carolina Department of Archives and History;
the records of the United States Commissioners under the Sixth Article of the
British Treaty of 1794, Henry E. Huntington Library, San Marino, California;
as well as Hamer, Rogers, and Chesnutt, eds., *The Papers of Henry Laurens*;
Leila Sellers, *Charleston Business on the Eve of the American Revolution* (Chapel
Hill, 1934), which relies heavily on Laurens; and Elizabeth Donnan, "The
Slave Trade into South Carolina Before the Revolution," *American Historical
Review*, XXXIII (July 1928), 804–828.

Governmental services are described in Richard Waterhouse, "The Responsible Gentry of Colonial South Carolina: A Study in Local Government,
1670–1770" in Bruce C. Daniels, ed., *Town and Country: Essays on the Structure
of Local Government in the American Colonies* (Middletown, Conn., 1978), 160–
185. One may also consult David M. Knepper, "The Political Structure of
Colonial South Carolina, 1743–1776" (unpublished Ph.D. dissertation, University of Virginia, 1972), which focuses primarily on the local level. Robert
M. Weir treats "The Role of the Newspaper Press in the Southern Colonies
on the Eve of the Revolution: An Interpretation," in Bernard Bailyn and John
B. Hench, eds., *The Press and the American Revolution* (Worcester, Mass., 1980),
99–150. Though this essay gives special attention to the printers of South
Carolina, Hennig Cohen, *The South Carolina Gazette, 1732–1775* (Columbia,
1953) and Christopher Gould, "Robert Wells, Colonial Charleston Printer,"
SCHM, LXXIX (January 1978), 23–49, provide more detail. For the military
and naval units stationed in South Carolina, see William A. Foote, "The
South Carolina Independents," *SCHM*, LXII (October 1961), 195–199; John
Shy, *Toward Lexington, The Role of the British Army in the Coming of the American*

Revolution (Princeton, 1965); and W. E. May, "His Majesty's Ships on the Carolina Station," *SCHM*, LXXI (July 1970), 162–169.

Charles M. Andrews, *England's Commercial and Colonial Policy*, volume IV of *The Colonial Period of American History*, remains one of the most convenient sources of information about commercial legislation pertaining to the colonies. How this legislation affected manufacturing and shipbuilding in South Carolina can be inferred from the cartographic representations and accompanying citations in Cappon et al., *Atlas of Early American History*; as well as from Richard Walsh, *Charleston's Sons of Liberty: A Study of the Artisans, 1763–1789* (Columbia, 1959); and Joseph A. Goldenburg, *Shipbuilding in Colonial America* (Charlottesville, 1976). For locally built and owned vessels, see R. Nicholas Olsberg, ed., "Ship Registers in the South Carolina Archives, 1734–1780," *SCHM*, LXXIV (October 1973), 189–279.

General attempts to assess the economic burdens and benefits of the imperial system which contain information specifically relevant to South Carolina are Lawrence A. Harper, "The Effects of the Navigation Acts on the Thirteen Colonies," in Richard B. Morris, ed., *The Era of the American Revolution* (1939; Gloucester, Mass., 1971), 3–39; Roger L. Ransom, "British Policy and Colonial Growth: Some Implications of the Burden from the Navigation Acts," *Journal of Economic History*, XXVIII (September 1968), 427–440; and R. P. Thomas, "A Quantitative Approach to the Study of the Effects of British Imperial Policy upon Colonial Welfare: Some Preliminary Findings," *ibid.*, XXV (December 1965), 615–638. Gordon C. Bjork, "The Weaning of the American Economy: Independence, Market Changes, and Economic Development," *ibid.*, XXIV (December 1964), 541–560, deals with postwar shifts in the pattern of trade. Anxiety over the restricted market for rice was widely evident in the governors' reports, lobbying activities of the colonial agents, private correspondence, and the newspapers. For the Carolina agents, see Ella Lonn, *Colonial Agents of the Southern Colonies* (Chapel Hill, 1945); Lewis Namier, "Charles Garth and His Connexions," and "Charles Garth, Agent for South Carolina," *English Historical Review*, LIV (July and October, 1939), 443–470, 632–652; and Michael G. Kammen, *A Rope of Sand: The Colonial Agents, British Politics, and the American Revolution* (Ithaca, 1968). Worrisome changes in land policy are described in St. George L. Sioussat, "The Breakdown of the Royal Management of Lands in the Southern Provinces, 1773–1775," *Agricultural History*, III (April 1929), 67–98, while Jack P. Greene and Richard M. Jellison deal with "The Currency Act of 1764 in Imperial-Colonial Relations, 1764–1776," *WMQ*, XVIII (October 1961), 485–518, as does Joseph A. Ernst, *Money and Politics in America, 1755–1775: A Study in the Currency Act of 1764 and the Political Economy of the Revolution* (Chapel Hill, 1973).

Meriwether, *Expansion of South Carolina* is still perhaps the most helpful on the development of the town of Ninety Six; Rogers deals with *The History of Georgetown County*, while Lawrence S. Rowland treats "Eighteenth Century Beaufort: A Study of South Carolina's Southern Parishes to 1800" (unpublished Ph.D. dissertation, University of South Carolina, 1978). Joseph A. Ernst and H. Roy Merrens provide a functional explanation of Camden's development in "'Camden's turrets pierce the skies!': The Urban Process in the Southern Colonies during the Eighteenth Century," *WMQ*, XXX (October 1973), 549–574. For the physical layout of the town, consult Kenneth E. Lewis, *Camden: A Frontier Town in Eighteenth Century South Carolina* (Institute of Archaeology and Anthropology, University of South Carolina, 1976). Jacob M. Price, "Economic Function and the Growth of American Port Towns in the Eighteenth Century," *Perspectives in American History*, VIII (1974), 123–188, includes a number of explicit and implicit comparisons between Charles Town and the other ports, while the Liverpool Papers, Additional Manuscripts, British National Library, London, contain figures for the number of colonial seamen.

8. Blacks, Whites, and Slavery

Perhaps to an even greater extent than native Americans, blacks have been the beneficiaries of an historiographical revolution in recent years. "'I Did the Best I Could for My Day': The Study of Early Black History during the Second Reconstruction, 1960 to 1976," *WMQ*, XXXV (April 1978), 185–223, by Peter Wood is the indispensable guide to this rapidly expanding literature. Wood's own volume, *Black Majority*, is also an important example of the new scholarship. John D. Duncan, "Servitude and Slavery in Colonial South Carolina, 1670–1776" (unpublished Ph.D. dissertation, Emory University, 1972) provides an encyclopedic collection of detail, while Michael Mullin, "British Caribbean and North American Slaves in an Era of War and Revolution, 1775–1807," in Jeffrey J. Crow and Larry E. Tise, eds., *The Southern Experience in the American Revolution* (Chapel Hill, 1978), 235–267, and Ira Berlin, "Time, Space, and the Evolution of Afro-American Society on British Mainland North America," *American Historical Review*, LXXXV (February 1980), 44–78, suggest how the situation in South Carolina differed from that in the other colonies. Mullin's collection of documents on *American Negro Slavery: A Documentary History* (Columbia, 1976) is also relatively strong on South Carolina during the colonial period. Olaudah Equiano, "The Interesting Narrative of the Life of Olaudah Equiano, or Gustavus Vassa, The African" (1789), conveniently available in Arna Bontemps, ed., *Great Slave Narratives* (Boston, 1969), 1–192, is a classic example of a genre rare in the eighteenth century.

The relative importance of naval stores and rice in initially stimulating the demand for slaves is discussed in VerSteeg, *Origins of a Southern Mosaic*, which emphasizes naval stores, and George D. Terry, "'Champaign Country': A Social History of an Eighteenth-Century Lowcountry Parish in South Carolina, St. John's Berkeley County" (unpublished Ph.D. dissertation, University of South Carolina, 1981), which contends for rice. For the slave trade to colonial South Carolina, see Elizabeth Donnan, "Slave Trade into South Carolina Before the Revolution," *American Historical Review*, XXXIII (July 1928), 804–828, as well as her collection of *Documents Illustrative of the History of the Slave Trade to America*, 4 vols. (1930–1935, reprinted New York, 1965), and Hamer, Rogers, and Chesnutt, eds., *The Papers of Henry Laurens*, passim. W. Robert Higgins, "Geographical Origins of Negro Slaves in Colonial South Carolina," *South Atlantic Quarterly*, LXX (Winter 1971), 34–47, establishes that most slaves arrived directly from Africa, while Higgins, "Charleston: Terminus and Entrepôt of the Colonial Slave Trade" in Martin L. Kilson and Robert I. Rothberg, eds., *The African Diaspora: Interpretive Essays* (Cambridge, Mass., 1976), 114–131, discusses the trade in more general fashion. Though dealing mainly with a later period, Albert J. Raboteau, *Slave Religion: The "Invisible Institution" in the Antebellum South* (New York, 1978) is helpful for the African religious background. The composition and growth of the black population in South Carolina are analyzed by Peter Wood, "'More Like a Negro Country': Demographic Patterns in Colonial South Carolina, 1700–1740," in Stanley L. Engerman and Eugene D. Genovese, eds., *Race and Slavery in the Western Hemisphere: Quantitative Studies* (Princeton, 1975), 131–171, and by Daniel C. Littlefield in "Plantations, Paternalism, and Profitability: Factors Affecting African Demography in the Old British Empire," *JSH*, XLVII (May 1981), 167–182, and *Rice and Slaves: Ethnicity and the Slave Trade in Colonial South Carolina* (Baton Rouge, 1981).

Philip D. Morgan's unpublished paper on "Afro-American Cultural Change: The Case of Colonial South Carolina Slaves" (given at the Waterloo Slave Studies Conference, March, 1979) is helpful on the drivers, while Morgan's "Work and Culture: The Task System and the World of Lowcountry Blacks, 1700 to 1880," *WMQ*, XXXIX (October 1982), 563–599, provides an insightful discussion of work patterns and the degree of relative autonomy among slaves. Herbert G. Gutman, *The Black Family in Slavery and Freedom, 1750–1925* (New York, 1976) draws heavily on evidence from South Carolina only for the period after the Revolution, but it is nevertheless suggestive for the earlier period. See also Cheryll Ann Cody, "A Note on Changing Patterns of Slave Fertility in the South Carolina Rice District, 1735–1865," *Southern Studies*, XVI (Winter 1977), 457–463, and Cody, "Naming, Kinship, and Estate Dispersal: Notes on Slave Family Life on a South Carolina Plantation,

1786–1833," *WMQ*, **XXXIX** (January 1982), 192–211. Much material about slaves in general as well as about Garden's attempt to educate black preceptors is contained in Frank J. Klingberg, *An Appraisal of the Negro in Colonial South Carolina: A Study in Americanization* (1941; reprinted Philadelphia, 1975) which is drawn from the reports of ministers supplied by the SPG. Information about slave medicine and housing is scarce, but see Peter Wood's two articles in *Southern Exposure*, "People's Medicine in the Early South," VI (1978), 50–53, and "Black Builders in the Early South," VIII (1980), 3–8, which include examples from South Carolina. M. Foster Farley, "The South Carolina Negro in the American Revolution, 1775–1783," *SCHM*, LXXIX (April 1978), 75–86, and Benjamin Quarles, *The Negro in the American Revolution* (Chapel Hill, 1961) are detailed treatments, but a few black South Carolinians appear in Mary Beth Norton, "The Fate of Some Black Loyalists of the American Revolution," *Journal of Negro History*, LVIII (October 1973), 402–426, and James W. St. G. Walker, *The Black Loyalists: The Search for a Promised Land in Nova Scotia and Sierra Leone, 1783–1870* (New York, 1976).

Wood, *Black Majority*, is especially useful on black resistance to slavery and the Stono Rebellion, but see also Philip D. Morgan and George D. Terry, "Slavery in Microcosm: A Conspiracy Scare in Colonial South Carolina," *Southern Studies*, forthcoming, and Daniel E. Meaders, "South Carolina Fugitives as Viewed through Local Colonial Newspapers with Emphasis on Runaway Notices, 1732–1801," *Journal of Negro History*, LX (April 1975), 288–319; as well as Littlefield, *Rice and Slaves*; and Philip Morgan, "En Carline Du Sud: Marronnage et Culture Servile," *Annales*, XXXVII (Mai-Juin 1982), 574–590, the last two of which provide the most systematic analysis of runaways during the colonial period. For the haven that some blacks found outside of St. Augustine, consult John T. TePaske, "The Fugitive Slave: Intercolonial Rivalry and Spanish Slave Policy, 1687–1764," in Samuel Proctor, ed., *Eighteenth-Century Florida and Its Borderlands* (Gainesville, 1975), 1–12.

The effect of slavery on the South Carolina militia system is treated in Benjamin Quarles, "The Colonial Militia and Negro Manpower," *Mississippi Valley Historical Review*, XLV (March 1959), 643–652, and John W. Shy, "A New Look at Colonial Militia," *WMQ*, XX (April 1963), 175–185. Discussions of the legal system governing blacks are to be found in A. Leon Higginbotham, Jr., *In the Matter of Color: Race and the American Legal Process, the Colonial Period* (New York, 1978); M. Eugene Sirmans, "The Legal Status of the Slave in South Carolina, 1670–1740," *JSH*, XXVIII (November 1962), 462–473; William M. Wiecek, "The Statutory Law of Slavery and Race in the Thirteen Mainland Colonies of British America," *WMQ*, XXXIV (April 1977), 258–280; and Michael S. Hindus, *Prison and Plantation: Crime, Justice, and Authority in Massachusetts and South Carolina, 1767–1878* (Chapel Hill, 1980). Winthrop D. Jordan's massive *White Over Black: American Attitudes Toward the Negro, 1550–1812* (Chapel Hill, 1968) discusses interracial sex in South Carolina as well as elsewhere.

Free blacks in the colonial period need more study, but see Marina Wikramanayake, *A World in Shadow: The Free Black in Antebellum South Carolina* (Columbia, 1973) and Lawrence D. Watson, "The Quest for Order: Enforcing Slave Codes in Revolutionary South Carolina, 1760–1800" (unpublished Ph.D. dissertation, University of South Carolina, 1980). The Jerry affair appears in Peter Wood, "'Taking Care of Business' in Revolutionary South Carolina: Republicanism and the Slave Society," in Crow and Tise, eds., *The Southern Experience in the American Revolution*, 268–293, and David Zornow, "A Troublesome Community: Blacks in Revolutionary Charles Town, 1765–1775" (unpublished undergraduate paper, Harvard University, 1976). Samuel Wragg's will is to be found in the Probate Records, British Public Record Office.

9. Society: The Social Aggregate

The most useful population figures are in Clowse, *Economic Beginnings*, Petty, *The Growth and Distribution of Population in South Carolina*, and chapter Z of the U. S. Census Bureau's *Historical Statistics of the United States*, but see also Evarts B. Greene and Virginia D. Harrington, *American Population Before the Federal Census of 1790* (New York, 1932) and Stella H. Sutherland, *Population Distribution in Colonial America* (New York, 1936).

Daniel B. Smith's review article, "The Study of the Family in Early America: Trends, Problems, and Prospects," *WMQ*, XXXIX (January 1982), 3–28, provides general guidance to the rapidly expanding literature on the family and related subjects such as childhood mortality; so far not much of this scholarship dealing with South Carolina has been published, but George Terry's "'Champaign Country,'" (unpublished Ph.D. dissertation, University of South Carolina, 1981) is helpful about these matters. Additional mortality figures are given in H. Roy Merrens and George D. Terry, "Dying in Paradise: Malaria, Mortality, and the Perceptual Environment in Colonial South Carolina" (forthcoming, *Journal of Southern History*, scheduled for publication in 1984).

For the effect of immigration on the expansion of South Carolina and the composition of its white population, the key work is Meriwether, *Expansion of South Carolina*, a meticulously researched but not very lively volume. "The Report of the Committee on Linguistic and National Stocks in the Population of the United States" by the American Council of Learned Societies in the *Annual Report of the American Historical Association*, I (1931), 107–441, is summarized in *Historical Statistics of the United States*; Forrest and Ellen Shapiro McDonald's revisions appear in "The Ethnic Origins of the American People, 1790," *WMQ*, XXXVII (April 1980), 179–199. Information about the size of various religious denominations and the distribution of their adherents can be gleaned from Patricia U. Bonomi and Peter R. Eisenstadt, "Church Adherence in the Eighteenth Century British American Colonies," *WMQ*, XXXIX (April 1982), 245–286; Cappon et al., *Atlas of Early American History*; Edwin S. Gaustad, *Historical Atlas of Religion in America* (rev. ed., New York, 1976); "The Writings of Rev. William Tennent, 1740–1777," edited by Newton B. Jones, *SCHM*, LXI (July and October 1960), 129–145, 189–209; and Marion C. Chandler, "Church Incorporation in South Carolina Under the Constitution of 1778" (unpublished M.A. thesis, University of South Carolina, 1969). Most of the relevant studies of ethnic and religious groups in South Carolina are now sufficiently dated to appear in the standard bibliographies mentioned earlier, but more recent work includes Kenneth L. Carroll, "The Irish Quaker Community at Camden," *SCHM*, LXXVII (April 1976), 69–83; Harold W. Gardner, "The Dissenting Sects on the Southern Colonial Frontier, 1720–1770" (unpublished Ph.D. dissertation, University of Kansas, 1969); and Amy E. Friedlander, "Carolina Huguenots: A Study in Cultural Pluralism in the Low Country, 1679–1768" (unpublished Ph.D. dissertation, Emory University, 1979), which is more analytical than Arthur H. Hirsch, *The Huguenots of Colonial South Carolina* (1928; reprinted London, 1962). A forthcoming study of the Huguenots by Jon Butler also promises to be helpful in placing the immigrants to Carolina in a broad context.

An entertaining source of information about the upcountry is *The Carolina Backcountry on the Eve of the Revolution: The Journal and Other Writings of Charles Woodmason, Anglican Itinerant* edited by Richard J. Hooker (Chapel Hill, 1953). Woodmason was there, but he seldom was an impartial observer and his work needs to be used with care. Carl Bridenbaugh, *Myths and Realities: Societies of the Colonial South* (1952; reprinted New York, 1963) provides a readable overview while Jackson Turner Main, *The Social Structure of Revolutionary America* (Princeton, 1965) contains some data about the distribution of property. Richard M. Brown, *The South Carolina Regulators* (Cambridge, Mass., 1963) and Rachel Klein, "The Rise of the Planters in the South Carolina Backcountry, 1757–1808" (unpublished Ph.D. dissertation, Yale University, 1979) not only supply more of this kind of data but also, as the title of Klein's recent article implies, deal with the question of "Ordering the Backcountry: The South Carolina Regulation," *WMQ*, XXXVIII (October 1981), 661–

680. William A. Schaper, *Sectionalism and Representation in South Carolina* (1901; reprinted New York, 1968) exaggerates the sectionalism of the late colonial period.

Studies of the distribution of wealth that are based on the recorded inventories of estates often turn out to be primarily studies of the lowcountry around Charles Town. Though marred by some basic misconceptions about the region, William G. Bentley, "Wealth Distribution in Colonial South Carolina" (unpublished Ph.D. dissertation, Georgia State University, 1977) is useful, even if (as is probable) it underestimates the increasing concentration of wealth in the late colonial period. Another study of inventories, Alice Hanson Jones, *Wealth of a Nation to Be: The American Colonies on the Eve of the Revolution* (New York, 1980), is an extraordinary work that suggests just how wealthy Carolinians were compared to other Americans. The presence of poor, however, can be seen in J. H. Easterby, "Public Poor Relief in Colonial Charleston: A Report to the Commons House of Assembly about the Year 1767," *SCH & GM*, XLII (April 1941), 83–86, and in "A Profile of a Mid-Eighteenth Century South Carolina Parish: The Tax Return of Saint James', Goose Creek," edited by Philip D. Morgan, *SCHM*, LXXXI (January 1980), 51–65, which cites and tabulates data from some other tax returns. See also Robert M. Weir, ed., "Muster Rolls of the South Carolina Granville and Colleton County Regiments of Militia, 1756," *SCHM*, LXX (October 1969), 226–239, which, when analyzed, also reveal that not all Carolinians were men of property.

Useful treatments of more established segments of society are Walsh, *Charleston's Sons of Liberty*; Stuart O. Stumpf, "The Merchants of Colonial Charleston, 1680–1756" (unpublished Ph.D. dissertation, Michigan State University, 1971); Waring, *A History of Medicine in South Carolina*; and Diane M. Sydenham, "Practioner and Patient: The Practice of Medicine in Eighteenth-Century South Carolina" (unpublished Ph.D. dissertation, Johns Hopkins University, 1974). John Belton O'Neall, *Biographical Sketches of the Bench and Bar of South Carolina*, 2 vols. (1859; reprinted Spartanburg, S.C., 1975) is anecdotal but helpful. The most complete treatment of the lawyers is now to be found in Hoyt P. Canady, Jr., "Gentlemen of the Bar: Lawyers in South Carolina" (unpublished Ph.D. dissertation, University of Tennessee, 1979).

Indentured servitude and social mobility have been treated most recently by Aaron M. Shatzman, "Servants Into Planters, the Origin of An American Image: Land Acquisition and Status Mobility in Seventeenth Century South Carolina" (unpublished Ph.D. dissertation, Stanford University, 1981) whose findings suggest that during the seventeenth century, at least, indentured servants, who survived, fared better in South Carolina than Abbot E. Smith, *Colonists in Bondage: White Servitude and Convict Labor in America, 1607–1776* (1947; reprinted New York, 1965) found was the case in other colonies.

Though insufficiently analyzed, the data assembled by Warren B. Smith, *White Servitude in Colonial South Carolina* (Columbia, 1961) indicate that the same probably continued to be true during the eighteenth century. David Galenson, *White Servitude in Colonial America* (New York, 1982) will help to provide a further basis for comparison.

For religious conditions before and after the Great Awakening, see George W. Williams, ed., "Letters to the Bishop of London from the Commissaries in South Carolina," *SCHM*, LXXVIII (January, April, July, and October 1977), 1–31, 120–147, 213–242, 286–317; Bolton, *Southern Anglicanism*; William H. Kenny, III, "Alexander Garden and George Whitefield: The Significance of Revivalism in South Carolina, 1738–1741," *SCHM*, LXXI (January 1970), 1–16; David T. Morgan, Jr., "George Whitefield and the Great Awakening in the Carolinas and Georgia, 1739–1740," *Georgia Historical Quarterly*, LIV (Winter 1970), 517–539, "The Consequences of George Whitefield's Ministry in Georgia and the Carolinas, 1739–1740," *ibid.*, LV (Spring 1971), 62–82, and "The Great Awakening in South Carolina, 1740–1775," *South Atlantic Quarterly*, LXX (Autumn 1971), 595–606. Divergent views of poor relief appear in Barbara Ulmer, "Benevolence in Colonial Charleston," *Proceedings of the South Carolina Historical Association* (1980), 1–12; and Walter J. Fraser, Jr., "Controlling the Poor in Colonial Charles Town," *ibid.*, 13–30. Carl Bridenbaugh, *Cities in Revolt: Urban Life in America, 1743–1776* (London, 1955), Canady, "Gentlemen of the Bar," and Hindus, *Prison and Plantation*, provide information about crime.

10. Society: Aspirations and Achievements

Two unpublished studies offer excellent introductions to the elite of colonial South Carolina: John C. Dann, "Low-Country Planter Society in Colonial South Carolina" (unpublished M.A. thesis, College of William and Mary, 1970) and Richard Waterhouse, "South Carolina's Colonial Elite: A Study in the Social Structure and Political Culture of a Southern Colony, 1670–1760" (unpublished Ph.D. dissertation, Johns Hopkins University, 1973). Waterhouse's unpublished paper, "The Development of Elite Culture in the Colonial South: A Study of Charles Town, 1670–1770" (presented at the annual meeting of the Organization of American Historians, 1979) distills and extends material and arguments from the dissertation.

For general guidance to recent scholarship on the family, see Smith, "The Study of the Family in Early America," *WMQ*, XXXIX (January 1982), 3–28. Testamentary practices have been studied by John E. Crowley in two unpublished papers: "Kinship and Family Reliance in Early South Carolina,"

and "Family Relations and Inheritance in Early South Carolina," a paper given
at the annual meeting of the Canadian Historical Association in 1981. Linda
K. Kerber, *Women of the Republic: Intellect and Ideology in Revolutionary America*
(Chapel Hill, 1980) and Mary Beth Norton, *Liberty's Daughters: The Revolu-
tionary Experience of American Women, 1750–1800* (Boston, 1980) contain
information about the role of women in South Carolina, as does Norton,
"Eighteenth-Century American Women in Peace and War: The Case of the
Loyalists," *WMQ*, XXXIII (July 1976), 386–409. The works by Norton and
Kerber are first-rate, but Julia C. Spruill, *Women's Life and Work in the Southern
Colonies* (Chapel Hill, 1938) still provides much useful information. Although
it appeared too late to influence the present work, Marylynn Salmon, "Women
and Property in South Carolina: The Evidence from Marriage Settlements,
1730–1830," *WMQ*, XXXIX (October 1982), 655–685, presents compatible findings and adds significantly to our understanding of these matters.
For Eliza Lucas Pinckney, one may consult her *Letterbook*, edited by Pinckney
and Zahniser, and the sketch by Sam S. Baskett, "Eliza Lucas Pinckney:
Portrait of an Eighteenth Century American," *SCHM*, LXXII (October 1971),
207–219. David Ramsay, *Memoirs of the Life of Martha Laurens Ramsay* (1812;
Philadelphia, 1845) is both a primary and a secondary source. Marriage settlements as a source for historians are discussed by Ruth S. Green and Charles
H. Lesser, "South Carolina Marriage Records," *SCHM*, LXXIX (April 1978),
155–162. Robert M. Weir, "Rebelliousness: Personality Development and
the American Revolution in the Southern Colonies," in Crow and Tise, eds.,
The Southern Experience in the American Revolution, 25–54, and Michael Zuck-
erman, "Penmanship Exercises for Saucy Sons: Some Thoughts on the Colonial
Family" (unpublished paper delivered at the annual meeting of the South
Carolina Historical Society, 1981) make some preliminary observations about
the character of parent-child relationships in early South Carolina.

Bonomi and Eisenstadt, "Church Adherence in the Eighteenth Century
British American Colonies," *WMQ*, XXXIX (April 1982), 245–286; Bridenbaugh, *Myths and Realities*; Jack P. Greene, "Search for Identity: An
Interpretation of the Meaning of Selected Patterns of Social Response in
Eighteenth-Century America," *Journal of Social History*, III (Spring 1970),
189–220; and Lewis Frisch, "Changing Social Attitudes in South Carolina,"
(unpublished undergraduate paper, Johns Hopkins University, 1968) are
suggestive regarding the relative materialism and religiosity of South Carolinians.

For the recreations and cultural life of the lowcountry in general, see Davis,
Intellectual Life in the Colonial South, Frederick P. Bowes, *The Culture of Early
Charleston* (Chapel Hill, 1942); and Samuel A. Lilly, "The Culture of Revo-
lutionary Charleston" (unpublished Ph.D. dissertation, Miami University,

1972), as well as Carl Bridenbaugh, *Cities in the Wilderness: The First Century of Urban Life in America, 1625–1742* (New York, 1938) and *Cities in Revolt.* Cohen, *The South Carolina Gazette*, also includes information about a wide range of topics. Hugh F. Rankin, *The Theater in Colonial America* (Chapel Hill, 1965) and Eola Willis, *The Charleston Stage in the Eighteenth Century, with Social Settings of the Time* (Columbia, 1924) are more specialized. Lewis Frisch, "The Fraternal and Charitable Societies of Colonial South Carolina: A Study of Aristocratic Social Structure" (unpublished undergraduate paper, Johns Hopkins University, 1969) discusses the subject broadly, while J. H. Easterby, *History of the St. Andrew's Society of Charleston, South Carolina, 1729– 1929* (Charleston, 1929) is perhaps the most readable among a group of similar older works. Raymond P. Stearns, *Science in the British Colonies of America* (Urbana, Ill., 1970) deals with local intellectual circles and their British contacts. Information about libraries and reading habits can be found in Anne King Gregorie, "The First Decade of the Charleston Library Society," *Proceedings of the South Carolina Historical Association* (1935), 3–10; Richard B. Davis, *A Colonial Southern Bookshelf: Reading in the Eighteenth-Century* (Athens, Ga., 1979); Walter B. Edgar, "Notable Libraries of Colonial South Carolina," and "Some Popular Books in Colonial South Carolina," *SCHM*, LXXII (April and July 1971), 105–110, 174–178; and Herbert A. Johnson, *Imported Eighteenth-Century Law Treatises in American Libraries, 1700–1799* (Knoxville, 1978). Gerald Stourzh, "William Blackstone: Teacher of Revolution," *Jahrbuch Für Amerikastudien*, Band XV (1970), 184–200, and Robert M. Weir, ed., *The Letters of Freeman, Etc.: Essays on the Nonimportation Movement in South Carolina Collected by William Henry Drayton* (Columbia, 1977) give examples of the ways in which South Carolinians put some contemporary English writings to use, while Dennis R. Nolan, "Sir William Blackstone and the New Republic: A Study of Intellectual Impact," *New York University Law Review*, LI (1976), 731–768, assesses Blackstone's indirect but pervasive influence on Americans generally.

Architecture in South Carolina deserves more scholarly attention than it has received but useful recent works include Davis, *Intellectual Life in the Colonial South*, vol. III; Frederic R. Stevenson and Carl Feis, "Charleston and Savannah," *Journal of the Society of Architectural Historians*, X (December 1951), 3–9; Harley J. McKee, "St. Michael's Church, Charleston, 1752–1762: Some Notes on Materials and Construction," *ibid.*, XXIII (March 1964), 39–42; and Caroline W. Dixon, "The Miles Brewton House: Ezra Waite's Architectural Books and Other Possible Design Sources," *SCHM*, LXXXII (April 1981), 118–142. A. S. Salley, Jr., *The State Houses of South Carolina, 1751– 1936* (Columbia, 1936) provides a very brief introduction to the subject. There is also an unpublished report by John Bryan, "The Exchange Building,

Charleston, 1766–1973: An Architectural History and Restoration Proposal" done in 1973 (available at the South Carolina Department of Archives and History). The original contractural specifications for the building are printed in the *Yearbook of the City of Charleston* (1898), 357–379.

Among the most helpful studies of the graphic arts are Anna W. Rutledge, *Artists in the Life of Charleston: Through Colony and State from Restoration to Reconstruction* (*Transactions of the American Philosophical Society*, **XXXIX**, pt. 2, 1949, 101–260); and two works by Margaret S. Middleton, *Jeremiah Theus* (Columbia, 1955) and *Henrietta Johnston of Charles Town, South Carolina, America's First Pastellist* (Columbia, 1966). For examples of local art, one can consult Francis W. Bilodeau et al., *Art in South Carolina, 1670–1970* (Charleston, 1970) and *Selections From the Collections of the Carolina Art Association* (Charleston, 1977). Bradford L. Rauschenburg, "The Royal Governors' Chair: Evidence of the Furnishing of South Carolina's First State House," *Journal of Early Southern Decorative Arts*, VI (November 1980), 1–32, suggests that even the best of local craftsmen were "out of the mainstream of design." A useful example of another approach to the material culture of colonial South Carolinians is Lynne G. Lewis, *Drayton Hall: Preliminary Archaeological Investigation at a Low Country Plantation* (Charlottesville, 1978).

The most convenient introduction to education in colonial South Carolina is perhaps now to be found in Davis, *Intellectual Life in the Colonial South*, vol. II, but Hoyt Canady, "Legal Education in Colonial South Carolina," in Johnson, ed., *South Carolina Legal History*, 99–118, is more complete on that of the lawyers. J. H. Easterby, *A History of the College of Charleston* (Charleston, 1935) is also useful. Most suggestive but relatively thin on South Carolina is Philip Greven, *The Protestant Temperament: Patterns of Child-Rearing, Religious Experience, and the Self in Early America* (New York, 1977).

For the ethos of the colonial elite, see especially Jack P. Greene, "'Slavery or Independence': Some Reflections on the Relationship Among Liberty, Black Bondage, and Equality in Revolutionary South Carolina," *SCHM*, LXXX (July 1979), 193–214; Waterhouse, "South Carolina's Colonial Elite" (unpublished Ph.D. dissertation, Johns Hopkins University, 1973); Robert M. Weir, "'The Harmony We Were Famous For,'" *WMQ*, XXVI (October 1969), 473–501, "Portrait of a Hero" (John Laurens), *American Heritage*, XXVII (April 1976), 16–19, 86–88, and "Rebelliousness: Personality Development and the American Revolution in the Southern Colonies," in Crow and Tise, eds., *The Southern Experience in the American Revolution*, 25–54, as well as Zahniser, *Charles Cotesworth Pinckney*.

Larry M. Boyer, "The Justice of the Peace in England and America from 1506 to 1776: A Bibliographical History," *Quarterly Journal of the Library of*

Congress, **XXXIV** (October 1977), 315–326, provides perspective on the situation in South Carolina. Beverly Scafidel, "The Bibliography and Significance of Trott's Laws," in Johnson, ed., *South Carolina Legal History,* 53–61, introduces the reader to its subject, while L. Lynn Hogue, "An Edition of 'Eight Charges Delivered, at So Many General Sessions, and Gaol Deliveries: Held at Charles Town...1703, 1704, 1705, 1706, 1707...by Nicholas Trott Esq., Chief Justice of the Province of South Carolina'" (unpublished Ph.D. dissertation, University of Tennessee, 1972) permits one to examine Trott's assumptions about the nature and function of law. Felix Rackow, "The Right to Counsel: English and American Precedents," *WMQ,* XI (January 1954), 3–27, is also useful.

Jack P. Greene, "Legislative Turnover in British America, 1696–1775: A Quantitative Analysis," *WMQ,* XXXVIII (July 1981), 442–463, gives figures that suggest the increasing social and political stability of local society.

11. *The Cherokee War and the Indirect*
Challenge to the Carolina Gentry

The most complete accounts of Lyttelton's administration are to be found in Clarence Attig, "William Henry Lyttelton, A Study in Colonial Administration" (unpublished PH.D. dissertation, University of Nebraska, 1958) and Sirmans, *Colonial South Carolina.* Jack P. Greene analyzes "The South Carolina Quartering Dispute, 1757–1758," *SCHM,* LX (October 1959), 193–204. Lyttelton's own letters in *The Correspondence of William Pitt,* 2 vols. (1906, reprinted New York, 1969) edited by Gertrude S. Kimball still provide the best view of his initial plans.

The background to the Cherokee War is treated in Corkran, *The Cherokee Frontier,* and Milling, *Red Carolinians,* as well as the general histories previously cited. Lawrence Henry Gipson, *The British Empire Before the American Revolution,* vol. IX (New York, 1956) provides an unusually full overview of the war from the British perspective, while Alan Calmes has a good account of "The Lyttelton Expedition of 1759: Military Failures and Financial Successes," *SCHM,* LXXVII (January 1976), 10–33. Much Grant material is available in the Amherst Papers, British Public Record Office (on microfilm at the South Carolina Department of Archives and History) and the "Journal of Lieutenant-Colonel James Grant, Commanding an Expedition Against the Cherokee Indians, June-July, 1761," *Florida Historical Quarterly,* XII (1933), 25–36, as well as in Scotland. For a description of the latter, see George C. Rogers, Jr., "The Papers of James Grant of Ballindoch Castle, Scotland,"

SCHM, LXXVII (July 1976), 145–160. Copies of journals of two subordinate British officers, Christopher French and Alexander Monypenny, are also conveniently available at the South Carolina Archives.

Edmund Atkin, the first British superintendent for Indian affairs, died during the war (of natural causes) and his successor, John Stuart, almost lost his life at the hands of the Indians, but Jacobs, ed., *The Appalachian Frontier: The Edmund Atkin Report and Plan of 1755* and John R. Alden, *John Stuart and the Southern Colonial Frontier* (1944; reprinted New York, 1966) provide excellent accounts of the superintendency and British policy toward the southern Indians in general. For the establishment of the boundary between Indian and white territories in particular, see Louis DeVorsey, Jr., *The Indian Boundary in the Southern Colonies, 1763–1775* (Chapel Hill, 1966). As befits a work by a historical geographer, the book contains valuable maps.

The best accounts of the disorders in the backcountry remain the previously cited works by Richard M. Brown and Rachael Klein, though Joseph A. Ernst, "Another View of the South Carolina Election of 1768 and the Regulators," in Patricia U. Bonomi, ed., *Party and Political Opposition in Revolutionary America* (Tarrytown, N.Y., 1980), 87–97, which emphasizes the potentially enduring political effects of the Regulator movement, is also worth consulting. Popular involvement in lowcountry politics is examined by David R. Chesnutt, "'Greedy Party Work': The South Carolina Election of 1768," *ibid.*, 70–86. For Carolinians' anger over British appointment policy, see especially James Kirby Martin, *Men in Rebellion: Higher Governmental Leaders and the Coming of the American Revolution* (New Brunswick, N.J., 1973); Vipperman, *Rise of Rawlins Lowndes*; and Robert M. Weir, "Who Shall Rule at Home: The American Revolution as a Crisis of Legitimacy for the Colonial Elite," *Journal of Interdisciplinary History*, VI (Spring 1976), 679–700.

Among several general works dealing with the relationship of the French and Indian War to the coming of the Revolution, the most relevant and useful for understanding the situation in South Carolina is now Jack P. Greene, "The Seven Years' War and the American Revolution: The Causal Relationship Reconsidered," in Peter Marshall and Glyn Williams, eds., *The British Atlantic Empire before the American Revolution* (London, 1980), 85–105.

12. *The Overt Challenge and the Coming of the Revolution*

Again, many of the general works cited earlier contain information about this period. More specifically, Robert M. Weir, "A Most Important Epocha": The

Coming of the Revolution in South Carolina (Columbia, 1970) provides an overview of developments, while Jack P. Greene supplies an excellent discussion of "The Gadsden Election Controversy and the Revolutionary Movement in South Carolina," *Mississippi Valley Historical Review*, XLVI (December 1959), 469–492. For the Stamp Act crisis, one can consult Maurice A. Crouse, "Cautious Rebellion: South Carolina's Opposition to the Stamp Act," *SCHM*, LXXIII (April 1972), 59–71, and Robert M. Weir, "'Liberty and Property and No Stamps': South Carolina and the Stamp Act Crisis" (unpublished Ph.D. dissertation, Western Reserve University, 1966), as well as the relevant sections of such standard works as Pauline Maier, *From Resistance to Revolution: Colonial Radicals and the Development of American Opposition to Britain, 1765–1776* (New York, 1972) and Edmund S. and Helen M. Morgan, *The Stamp Act Crisis: Prologue to Revolution* (rev. ed., New York, 1963). E. S. Morgan, ed., *Prologue to Revolution: Sources and Documents on the Stamp Act Crisis, 1764–1766 (Chapel Hill, 1959)* permits a comparison of the resolutions against the act by the various colonial assemblies, including the South Carolina Commons. C. A. Weslager, *The Stamp Act Congress* (Newark, Del., 1976) prints the spare extant journal of the meeting.

Volumes five and six of *The Papers of Henry Laurens* are full of his troubles with the customs service and the vice-admiralty courts. For the customs officers and judge's side of the controversy, see especially Barrow, *Trade and Empire*, and Robert M. Calhoon and Robert M. Weir, "'The Scandalous History of Sir Egerton Leigh,'" *WMQ*, XXVI (January 1969), 47–74. Carl Ubbelohde, *The Vice-Admiralty Courts and the American Revolution* (Chapel Hill, 1960) provides a succinct and thoughtful view of the vice-admiralty courts in general. Weir's introduction to *The Letters of Freeman* supplies some details about the nonimportation movement and cites the older literature. For the gift to John Wilkes and its constitutional implications, see Jack P. Greene, "Bridge to Revolution: The Wilkes Fund Controversy in South Carolina, 1769–1775," *JSH*, XXIX (February 1963), 19–52, and Greene, ed., *The Nature of Colony Constitutions: Two Pamphlets on the Wilkes Fund Controversy in South Carolina by Sir Egerton Leigh and Arthur Lee* (Columbia, 1970). George C. Rogers, Jr., deals with "The Charleston Tea Party: The Significance of December 3, 1773," *SCHM*, LXXV (July 1974), 153–168.

The last days of the colonial government and the first of the Revolutionary organizations can be followed in the journals of the Commons House and the published *Extracts from the Journals of the Provincial Congresses of South Carolina, 1775–1776* (Columbia, 1960) edited by W. Edwin Hemphill and Wylma A. Wates. Despite its title, this volume contains all that survives of the proceedings of this body. Less meticulously edited but still useful are the journals and papers of the First and Second Councils of Safety published, respectively, in the *Collections of the South Carolina Historical Society*, II and III (1858 and 1859), and *SCH & GM*, I–IV, various pages. Unpublished minutes of the Council of Safety, February 28–March 26, 1776, are available at the New York Public Library and, on microfilm, at the South Carolina Department of Archives and History. For the composition and work of the local committees, one can consult Eva B. Poythress, "Revolution by Committee, An Administrative History of the Extralegal Committees in South Carolina, 1774–1776" (unpublished Ph.D. dissertation, University of North Carolina, 1975).

William Henry Drayton looms large in this period, no doubt partly because his surviving papers provided the basis for John Drayton's *Memoirs of the American Revolution*, 2 vols. (1821; reprinted New York, 1969) compiled by William Henry's son. For a brief assessment of this work, see Solomon Lutnick, "William Henry Drayton's Memoirs," in Leder, ed., *The Colonial Legacy*, III and IV in one, 200–212. Drayton himself still needs a really good study, but in the interim one can consult William M. Dabney and Marion Dargan, *William Henry Drayton and the American Revolution* (Albuquerque, 1962).

Frank W. Ryan, Jr., deals with "The Role of South Carolina in the First Continental Congress," *SCHM*, LX (July 1959), 147–153. The ongoing work of the South Carolinians in the Continental Congresses is, however, best followed in *The Journals of the Continental Congress, 1774–1789* edited by Worthington C. Ford and others, 34 vols. (Washington, D. C., 1904–1937); *Letters of Members of the Continental Congress* edited by Edmund C. Burnett, 8 vols. (Washington, D. C., 1921–1936); and, now, Paul H. Smith, ed., *Letters of Delegates to Congress, 1774–1789* (Washington, D. C., 1976–   ), a collection which will eventually replace Burnett's edition. Recent studies of the Congress which reveal the position of the Carolina delegation on various questions—including independence—are H. James Henderson, *Party Politics in the Continental Congress* (New York, 1974) and Jack N. Rakove, *The Beginnings of National Politics: An Interpretative History of the Continental Congress* (New York, 1979). Milton M. Klein, "Failure of a Mission: The Drummond Peace Proposal of 1775," *Huntington Library Quarterly*, XXXV (August 1972), 343–380, describes an abortive attempt at reconciliation in which a leading Carolinian (Thomas Lynch, Sr.) was heavily involved. John M. Head, *A Time to Rend: An Essay on the Decision for American Independence* (Madison, 1968) is a stimulating study that nevertheless fails to recognize the extent to which the British connection undermined rather than bolstered the position of local elites.

13. *The Revolution*

The literature about South Carolina in the Revolutionary period is voluminous but uneven. In recent years, however, new finding-aids and editions of basic source material have appeared to facilitate future research. The latter include in particular W. Edwin Hemphill, Wylma A. Wates, and R. Nicholas Olsberg, eds., *Journals of the General Assembly and House of Representatives, 1776–1780* (Columbia, 1970), which is incomplete in chronological coverage but contains all the journals of this body known to have survived prior to 1782; Adele S. Edwards, ed., *Journals of the Privy Council, 1783–1789* (Columbia, 1971); Theodora Thompson and Rosa S. Lumpkin, eds., *Journals of the House of Representatives, 1783–1784* (Columbia, 1977); Lark Adams and Rosa S. Lumpkin, eds., *Journals of the House of Representatives, 1785–1786* (Columbia, 1979); and Michael E. Stevens and Christine M. Allen, eds., *Journals of the House of Representatives, 1787–1788* (Columbia, 1981). Serviceable but less satisfactorily edited journals of the House and Senate that met at Jacksonborough in 1782 were edited by A. S. Salley, Jr. (Columbia, 1916 and 1941).

Much information about South Carolina during the war years lurks in the papers of the Continental Congress housed at the National Archives and available on microfilm at a number of other repositories, including the South Carolina Department of Archives and History. This material is indexed in John P. Butler, *Index to the Papers of the Continental Congress, 1774–1789*, 5 vols. (Washington, D. C., 1978). In addition, "Revolutionary War Pension and Bounty-Land Warrant Application Files" are available on microfilm from the National Archives. For an introduction to the nature and utility of these records, one can consult J. Todd White and Charles H. Lesser, eds., *Fighters for Independence: A Guide to Sources of Biographical Information on Soldiers and Sailors of the American Revolution* (Chicago, 1977) or John C. Dann, ed., *The Revolution Remembered: Eye-Witness Accounts of the War for Independence* (Chicago, 1980), which prints a number of items from South Carolina. Less colorful than the pension applications but useful for establishing details are the South Carolina "accounts audited" which record payments for supplies and services during the war. A good capsule description of these records, which are available at the South Carolina Department of Archives and History, is Helen C. Carson, "Accounts Audited of Claims Growing out of the Revolution," *SCHM*, LXXV (July 1974), 201–204. Finally, the ongoing *Papers of Nathanael Greene* (Chapel Hill, 1976–) edited by Richard Showman et al. will soon reach the period in which Greene was in South Carolina. In the meantime, important unpublished collections of Greene's papers are available at the Library of Congress and William L. Clements Library.

For the British side, the most important collection of materials outside of the British Public Record Office is at the William L. Clements Library which houses the papers of Sir Henry Clinton. Some of Lord Cornwallis's papers were published by Charles Ross, ed., 3 vols. (London, 1859) but the mass of his unpublished material in the Public Record Office is available on microfilm at the South Carolina Department of Archives and History and elsewhere. George H. Reese, comp., *The Cornwallis Papers: Abstracts of Americana* (Charlottesville, 1970) provides a guide to this material. British Headquarters Papers in the Royal Institution, often known as the Carleton Papers, have been imperfectly calendared by the Historical Manuscripts Commission, 4 vols. (London, 1904–1909). Germans with the British Army made some interesting observations about South Carolina which can be consulted in Bernhard A. Uhlendorf, trans. and ed., *The Siege of Charleston with an Account of the Province of South Carolina: Diaries and Letters of Hessian Officers* (1938; reprinted New York, 1968) and Johann Ewald, *Diary of the American War: A Hessian Journal* (New Haven, 1979) translated and edited by Joseph Tustin; there is, however, some overlap in the two volumes.

Useful general studies of the war include the statistics compiled by Howard H. Peckham, *The Toll of Independence: Engagements and Battle Casualties of the American Revolution* (Chicago, 1974) and Charles H. Lesser, *The Sinews of Independence: Monthly Strength Reports of the Continental Army* (Chicago, 1976). Don Higginbotham, *The War of American Independence: Military Attitudes, Policies, and Practice, 1763–1789* (New York, 1971) is an excellent example of the newer style of military history which views tactical matters in a broad social and political context. Henry Lumpkin, *From Savannah to Yorktown: The American Revolution in the South* (Columbia, 1981) is a handsome volume in the older tradition, strong on technical details. Since 1973 the journal *Names in South Carolina* has also been publishing an ongoing series of articles by Terry Lipscomb which offer detailed discussions of local battles. Alden, *The South in the Revolution*, continues to provide a good overview of both military and political developments.

Memoirs and biographies of a number of key individuals are also helpful. William B. Willcox, *Portrait of a General: Sir Henry Clinton in the War of Independence* (New York, 1964) is a brilliant study, but too broad to provide much detail about South Carolina. Some of his subordinates spent more time there, and Franklin and Mary Wickwire, *Cornwallis: The American Adventure* (Boston, 1970) is a good biography, though some readers may believe it to be excessively laudatory. Banastre Tarleton recounts his own exploits in *A History of the Campaigns of 1780 and 1781 in the Southern Provinces of North-America* (1787; reprinted Spartanburg, S.C., 1967). Popular studies of *The Green Dragoon: The Lives of Banastre Tarleton and*

Mary Robinson (1957; reprinted Columbia, 1973), *The Gamecock: The Life and Campaigns of General Thomas Sumter* (New York, 1961), and *The Swamp Fox: The Life and Campaigns of General Francis Marion* (1959, reprinted Columbia, 1972) have been written by Robert D. Bass. More scholarly than Bass's work, Hugh F. Rankin, *Francis Marion: The Swamp Fox* (New York, 1973) also provides guidance to older works which remain valuable because of the inclusion of documentary material. Anne King Gregorie, *Thomas Sumter* (Columbia, 1931) is still standard. William Moultrie is well represented by his own *Memoirs of the American Revolution*, 2 vols. (1802), which has been reprinted in one volume (New York, 1968). The best study of Pickens is Clyde Ferguson, "General Andrew Pickens" (unpublished Ph.D. dissertation, Duke University, 1960), though Alice N. Waring, *The Fighting Elder: Andrew Pickens, 1739–1817* (Columbia, 1962) is more readily available. John C. Cavanagh, "American Military Leadership in the Southern Campaign: Benjamin Lincoln," in W. Robert Higgins, ed., *The Revolutionary War in the South: Power, Conflict, and Leadership* (Durham, 1979), 101–131, Paul D. Nelson, *General Horatio Gates: A Biography* (Baton Rouge, 1976) and Theodore Thayer, *Nathanael Greene: Strategist of the American Revolution* (New York, 1960) are all useful, while Charles Royster, *Light-Horse Harry Lee and the Legacy of the American Revolution* (New York, 1981) has a thoughtful chapter on the partisan war. Alden, *John Stuart and the Southern Colonial Frontier*, covers the last years of Stuart's life and his Indian policy during the early years of the war in a judicious manner. For later developments involving the Indians, one may consult James H. O'Donnell, III, *The Southern Indians in the American Revolution* (Knoxville, 1973).

Political and constitutional developments in South Carolina during the war and immediately thereafter have been most recently treated by Jerome J. Nadelhaft, *The Disorders of War: The Revolution in South Carolina* (Orono, Maine, 1981), which emphasizes change, and S. R. Matchett, "'Unanimity, Order and Regularity': The Political Culture of South Carolina in the Era of the Revolution" (unpublished Ph.D. dissertation, University of Sydney, 1980), which stresses political and ideological continuity. Another work which similarly concludes that "continuity and stability were the hallmarks of South Carolina lawmaking in the Critical Period" is James W. Ely, "American Independence and the Law: A Study of Post-Revolutionary South Carolina Legislation," *Vanderbilt Law Review*, XXVI (1973), 939–971. Although Walter J. Fraser, Jr., "Reflections of 'Democracy' in Revolutionary South Carolina?: The Composition of Military Organizations and the Attitudes and Relationships of the Officers and Men, 1775–1780," *SCHM*, LXXVIII (July 1977), 202–212, may read more into the evidence than it will support, both he and Ronald Hoffman, "The 'Disaffected' in the Revolutionary South," in

Alfred F. Young, ed., *The American Revolution: Explorations in the History of American Radicalism* (DeKalb, Ill., 1976), 273–316, as well as Pauline Maier, "The Charleston Mob and the Evolution of Popular Politics in Revolutionary South Carolina, 1765–1784," *Perspectives in American History*, IV (1970), 173–196, clearly demonstrate that the Revolutionary elite was under popular pressure during and immediately following the war. How it managed to keep its political footing comes out, at least in part, in Bolton, *Southern Anglicanism*, and Robert M. Weir, "The 'Violent Spirit,'" in Ronald Hoffman and Thad W. Tate, eds., *The Southern Backcountry in the Revolution* (Washington, D. C., forthcoming). A specialized work is Richard G. Stone, Jr., "The Privy Council of South Carolina, 1776–1790: A Study in Shared Executive Power" (unpublished Ph.D. dissertation, University of Tennessee, 1973). For the early course of the conflict and the initial "problem" of loyalism in the backcountry, see "A Fragment of a Journal Kept by the Rev. William Tennent Describing his Journey, in 1775 . . . ," *Yearbook of the City of Charleston* (1894), 296–312, also printed in Gibbes, *Documentary History of the American Revolution*, I, 225–239; James H. O'Donnell, III, ed., "A Loyalist View of the Drayton-Tennent-Hart Mission to the Upcountry," *SCHM*, LXVII (January 1966), 15–28; Gary D. Olson, "Loyalists and the American Revolution: Thomas Brown and the South Carolina Backcountry, 1775–1776," *SCHM*, LXVIII and LXIX (October 1967 and January 1968), 201–219, 44–56; Lewis P. Jones, *The South Carolina Civil War of 1775* (Lexington, S.C., 1975); Marvin L. Cann, "Prelude to War: The First Battle of Ninety Six, November 19–21, 1775, *SCHM*, LXXVI (October 1975), 197–214; as well as Klein, "Ordering the Backcountry," *WMQ*, XXXVIII (October 1981), 661–680. Subsequent attempts to deal with the loyalists are treated by Robert S. Davis, Jr., "The Loyalist Trials at Ninety Six in 1779," *SCHM*, LXXX (April 1979), 172–181, who supplies valuable detail, and Clyde R. Ferguson, "Carolina and Georgia Patriot and Loyalist Militia in Action, 1778–1783," in Crow and Tise, eds., *The Southern Experience in the American Revolution*, 174–199, which notes the effectiveness of the militia in controlling and intimidating Tories. Robert D. Bass, *Ninety Six: The Struggle for the South Carolina Back Country* (Lexington, S.C., 1978) is more colorful than analytical.

For the local loyalists' effect on British strategic thinking, one should consult Ira D. Gruber, "Britain's Southern Strategy," in Higgins, ed., *The Revolutionary War in the South: Power, Conflict, and Leadership*, 205–238, Paul H. Smith, *Loyalists and Redcoats: A Study in British Revolutionary Policy* (Chapel Hill, 1964), and K. G. Davies, "The Restoration of Civil Government by the British in the War of Independence," in Esmond Wright, ed., *Red, White and True Blue: The Loyalists in the American Revolution* (New York, 1976), 111–133. Robert M. Calhoon, *The Loyalists in Revolutionary America, 1760–1781*

(New York, 1973) includes perceptive insights about loyalists in South Carolina, while Wallace Brown, *The Kings' Friends: The Composition and Motives of the American Loyalist Claimants* (Providence, 1965), which has a chapter on South Carolinians, analyzes those who ultimately filed claims for compensation from the British government. Relying heavily on claimants from Carolina, Eugene R. Fingerhut, "Uses and Abuses of the American Loyalists' Claims: A Critique of Quantitative Analysis," *WMQ*, XXV (April 1968), 245–258, shows that these records must be used with caution. Some South Carolinians also appear in Mary Beth Norton, *The British-Americans: The Loyalist Exiles in England, 1774–1789* (Boston, 1972), Linda K. Williams, "East Florida as a Loyalist Haven," *Florida Historical Quarterly*, LIV (April 1976), 465–478, and Wallace Brown, "The Loyalists in the West Indies, 1783–1834," in Wright, ed., *Red, White and True Blue*, 73–96. Robert W. Barnwell, Jr., "Loyalism in South Carolina, 1765–1785" (unpublished Ph.D. dissertation, Duke University, 1941) remains a very useful study, well researched and thoughtful, while Robert S. Lambert, "A Loyalist Odyssey: James and Mary Cary in Exile, 1783–1804," *SCHM*, LXXIX (July 1978), 167–181, describes a particularly moving case. Guidance to local sources is provided by Lambert for "A Bibliography of Loyalist Source Material in the United States: Part III," edited by Herbert Leventhal and James E. Mooney, *American Antiquarian Society Proceedings*, LXXXVI, pt. 2 (1976), 360–367.

Additional sources and studies dealing with specialized topics include Pete Maslowski, "National Policy Toward the Use of Black Troops in the Revolution," *SCHM*, LXXIII (January 1972), 1–17, and George S. McCowen, Jr., *The British Occupation of Charleston, 1780–1782* (Columbia, 1972), a helpful but not exhaustive study. One of the most suggestive short introductions to the bitter warfare following the British invasion is Russell F. Weigley, *The Partisan War: The South Carolina Campaign of 1780–1782* (Columbia, 1970). "Colonel Robert Gray's Observations on the War in Carolina," *SCH & GM*, XI (January 1910), 139–159, provides a shrewd and interesting assessment by a loyalist, while Moultrie's *Memoirs of the American Revolution*— like the remarks of the Reverend Archibald Simpson reprinted in Katherine M. Jones, ed., *Port Royal Under Six Flags* (Indianapolis, 1960)—contain vivid descriptions of conditions at the end of the war.

A number of studies are helpful on the Confederation period and local attitudes toward a stronger central government. Not especially readable but still worth consulting is Charles G. Singer, *South Carolina in the Confederation* (Philadelphia, 1941). Robert A. Becker deals with local problems in "Salus Populi Suprema Lex: Public Peace and South Carolina Debtor Relief Laws, 1783–1788," *SCHM*, LXXX (January 1979), 65–75, and puts similar matters in wider perspective in his book, *Revolution, Reform, and the Politics of*

American Taxation, 1763–1783 (Baton Rouge, 1980). For specifics on the size of the local debt, see W. Robert Higgins, "A Financial History of the American Revolution in South Carolina" (unpublished Ph.D. dissertation, Duke University, 1970). E. James Ferguson, *The Power of the Purse: A History of American Public Finance, 1776–1790* (Chapel Hill, 1961) clarifies the question of assumption of this debt by the federal government. Forrest McDonald, *We the People: The Economic Origins of the Constitution* (Chicago, 1958) makes some suggestive but tenuous inferences about local alignments. Ernest M. Lander, Jr., "The South Carolinians at the Philadelphia Convention, 1787," *SCHM*, LVII (July 1956), 134–155, is a careful study, while George C. Rogers, Jr., "South Carolina Ratifies the Federal Constitution," *Proceedings of the South Carolina Historical Association* (1961), 41–62, is both reliable and more inclusive in its coverage than the title suggests.

Hitherto, Max Farrand, ed., *The Records of the Federal Convention of 1787*, 4 vols. (New Haven, 1911–1937); Jonathan Elliot, ed., *Debates in the Several State Conventions on the Adoption of the Federal Constitution as Recommended by the General Convention at Philadelphia in 1787 . . .*, 5 vols. (Washington, D. C., 1836–1845); and A. S. Salley, Jr., ed., *Journal of the Convention of South Carolina Which Ratified the Constitution of the United States, May 23, 1788* (Atlanta, 1928) have constituted the most readily available source material. Merrill Jensen et al., eds., *The Documentary History of the Ratification of the Constitution* (Madison, 1976–) promises to set a new standard.

14. Epilogue: Toward the Nineteenth Century

Attempts to understand the behavior of South Carolina in the nineteenth century have, of course, been legion. Here the following works are perhaps the most relevant. James M. Banner, Jr., "The Problem of South Carolina," in Stanley Elkins and Eric McKitrick, eds., *The Hofstadter Aegis: A Memorial* (New York, 1974), 60–83, seeks explanations in terms of aberrant institutional features and political practices, while Richard M. Brown emphasizes the effects of a violent heritage; see his *Strain of Violence; Historical Studies of American Violence and Vigilantism* (New York, 1975). More recently, the early chapters of Lacy Ford, "Social Origins of a New South Carolina: The Upcountry, 1840–1900" (Ph.D. dissertation in progress, University of South Carolina) argue ably that local politics were not as aberrational as has sometimes been assumed. Nevertheless, Kenneth S. Greenberg, "Representation and the Isolation of South Carolina, 1776–1860," *Journal of American History*, LXIV (December 1977), 723–743, demonstrates the unusual persistence of eighteenth century political assumptions. How this political culture influenced the behavior of South Carolinians in the context of the changing conditions of the nineteenth century is the subject of George C. Rogers, Jr., "South Carolina Federalists and the Origins of the Nullification Movement," *SCHM*, LXXI (January 1970), 17–32, and Robert M. Weir, "The South Carolinian as Extremist," *South Atlantic Quarterly*, LXXIV (Winter 1975), 86–103, which approach the matter from complementary perspectives.

BIBLIOGRAPHICAL
SUPPLEMENT

This bibliography is complementary to its predecessor in the first edition; thus most dissertations and works in progress listed there are not repeated here, though they may have been published in the meantime. Readers are also urged to consult the *South Carolina Historical Magazine* for the intervening years. It contains many relevant items too numerous to mention. Lengthy as it is, this bibliography represents a selective list that omits several good works. Those chosen have been picked for their coverage, significance, and readability.

BIBLIOGRAPHICAL GUIDES, SOURCES, AND GENERAL WORKS

The following are useful aids: John J. McCusker, "New Guides to Primary Sources on the History of Early British America," *William and Mary Quarterly* (hereafter abbreviated *WMQ*), XLI, (April 1984), 277–295, and Charles H. Lesser's prize-winning, *South Carolina Begins: The Records of a Proprietary Colony, 1663–1721* (Columbia, 1995). Brief introductions to the primary and secondary sources for the major religious denominations appear in volumes LXXXIV (1983) and LXXXV (1984) of the *South Carolina Historical Magazine* (hereafter abbreviated *SCHM*). John H. and Gary S. Wilson, *The Early South Carolina Newspapers: A Quick Reference Guide to Local News and Advertisements Found in the Early South Carolina Newspapers* (Mt. Pleasant, S.C., 1995) provide an index to the *South Carolina Gazette,* which will eventually cover from 1732 to 1782; ESCN Database Reports, Mt. Pleasant, S.C., will also search its database upon request. Christopher Gould and Richard P. Morgan give *A Descriptive Bibliography: South Carolina Imprints, 1731–1800* (Santa Barbara, 1985). David Fischer, comp., *Transactions of the Huguenot Society of South Carolina, Index to Volumes 1–96,* 2 parts (Charleston, 1994), facilitates use of this series. Robert H. Mackintosh, Jr., *Selected Bibliography of County, City, and Town Histories and Related Published Records in the South Carolina Archives Reference Library* (Columbia, 1994) is a handy booklet, while Lewis P. Jones, *Books and Articles on South Carolina History* (2nd ed., Columbia, 1991) is particularly helpful for teachers and interested readers. More comprehensive guidance to the colonial period as a whole can be found in David L. Ammerman and Philip D. Morgan, comp., *Books about Early America* (Williamsburg, 1989); Mary Beth Norton, *Guide to Historical Literature,* 2 vols. (3rd ed., New York, 1995); and Jack P. Greene and J. R. Pole, eds., *Colonial British America: Essays in the New History of the Early Modern Era* (Baltimore, 1984). America: History and Life on Disc, 1982–, ABC-Clio, Inc., Santa Barbara, Calif., provides convenient, computerized access to articles, book reviews, and dissertations. In addition, Michael O'Malley and Roy Rosenzweig, "Brave New World or Blind Alley? American History on the World Wide Web," *Journal of American History,* LXXXIV, no. 1 (June 1997), 132–155 provide assistance in dealing with expanding resources of varying reliability.

Recently printed primary sources include the multivolume *Early American Indian Documents: Treaties and Laws, 1607–1789,* under the general editorship of Alden T. Vaughan, in which the South Carolina volume will be forthcoming shortly. Scattered references to South Carolina and South Carolinians appear in John C. Van Horne and George Reese, eds., *The Letter Book of James Abercromby, Colonial Agent, 1751–1773* (Richmond, 1991). Abercromby, who served in the South Carolina Assembly, eventually became one of the few members of Parliament to have had such experience in the colonies.

Among works that provide relatively broad coverage of South Carolina history, the following are especially noteworthy. The revised edition of George C. Rogers, Jr. and C. James Taylor, eds., *A South Carolina Chronology, 1497–1992* (Columbia, 1994) includes more information about social and cultural matters than the first version. David R. Chesnutt and Clyde N. Wilson, eds., *The Meaning of South Carolina History:*

Essays in Honor of George C. Rogers, Jr. (Columbia, 1991) does not answer the question implicit in its title but it contains several excellent essays on various topics. Jane Iseley and Agnes L. and William P. Baldwin, *Plantations of the Lowcountry: South Carolina, 1697–1865* (Greensboro, N.C., 1985) provide a beautifully illustrated introduction to the low-country, useful to a wide range of readers. Another handsome volume, Suzanne C. Linder, *Historical Atlas of the Rice Plantations of the ACE River Basin—1860* (Columbia, 1995) covers the drainage area of the Ashepoo, Combahee, and Edisto rivers. Peter McCandless, *Moonlight, Magnolias, and Madness: Insanity in South Carolina from the Colonial to the Progressive Eras* (Chapel Hill, 1996); Richard Waterhouse, *A New World Gentry: The Making of a Merchant and Planter Class in South Carolina, 1670–1770* (New York, 1989); and Robert M. Weir, *"The Last of American Freemen": Studies in the Political Culture of the Colonial and Revolutionary South* (Macon, Ga., 1986) treat relevant topics. The South Carolina Department of Archives and History has also published a number of authoritative booklets directed to a general audience, a regularly updated list of which is available from the archives. Lewis P. Jones, *South Carolina: One of the Fifty States* (Orangeburg, S.C., 1991) and Archie V. Huff, *The History of South Carolina in the Building of the Nation* (Greenville, S.C., 1991) are eighth-grade textbooks by knowledgeable professional historians.

William L. Watkins, "South Carolina's Changing, Confusing, Controversial Boundary Line," *Carologue*, X (Spring 1994), 14–20, provides a brief overview; Louis DeVorsey, Jr., *The Georgia–South Carolina Boundary: A Problem in Historical Geography* (Athens, Ga., 1982) offers the Georgians' perspective on the recently settled boundary question. Regionally specific studies include Walter J. Fraser, Jr., *Charleston! Charleston! The History of a Southern City* (Columbia, 1989); John Hammond Moore, *Columbia and Richland County: A South Carolina Community, 1740–1990* (Columbia, 1993); and Lawrence S. Rowland, Alexander Moore, and George C. Rogers, Jr., *The History of Beaufort County, South Carolina*, vol. I, 1514–1861 (Columbia, 1996), all of which are well written and sound.

Useful works about important individuals and families are N. Louise Bailey, Mary L. Morgan, and Carolyn R. Taylor, *Biographical Directory of the South Carolina Senate, 1776–1985*, 3 vols. (Columbia, 1986); Malcolm Bell, Jr., *Major Butler's Legacy: Five Generations of a Slaveholding*

Family (Athens, Ga., 1987); Kinloch Bull, Jr., *The Oligarchs in Colonial and Revolutionary Charleston: Lieutenant Governor William Bull II and His Family* (Columbia, 1991), [which is more thorough than Geraldine M. Meroney's readable *Inseparable Loyalty: A Biography of William Bull* (Norcross, Ga., 1991)]; Alan Gallay, *The Formation of a Planter Elite: Jonathan Bryan and the Southern Colonial Frontier* (Athens, Ga., 1989); W. Stitt Robinson, *James Glen: From Scottish Provost to Royal Governor of South Carolina* (Westport, Conn., 1996); James A. Rogers, *Richard Furman: Life and Legacy* (Macon, Ga., 1985); Arthur H. Shaffer, *To Be an American: David Ramsay and the Making of the American Consciousness* (Columbia, 1991); James Haw, *Founding Brothers: John and Edward Rutledge of South Carolina* (Athens, Ga., forthcoming 1997); and J. Russell Snapp, *John Stuart and the Struggle for Empire on the Southern Frontier* (Baton Rouge, 1996). Several dissertations are also helpful: J. E. Buchanan, "The Colleton Family and the Early History of South Carolina and Barbados, 1646–1775" (University of Edinburgh, 1989); Dorothy G. Griffin, "The Eighteenth Century Draytons of Drayton Hall" (Emory University, 1985); George W. Lane, Jr., "The Middletons of Eighteenth Century South Carolina: A Colonial Dynasty, 1678–1787" (Emory University, 1990); Daniel J. McDonough, "Christopher Gadsden and Henry Laurens: The Parallel Lives of Two American Patriots" (University of Illinois, 1990); and Gregory D. Massey, "A Hero's Life: John Laurens and the American Revolution" (University of South Carolina, 1992).

Several general works also contribute to an understanding of where South Carolina fits in the overall picture of colonial development. Bernard Bailyn, *Voyagers to the West: A Passage in the Peopling of America on the Eve of the Revolution* (New York, 1987) examines emigration from the British Isles and provides detailed accounts of ventures in Florida and the backcountry that are relevant to South Carolina. David H. Fischer's *Albion's Seed: Four British Folkways in America* (New York, 1989) postulates the continuing influence of these cultural patterns; the thesis is controversial, but his description of the Borderers (mainly Scotch-Irish) is pertinent to South Carolina. Jack P. Greene has published several volumes of exceptionally stimulating essays; some individual items that deal specifically with South Carolina have been listed in the first bibliography of this volume. Greene's *Pursuits of Happiness: The Social Development of Early Modern British Colonies and the Formation of American Culture*

(Chapel Hill, 1988) couples an emphasis on regional diversity with a general model of colonial development. Both Greene and D. W. Meinig, *The Shaping of America: A Geographical Perspective on 500 Years of History* (New Haven, 1986) treat cultural diffusion to and from Carolina.

TOPICAL WORKS

1. *Prologue to Settlement*

David J. Weber, *The Spanish Frontier in North America* (New Haven, 1992) provides the best general account, while Michael Gannon, ed., *The New History of Florida* (Gainesville, 1996) has a number of sections relevant to the history of South Carolina. Paul E. Hoffman, *A New Andalucia and a Way to the Orient: The American Southeast During the Sixteenth Century* (Baton Rouge, 1990) is the standard treatment of exploration in the region. His contention that Ayllón's settlement was in the Sapelo Sound area—along with some criticisms of his thesis by other authors—also appears in Jeannine Cook, *Columbus and the Land of Ayllón: The Exploration and Settlement of the Southeast* (Valona, Ga., 1992), a volume that makes the scholarly debate accessible to general readers. Jerald T. Milanich and Charles Hudson, *Hernando de Soto and the Indians of Florida* (Gainesville, 1993) provides important ethnographic information and outlines the authors' thinking about de Soto's entire route. *The De Soto Chronicles: The Expedition of Hernando De Soto to North America in 1539–1543*, Lawrence A. Clayton, Vernon J. Knight, Jr., and Edward C. Moore, eds., 2 vols. (Tuscaloosa, Ala., 1993) publishes the basic documents in translation, while David E. Duncan depicts *Hernando de Soto: A Savage Quest in the Americas* (New York, 1995). Charles Hudson, *The Juan Pardo Expeditions: Exploration of the Carolinas and Tennessee, 1566–1568* (Washington, D.C., 1990) locates Cofitachequi near Camden, South Carolina, and Charles Hudson and Carmen C. Tesser, eds., *The Forgotten Centuries: Indians and Europeans in the American South, 1521–1704* (Athens, Ga., 1994) brings together the views of a number of scholars about these and other matters. "The New Alliance of History and Archaeology in the Eastern Spanish Borderlands," *WMQ*, XLIX

(April 1992), 321–334, by Michael Gannon, describes recent archaeological work on Santa Elena, South Carolina, and St. Augustine, while Elizabeth J. Reitz and C. Margaret Scarry, *Reconstructing Historic Subsistence with an Example from Sixteenth-Century Spanish Florida* (Pleasant Hill, Calif., 1985) combines documentary evidence with insights from ethnobotany and zooarchaeology to discover what people ate. More recently, the Institute of Anthropology and Archaeology of the University of South Carolina announced the discovery of the remains of the French fort in the Port Royal area, Charles Fort. See *The State* (Columbia), June 6, 1996.

2. *The Indians*

Wes Taukchiray provides two helpful lists in "American Indian References in the *South-Carolina Gazette*," *SCHM*, XCIV (July 1993), 185–192 and "American Indian References in the *South-Carolina and American General Gazette, The Gazette of the State of South Carolina*, and *The Royal Gazette*," *SCHM*, XCVII (January 1996), 65–76; while Thomas J. Blumer has compiled a useful chronological *Bibliography of the Catawba* (Metuchen, N.J., 1987). Gregory A. Waselkov and Kathryn E. H. Braund, eds., *William Bartram on the Southeastern Indians* (Lincoln, Nebr., 1995) is an important source. Peter H. Wood, Gregory A. Waselkov, and M. Thomas Hatley, eds., *Powhatan's Mantle: Indians in the Colonial Southeast* (Lincoln, Nebr., 1989) provides several significant essays, including Wood's "The Changing Population of the Colonial South." *The Indians' New World: Catawbas and Their Neighbors from European Contact through the Era of Removal* (Chapel Hill, 1989) by James H. Merrell is a prize-winning study of survival in an increasingly alien world. Four fine books cover Indian-white interaction on the Carolina periphery: Tom Hatley, *The Dividing Paths: Cherokees and South Carolinians through the Era of Revolution* (New York, 1993); Kathryn E. H. Braund, *Deerskins & Duffels: The Creek Indian Trade with Anglo-America, 1685–1815* (Lincoln, Nebr., 1993); Daniel H. Usner, Jr., *Indians, Settlers, & Slaves in a Frontier Exchange Economy: The Lower Mississippi Valley Before 1783* (Chapel Hill, 1992); and Gregory E. Dowd, *A Spirited Resistance: The North American Indian Struggle for Unity, 1745–1815* (Baltimore, 1992). Gregory E. Dowd, "The Panic of 1751: The Significance of Rumors on the South Carolina–Cherokee Frontier," *WMQ*, LIII (July 1996), 527–560, is an interesting study of a specific incident with wider implications.

3. *The Land*

Charles F. Kovacik and John J. Winberry, *South Carolina: A Geography* (Boulder, 1987) is the standard account by two historical geographers. David P. George, Jr., "Ninety Six Decoded: Origins of a Community's Name," *SCHM*, XCII (April 1991), 69–84, is an ingenious attempt to account for the name of the settlement by the configuration of streams in the area. Timothy Silver, *A New Face on the Countryside: Indians, Colonists, and Slaves in South Atlantic Forests, 1500–1800* (New York, 1990) provides a comprehensive account of environmental change. Jack P. Greene, ed., *Selling a New World: Two Colonial South Carolina Promotional Pamphlets* (Columbia, 1989) depicts the attractions of Carolina, while a darker side of the picture appears in Karen O. Kupperman, "Fear of Hot Climates in the Anglo-American Colonial Experience," *WMQ*, XLI (April 1984), 213–240; H. Roy Merrens and George D. Terry, "Dying in Paradise: Malaria, Mortality, and the Perceptual Environment in Colonial South Carolina," *Journal of Southern History* (hereafter abbreviated *JSH*), L (November 1984), 533–550; and Suzanne Krebsbach, "The Great Charlestown Smallpox Epidemic of 1760," *SCHM*, XCVII (January 1996), 30–37.

4. *Settlement and Politics to 1748*

An important, hitherto unknown source comes from a member of Robert Sandford's exploring expedition of 1666, Lt. James Woory. His report, entitled "A Discovery of the Coasts, Islands, Rivers, Sounds & Creeks of that part of the province of Carolina between Cape Romano and Port Royall," provides significant detail about the Indians as well as other matters. The Clements Library will publish it in 1997 or 1998. Warren Alleyne and Henry Fraser discuss *The Barbados-Carolina Connection* (London, 1988) for a popular audience, while Kinloch Bull, "Barbadian Settlers in Early Carolina: Historiographical Notes," *SCHM*, XCVI

(October 1995), 329–339, questions the presumed Barbadian origins of many prominent South Carolinians. Agnes L. Baldwin, *First Settlers of South Carolina, 1670–1700* (2nd ed., Easley, S.C., 1985) provides a useful list of names that nevertheless needs to be used with caution. Alexander Moore, ed., " 'A Narrative of an Assembly . . . January the 2d, 1705/6: New Light on Early South Carolina Politics," *SCHM*, LXXXV (July 1984), 181–186, prints a contemporary description that fills a gap for which no official journal survives. J. D. Alsop, "Thomas Nairne and the 'Boston Gazette No. 216' of 1707," *Southern Studies*, XII (Summer 1983), 209–211, argues that Nairne may in fact have been a Jacobite. The effects of war appear in John H. Hann, *Apalachee: The Land Between the Rivers* (Gainesville, 1988), which discusses destruction of the missions in the Tallahassee area by Carolinians. Thomas C. Parramore, "With Tuscarora Jack on the Back Path to Bath," *North Carolina Historical Review*, LXIV (April 1987), 115–138 argues that Barnwell's expedition was "a tragic farce" that made accommodation with the Tuscarora Indians impossible. Richard L. Haan provides a sophisticated account of "The 'Trade Do's not Flourish as Formerly': The Ecological Origins of the Yamassee War of 1715," *Ethnohistory*, XXVIII (Fall 1981), 341–358, while John H. Hann, "St. Augustine's Fallout from the Yamasee War," *Florida Historical Quarterly*, LXVIII (October 1989), 180–200, follows the Yamasees who settled in Florida after their defeat.

Alexander Moore gives the most complete account of "Royalizing South Carolina: The Revolution of 1719 and the Evolution of Early South Carolina Government" in his dissertation (University of South Carolina, 1991) that draws parallels between the situation in South Carolina and the Bahamas. In "Judiciary Without Jurisdiction: South Carolina's Experiment with a County and Precinct Court System, 1720–1730," *SCHM*, XC (July 1989), 237–256, John E. Douglass attributes the destruction of the regional courts to the machinations of inconvenienced lawyers; for the influence of the lawyers, see also John E. Douglass, "Power of Attorneys: Formation of Colonial South Carolina's Attorney System, 1700–1731," *American Journal of Legal History*, XXXVII (January 1993), 1–24. Phinizy Spalding and Harvey H. Jackson, eds., *Oglethorpe in Perspective: Georgia's Founder After Two Hundred Years* (Tuscaloosa, Ala., 1989) contains several relevant essays. Carl E. Swanson, *Predators and Prizes: American Privateering and Imperial Warfare, 1739–1748* (Columbia, 1991) shows that South Carolina's privateering efforts were considerable though less than those of Newport and New York.

5. *The Economy*

John J. McCusker and Russell R. Menard, *The Economy of British America, 1607–1789* (Chapel Hill, 1985) provides the context for understanding South Carolina. Linda M. Pett-Conklin, "Cadastral Surveying in Colonial South Carolina: A Historical Geography" (dissertation, Louisiana State University, 1986) describes the process of parceling out the land. John S. Otto and Nain E. Anderson, "The Origins of Southern Cattle-Grazing: A Problem in West Indian History," *Journal of Caribbean History*, XXI, No. 2 (1988), 138–153, conclude that the cattle industry on the mainland arose from the complex interaction of Indian, African, and European traditions.

Who and what provided the capital for the expansion of the South Carolina economy comes out in Russell R. Menard, "Financing the Low-country Export Boom: Capital and Growth in Early South Carolina," *WMQ*, LI (October 1994), 659–676, which argues that the local mortgage market made "a key contribution." Peter A. Coclanis, *The Shadow of a Dream: Economic Life and Death in the South Carolina Low Country, 1670–1920* (New York 1989) paints a brilliantly evocative picture of the power of the market, while Henry C. Dethloff provides a sound, if more prosaic account, in *A History of the American Rice Industry, 1685–1985* (College Station, Tex., 1988). See also James M. Clifton, "The Rice Industry in Colonial America," *Agricultural History*, LV (July 1981), 266–283. Joyce E. Chaplin, *An Anxious Pursuit: Agricultural Innovation and Modernity in the Lower South, 1730–1815* (Chapel Hill, 1993) depicts the tensions inherent in a slaveholding society bent on "improvement." "South Carolina and the Atlantic Economy in the Late Seventeenth and Eighteenth Centuries," *Economic History Review*, XLV (November 1992), 677–702, by R. C. Nash, argues that the growth of the South Carolina rice industry resulted mainly from changes in the European supply of competing cereals.

A number of works depict trading practices and patterns: Kenneth Morgan, "The Organization of the Colonial American Rice Trade," *WMQ*, LII (July 1995), 433–452; Stuart Stumpf, "Trends in Charleston's Inter-Regional Import Trade, 1735–1764," *Southern Studies*, XXIII (Fall 1984), 243–265, and "South Carolina Importers of General Merchandise, 1735–1765," *SCHM*, LXXXIV (January, 1983), 1–10, which gives an extensive list of importers. R. C. Nash, "Trade and Business in Eighteenth-Century South Carolina: The Career of John Guerard, Merchant and Planter," *SCHM*, XCVI (January 1995), 6–29, focuses on the operations of a substantial individual. Converse D. Clowse surveys "Shipowning and Shipbuilding in Colonial South Carolina: An Overview," *American Neptune*, XLIV (Fall 1984), 221–244, to conclude that they were significant though limited economic activities. Written by a professional model ship builder, P. C. Coker, III, *Charleston's Maritime Heritage, 1670–1865: An Illustrated History* (Charleston, 1987) clarifies technical matters for popular as well as professional audiences. Marcus Rediker depicts class conflict in *Between the Devil and the Deep Blue Sea: Merchant Seamen, Pirates, and the Anglo-American Maritime World, 1700–1750* (Cambridge, Eng., 1987), which includes scattered material on South Carolina—including a striking contemporary illustration of the hanging of Stede Bonnet at Charleston in 1719. Ian K. Steele, *The English Atlantic, 1675–1740: An Exploration of Communication and Community* (New York, 1986) depicts communications and tabulates sailings from Charleston and other ports. Lawrence Rowland, *Beaufort County*, and Ronald E. Bridwell, *". . . That We Should Have a Port . . .": A History of the Port of Georgetown, South Carolina, 1732–1865* (Georgetown, 1982) provide information on the secondary seaports, while W. J. Fraser describes South Carolina's major port in *Charleston! Charleston!*. R. C. Nash, "Urbanization in the Colonial South: Charleston, South Carolina, as a Case Study," *Journal of Urban History*, XIX (November 1992), 3–29, stresses the role of the local merchant community. The changing location of that community appears in Jeanne A. Calhoun, Martha A. Zierden, and Elizabeth A. Paysinger, "The Geographic Spread of Charleston's Mercantile Community, 1732–1767," *SCHM*, LXXXVI (July 1985), 182–220, which contains the names of women and craftsmen as well as merchants and males. Several articles treat the development of local industries.

See particularly Bradford L. Rauschenberg's works in the *Journal of Early Southern Decorative Arts*, XVII (1991). For ironworks in the up-country, consult Thomas Cowan, "William Hill and the Aera Ironworks," *Journal of Early Southern Decorative Arts*, XIII (November 1987), 1–31.

John J. McCusker, *How Much is That in Real Money? A Historical Price Index for Use as a Deflator of Money Values in the Economy of the United States* (Worcester, 1992) helps one understand price and production figures. Different explanations for the relative stability of the currency appear in Elmus Wicker, "Colonial Monetary Standards Contrasted: Evidence from the Seven Years' War," *Journal of Economic History*, XLV (December 1985), 869–884, and Ivan A. Marcotte, "Colonial South Carolina: A Quantity Theoretic Perspective" (dissertation, University of South Carolina, 1989).

Lobbying by merchants and others, Alison G. Olson, *Making the Empire Work: London and American Interest Groups, 1690–1790* (Cambridge, Mass., 1992) contends, provided a bond of union before 1754; the breakdown of these networks thereafter contributed to the coming of the Revolution, while Russell Menard, "Slavery, Economic Growth, and Revolutionary Ideology in the South Carolina Lowcountry," in Ronald Hoffman, John J. McCusker, Russell R. Menard, and Peter J. Albert, eds., *The Economy of Early America: The Revolutionary Period, 1763–1790* (Charlottesville, 1988) finds that economic success bred the necessary self-confidence. For the earlier celebration of their accomplishments by South Carolinians and others, see David S. Shields, *Oracles of Empire: Poetry, Politics, and Commerce in British America, 1690–1750* (Chicago, 1990).

6. Blacks, Whites, and Slavery

The major themes of the burgeoning literature on African Americans and slavery appear in Jon F. Sensbach, "Charting a Course in Early African-American History," *WMQ*, L (April 1993), 394–405, which unfortunately gives little attention to South Carolina per se. David Richardson outlines changing patterns in "The British Slave Trade to Colonial South Carolina," *Slavery & Abolition*, XII, No. 3 (1991), 125–172, while Daniel C. Littlefield, "The Colonial Slave Trade to South Carolina: A Profile," *SCHM*, XCI (April 1990), 68–99, gives useful information about ships and cargos. African origins and cultural backgrounds appear in John K. Thornton's wide-ranging *Africa and Africans in the Making of the Atlantic World, 1400–1680* (New York, 1992). Margaret W. Creel argues for the persistence of African religious patterns in *"A Peculiar People": Slave Religion and Community-Culture Among the Gullahs* (New York, 1988), a stimulating but controversial work. Michael A. Gomez, "Muslims in Early American History," *JSH*, LX (November 1994), 671– 710, finds evidence of their presence in South Carolina runaway ads. "From Creole to African: Atlantic Creoles and the Origins of African-American Society in Mainland North America," *WMQ*, LIII (April 1996), 251–288, by Ira Berlin, maintains that long experience in the Atlantic trading world made the first generations of African Americans savvy Creoles. How they and their successors fared in South Carolina appears in Russell R. Menard, "Slave Demography in the Lowcountry, 1670–1740: From Frontier Society to Plantation Regime," *SCHM*, XCVI (October 1995), 280–303, which revises previous estimates of population growth.

Numerous works treat African American life and work patterns, evidence for which appears in the archaeological record. See Leland Ferguson, *Uncommon Ground: Archaeology and Early African America, 1650–1800* (Washington, D.C., 1992) for a discussion of African American Colono-Ware ceramics and the excavations at Middleburg Plantation. African skills also contributed to rice-growing techniques; see Judith A. Carney, "From Hands to Tutors: African Expertise in the South Carolina Rice Economy," *Agricultural History*, LXVII (Summer 1993), 1–30. Philip Morgan—in an excellent example of his many wide-ranging articles on African American life—treats various manifestations of the "Task and Gang Systems: The Organization of Labor on New World Plantations" in Stephen Innes, ed., *Work and Labor in Early America* (Chapel Hill, 1988). Another of Morgan's essays, "Black Life in Eighteenth-Century Charleston, *Perspectives in American History*, I (1984), 187–232, stresses the relative autonomy of African Americans in this setting and tabulates their occupations. Allison Carll-White's "South Carolina's Forgotten Craftsmen," *SCHM*, LXXXVI (January 1985), 32–38, and " 'Great Neatness of Finish': Slave Carpenters in South Carolina's Charleston District, 1760–1800," *Southern Studies*, XXVI (Summer 1987), 89–100, provides names and specifics. Other articles find kinship patterns and various degrees of autonomy in naming practices. See especially Cheryll A. Cody, "There Was No 'Absalom' on the Ball Plantations: Slave-Naming Practices in the South Carolina Low Country, 1720–1865," *American Historical Review*, XCII (June 1987), 563–596; John C. Inscoe, "Carolina Slave Names: An Index to Acculturation," *JSH*, XLIX (November 1983), 527–554; John Thornton, "Central African Names and African-American Naming Patterns," *WMQ*, L (October 1993), 727–742; Shane White and Graham White, "Slave Hair and African American Culture in the Eighteenth and Nineteenth Centuries," *JSH*, LXI (February 1995), 45–76 concludes that white indifference permitted considerable "expressive space" during the eighteenth century.

For efforts to educate and convert African Americans, see John C. Van Horne, ed., *Religious Philanthropy and Colonial Slavery: The American Correspondence of the Associates of Dr. Bray, 1717–1777* (Urbana, Ill., 1985) and Alan Gallay, "The Origins of Slaveholders' Paternalism: George Whitefield, the Bryan Family, and the Great Awakening in the South," *JSH*, LIII (August 1987), 369–394, as well as John S. Strickland, "Across Space and Time: Conversion, Community and Cultural Change among South Carolina Slaves" (dissertation, University of North Carolina, 1985) and the work on the Bryan family and the Great Awakening cited later. Barbara E. Lacey, "Visual Images of Blacks in Early American Imprints," *WMQ*, LIII (January 1996), 137–180, includes South Carolina items. Michael Mullin discusses *Africa in America: Slave Acculturation and Resistance in the American South and the British Caribbean, 1736–1831* (Urbana, Ill., 1992) with emphasis on variations in the patterns, while Robert A. Olwell's forthcoming book *"Kings & Slaves": The Culture of Power in a Colonial Slave Society, the South Carolina Lowcountry, 1740–1782* depicts the subtle interplay of authority and resistance. Philip D. Morgan, *Slave Counterpoint: Black Culture in the Eighteenth-Century Chesapeake and Lowcountry* has been much anticipated and will appear in 1997. John K. Thornton, "African Dimensions of the Stono Rebellion," *American Historical Review*, XCVI (October 1991), 1101–1113, finds them in the religion and military tactics of the rebels. Jane Landers, "Gracia Real de Santa Teresa de Mose: A Free Black Town in Spanish Colonial Florida," *American Historical Review*, XCV (February 1990), 9–30, depicts the haven of fugitives who reached Florida. Peter H. Wood, " 'Liberty is Sweet': African-American Freedom Struggles in the Years Before White Independence," in Alfred F. Young, ed., *Beyond the American Revolution: Explorations in the History of American Radicalism* (DeKalb, Ill., 1993), emphasizes African American initiative; while Lathan A. Windley, comp., *Runaway Slave Advertisements: A Documentary History from the 1730s to 1790*, vol. 3: *South Carolina* (Wesport, Conn., 1983) provides transcripts of nearly 2,500 runaway ads from South Carolina. For regional and chronological correlates of resistance, see Edward A. Pearson, "From Stono to Vesey: Slavery, Resistance, and Ideology in South Carolina, 1739–1822" (dissertation, University of Wisconsin, 1992).

Sylvia R. Frey, *Water from the Rock: Black Resistance in a Revolutionary Age* (Princeton, N.J., 1991), gives considerable attention to the situation in South Carolina; George F. Jones discusses "The Black Hessians: Negroes Recruited by the Hessians in South Carolina and Other Colonies," *SCHM*, LXXXIII (October 1982), 287–302, and Graham R. Hodges, ed., *The Black Loyalist Directory: African Americans in Exile after the American Revolution* (New York, 1996) prints the names and some particulars about the African Americans who evacuated New York with the British in 1783. Many of them were from South Carolina. Morgan's essay in Ira Berlin and Ronald Hoffman, *Slavery and Freedom in the Age of the American Revolution* (Charlottesville, 1983) observes the Revolution's paradoxical entrenchment of both slavery and increased autonomy for African Americans. How it was for those who remained in the South Carolina lowcountry appears in Charles W. Joyner, *Down by the Riverside: A South Carolina Slave Community* (Urbana, Ill., 1984), a beautifully written and perceptive work that deals with a later period.

7. *Society: The Social Aggregate*

"The Population of the United States, 1790: A Symposium," *WMQ*, XLI (January 1984), 85–135, gives little specific information on South Carolina, but raises important methodological questions that cast doubt on earlier estimates. Bernard Bailyn and Philip D. Morgan, eds., *Strangers within the Realm: Cultural Margins of the First British Empire* (Chapel Hill, 1991) provides an intellectual framework for understanding English encounters with and recruitment of alien peoples; it includes essays on Native Americans, African Americans, Germans, and the Scotch-Irish that are relevant to the history of South Carolina. Historians' increasing sensitivity to ethnicity in the colonial period also appears in Albert H. Tillson, Jr., "The Southern Backcountry: A Survey of Current

Research," *Virginia Magazine of History and Biography*, XCVIII (July 1990), 387–422.

Works that give particular attention to groups in South Carolina include the following: David Dobson, *Scottish Emigration to Colonial America, 1607–1785* (Athens, Ga., 1994); Jon Butler, *The Huguenots in America: A Refugee People in New World Society* (Cambridge, Mass., 1983) seeks to explain their rapid assimilation, while Bertrand van Ruymbeke treats "The Huguenot Emigration from the French Perspective," *Proceedings of the South Carolina Historical Association* (1992), 19–28. James W. Hagy, *This Happy Land: The Jews of Colonial and Antebellum Charleston* (Tuscaloosa, Ala., 1993) also notes how the Jews soon became like other South Carolinians in all but religion; this volume includes an appendix listing names and biographical information for every Jew in Charleston through 1861. Jo Anne McCormick studies "The Quakers of Colonial South Carolina, 1670–1807" (dissertation, University of South Carolina, 1984). For German-speaking immigrants, see Marianne Wokeck's essay in Ida Altman and James Horn, eds., *"To Make America": European Emigration in the Early Modern Period* (Berkeley, 1991), which provides a good overview of the German emigrant flow from 1683 to 1783. A. G. Roeber, *Palatines, Liberty, and Property: German Lutherans in Colonial British America* (Baltimore, 1993) discusses the most numerous group, the Lutherans, and their adjustment to the English legal system; the material on Carolina is informative but not easy reading. Robert A. Selig, "Emigration, Fraud, Humanitarianism, and the Founding of Londonderry, South Carolina, 1763–1765," *Eighteenth-Century Studies*, XXIII (Fall 1989), 1–23, traces the fortunes of several hundred Palatines who were stranded in London by an unscrupulous promoter and eventually wound up on the South Carolina frontier. Arlin C. Migliazzo, "A Tarnished Legacy Revisited: Jean Pierre Purry and the Settlement of the Southern Frontier, 1718–1736," *SCHM*, XCII (October 1991), 232–252, provides a sympathetic treatment; George F. Jones supplies a "Compilation of Lists of German-Speaking Settlers of Purrysburg," *SCHM*, XCII (October 1991), 253–268. *Travels in the Colonies in 1773–1775: Described in the Letters of William Mylne*, Ted Ruddock, ed., (Athens, Ga., 1993) provides a first-hand account of the Carolina backcountry, while Kaylene Hughes, "Populating the Back Country: The Demographic and Social Characteristics of the Colonial South Carolina Frontier, 1730–1760" (dissertation, Florida State University, 1985) employs modern techniques to study the eighteenth-century mosaic. Rachel N. Klein's prize-winning *Unification of a Slave State: The Rise of the Planter Class in the South Carolina Backcountry, 1760–1808* (Chapel Hill, 1990) tells a complex story readably.

For the Great Awakening and related religious developments, see Patricia U. Bonomi, *Under the Cope of Heaven: Religion, Society, and Politics in Colonial America* (New York, 1986), which depicts religious vitality in the eighteenth century but is relatively slight on South Carolina, and Jon Butler, *Awash in a Sea of Faith: Christianizing the American People* (Cambridge, Mass., 1990), which contends that the Great Awakening is "an interpretive fiction" and argues that slavery produced a "spiritual holocaust" making slaves vulnerable to European versions of Christianity in the late eighteenth century (African elements came later). For attempts to convert the slaves, see the works by Alan Gallay listed in previous sections and Harvey H. Jackson, "Hugh Bryan and the Evangelical Movement in Colonial South Carolina," *WMQ*, XLIII (July 1986), 594–614. Lyon G. Tyler, "The Gnostic Trap: Richard Clarke and His Proclamation of the Millennium and Universal Restoration in South Carolina and England," *Anglican and Episcopal History*, LVIII (June 1989), 146–168, traces the career of an Anglican rector whose visions may have influenced the English poet William Blake. Erskine Clarke, *Our Southern Zion: A History of Calvinism in the South Carolina Low Country, 1690–1990* (Tuscaloosa, Ala., 1996)—which recognizes the vigor of the Reformed community—and Robert M. Calhoon, *Evangelicals and Conservatives in the Early South, 1740–1861* (Columbia, 1988) put developments in a broad perspective, while *The Churches of Charleston and the Lowcountry* (Columbia, 1994) by the Preservation Society of Charleston offers short histories of the various congregations and gorgeous photographs of the extant buildings. Barbara L. Bellows treats religious and secular impulses for *Benevolence Among Slaveholders: Assisting the Poor in Charleston, 1670–1860* (Baton Rouge, 1993).

8. *Society: Aspirations and Achievements*

For the family and women, a place to begin is Marylynn Salmon, *Women and the Law of Property in Early America* (Chapel Hill, 1986), which reveals that women had more property rights in South Carolina than in most other colonies. Their exercise of some of them appears in Susan Henry, "Exception to the Female Model: Colonial Printer Mary Crouch," *Journalism Quarterly*, LXII (Winter 1985), 725–733, and Mary R. Parramore, "For Her Sole and Separate Use: Feme Sole Trader Status in Early South Carolina" (Master's thesis, University of South Carolina, 1991) and Cara Anzilotti, " 'In the Affairs of the World': Women and Plantation Ownership in the Eighteenth Century South Carolina Lowcountry" (dissertation, University of California, Santa Barbara, 1994). Cynthia A. Kierner, "Hospitality, Sociability, and Gender in the Southern Colonies," *JSH*, LXII (August 1996), 449–480, finds some improvement in women's status before the Revolution, while Marylynn Salmon, in Ronald Hoffman and Peter J. Albert, eds., *Women in the Age of the American Revolution* (Charlottesville, 1989) observes that the post-Revolutionary inheritance law of South Carolina was unique in putting husbands and wives on an equal footing. Studying earlier patterns, John E. Crowley, "The Importance of Kinship: Testamentary Evidence from South Carolina," *Journal of Interdisciplinary History*, XVI (Spring 1986), 559–577, discovered little patriarchal emphasis on kinship. Burial customs are covered in Bradford L. Rauschenberg, "Coffin Making and Undertaking in Charleston and its Environs, 1705–1820," *Journal of Early Southern Decorative Arts*, XVI (May 1990), 18–63, and Diana W. Combs, *Early Gravestone Art in Georgia and South Carolina* (Athens, Ga., 1986).

Cary Carson, Ronald Hoffman, and Peter J. Albert, eds., *Of Consuming Interests: The Style of Life in the Eighteenth Century* (Charlottesville, 1994) provides an intellectual framework for understanding local consumption patterns. Some of these appear in Robert F. Neville and Katherine H. Bielsky, "The Izard Library," *SCHM*, XCI (July 1990), 149–169, and Gail Gibson, "Costume and Fashion in Charleston, 1769–1782," *SCHM*, LXXXII (July 1981), 225–247. Jessie Poesch, *The Art of the Old South: Painting, Sculpture, Architecture and the Products of Craftsmen, 1560–1860* (New York, 1983) covers South Carolina as well as other areas in a beautifully illustrated survey. Another handsome volume, Mills Lane, *Architecture of the Old South: South Carolina* (Savannah, 1984) includes architectural drawings as well as buildings from the interior of the state. Shirley Abbott, "The Charleston Inheritance," *American Heritage*, XXXVIII (April 1987), 62–69, is a lavishly illustrated tour, while Jane B. Gillette, "American Classic," *Historic Preserva-*

tion, XLIII (March/April 1991), 22–29, 71–72, provides a good popular introduction to Drayton Hall. *The Early Architecture of Charleston* (1927; Columbia, 1990), edited by Albert Simons and Samuel Lapham, Jr., is a classic that contains photographs of some buildings since demolished. Gardens are treated in George C. Rogers, Jr., "Gardens and Landscapes in Eighteenth-Century South Carolina," *Eighteenth-Century Life*, VIII (January 1983), 148–158, and Elise Pinckney, " 'Still Mindful of the English Way': 250 Years of Middleton Place on the Ashley," *SCHM*, XCII (July 1991), 149–171.

Wayne Craven, *Colonial American Portraiture: The Economic, Religious, Social, Cultural, Philosophical, Scientific, and Aesthetic Foundations* (Cambridge, Eng., 1986) is a sophisticated general study that recognizes Carolinians' affinity with the English aristocracy, while Martha R. Severens, "Jeremiah Theus of Charleston: Plagiarist or Pundit?" *Southern Quarterly*, XXIV (Fall-Winter 1985), 56–70, notes that the artist copied English works for settings. See also Richard H. Saunders and Ellen G. Miles, *American Colonial Portraits, 1700–1776* (Washington, D.C., 1987); Martha R. Severens, *The Miniature Portrait Collection of the Carolina Art Association* edited by Charles L. Wyrick, Jr. (Charleston, 1984); and National Society of the Colonial Dames of America in the State of South Carolina, comp., *South Carolina Portraits: A Collection of Portraits of South Carolinians and Portraits in South Carolina* (Columbia, 1996), which contains numerous examples previously unpublished.

Civic aspirations of the Carolina elite appear in Richard Waterhouse, "Merchants, Planters, and Lawyers: Political Culture and Leadership in South Carolina, 1721–1775," in Bruce C. Daniels, ed., *Power and Status: Officeholding in Colonial America* (Middletown, Conn., 1986), which concludes that they maintained "a responsible, responsive and inclusive political system" during most of the royal period, and in David C. R. Heisser, " 'Warrior Queen of Ocean': The Story of Charleston and Its Seal," *SCHM*, XCIII (July/October 1992), 167–195, which discusses iconography as well as use.

9. *The Revolutionary Era*

For the Cherokee War and its effects, see Thomas Hatley, *The Dividing Paths;*, Douglas E. Leach, *Roots of Conflict: British Armed Forces and Colo-*

nial Americans, 1677–1763 (Chapel Hill, 1986); and Paul D. Nelson, *General James Grant: Scottish Soldier and Royal Governor of East Florida* (Gainesville, 1993). J. Russell Snapp, *John Stuart and the Struggle for Empire on the Southern Frontier* and Marc Egnal, *A Mighty Empire: The Origins of the American Revolution* (Ithaca, 1988) find origins of the Revolution in the frustrations of Indian traders and ambitious expansionists from South Carolina as well as elsewhere. Alan D. Watson provides the most complete account of "The Beaufort Removal and the Revolutionary Impulse in South Carolina," *SCHM*, LXXXIV (July, 1983), 121–135, while J. Russell Snapp, "William Henry Drayton: The Making of a Conservative Revolutionary," *JSH*, LVII (November 1991), 637–658, argues for Drayton's consistency. Robert A. Olwell, " 'Domestick Enemies': Slavery and Political Independence in South Carolina, May 1775–March 1776," *JSH*, LV (February 1989), 21–48, shows that South Carolinians revolted partly to maintain authority over their slaves.

Military developments in the Lower South can be found in Terry Lipscomb, *The Carolina Lowcountry, April 1775–June 1776* (Columbia, 1991), an authoritative reference as well as an accessible introduction for the general reader. Martha C. Searcy covers *The Georgia-Florida Contest in the American Revolution, 1776–1778* (Tuscaloosa, Ala., 1985). Successive commanders of the southern army are subjects of Charles E. Bennett and Donald R. Lennon, *A Quest for Glory: Major General Robert Howe and the American Revolution* (Chapel Hill, 1991) and David B. Mattern, *Benjamin Lincoln and the American Revolution* (Columbia, 1995). Bobby G. Moss provides an exhaustive *Roster of South Carolina Patriots in the American Revolution* (Baltimore, 1983). Its counterpart for the British side is Murtie J. Clark, *Loyalists in the Southern Campaign*, 3 vols. (Baltimore, 1981). Anthony J. Scotti, "Brutal Virtue: The Myth and Reality of Banastre Tarleton" (dissertation, University of South Carolina, 1995) is the most thorough study, but see also J. Tracy Power, " 'The Virtue of Humanity was Totally Forgot': Buford's Massacre, May 29, 1780," *SCHM*, XCIII (January 1992), 5–14. Stephen Conway, "To Subdue America: British Army Officers and the Conduct of the Revolutionary War," *WMQ*, XLIII (July 1986), 381–407, does not treat South Carolina in detail but is suggestive on the hardliners and the failure of their tactics. John S. Pancake, *This Destructive War: The British Campaign in the Carolinas, 1780–1782* (Tuscaloosa, Ala., 1985) is readable but contains some errors.

There are several helpful works on the loyalists. See Robert S. Lambert, *South Carolina Loyalists in the American Revolution* (Columbia, 1987), which is the most comprehensive; John L. Nichols, "Alexander Cameron, British Agent among the Cherokee, 1764–1781," *SCHM*, XCVII (April 1996), 94–114; Edward J. Cashin, *The King's Ranger: Thomas Brown and the American Revolution on the Southern Frontier* (Athens, Ga., 1989); Kathy R. Coker, "The Punishment of Revolutionary War loyalists in South Carolina" (dissertation, University of South Carolina, 1987); Coker on the loyalist artisans of Charleston and Rebecca Starr on Daufuskie Island in Robert M. Calhoon, Timothy M. Barnes, and George A. Rawlyk, eds., *Loyalists and Community in North America* (Westport, Conn., 1994); and Carole W. Troxler, "Refuge, Resistance, and Reward: The Southern Loyalists' Claim on East Florida," *JSH*, LV (November 1989), 563–596.

For state politics, consult Jerome J. Nadelhaft's essay in Ronald Hoffman and Peter J. Albert, eds., *Sovereign States in an Age of Uncertainty* (Charlottesville, 1982), which argues for a substantial democratization of the system; as well as John A. Hall, "Quieting the Storm: The Establishment of Order in Post-Revolutionary South Carolina" (dissertation, University of Oxford, 1989), and Christopher F. Lee, "Establishing a Republic: The South Carolina Assembly, 1783–1800" (dissertation, University of Virginia, 1986), both of which recognize the limits of change. "Thomas Bee's Notes on the State of South Carolina," edited by Alexander Moore, *Journal of the Early Republic*, VII (Summer 1987), 115–122, and "William Henry Drayton's Journal of a 1784 Tour of the South Carolina Backcountry," edited by Keith Krawczynski, *SCHM*, XCVII (July 1996), 182–205, provide firsthand accounts of conditions in the early 1780s.

Two new items make the state's relations with the Continental Congress and foreign nations easier to trace. Letters of the Delegates to Congress are now available on CD-ROM by Historical Database, Summerfield, Fla. 34491, while Mary A. Giunta, ed., *The Emerging Nation: A Documentary History of the Foreign Relations of the United States under the Articles of Confederation, 1780–1789* (Washington, D.C., 1996–) is a well-indexed compilation. See also Paul A. Horne, Jr., "Forgotten Leaders: South Carolina's Delegation to the Continental Congress, 1774–1789" (dissertation, University of South Carolina, 1988), and James Haw, "A Broken Compact: Insecurity, Union, and the Proposed Surrender of Charleston, 1779," *SCHM*, XCVI (January 1995), 30–53. Calvin Jillson and Rick K. Wilson, *Congressional Dynamics: Structure, Coordination, and Choice in the First American Congress, 1774–1789* (Stanford, Calif., 1994) provide a sophisticated explanation of Congress's declining effectiveness; their statistical analysis periodically illuminates the position of South Carolina delegates.

Calvin C. Jillson, *Constitution Making: Conflict and Consensus in the Federal Convention of 1787* (New York, 1988) provides a similar statistical analysis of alignments in the convention. For the voluminous body of scholarship generated by the bicentennial celebration, see Peter S. Onuf, "Reflections on the Founding: Constitutional Historiography in Bicentennial Perspective," *WMQ*, XLVI (April 1989), 341–375. Representative samples of work pertinent to South Carolina can be found in *SCHM*, LXXXIX (1988) which contains essays by M.E. Bradford, David Moltke-Hansen, Lacy K. Ford, Herbert A. Johnson, Robert E. Shalhope, and Robert M. Weir. Patrick T. Conley and John P. Kaminski, *The Constitution and the States: The Role of the Original Thirteen in the Framing and Adoption of the Federal Constitution* (Madison, 1988) includes Nadelhaft's essay treating South Carolina's ratification as a manifestation of controlled change. James W. Ely, Jr., in *The South's Role in the Creation of the Bill of Rights,* Robert J. Haws, ed. (Jackson, 1991) argues that the ratification debates reflected and exacerbated sectional and class differences, while Weir maintains in Michael A. Gillespie and Michael Lienesch, *Ratifying the Constitution* (Lawrence, Kan., 1989) that consensus on the desirability of slavery facilitated ratification. John C. Meleney, *The Public Life of Aedanus Burke: Revolutionary Republican in Post-Revolutionary South Carolina* (Columbia, 1989) studies an Anti-Federalist. Patrick Conley and John Kaminski, *Bill of Rights and the States: Colonial and Revolutionary Origins of American Liberties* (Madison, 1992) contains a good bibliographic essay and Michael Stevens's discussion of "Civil Liberties in South Carolina, 1663–1791."

10. *Epilogue: Toward the Nineteenth Century*

Perhaps the most cogent recent contributions to solving the "problem of South Carolina" are Lacy K. Ford, *Origins of Southern Radicalism: The South Carolina Upcountry, 1800–1860* (New York, 1988); Don Higginbotham, "Fomenters of Revolution: Massachusetts and South Carolina," *Journal of the Early Republic*, XIV (Spring 1994), 1–34; and Rebecca K. Starr, "A School for Politics: Interest-Group Strategies and the Formation of South Carolina's Political Culture, 1763–1794" (dissertation, University of Oxford, 1989). Higginbotham provides citations to the most recent literature, while Mark D. Kaplanoff, "Making the South Solid: Politics and the Structure of Society in South Carolina, 1790–1815" (dissertation, Cambridge University, 1979) remains useful.

INDEX